RETAILISATION:

THE HERE, THERE AND EVERYWHERE OF RETAIL

by

FRANCESCA de CHÂTEL

and

ROBIN HUNT

'You only work in a shop, you know. You can drop the attitude.'

Eddie, *Absolutely Fabulous*

RETAILISATION:
THE HERE, THERE AND EVERYWHERE OF RETAIL

by

FRANCESCA de CHÂTEL

and

ROBIN HUNT

Europa Publications
Taylor & Francis Group plc

© Francesca de Châtel and Robin Hunt 2003

Published by Europa Publications Limited 2003
2 Park Square, Milton Park, Abingdon,
Oxon, OX14 4RN

(A member of the Taylor & Francis Group)

Transferred to Digital Printing 2005

ISBN 085142 4589

Contents

Acknowledgements

Thanks to Tim Mason, Head of Marketing at Tesco; Steve Richards, Managing Director of Manchester United; David Smith, Commercial Manager of the British Football Association; Susan Sullivan, Head of Marketing and Communications at Sony Style store and Sony WonderTech Lab; Tom Dixon, Head of Design at Habitat UK; Tyler Brûlé, founder of *Wallpaper** magazine; Ben Van Berkel and Caroline Bos of UN Studio in Amsterdam; Mike Pilbeam, Technical Director of Cisco Systems; Emma Haughty at the Laing Homes; Celia Clear, Managing Director of Tate Publishing; Alex Beard of Tate; Carlos Virgile of Virgile and Stone Associates; Charles Ponsonby, Group Strategy and Marketing Director of Open Television and British Interactive Broadcasting; James Gundell, President, MoMA Retail; Jan Hol, Director of Marketing at Ahold; Richard Baker, Head of Marketing at Asda; Rem Koolhaas and Markus Schaefer of the Office of the Metropolitan Architecture in Rotterdam; the Jerde Partnership; Kas Oosterhuis; Professor Steven Gage at the Bartlett School of Architecture; Emma McNamara; Jimmy Evans; Susanne Düsing, Stefan Vogel and Otto Wachs at Autostadt; Professor Benjamin Barber; Naomi Klein; Stovin Hayter; Kate Meyrick, Director of Corporate Relations at Bluewater; Mark Squires at Nokia; Michael Sastry at lastminute.com; Louis Wahl, Head of Public Relations at Waterstone's, Piccadilly; Dr Jonathan Reynolds at the Oxford Institute for Retail Management; Paco Underhill at Envirosell; Professor Daniel Miller at University College London; the CAVE at SARA in Amsterdam; Professor Adrienne Baker; Nicolas Bos at the Fondation Cartier; Andrew de Vigal; Peter de Coster at Cabvision; Mirjam Snoerwang, Press Officer at Schiphol Airport and Johan van Streun, Manager of Commercial Business at Schiphol Airport; Alice Ciccolini; Peter de Châtel; Colette Forder, *The Times*; Ray Main, Alison Scammell and Sarah Blair at ASLIB; the hotel staff at the Gramercy Park, Boston Hilton and the Helnan Marina hotels; Sharm al Sheikh, Tim Gentles and Liz Citron at arehaus; the staff at the V&A Archives; Lindsay Keenan, Markets Campaigner at Greenpeace; Alex Wijeratna at Action Aid; Sian Lloyd; Professor David Nicholas at City University; Peter Hunt; and Helen Martin at the *Guardian*.

Special thanks to David Peek, Professor William Mitchell and Jon Jerde.

Introduction

You step off the plane, look around, take a deep breath – and come to somewhere south of SoHo, or on a midtown traction table with a silver tray and a tasselled tab on your chest and a guy in white saying 'Good morning, sir. How are you today? That'll be fifteen thousand dollars...'

Martin Amis, *Money*[1]

This book is out of date and then again, so is Martin Amis's – his is *really* wrong: only $15,000 for a detox and a little light plastic surgery after a big bad night out in Manhattan in the 21st century? *Get out of here.* Then again, every book we have read and referenced in *Retailisation* – whether bought in Waterstone's or Barnes & Noble bookshops, ordered from amazon.com or read via database screen or in an old-fashioned library, and every interview we have undertaken – is out of date. All our research is past it, superseded by the relentless speed of information – knowledge – being produced about our behaviour as consumers and people in newspapers, online, in research papers, in prognostications made at expensive retail conferences around the world, in life as we experience it osmotically. Every interview has dated, rusted, flirted with the trashcan on our desktops, is in need of an upgrade, a makeover. Every piece of information has had its time. Is past its sell-by date.

We're looking in this book for retail principles as an extension of the way we live, and we're looking at a very confusing time, a time often characterised as one of 'information overload'. We wish to illustrate that this is in fact also an era of retail overload, of *everything* overload. Retailing, that is, of goods that range from packaged soups to film channels on subscription television; stories emanating from tabloid newspapers and delivered through mobile phones to medical diagnosis coming from human practitioners or accessed through debatable websites; from vampire holidays in the hills of Transylvania to the latest home entertainment systems.

At the core of what we consider to be 'retail overload' is the issue of time. For, as life and work merge with travel for so many of us to form a seamless core of 'labour-time', which no longer stops as we catch the 6.45 train home, nor when we close the front door and enter our house or apartment, free time is one of the few valued commodities that retail can't really provide for us. While money buys us the 'things' we want and can afford (or not quite afford, but buy *anyway*) we find that in the retailisation era more free time is a luxury good far grander than any Fifth Avenue purchase or satellite-enabled holiday home. Time, like common culture, democracy, contentment, citizenship and public service

---

[1] Martin Amis, *Money* (London: jonathan Cape, 1984).

1

broadcasting, is a scarce commodity, something you can't buy. For this reason time is a new battlefield on which retail engages, an extension of the historic arena of retail competition: geography. Price too remains a huge factor – some things never change – but for most of us, overwhelmed by working hours or commuting times, choices to make and credit card bills to pay, time for 'ourselves' is frequently rare. And there are many who want to buy even this freedom back from us. There are many who want to be always in our face, enticing us to spend on.

Money is a novel written well before many of the trends, fads and social shifts that have speeded up our lives, taken our time and made more sophisticated the processes by which we live. The combination of relentless consumer analysis, technological progress, and the cultural changes in work, travel, relationships and the very way we decide to live has led to a multitude of phenomena, some permanent, most transient, that affect us. For instance, *Money* precedes the yuppies, the guppies, the nesters, the grey panthers, the single online investors, the Internet, WAP, the mobile PDA, the cellphone, the hypermall, the endless number of shifts, paradigm shifts and management books about the new economy, the wired digerati, the pursuit of lifelong 'cool'. *Money* was written before The Gap and Tommy Hilfiger; it is oblivious to Playstation culture or Britney. It could not have conceived of e-commerce, Pokemon, viral love bugs, chat rooms, shrines to motor cars; will not have enjoyed the disaster that was the dot.com debacle of 2001, the stock crashes and 'egregious' accounting errors of 2002. It was written before mainstream newspaper media became the vehicle not just for news but for wide-scale daily editorial endorsements of the perfect way to cook, decorate or give birth; the perfect way to 'live'. It was written before 'Seattle' and 'Washington', 'September 11' and the spread of the 'new' counter-corporationism. It was written long before Naomi Klein's groundbreaking investigation into the darker sides of global brands, *No Logo*, became a best-selling global brand in itself.

In its defence, though it hardly needs it, *Money* is also great comic dystopian fiction, which as we shall see is an apt description for a lot of non-fiction written about the consumer world in the past decade. To explain our position: *Retailisation* is not a management book, not a how to get rich in retail '101'; there are few PowerPoint bullet-points to be found here. It describes instead the informational processes by which life choices are presented and sold to us. It is thus about retail and space and time, not about Panglossian e-commerce nirvanas or, indeed, South Sea Bubbles or perfect brand campaigns to come. Martin Amis can't help that he missed out on the last 20 years of extraordinary life-changes in the post-modern world; his book nevertheless describes the velocity of such trends perfectly: fast, faster, fastest; slower, slow. Amis once wrote that *Money* was about speed, that it featured a semi-colon in the last sentence because it was about the ultimate, inevitable, slowing down of human life in the face of the speed-lusting 1980s.

Now, at the beginning of another century, the wild, wired world of *Money's* Manhattan mayhem can itself seem very slow.[2] That is because retail, making a profit by selling 'things', a constant share-holder-value, quarterly profit cycle of necessary refreshment – or upgrade culture – works at global digital speed. This pressure to per-form means that retail's DNA is constantly evolving. It has to, and so its cells increasingly infect the bloodstream of contemporary life, responding to and cajoling 'us', whoever 'we' are trying to be. Retail chains may slow in growth, entire Internet franchises may crash and burn, new economic models of buying and selling may 'lose their juice' – just look at the speed with which Enron turned out the lights in 2001 – but, despite all, selling us things goes on. And on.

So we are very aware that our book was out of date as the last chapter, this one, was being written, designed and edited, and that it fell behind the here and now a little more when it went to the printers and further still when it arrived finally in bookshops. It is, after all, only a book, not CNN television, not the NASDAQ, not real-time news. It is not a bike package delivered within the hour to your home, office or hotel room. It is not immediately, organi-cally and speedily responsive to the last minute's news, informa-tion or price change – it is not the Internet, as though that is as speedy as was promised. It is instead matter, material, and the pro-duction of matter takes time. And in these increasingly digital days we are allowed little time before there is something else we are offered to buy, something newer, better, more fashionable, differ-ent: a new insurance deal, another way to package Coke, a new form of pyramid selling, a DVD, a third-generation mobile phone with a camera built in.

This book is out of date precisely because of this speed, retail's ever-diminishing cycles; it is an analysis of the state of retail, shop-ping, the processes of buying and selling goods or services up to the year 2001. It is an analysis of how the disciplines and proce-dures of retail significantly affect all parts of our life, seemingly hur-rying us ever forward towards a 'perfect' time when we can – if we have the money, virtually through plastic credit cards or 'smart'

---

[2] 'In 1982 Pauline Kael, in the *New Yorker*, assailed the turn to hyperactivity represented, for her, by *Star Wars* and *Raiders of the Lost Ark* – two films that stretched the limits for fast-action sequences. At the century's end, these films already seem like classics; they had structure, character, and wit. Now we have what Anthony Lane, one of Kael's successors, calls "our ever-growing predicament: there is nothing so boring in life, let alone in cinema, as the boredom of being excited all the time".' James Gleick, *Faster* (Little, Brown & Company), 1999, p. 176.

cards, or in old-fashioned notes and coins – buy what we need, and what we don't need, wherever we are; and that this new world of buying processes includes the illusion of buying time, of escape from the quark velocity embrace of what was once, prosaically, named the rat race. We may be buying to escape the pressures of life or to fortress behind our front door; we may be buying to survive or as a tax loss activity – but know this: however we spend, on whatever commodities, there is a process awaiting and evolving to make us spend more.

Whether we consider the high street or the website, politics or education, entertainment or recreation, retail affects us because it is apparently *everything*. For some it is the new symbolic enemy, its markets a war zone, replacing the competing ideologies of communism or capitalism from Cold War times with the 'threat' that comes from the power and control over our perceived landscapes given to the largest global brands, the notion that the Fortune 500 runs America, not its President. For others retail is the nuts, bolts and shop window of that grander ideological conceit, the global economy. For some it is 20 cents an hour working in sweatshops to create computer chips or the latest trainers or ski pants. For others it is the possibility of starting a new e-commerce retail business unencumbered by the physical. For many retail's temples and communications strategies represent the high triumph of democracy, the 'free' market: 'shopping is my religion' they say as they pile on the plastics. For others these places are the decadent symbols of Western hegemony. Whatever the position taken, and however uncomfortable the notion, the fact remains that retail is here, will always be and will always resist easy definitions; it will alienate some and make multi-millionaires of others. And that is as true at an arms fair in Delhi as it is in a strip mall in Iowa.

Part of our definition of retailisation includes the psychological process by which we believe we stand outside the loop of buyer and seller, while simultaneously being an active participant in its dynamic. For retailisation holds within itself a paradox of retail: expanded, speed-driven, immersive consumer choice does not make us happy – for long – nor is its mission to sate all our needs. Retail is trained on the short term, speeding on to the next, the bigger, the different, *next season, the upgrade, the sequel, Star Wars X,* as fast as we will let it (as fast as we can tolerate): just see how quickly retail businesses can lose their way if their short-term profits fall significantly. To paraphrase the Bloomsbury economist John Maynard Keynes, these days even in the medium term you are dead. So retailisation is partly about its implicit requirement to stealth bomb our acquisitive genes, about the way it seeks immersion in our lives, wherever we are, to create the *ability and the desire* for us to buy things.

This is a book about retail at a breakthrough time. Classical high street or mall retail is now facing a range of new challenges: the digital world of e-commerce, interactive television and mobile-phone shopping are its much trumpeted technological face. But it is also confronted by a world of consumers who grow more individual, more distinct and more difficult to categorise. It is faced by a culture of speed and change that nobody can ultimately understand or rationalise – merely 'model' if they are 'quantitative' analysts, or stick a finger in the air and hypothesise about if they are 'qualitative' ones. Retail is thus forced to seek opportunities wherever it can, and whenever it can, using anything it can find to help it. In the winter months of 2002, who would have predicted the six million red and white flags of St George sold in June as part of the English nation's support for its football team in the World Cup? Answer? A lot of retailers, obviously. Retailisation is about this kind of nudging at the gaps in our fiscal defences. The drivers: greed and narcissism, need and hunger, early adoption and week-end boredom and – in the case of the six million flags – a collective patriotism that seems quite at odds with the me-focused, celebrity-obsessed, England we experience daily. *Things change.* And quickly.

Retailisation is the process by which retail is fighting back against a knowledge-rich consumer who has grown up in an era of mass 'quality' information about the things he or she consumes. It is also about the impact and effectiveness of architecture, branding, experience, location, money, motion, politics, policy, space and speed in this process, but mostly it is about consumers. It is about *us*: who we are and how we are got at, and how we get at retail.

We all shop, whether it is for knowledge or onions, medicine or trainers. Some of us are unashamed shoppers, others pretend it doesn't really happen. It does. Here's how.

Chapter 1 – The speed of choice: asses' values?

'Well, but what did you buy this mass of things for?' said the Princess, smiling, and handing her husband a cup of coffee.
'One goes for a walk, one looks in a shop, and they ask you to buy. "Erlaucht, Excellenz, Durchlaucht?" Directly they say "Durchlaucht" I can't hold out – and ten thalers are gone.'
'It's simply from boredom,' said the Princess.
'Of course it is. Such boredom, my dear, that one doesn't know what to do with oneself.'
'How can you be bored, Prince? There's so much that's interesting now in Germany,' said Marya Eugenyevna.
'But I know everything that's interesting: the plum soup I know and the pea sausages I know. I know everything.'

Leo Tolstoy, *Anna Karenina*[3]

'Could we? I mean, it is nearly lunchtime.'
'10:30, Patsy!'
'Um-hum?'
'Well, look, we can do Harvey Nichols quickly.'

Patsy and Eddie discuss time, speed and shopping, *Absolutely Fabulous*

Imagine for a moment that you are in your giant out-of-town local supermarket or mall. You know its layout well because you have been coming here to shop for years and you have found everything you need to buy for the next week in record time. The stately procession of you and your family with your piled-high trolley filled with your standard weekly shopping hasn't been derailed by sudden excursions to unusual store aisles featuring new, highly advertised, impeccably branded luxury products, and the flow of fellow-shoppers is as logical as your own. Nobody u-turns to pick up the missed toothpaste or hesitates over the cheese counter, or drops a child off their trolley. You haven't been seduced by any special offers, the children haven't insisted on having the latest chocolate bar that is tied into a blockbuster movie and your partner has resisted arguing over the merits of Chilean Merlot against German lager – you've bought both without friction. You haven't been immersed by the vastness of the space and fallen into a kind of dream state of irrational purchasing, nor become so irritated that you have missed half the things you meant to buy.

And so now it is time to queue to pay. Speed is probably the last thing to expect from now on. Frustration, anger, irritation, dreams of robotic pay-out till minders: these are our thoughts. And when we have finally signed our credit card or handed over our cash, packed our groceries and left the store do we feel that life will

---

[3] Leo Tolstoy, *Anna Karenina*, translated by Constance Garnett in 1908, chapter 35.

quicken again? No, we have the car park and traffic to navigate, the bus to wait for, the taxi to holler at, the heavy bags to carry home. No, retail is not a speedy experience. Not unless, that is, you shop at 3 a.m. in the morning.

Now imagine instead that you are at home. Or at work. Or in your car. Or on a plane, at sea, walking in the Lake District or skiing down the Rocky Mountains – anywhere but in the supermarket, in fact. You are still wanting to fill your fridge and kitchen cabinets at home with the provisions to keep you fed for the next week, but you haven't got the time – or you are not in the right place – to make the purchases from your usual store. Or you simply don't want to be there.

So, instead of the 20-minute trawl of the supermarket aisles to gather your groceries followed by the 20-minute queue to pay, you use a computer or a personal digital assistant or a mobile phone to access an online grocery store. You have a standard order of provisions, which you've previously set up. So now you click on the purchase button, select a time that is convenient to you for delivery of your goods, add your credit card details, and then sit back and enjoy all the time you have saved. Four hours or two weeks later (it is all up to you) a delivery truck arrives, someone carries your goods inside and your weekly shopping is complete. The result: no queuing, no stress, no traffic – just a slightly higher bill to pay for the service and delivery. E-commerce or electronic retailing, digital home shopping is king: speedy and needful of your needs, not those of the retailer.

Simple. Except that right now the majority of us are far more likely to find ourselves in that checkout queue than online and buying goods. We know we waste time in shops, particularly supermarkets, but we don't yet trust the Internet to deliver to us reliably. Many of us don't have delivery services in our area yet. We don't all have Internet access (though the growth figures for the Web suggest that it will be as ubiquitous as the telephone within a decade). Or computers. We aren't always, or ever, able to say when we will be home to receive a delivery. But we all would love to save time, because none of us ever has a perfect supermarket experience. We'd all love to cut out this unnecessary trip, this time-waste (unless we are looking for more than frozen peas when we visit our supermarket; for example, we could be looking for love – people do).

Now imagine that you are thinking about buying a business suit, a party dress, a swimsuit for the holidays, a new sofa – or even a new home. Again, as with our supermarket odyssey, there are many options, both physical and virtual. Again, though we are still strapped for time, we will probably find some, one way or another, to ensure we make a smart purchasing decision. We will, perhaps, visit a store that has many of the brands we like. We will perhaps visit one branded store we have bought from before. We could visit, say, a Selfridges or Macy's department store or a particular Topshop. We could visit a Habitat or a Crate and Barrel store where we know a member of the staff and we trust them. If we are looking for a house we could visit one estate agency, or every agency on the relevant high street. We could talk to the person we bought our last house from and ask advice about the market. We will have our favourite stores, and the most convenient ones; stores that are likely to have *something*, at least.

Or we could visit all of the above online – search through the ranges of £600 suits or £2,000 sofas, or £200,000 homes – and make a decision. That decision is twofold, and is core to the decisions we investigate in this book. Do we negate time and space and buy the object online using a credit card, waiting for delivery by the agency we have bought from? Do we make a choice by researching all the available information and opinion to guide us, find out how to buy what we want using the Internet, then purchase it in physical space? Or do we almost make a decision, then visit the most convenient store, mall, or agency to make the final purchase even if the choices are not perfect? We could just want to buy a pair of trousers, or just *want* to go shopping. In this case, research, the elimination of time and space, and any other considerations about improving our chances of a rational, best-buy experience all but vanish.

All options have their fans. Retailers would love us to buy leather sofas or linen Armani jackets online. After all, if everyone bought their luxury purchases online there would be no need for the high street. There would be no need for retailers to spend so much money on buildings and interior decorations. There would be no need constantly to refresh the window displays. There would be no need to employ all those expensive, temperamental staff. That hasn't happened yet, and won't for two reasons.

First, as consumers we still feel a little unsure about e-commerce and large, luxury purchasing – particularly after the first generation of dot.coms and websites imploded in such spectacular ways, leaving us apparently with only eBay and Amazon as the safe, sure bet. Sure, people have bid $25,000 for art online; sure they buy cars online; sure, they scoop up great auction bargains online at enormous prices. But what if the dress we've bought online doesn't feel right when we've got it on? What if the pixilated colours of the sofa or car aren't true on the website? What if the necklace isn't exactly as it is photographed? It is a lot of money that we are spending on this luxury item, after all.

With simpler purchases we will suspend our disbelief a little, but not with these complex choices. That's why books and CDs have proved such an allure online: we know what we are getting when we buy Martin Amis or Harry Potter from amazon.com – we are getting the same thing as we would if we visited Waterstone's or Barnes & Noble bookshops. Except that it might be a little cheaper, and we will have to wait a few days before we can read it. In which case there is usually a bookshop somewhere around to buy from straight away.

The same is true with computers – we don't test-drive computers before we buy them. We research which chips we want inside, what software we need and thus what capacity of machine we need. We would and could buy computers or software online – which is why Dell computers have been so successful with their e-commerce-enabled website. It is when we are thinking about ourselves and how a purchase could change us – when we think about buying that perfect suit or dress, that car or house – that we're more likely to go and try it physically. We want to look at ourselves in a mirror and sometimes ask the opinion of someone else – a retailer or a friend – before we hand over our money.

Curiously, given its growing influence and impact, the wired world has failed to seduce us when it comes to the pleasures of random retail: we will not buy on impulse online in the way we often do in a store. The textures and metaphors of online shops are those of ease and efficiency, not of sophisticated, immersive experiences such as we find increasingly in the high street and mall.

This all boils down to a simple series of questions. Do we have time to make the most rational retailing decisions when we need or want to shop, or will we use filters to screen the myriad of options we now have? Will these filters be information sources, other people, or the amount of time we have? Will we use technology or visit the most efficient (or entertaining) new forms of retail experience to curtail the normal processes of Saturday afternoon queuing, instant decisions made in the heat of the moment or simply in irritation or because we want to buy *something*? Will we use the virtual, the physical, or a combination of the two to buy the things that define us? Will we keep going to shops, or will they begin to come to us?

Actually, they have come already. Home is where we escaped retail once; now it is becoming the perfect immersive environment. In a nirvana economy for retail we would be able to shop 24 hours a day, 365 days a year. There would be no such thing as no time to choose, because we would have options all the time. Well, now we are entering a time when this dream – however bleak it might seem to some – appears to be possible. As each year passes, and often faster, barriers to our being able to shop are crumbling.

In the physical world we have few religious or political impediments any longer – how quickly did Sunday become a day of retail rather than rest? We can now travel far further than ever before to find what we want. We now have many all-night stores to service those must-have last minute needs, and – even if we are frightened of venturing out at 3 a.m. – retail is now in our homes via almost all of the technologies with communications facilities: welcome to the virtual world. So now it is all up to us.

We have let retail surround us because it makes our way of living easier: many of us lead busy lives where every minute counts. Where once we would tolerate the slow, we now value the fast – whether we term this 'business efficiency' whether we must be *first to the market or die*, or whether we merely believe and perceive ourselves never to have enough time because we are so often being told so – we demand things *now* rather than *then*. We demand speed because of the increasing demands on our time: long hours of work, long hours of travel to work, the strains of working from home, mobile working, relearning for new jobs, our 'time rage'. In a world of low certainty about anything, from our jobs to what's actually good on television, the virtues of patience and calm are losing out to the efficiencies of an on-demand world. We enter a McDonald's and expect to be eating a Big Mac within 90 seconds. We use public transport and quickly decide – if we can afford it (and sometimes when we cannot) – that a car will be more effective. We send an email, where once we would have written a letter, and expect a reply within hours, not days. We visit a shopping mall because everything we want is located in a single environment where once we would happily have traversed high streets and side roads for hours to find what we want.

Some of us use websites to compare the prices of everything from jeans and cars to insurance policies and medicines because we don't have time to shop around any more. We go on time-management courses where we learn to prioritise our workloads, to project manage not just our work, but our lives. We want mission statements, not complex documents about ambiguity. We want one-page summaries, not 600-page directories. We want to defeat time and speed through knowledgeable choice. We want literally *everything*. But most of all we want control in a world spinning out of control.[4]

Information

Despite the appeal of the purely random shopping experience and the overt fact that we can seemingly now shop any time, day or

---

[4] In 1995 many of us got very excited by *Out of Control*, a marvellous book written by Wired Executive Editor, Kevin Kelly. His thesis: 'Why you should read this book. This is a book about how our manufactured world has become so complex that the only way to create yet more complex things is by using the principles of biology. This means decentralised, bottom-up control, evolutionary advances and error-honouring institutions. I also get into the new laws of wealth in a network-based economy, what the Biosphere 2 project in Arizona has or has not to teach us, and whether large systems can predict or be predicted.' The author, at *http://www.wired.com/staff/kevin*, 24 May 1996.

night, there are many of us who would like to feel we have all or at least some of the information available about goods – be it about Harry Potter's latest wizard war or about the resolution and Internet facilities of a particular wide-screen television new to the market – before we make a purchase. Most things we can buy come with promotional literatures that connote information: the specifications of all technological purchases from cameras to televisions and computers; the catalogues and glossy images produced by car manufacturers; the dense brochures that underpin mortgages and insurance policies; the texts that augment striking advertising images in newspapers and magazines.

Then there is the centralised, polyglot, information dreamscape that is the media itself. Our media is now about far more than information, news and comment – it is about reflecting us, our lifestyles, our needs. The exponential growth of news outlets through television, radio and the Internet has to an extent commoditised *news* – we find *things* out however we can from radio, television, newspapers, the Internet, or from people who have consumed one or more of these channels. Thus, it is in the realm of how *useful* media is to us that we make our choices of purchase. A newspaper that is full of stories of soap stars and sex scandals is of little use to the merchant banker trying to buy a Swiss pharmaceutical company, the *Financial Times* of little use to a McDonald's worker in the borders of Scotland. Consequently, a newspaper is now both a record of a news event, such as September 11, and also a take on that news, which appeals to, or shapes, our take on the world. In fact the papers are now much more than this concept of targeted news and analysis: each in its way recommends travel destinations, clothes, Internet sites, insurance policies and banks. And specialised magazines take this 'educational element'[5] far further, with tips on every part of their editorial remit – be it high fashion or graphics software for the computer.

Thus media has a far closer relationship with retail than it might at first appear to – with the exception, largely, of the BBC, there is no longer a sense that one newspaper or television channel is the agency of public 'record' and thus somehow beyond retail's murky grip. In fact we can say that most newspapers are now, during heavy promotional seasons such as early autumn, agencies merely of free CDs rather than 'record', and that's about as good as it gets. Instead they are – to an extent – about editing our consumer choices, giving us information, but from a highly specific position, one that we may not totally agree with.

In an era of consumer choice, empowerment, total quality management, the service economy and comparison websites, we can

---

[5] Some people call this 'infotainment'.

believe, like Mulder and Scully, our culture's high priests of contemporary scepticism, that all the information is out there, somewhere, for us to make the best choice. We live, we are repeatedly told, in the Information Era, but we know also that there is too much information, that every commentator from the media critic to the sociologist and psychiatrist tells us we are in a state of overload. And so contemporary media steps into the gap to provide an edited commentary: it makes choices for us in everything from the number of columns it devotes to the euro to the number of photographs it features of David Beckham, Madonna or Elizabeth Hurley. Online 'weblogs' create easy links to the best stories of the day, irrespective of their source. Some say that a corollary to this process of necessary information editing is that we have dumbed down as cultures to cope with the too-muchness of the world.

We have argued elsewhere[6] that dumbing down, making choices about what we choose to know – football rather than opera, literary theory or information on Brad Pitt's love life rather than 'political news' – is probably the only answer in an era of too much information, as James Gleick points out in his book *Faster*.[7]

Even the *New York Times* altered its traditions to accommodate a time-pressured reading style, with modulated layouts and new tables of contents. This great purveyor of text conducted market surveys of people who matched *Times'* readers socio-economically in every way but one: they did not read the *Times*. Why not? The surveys found that non-readers felt intimidated by the sheer time-consuming bulk – that mass of words spread daily across broadsheet. Thus, without explicitly repudiating its 'All the News That's Fit to Print' history, the newspaper began trying a new slogan, still words of one syllable but fewer of them: 'Read What you Like.' 'Think of the newspaper as a sort of tasting menu.'

James Gleick, *Faster*[8]

We have also argued that much of the information out there is not true.[9] But that hardly seems to matter in many cultures where politics and leadership have been so deconstructed by journalists and theorists as to have elections become an experience not so different from choosing a fairground ride or a favourite pop band. It hardly seems to matter in societies where the nature of growth and development is about the market – and how we are all middle class now (and those who aren't don't count). Where, as the academic

---

[6] Robin Hunt, 'Dumbing down, the only way is up', *Aslib Proceedings*, Vol. 51, No. 2, February 1999, p. 46.
[7] James Gleick, 'Jog more, read less', in *Faster* (Little, Brown & Company), 1999, p. 140.
[8] Ibid.
[9] '"Information wants to be free" was the clarion cry as the Internet first took its place amongst its wiser media elders…the mistake was that freedom also brings 200 Diana conspiracy websites, it brings live sex from Amsterdam and naked celebrities, it brings email spam gushing onto our computers.' Hunt, 'Dumbing down, the only way is up', p. 46.

Benjamin Barber and the journalist Naomi Klein argue, governments have all but given in to the seductions of the free market, whatever the implications for freedom of access to a diversity of opinions.[10] Others, such as Tim Berners-Lee, the guru behind the World Wide Web, argue that it is merely a case of waiting for a digital nirvana when all information will be available to everyone to use how they will for a better world. In his autobiography, *Weaving the Web*, Berners-Lee writes: 'The ultimate goal of the Web is to support and improve our web-like existence in the world...We develop trust across the miles and distrust around the corner. What we believe, endorse, agree with and depend on is representable and, increasingly, represented on the Web. We have to ensure that the society we build with the Web is the sort we intend.'[11]

But this is an extremely optimistic position: for all the good information out there, there is an equal measure of bad. As some of the major telecommunications companies such as AOL, Time Warner, Yahoo!, Microsoft and Disney, who are all trying to publish good and immersive content, create giant Internet businesses – 'portals', which we can personalise to cover many aspects of our lives and buy things from – it becomes more difficult to judge what we are reading and consuming. If companies must pay for the optimum placement in a search engine how can we trust we are getting the best results when we search? Internet content is media, whether it is the online version of the *New York Times* or the corporate website for General Motors. The problem is that it becomes increasingly difficult to distinguish the motives underpinning media (a world of speed of light competition for audiences with the maximum options and choices to change channel or information source) from classical retail of goods and services, which is speedily chasing it.

Media is everywhere. The television news is available 24 hours a day; we can watch or we can zap from channel to channel, from home shopping to live sport and movies and back again, and we can find things that amuse or engross us but rarely for long. In any newsagent, magazines laden with advertisements aimed at each market sector, each *slice* of our worlds, now exist for seemingly any and every grouping within a culture: from the elderly gay community[12] through the early adopters of new technologies to the über-wealthy (and those who aspire to be) furniture fetishists. Technology – in this case desktop publishing – has enabled the costs of entry to the print world to be greatly reduced, and retail-

---

[10] See discussion in chapter 9 (Barber and Klein).
[11] Tim Berners-Lee, *Weaving the Web* (London: Harper Collins, 1999), chapter 10.
[12] J. Blotcher, 'For gay and lesbian elderly a paper of their own', *New York Times*, 12 March 2000, p. 7.

ers, only too pleased to be offered up the 'correct' market segments for their commodities, however well distinguished by branding or design they are, buy into these pages to gain association. And sales.

As consumers we don't use all or indeed know about many of the information offerings that are available to us because we don't have the time. If we investigated half of the things there for us, we would quickly become gibbering wrecks. Consider the end of the century lists of the 'best' that featured in every magazine and newspaper in December 1999.[13] These showed us, as if we needed it, that we haven't seen, heard, been, experienced, bought, thought even half of a shopping basket of what is – allegedly – the best art, music, travel location, concert, dress, book, philosophy of even the past 10 years, let alone our last century. These lists make it clear that being a specialist is the only rational route: to pare down, to simplify the things we want or need to know, to 'expert up'. These seem the logical next steps. And yet, how many of us want to be good at just one thing...to be in one place only? How, in this age of the Internet, of alleged globalisation, of uncertainty, can we feel secure, tenured, tethered to anything or anyone?[14] We are bedevilled by the reliability of our information sources: is the *Daily Mail* telling us the best fashion tips or merely the tips that they have been 'sold' by the PR company of a big perfume manufacturer that advertises in its pages? Is *Vogue*'s choice right or merely Vogueish? Is the holiday to Martinique described in *The Times* Saturday weekend section an accurate reflection of the island, or a rose-tinted version written by a journalist who has just enjoyed the largesse of the French tourist board for a week? Or to put it another way, is *Which?*[15] magazine right? Is amazon.com right when it makes choices for us? Are lastminute.com's holidays the best value, cheapest, last-minute choices? Is a computer bought online more of a bargain than one bought at the PC warehouse if the service isn't so good when it needs repairing? Is the online news written and consumed in eight minutes, but copied from a wire service such as Reuters, better than the news written over two hours available in print the next day? Who is in control? The answer, of course, is nobody.

We try to choose the most effective route to live our lives, to learn things, and technology helps us in many ways. It is easier to search for hotels in Paris from a website than by phoning 20 establishments there. It is cheaper to use the website than to buy a

---

[13] *Artforum International*'s December 1999 edition was a 'Best of the 90s' special edition, consisting almost entirely of lists.
[14] Consider the increase in divorce rates, the frequency with which people move house, and the growth of websites.
[15] A leading British consumer magazine.

guidebook (which will probably be out of date, even if it has been published recently). We shop locally late at night in a neon-lit supermarket or early in the morning from our gloomy local corner store, paying the often costly premium for 24-hourness on one hand, and ease and familiarity on the other. We suffer the supermarket shuffle because one shop, however painful, can feed us for a week. We suffer the changing room queue because one new suit may keep us in employment for a few more months. Because one new pair of trousers might get us a date on Saturday night.

In the end all of the processes of retailisation are about information: our access to it and the speed and timeliness at which it arrives, and the time we will commit to the process, consciously and unconsciously, of deciding whether or not we believe it – and whether or not we will 'buy' into it.

The identity parade

'Who are you really, and what were you before? And what did you do? And what did you think?'

Humphrey Bogart to Ingrid Bergman, *Casablanca*, 1942

It is almost more difficult for the retailers than for us to understand (and merely to see and comprehend) all the information out there. For them the arrival of the digital retail selling points means these are not so much times of change – change management has been a mantra in business for years, after all. These are times of transformation for them as well. That means becoming new kinds of businesses, new kinds of retailers – becoming everything. 'We are now faced with abandoning many of the things we have done in the past,' the chairman of Lloyds TSB, Sir Brian Pitman, told *Management Today*. He continued: 'Abandonment is a much more difficult concept to accept than mere change. What we are managing today is not evolution or even rapid change. We are having to manage transformation.'[16]

And that transformation is not simply a case of technological revolution, of the moving towards the digital; it is also a social one. For just as retailers, manufacturers and producers of services are getting to grips with a world in which bricks and mortar techniques grow ever more sophisticated and need to be combined with the nascent world of virtual clicks to online stores, so too we are now overloading with people we *might* be. Consumers as well as retailers are now both physical and virtual. This process of changing our needs and wants used to be called aspirationalism or just 'getting married' or merely 'growing old'. Nowadays it is everything from

---

[16] Sir Brian Pitman, 'My opinion', *Management Today*, June 2000, p. 14.

being canny shoppers by using software agents to find us the cheapest goods to being crazed debt-laden over-spenders following fashions in clothes, interiors, drugs, drinks or holidays, which we cannot rationally afford. It is about an 'ageing population' that resolutely refuses to act 'old' – whatever that is. It is about a constantly changing perspective on who we are, about a world where the definite has been replaced by the perhaps. It is about *options*. About *probably*.

It is also about the things we *could* buy. Do we buy a diary or a Filofax? A Filofax or a software program diary for our computer? Software or a Palm Pilot? A Palm Pilot or a programmable mobile telephone? A mobile or a WAP phone? Or a diary? As David Redhead writes in *Products of our Time*: 'Most of us living in the wealthy parts of the world have never had it so good or so cheap or so fast and that's the way we like it. Literally and metaphorically, we are speed addicts, relishing every new speedy accessory, lapping up production's growing ability to get us everything we want as soon as we want it.'[17]

We are, despite our upbringings, despite education, finally the inheritors of *The Great Gatsby* myth: we can – *we think* – become other people, can transform ourselves through what we buy. We can control the person or people we are. And, unlike Jay Gatsby, seduced by a woman whose voice sounded of money,[18] we don't need huge amounts of money to do this. At first.

Our transformation may be for a few hours when we are in a club, or shopping when we buy a new brand and an unsuitable fashion idea because of celebrity endorsement or cool placement in trendy magazines. This may be when we are on holiday, 'liberated' by the credit that our plastic gives us to live out a short-break, rich-and-famous lifestyle. It may be because we have reinvented ourselves professionally through adult re-education or, at the most extreme, we may have truly become someone else: 'Of the 250,000 people who go missing each year in the United Kingdom, many have vanished voluntarily according to the National Missing Persons Helpline,' Jocasta Shakespeare wrote in *The Times*. 'They have changed their identity; they may even have bought a copy [for where there are people seeking transformation, there are retail opportunities] of *Get Lost,* a new guide on how to disappear from your old life and reinvent yourself as a new person.'[19]

On the retailers' side this issue of who people are, and how *they* reinvent themselves to appeal both to this confusing new us, and

[17] David Redhead, *Products of our Time* (Belgium: Birkhäuser, 2000).
[18] F. Scott Fitzgerald, *The Great Gatsby* (first published 1925, London: Abacus Books, 1991 edn), p. 113.
[19] Jocasta Shakespeare, 'I'm sorry I didn't recognise you', *The Times*, 10 June 2000, p. 19.

to their very unconfusing, profit-driven shareholders, is even more complex. In 1995 large retail chains, faced with enormous rental charges, saw the promises of the virtual world and grew giddy with excitement. What if, they (and their shareholders) chanted, we could close all our stores, or sack all our salespeople, or sell everything from a website? At the same moment millions of managers, students and just about anyone on the lookout for a fast buck, thought: what if we set up a rival to that established brand, which *can't* sack all its staff, get rid of its stores – can't disintermediate? Thus was born the first retail world war of bricks and mortar versus the digital: it lasted about four years. Amazon.com suddenly became a threat to Barnes & Noble and Waterstone's bookstores. eBay became a threat to every newspaper with revenues from small ads. Thousands of dot.com start-ups could suddenly offer retail with choice, control and – very often – cheaper prices. But online, as an early geek said, nobody knows if you are a dog. That goes for us as consumers – the only way retailers can define us in online retail is if we buy something – but it also goes for dot.coms and e-commerce websites. Why should we trust them? Why should we use them? In many cases we didn't.

So it is not surprising in this interim environment of physical and virtual confusion that classical high street brands – indeed all retail businesses – who don't effectively embrace either speedy change or these new potential selling vehicles, find themselves in trouble. At the very basic level they are in trouble with their e-commerce obsessed shareholders. For example, media organisations are told they need to be partnered with a retailer within a few years or go bankrupt. A *Financial Times* Information Technology Survey in June 2000 began: 'What do you get when you cross traditional media with the Internet? Many music publishers, broadcasters and film studios [they could have added high street retailers] would dearly love to know…the Internet today is metamorphosing into a complex and radically different medium that creates as many challenges as it does opportunities for the traditional media giants.'[20]

Transformation

So we are living in an interim world somewhere between the physical and the virtual. A prelapsarian world, perhaps, before e-commerce really works; before the secrets of DNA code enable The Chosen to live for 500 years; before we decide if science and technology can make a difference to retail.[21] We don't know if we will

---

[20] Geoffrey Nairn, 'Internet heralds a new media age', *Financial Times*, 7 June 2000.
[21] See chapter 7 for more discussion about this.

still quite happily allow a human to guide us in our purchasing decisions, a shop assistant or a 'personal shopper' to give advice to us in a store.[22] Or whether, more significantly, we will allow a database to make suggestions, for example the 'recommendations' made for registered users of the website amazon.com? (The 'you've bought *Pride and Prejudice* by Jane Austen, have you considered trying *Bridget Jones's Diary?*' school of matching association that is now possible using computer database techniques.) Will we finally learn to love and trust the computers that improve the data-processing aspects of our lives enough to let them make retail choices on our behalf? Or will we just allow ourselves to be swept up into a physical retail experience such as Disneyland or Bluewater and leave rationality behind us, replacing it with pleasure?[23]

Would we; will we? We don't know. We know that some of the metaphors of contemporary retail are about us being in control, about being 'helped' to be in control. We know that some of these metaphors are about choice and information. We know that the promises of e-commerce are of a world where at the click of a mouse we can compare, contrast, be expertly and rationally guided – and *buy*. We also know that many of the physical retailers' metaphors are about entertainment and immersion; these are not about our control or rational guidance. They are about creating a world in which we feel comfortable enough to spend, despite our rational thought.

We know that the metaphors of contemporary business are about transformation. For example, the world's leading computer chip manufacturer, Intel, is not in the business of creating silicon interiors for personal computers: it is in the business of 'the delivery of information and lifelike interactive experiences', chairman Andy Grove stated five years ago.[24] Volkswagen is not in the business of selling cars at its flagship $500 million theme park, Autostadt: it is about building relationships. Whether retailers are transforming faster or slower than us it is always hard to know or predict, but in so doing they are transforming the promises of retail. Retail tells us Gap or Nike will make you cool; Disney will take over your imagination and create your histories; the Internet

---

[22] Harvey Nichols' personal shopping team has been visiting the growing number of European and US investment banks and institutions in London that have ditched pinstripe suits in favour of more relaxed dress codes. Chief Executive Joseph Wan said: 'We are teaching investment banks and institutional organisations on how to adapt to this trend. We can tailor our presentation to individual companies.' *Retail Week*, 23 June 2000, p. 3.
[23] 'Creating the ultimate retail and leisure experience is the aim of Bluewater', in 'Welcome to Bluewater', LendLease Ltd, 1999.
[24] Comdex. Quoted in B. Joseph Pine and James H. Gilmore, *The Experience Economy* (Harvard Business Press, Boston, Mass.: Harvard Business School Press, 1999), p. 3.

will save your business; the Millennium Dome in London will bring you 'One Amazing Day'; Manchester United can take us from cradle to grave.

The allure of such transformations was trumped by the promise of techology. Its ability to guide us, to speed us, to help us overcome our apparent time imbalance has become the dominant part of the discourse of the digital era, just as it was part of every culture's in times of technological change. Whether it is billable hours, leading to longer working, whether it is the time disruptions and instant requirements of the mobile, email-using world, or whether it is merely that there are more things to distract us, there really doesn't ever seem to be enough time and technology appears to be there to aid us. Perhaps this is all in our imaginations, perhaps not. Consider these lists for a moment and decide.

Speed of banking transactions, 1880–2005:

- 1880 – We write a letter to the bank manager asking for an overdraft; we get a letter back making an appointment. We reply. We meet and discuss. A letter confirming our arrangement is sent to our house. Approximate time to do business: *three weeks to one month*.
- 1910 – We send a telegram; we get a letter back and the process continues as above. Approximate time to do business: *three weeks*.
- 1930 – It is possible that a few of us now phone to discuss business; sometimes we can agree over the phone, but usually we ring to arrange a meeting. Approximate time to do business: *two weeks*.
- 1970 – We fax our point of view; the bank phones us back with a decision. Approximate time to do business: *two days*.
- 1990 – We phone on our mobile; the bank phones us back. Approximate time to do business: *one day*.
- 1995 – We arrange a meeting via our ATM; sometimes the ATM can even sort out our problems, pay all bills, move money from one account to another. Approximate time to do business: *half an hour*.
- 1998 – We email to discuss or we arrange everything from home via our Internet bank account. Approximate time to do business: *half an hour to two hours*.
- 2003 – We phone via our Internet connection and our video link. Approximate time to do business: *15 minutes*.
- 2005 – All communication is via our bank smart card, which always knows where we are, worldwide, because of its global positioning system. We are always in communication – albeit with an intelligent database, rather than a human. Approximate time to do business: *none*.

Speedy knowledge of, or influence over, our lives, however they are led, is central to retail – and banking is retail as much as anything else. The new services that technology allows might have helped banks to keep us as customers, might have appeared to offer us a new flexibility. But in these times services, however clever and real-time, are on their own not enough. For we also don't any longer all behave in a classically linear way, don't repeat actions in the way we might have 20 or 50 years ago, don't all end up in 40-year marriages with 2.3 kids living in the suburbs. We have, instead, tendencies that change with speed. 'The days of predictable, packaged audiences and comfortable media dominance are waning,' Dan O'Brien, senior analyst with Forrester Research, wrote.[25] That's because most Western consumer cultures allow difference, allow us to choose how we live. Or appear to. We are transforming ourselves: experiencing more (we can now travel the world more easily and more cheaply than any generation before us), knowing more (in 50 years the number of books published per year in the United States has risen from 85,000 to 1.8 million)[26] and working with many different kinds of people (where in 1950 the average number of jobs someone would have in their life was one or two, people entering their first jobs in 2000 might reasonably expect to have another 40 before they retire). This all leads to an unstable concept of consumers, and unstable times for retailers, as we shall see. And certainly technology does not *per se* offer all the solutions to this new kind of melting pot.

Of course, we do have time for some stable things. We have time for experiences: for television dramas, sports events, movies, weddings, holidays; for people. Somehow we find time for some of these things. So we have time to eat with family or friends and we have time to visit a church or a music festival. We have time because we choose to. We have the choice to do many things when we are at home, when we are out in cities or in the countryside and when we are travelling – even when we are at work. But what retailisation attempts to do is to emphasise that the thing we have the choice to do most is to…buy things. In fact, increasingly, what we are being offered to buy is *personal experiences*. Retail has learnt that we give our time to experiences not goods or services. If you like, retailisation is about us buying a good experience with our bank, not online banking, or a new kind of mortgage. So retail is in the experience business too.

This confusing physical (and metaphysical) choice is spiralling before us now. We can buy things to make ourselves 'individual'.

---

25 'UK media companies must build universal destinations and strong retail partnerships to survive beyond 2005', Forrester Research, 27 June 2000.
26 Gleick, *Faster*, p. 142.

We can buy to be a part of a group, or we can join the visual culture.[27] By this we mean we can be self-aware as we allow ourselves to be immersed in the iconography of retail and its many tribal groups (from an H&M girl to a Prada power dresser, from Gap-weekender or Niked-up gym-goer to a summer-long Aya Napa clubber: each has their 'look' each season). We can and do consume beguiling images of retail and selling almost everywhere: from the poster billboard to the banner advert on a website; from the television to the mobile phone; from the airport cabin to the bar urinal. It has been estimated that we consume around 17,000 advertising messages a day and most of them are visual.[28] This visual culture is packed with even more information than the verbal or the textual: it immerses us in images of worlds we half recognise and often aspire to, and we take these in, willingly or not. Thus many of our choices in life are proscribed by a space where speed, image and retail meet with location to provide us with what can, positively, be described a process that brings us the experience that we have control over who we are and how we live. It can also be seen negatively as a process that can leave us numb, in debt, and totally confused. Overloaded, in fact, with retail information.

Don't look down
Cool lunch, great chat, new and old media converge:
lunch on Fifth Avenue, Manhattan – a nice meeting.
Stovin Hayter, editor of *Revolution* is in expansive
mood. Over coffee, he disappears to the bathroom and
returns in a state of high excitement. We have been

---

[27] On 14 October 1999 a storefront of Waterstone's in Long Acre, London, celebrated a six-magazine 'book' called *Symbol Soup*. Among the longueurs of graphic designers given their head to 'talk' in these books there were some insights: 'Due to the ever-increasing mediatisation and the growing opportunities to travel, including on the World Wide Web, we are now more entitled than ever to talk about a global youth generation. Since the late Eighties MTV and its pop stars play everywhere – as another kind of soap. Lara Croft and Mario Bros. have evolved from interactive play figures to worldwide heroes. Well-known world brands, from Calvin Klein to McDonald's and from Nike to Netscape, add another series of important ingredients to the symbols and lifestyles of global youth. These brands and their products not only fulfil instrumental, material needs; at least as important is the symbolic function they exert. Nike, for instance, is far more than just a sports shoe. The brand touches the mindset and heartstrings of a large proportion of VG [the Visual Generation] by offering an attitude for living: "Just Do It". Today, the dynamics of production and consumption have shifted from the "logic of utility" towards the "logic of desire", making symbols even more important than ever....' 'The fear of being swallowed by the global triangle of mediatisation, Americanisation and commercialisation is real to VG (as is its seductiveness). This explains youth's fascination for the underground and its veneer of illicitness, danger, adventure, escape from branding...'
[28] James Gleick, *Faster* (Little, Brown & Company), 1999, p. 76.

> describing the processes of 'peripheral space' and the
> way that retail has invaded them. 'First urinal on the
> left,' he says breathlessly. 'Go pee now!' We obey. As the
> course of nature takes place, a voice says, 'Hey, look
> here.' At eye level a plasma screen advert for the Sci-Fi
> channel is 'speaking' to us. It tells us when the new
> 'Invisible Man' show first airs, and not to miss it. We've
> been retailed in peripheral space – while peeing.
> *Revolution*, a British new media magazine, folded in the
> US within a year of being launched as part of the down-
> turn in the dot.com world, it wasn't of the 'right' time.
> The market folded.

The process of retail and its evolution over the previous centuries
can be described in a simple progression:

- from selling goods – because we needed or wanted them – to
  selling services that bring added value to us as consumers
  (because goods such as toothpaste or baked beans, and with
  the Internet and its cost-checking search engines, cars or Nike
  trainers, have become so commoditised they are bought by their
  price alone)
- from selling services – such as financial advice or having knowledgeable, well-read booksellers to advise on that summer read
  – to selling 'experiences' that in some way and in some or many
  places engage us in a relationship over time, so that as consumers we will return again and again, less mindful of cost or
  time issues
- from selling experiences – the perfect drive in a car; the perfect
  fun day with the kids at Disney World captured forever on video
  and made manifest by the purchase of t-shirts, books and memorabilia; the perfect day in a bookshop where we find not only
  our book choice, but enjoy passing the time by reading it over
  a cappuccino and ciabatta – to the selling of 'transformations'
  whereby the experiences we have as consumers (of life) change
  the people we are, even if only temporarily
- from selling transformations – as a possibility for anyone who
  buys in – to the selling of individualised transformations as a
  given. Think of it as the mylife.com transformation. So Nike
  transforms me into a better athlete: even if I only run for 10
  minutes a week, Nike shoes, if I choose the correct model for
  me, will help to make me a better runner. Amazon.com transforms me as a reader because it recommends new books to me
  each time I visit its site from its knowledge (gained by monitoring my use of the site) about what I buy and read. Barnes &
  Noble bookshop could transform me as a person because, sit-

ting over my book or magazine in its peaceful café, I might meet my partner for life.[29]

This may sound overtly schematic and it is important to explain that we are not here entering a critique or concrete methodology of retail – creating an us and them-ness around the relationship of buyer and seller – though in chapter 9 we will explore who is opting out of retail's globalised economy. What we are exploring is retail's role, our relationship to it and how these relationships have changed dramatically, though far from perfectly, with the arrival of the digital world.

To prove a point about the new Internet dot.com nirvana of home e-commerce that will revolutionise our world, an American man once named Mitch Maddox has chosen to take to his home and live a normal life without leaving it.

Can humankind live by the Internet alone? A 26-year-old Dallas man who legally changed his name late last year to DotComGuy thinks so, and he and some associates are hoping to make a career out of proving it.

To demonstrate that we need never walk into a store, grocery, library, school, government office, movie house, arcade or repair shop again, the man formerly known as Mitch Maddox of Highland Park put his career as a computer systems manager on hold and moved into a Dallas townhouse Jan. 1. He has restricted himself to the townhouse and its back yard for a year.

DotComGuy is relying on his computer and Internet connections to locate and supply all his material needs – food, clothing, furnishings, entertainment, medical care, essentially everything.

Paula Felps, *Dallas Morning News*[30]

It isn't that bad really. Not yet. For every academic or performance artist who has implanted chips to dot.com themselves into a world that seems inspired by the terrifying dystopian novels of author William Gibson,[31] there are millions who haven't reneged on their analogue, corporeal way of life. Who are all these weird

---

[29] 'You May Not Find a Book But You May Find a Partner For Life', was an advertising campaign for Barnes and Noble stores in spring 1999.
[30] Paula Felps, 'E-tailers keep an eye on DotComGuy', *Dallas Morning News*. But although DotComGuy may have chosen to be cut off from much of the physical world for 12 months, he's definitely not alone. DotComGuy has managers, producers, a public relations handler and a personal trainer all dedicated to him. The attention of multitudes of mass media is fast developing his celebrity. For example, the 24 January edition of *People* chronicled DotComGuy's challenge to have beer delivered to his home. His every move is caught on video cameras – 16 inside and outside – which are monitored in a control room by a fleet of technicians in the adjoining townhouse. Only his bedroom and the bathroom are off limits. Anyone with access to the Internet can tune into the continuing adventures of DotComGuy as he tries to make it after all. But why do it? For $98,280 (along with set payments for all his online purchases) from a host of sponsors, including NetBank, Gateway computers, United Parcel Service, Service911.com, TheMall.com and the *Dallas Morning News* – if DotComGuy completes his year on the Net.
[31] Kevin Warwick, *i in the Sky* (London: Aslib, 1999).

web-hermit-like people, you might ask. Well, they are either a newly 'transformed' market sector or a new 'media' invention – or both. Are they true people? Do they accept that everything 'we believe, endorse, agree with and depend on is representable and, increasingly, represented on the Web?', as Berners-Lee puts it when writing of the Internet?[32] Or are we just a little cynical about Vogue Woman or DotComGuy? Will the market segments they represent be sliced up into ever new slices to entertain us over the coming months and years? Yes. Do they even exist, six months after they were invented? Who knows? Retailers will have taken note, for sure, but will only have acted if it helps them to sell things.

The new technologies

DotComGuy is but one example of how speed and change have become manifest most strikingly during the past eight years in which the Internet has undergone the kind of economic and social revolutions that historically take many generations. Since 1994 and the beginnings of the World Wide Web we have seen gurus come and go and early adopters tell us the Web would change everything.[33] We have seen the educators promising universal access to all knowledge, then noted the arrival of pornographers, the media, money, millions of home pages (*Time* magazine described the Internet as 'the invention that puts the 'me' into 'medium'),[34] the invasion by cults such as Heaven's Gate – the infamous web-agency cult that exploded so violently and tragically in 1998 – freaks and gamblers. The Web has inveigled its way into our homes, our work and our cafés. It is accessible through some of our phones, and will soon be part of all phone networks. It is already in some cars and aeroplanes; there are even those who believe it will become part of our bodies. Between 1994 and 1999 speed was the reason why a new dot.com was created every five seconds and why so many dot.com businesses whose aim was to sell things online got massive investment funds. Speed is the reason why Bob Foster, the Executive Director of the Centre for Management in the Information Economy at UCLA, can say: 'I see a lot of people who are coming up with an idea that uses the tech-

---

32 Tim Berners-Lee, *Weaving the Web* (London: Harper Collins, 1999).
33 'Because the Digital Revolution is whipping through our lives like a Bengali typhoon – while the mainstream media is still groping for the snooze button. Because the more fascinating and powerful people today are not politicians or priests, generals or pundits, but the vanguard who are integrating digital technologies into their business and personal lives, and causing social changes so profound their only parallel is probably the discovery of fire...' 'Why wired?', leader in the first edition of *Wired UK*, March 1995. The magazine closed in 1997.
34 James Poniewozik, 'We like to watch', *Time*, 26 June 2000, p. 56.

nical ability of the Internet, but haven't the foggiest idea of the real business they're going into.'[35] My, how right was Bob.

In Spring 2000 a retail e-commerce 'dot.com millionaire' – soon, real soon, maybe – friend of our business phoned to recommend a guy he'd met at an Internet 'social' event. The man was a 'great entrepreneur' with a b2b[36] retail idea in which our company might invest, our friend thought. So we phoned him and within two hours we are eating hamburgers in the upstairs room of an anonymous City of London pub. 'Sorry about the pub, we can't go to my local for obvious reasons,' he said, edgily. The guy is 23 years old, Scandinavian, with a Harvard Business School education. He has been in the United Kingdom for four months. His b2b knowledge-retail idea is lukewarm; we've heard it at least six or seven times before in the past two years. It is being done by better people than the group he has put together. 'I need to know how much it will cost to build the website,' he said. 'You have four hours.'

The next day, and nothing done about the plan – we have not had time to even think about it – he phones, emails and finally sends grim fax warnings about us stealing the idea. When we finally speak and we question his anxiety, he merely says, 'We have a week to get this right, four weeks to launch it, otherwise it is too late.'

We never speak again. A few weeks later we lunch with our friend, but we never get to talk about the Scandinavian man, because he himself has come within 'two hours of meltdown'. The venture capitalists wouldn't cough up for the second-round funding of his e-commerce company. 'The environment has changed a 180 degrees,' Merrill Lynch analyst Henry Blodget told the *New Yorker*.[37] 'Six months ago your biggest problem if you were an e-commerce start-up was to avoid being drowned in the money that was being thrown at you. Today, it's persuading your investors to give you that extra 20 million you need not to go under.'

Our friend had made the oh-too-real millennium year journey from dot.com millionaire manqué to dot.com monkey who just wants to keep his head above water in

---

[35] Quoted in Adam Bryant, 'I'm in the garage', *Newsweek*, 29 May 2000, p. 73.
[36] business-to-business
[37] Blodget, *New Yorker*, 17 October 2000.

> around five weeks. His business was about nine months old. 'It's too late to think about a flotation now,' he said wistfully over the à la carte menu – my, things have changed; it used to be £60 bottles of wine – 'we're just thinking about a trade sale'.
>
> Too late. We hear the phrase all the time. It is too late to have a unique Internet idea, too late to enter the digital world, too late to get money from the generous venture capitalists, too late to say you are sorry, as that great philosopher, Carlos Santana, once sang. Or as the author and journalist, James Gleick, wrote in 1999: 'We are in a rush. We are making haste. A compression of time characterises the life of the century now closing.'[38]

And even when they are unconditionally out there and marketing heavily, the e-commerce promises such as 'Thousands of Stores. Millions of Products. All with one Wallet' – the strapline for Yahoo!'s shopping channel, one of the most favoured destinations on the Internet – don't always bear fruit:

The ordering may be express, but the delivery seems Pony Express. That is shaping up as a central issue in the highly competitive world of online shopping, and it is spawning creative solutions for getting goods to customers more quickly. 'I can order a book on my lunch break, but if I have to wait a week to get something, it becomes less valuable,' said Stacey McCullough, a senior analyst at Forrester Research, in Cambridge, Mass., explaining the frustration that sends many potential online shoppers to the mall. Delivery delays are often attributed to the parcel carrier, but mishaps frequently occur before an order leaves the warehouse. Not that this matters to the customer, who knows only that the order did not arrive on time.

Jonathan Burton, *New York Times*[39]

For while the promise of e-commerce is in many ways irresistible – you don't have to fight in the mall, don't have to queue at the till – there is the other side: you do have to wait in for the delivery. If it comes at all. In a recent study in the United States, 19 per cent of online customers said the delivery of their order either took longer than they expected or simply never occurred. As a result, many stopped shopping online, while others removed the offending e-tailer from their bookmarks.

But, whatever the reality, we plough on. Those of us who use the Internet and all its retail information do sometimes find great e-commerce solutions: Amazon books, Buzz airlines, lastminute.com. But in the physical world we still find ourselves

---

[38] Gleick, *Faster*, p. 9.
[39] Jonathan Burton, 'Creating ways to cut the delivery, time from mouse to house', *New York Times*, 7 June 2000, p. 38.

queuing at stand-by gates, or outside changing rooms, growing ever more time-raged. And when we see so many adverts for this brave new world of instant retail gratification, or when we are assailed in the most ludicrous of places with marketing messages about the great digital, we are torn. We want this electronic on-demand world, but we want the electronic world to work now, not merely be learning the tricks of the retail trade that physical shops and retailers have been honing for the past 150 years (see chapter 2). We want to avoid being guinea-pigs in the first few years of the Internet's speedy progress towards its retail nation-state status – the ultimate, no place, no tax, über shopping mall – because it often wastes our time and is not so pleasurable to use.

As humans we believe we want to run, not walk. And so we definitely want the high-profile, high-living newbies of electronic commerce to run really fast.

Controlled transformation: the personalisation effect

We live, we think, in an era of control over the worlds around us. We are all individuals now, it seems.[40] Now we all want to be unique and special. As Toyota advertised its cars in the United States in 1999: 'It's not for everyone, just for you.' We have seemingly bought this notion that despite mass-production – given variety by new production processes that efface time (which, as with, say, the Audi 8 car, build out one piece of aluminium, and yet hide this commoditisation through design variation: colour, seating, CD player and in-car global position system) – we are made uniquely special, we are transformed yet in control. Think of that next time you see Tom Cruise in his sexy, sleek Audi Roadster in *Mission: Impossible 2*, or Madonna in the latest pair of $300 faded jeans. Special? Well, up to a point we are. Unique, just for us? Is this what retail can do? No, it can merely allude to and play on our desire to be. It can merely play on our faith that it will transform us.

Human resources experts tell us that it is we who choose a company to join, not the other way around. It is we who dress as we like, who live where we wish, who go where we want. But we

---

[40] In 2000, in a stressful meeting with a pent-up, no-time-to-think, tetchy television executive, the atmosphere lightened considerably when the executive's mobile phone went off – playing the Lalo Schiffrin theme music from *Mission: Impossible* rather than the more prosaic ringing tone or an extract from disco Mozart. 'It's great,' he said. 'You go to the Nokia website, choose a piece of music and it downloads – *straight* to your phone.' The vision of this executive sitting at home flicking between music samples of *Mission: Impossible*, *Starsky and Hutch* and James Bond is too striking to ignore: this man never returns phone calls or emails and apparently has no time for anyone. Retailisation has got to him, has *immersed* him.

very often don't have the time to know what we want, or indeed who we are; don't have time to be transformed, are too busy solving the problems of being us. Retailers exploit this time problem (or, as we shall argue as well, help us by being constantly near at hand to guide us in our decision-making). And yet for most of us there is the nagging doubt that we are not controlled individuals at all, as we leer at that Audi TT Roadster or pair of twisted jeans, as we buy online our 'cheap' airline tickets from our 'MyFlight' page to escape, only to discover we have paid a small fortune.

We believe that the future of retail will be about a process of colonisation of every space: from the high street to the home, from the virtual world to the physical handset technologies we carry with us wherever we are, to our very imaginations, to each of our imaginations as individuals. Retailisation is, in fact, about the ultimate colonisation: a no-border light-speed global thrust, which will travel to every space in which people pay money to buy things. What is core to the concept is that we can, if we choose, believe it will be a force for good. We can imagine.

So let us imagine for a moment. What follows is one very speedy vision of experience-driven, transformational retail in its broadest sense. It is a very personal vision of the consumer life as it can be – and in some cases is – lived today. However, this is the vision of retail possibilities that is promised for all of us through the wonders of the networked world, through the extravagances of the shopping experience and, most fundamentally, through the choices and speed with which we can make them available to us. But remember, for every moment you think of the following experience as a psychotic impossibility, think of yourself or your kids watching MTV or playing a computer game, think of your experiences with a television zapper or in a shopping mall, think of the future when your DNA will be on your credit card and 'corrective' drugs available at the click of a mouse.

Saturday night fever

The whole day long there was fever, delirium, and unconsciousness. At midnight the patient lay without consciousness, and almost without pulse. The end was expected every minute.

Leo Tolstoy, *Anna Karenina* [41]

It is 9 p.m. – realtime – on a wet spring stay-at-home Saturday night in London and there's nothing much to watch on the 350 satellite television channels we pay around £50 a month to possess. We've already seen most of the half-good pay-for movie options that have been promoted heavily during the early evening ad-breaks, apart, that

---

[41] Leo Tolstoy, *Anna Karenina*, trans. George Gibiart (London: Norton Critical Editions, 1995), part IV, chapter XVII, p. 397.

is, from the soft-porn channels and they hold no interest. Even if they did, there are at least six late-night erotic films available on the foreign channels without further expense as long as you don't mind the German dubbing and another half an hour or so wait. We pick at the last of the takeaway food and check the time on Teletext. Then we try a listings magazine: Tate Modern – the place everyone is going right now – is open only for another hour, and we live 40 minutes away.

Our date for the evening has emailed to say she's ill, and our other tentative evening companion has her mobile switched off. The *Frasier* episodes being re-run on the Comedy Channel we've seen just once too often, and there's no Larry Sanders just when we want it. It is a 20-minute walk to the video store from the flat and it is pouring with rain, and they don't do home delivery – yet – nor can we download the movies we might want from the Internet, even though it seems as though the new media gurus have been telling us about convergence, broadband and video-on-demand for centuries now. The radio doesn't work, it has no batteries, but we've been about six months without it with no discernible effect on our culture or our persistent condition of information and experience overload.

The Web doesn't hold any appeal tonight, not even 'my' Yahoo!, and in the flat below us two small children will be sleeping, we were informed tersely by email the previous day, making a mid-evening dose of Basement Jaxx or Jacques Brel CDs – well, they're actually MP3 (the audiocompression system) burnt on to CDs – out of the question. We try a book that has arrived by post from amazon.com but we're not in the mood for another novel about how difficult it is to be a 'bloke' in an era of equality, six-pack 'abbs' and no commitment on any side of the gender war. The nearby pub is heaving with satellite-less punters watching the re-run of England versus Brazil at football, and it is too late even for last-minute.com to whisk us away for the rest of the weekend to a country hotel. We could go clubbing to one of the new breed of slick East London nightclubs for old people who still think themselves to be 17, but we want to be up early tomorrow to work. We can't check my stocks on my phone or the Web – or even in the paper, because it is the weekend, and nobody's trading. And because we choose not to have a car – unnecessary in London, which is overcrowded and over-polluted enough without our contribution – we can't even visit family as public transport at this time of night in the capital veers towards the Bermuda Triangle rather than the south of London. There's always a taxi. We ring the local mini-cab rank to discover there is an hour and a half wait. 'The rain, you see, very busy with the rain, and the bank holiday weekend,' the admin controller tells us. As for neighbours? Don't be ridiculous, never spoken to them. They're different from us, not our market cluster at all. We know the guy and his family at the off-licence and the convenience store, but only to say hello.

The Saturday night we describe, however accelerated and exaggerated its possible activities seem, is about the physical newsrack of retail choice and the virtual portal of purchasing opportunities, too. It is about the confusion that such choice engenders in us as individuals and collectively. Retailisation is, to paraphrase the philosopher Soren Kierkegaard, about the dizziness that comes with 'freedom' – however constructed – that can cause either delight or despair. Consider the parable of Buridan's Ass, attributed to a 14th-century French philosopher and logician named Jean Buridan. Buridan, who has also been credited with originating probability theory, poses a simple idea, which goes as follows. An ass is hungry and there are two similar piles of hay in front of him, one to the right, and one to the left. The ass has an exactly equally balanced tendency to go either right or left. Therefore, given such equality of choice, it will not be able to move, and will thus starve to death.

Retailers, be they of artificial intelligence software, architectural plans, coffee or condoms, try to ensure that none of us has that 'equally balanced tendency' so that we always do finally go to eat from one bale or the other, Volvo or Volkswagen, Viagra or Virgin. They want to remove the barriers of control and rationality we erect as humans, to make us question why we choose one thing and not another. However, they do not want us to die; that isn't a cool demographic. But increasingly they have ensured that we 'eat' not merely to live, but to exert a power over the world, to make a statement about ourselves. To buy in to the consumer dream – or rather the set of collected dreams we inhabit, which we call modern life. Retailers tell us that by making one decision – Volkswagen rather than Peugeot, for example – we are in control. The reality is that, modern car technology being what it is, we would also be in control if we had made the opposite decision.

So we choose, but we don't choose. We seek to control as, for example, when the anti-globalisation protesters attempt to disrupt World Bank meetings, or when they trash a Nike superstore or a McDonald's; or, more awfully, when ideological groups seek a kind of mental control by flying into the Twin Towers.

We seek control when we go shopping to the high street with a definite budget, but our credit cards tell us *we can afford it anyway*. We seek control when we use home shopping rather than the supermarket, but do we know the vegetables will be as good? Do we know we will get what we ordered? We seek control, but sometimes we give up and immerse ourselves in a pleasing experience and spend spend spend. As even the most engaged of anti-consumers admits, retail is seductive. Naomi Klein, author of the anti-corporate best-seller, *No Logo*, and an activist and reporter on the anti-globalisation movements such as the Seattle demonstrations of December 1999, said: 'I go to SoHo [in New York] and I see something and I admit I go crazy. I can resist it here in Toronto, it doesn't do it for me, but when I see the shops in New York or Paris it's all over for me. *Finished. I'm lost.'* [42]

Immersion

Captain Nemo's first care was to recall the unfortunate man to life again. I did not think he could succeed. I hoped so, for the poor creature's immersion was not long; but the blow from the shark's tail might have been his death-blow. Happily, with the Captain's and Conseil's sharp friction, I saw consciousness return by degrees. He opened his eyes. What was his surprise, his terror even, at seeing four great copper heads leaning over him! And, above all, what must he have thought when Captain Nemo, drawing from the pocket of his dress a bag of pearls, placed it in his hand!

Jules Verne, *20,000 Leagues Under the Sea* [43]

Finished. Lost. These are not the words of someone defeated, these are the metaphors of immersion. Immersion comes from retail being everywhere and selling itself as everything. Immersion comes from the transformation of retail, architecture, media and information into a fluid current of experiences and services dependent on pleasing us, somehow. What follows are just a few of the transformations of retail as it invades our lives everywhere, becoming, it appears, everything. The car is a shop, the phone a salesman, the motorway a high street. That's the promise. Everything is everything now: that is the retailers' implicit message. What do we mean by this opaque statement? Is this another example of dumbing down, another debasement of our culture? Is this what happens when the Microserfs get to pontificate from their virtual towers, freed of logical thought by the riches of Croesus promises of flotation on the National Association of Securities Dealers Automated Quotations (Nasdaq)? [44] We don't think so. Then again, we don't care. We believe it is simple. Over the past decade shopping, along with technology, social systems, politics, the media, travel, music, art, literature, sport, corporate organisation, nation states – everything – has changed beyond recognition.

Shopping malls, as we will discover, are now 'metaphysical brands'. Television is to be an interactive shopping experience. The Internet is now – and the World Wide Web is, please remember, barely ten years old – seemingly merely a series of e-commerce opportunities and share-price wonders. Architecture is virtual, three dimensions rendered on two-dimensional screens. Avatars

---

[42] Naomi Klein in personal interview; all quotes from interview.
[43] Jules Verne, *20,000 Leagues Under the Sea* (London: Bloomsbury Books, 1994) chapter 3, p. 32.
[44] Douglas Coupland.

have moved away from Eastern religions towards the non-existent spaces of virtual worlds.[45] Computer games make great films. Nearly. Medicine is going remote, a phone call or touch pad – and insurance policy – away. Academia is now big business. The home is a shop; the shop – increasingly – a home. In between, in the spaces we used to call outside, the periphery, the mobile phone is now a digital mail-order catalogue, a radio, a stock checker, a Walkman substitute; the touch screen a commonplace in malls and airports, the focus group and questionnaire a given at the shopping mall; the ATM is taking over from the bank manager. In the cinema feature films are now also mall experiences, DVDs, videos, pay-for satellite features, satellite fodder, television fodder, theme parks, marketing opportunities, soundtracks, breakfast cereals – and websites. (Architecture is now cinema, and vice versa.)[46] Haptics are coming,[47] so get ready to feel those bytes. In supermarkets and grocers food is now about genetic modification stickers and eco-campaigners' banners. Sport is about television rights. Pubs are about chains (we have nothing to gain but our chains).[48] Journalists are now content providers for shopping portals; print journalists are historians, so late, so dated, is their 'news'. Teenage geeks are now multimillionaires. State pensions will soon be (commercial) stakeholding opportunities. Computer games designers are now signing the Official Secrets Act to work with the Ministry of Defence. Government is waiting for the virtual ballot box, and is itself now an anxious wag-the-dog extension of advertising, film-making and focus grouping. And Bill Clinton did not lie.

Everything is everything.

No? Try this.

UK Media Companies Must Build Universal Destinations And Strong Retail Partnerships To Survive Beyond 2005, Forrester advises

Media companies must develop ultimate destinations – sites which provide a one-stop shop for all the information and product needs for a given interest group. These will be achieved through partnerships with retailers with the same target audience and strategy.

Forrester Research[49]

---

[45] Avatars are on-screen icon-based representations of human life. At present they are basic, lacking the mobility even of a good computer game hero such as Lara Croft. However, it is expected that in time these will be accurate mirrors of ourselves, but on screen.

[46] François Penz and Maureen Thomas, editors, *Cinema & Architecture* (London: British Film Institute, 1997).

[47] Mark Frauenfelder, 'The feel of things to come', *International Design Magazine*, November 1999, p. 106.

[48] See Barlife at http://www.barlife.co.uk.

[49] 'UK media companies must build universal destinations and strong retail partnerships to survive beyond 2005', Forrester Research, 27 June 2000. For the report 'UK Media's Retail Revolution' Forrester interviewed 26 executives from key media and retail companies and drew on information from a survey of 57 commercial websites.

Few offline brands are equipped to create one-stop ultimate destinations alone. Online, some media companies will bring several of their brands together to exploit a range of content, while some ultimate Web destinations require content from diverse owners. Forrester advises all 'ultimate destinations' to partner with retailers that complement their content strengths, and demonstrate a dedication to long-term co-operation. Both parties must be prepared to co-brand and co-develop where necessary; operating jointly, they will reduce the cost of participation for both players, reducing time to break-even.

So mind the gap. There isn't one any more between media or architecture or our living room or our favourite footballers and *selling things to us*. Everything is everything. Or rather, that's what light speed, which puts us in two places at the same moment, tells us. That is why we feel we can argue that, as consumers, we are often all but rendered out of control – or inert – by such facts. Despite the control we have – to change our clothes, our jobs, our computers, our home, our lives – retail is pursuing us with its processes of metamorphosis: this means there are 200,000 of Buridan's bales to chose from, not two.

Consider the last time you were genuinely away from retail. Think about the last time you were away from retail's siblings, branding and advertising, away from advertising targeted through media such as radio, television, the Web, or posters. Think about the last time you were away from viral marketing such as 'must have' trends your children demand to own (think Harry Potter, Pokemon, Stuart Little; a few years ago Spice Girls dolls; before that Playstations ... the list is endless). Think about the last time you were away from any retail opportunity.

Our Buridian confusion comes from *ennui* and tiredness (do we have enough time to sleep these days?) as much as from the rational understanding that we can never know everything. The confusion comes from overload as much as a simple two-way choice. It comes from our budgets and the possibilities that come from potential credit facilities. And our confusion comes as much from our desire for control as from a lack of control brought about by seemingly limitless choice. We find ourselves asking how can we buy anything, a newspaper or a toothpaste, a car or a mobile phone when we are confronted with so many *things?* We respond, sometimes, by buying the most convenient thing, the best-known thing – but is that necessarily the best? We know, because we are constantly being told, that we can now make the best – and the most convenient – retail decisions. It is merely that we don't quite believe it.

The plethora of choices now available – from numerous mobile phone tariffs to 180 TV channels, 40,000 products in the supermarket, including 18 types of organic cheese and over 400 different kinds of shampoo – is literally driving consumers to distraction according to new research by Abbey National. 'One of life's biggest irritations for nearly half of all women and one in five men is deciding what to eat each evening. And, perhaps surprisingly, this decision is more taxing for those with potentially more time on their hands to shop and cook, with 51 per cent of part-time working women labelling it as their worst bugbear.'[50]

Slow

To begin with clear and self-evident principles, to advance by timorous and sure steps, to review frequently our conclusions, and examine accurately all their consequences; though by these means we shall make both a slow and a short progress in our systems; are the only methods, by which we can ever hope to reach truth, and attain a proper stability and certainty in our determinations.

David Hume, *An Essay on Human Understanding*, section XI

Very well,' said the wolf, and he dashed away at full speed, followed by the others.

Frank L. Baum, *The Wizard of Oz*, chapter XII

We travel at light speed when the Internet's around. Except we don't really. We have the illusion of speed, which we try to escape when we are at home. Speed really happens when light travels in space, or at a trading desk in Berlin or on Wall Street.[51] But speed, the description of speed, the marketing of it, the branding of it, plays at us, plays with us to make us feel dissatisfied, telling us there is always a next, another: a summer blockbuster or a twisted pair of jeans; a pack of washing powder or a leather jacket for two-year olds from Gap for Kids. Speed takes us to the brink of joy that the latest *Star Wars* movie is arriving, and then despair that it is so. Speed build us up for events such as the Millennium or a football championship, Easter or Thanksgiving, holidays or school. Speed is foreplay, what happens next is often very disappointing.

Speed effaces many things, and quality and longevity are two of

---

[lii] 'How choosing the right clothes is wearing us out', research from the Abbey National Building Society in conjunction with the think-tank The Future Foundation, April 2000.

[liii] See Jonathan Leake, 'Eureka! Scientists break speed of light', *Sunday Times*, 4 June 2000, p. 1. 'Scientists claim they have broken the ultimate speed barrier: the speed of light. In research carried out in the United States, particle physicists have shown that light pulses can be accelerated to up to 300 times their normal velocity of 186,000 miles per second. The implications, like the speed, are mind-boggling. On one interpretation it means that light will arrive at its destination almost before it has started its journey. In effect, it is leaping forward in time. Exact details of the findings remain confidential because they have been submitted to *Nature*, the international scientific journal, for review prior to possible publication.'

the many victims. Yet retailisation and the texts promoting it posit a speeding transforming experience where it is never too late: a veritable Last Minute world where, whether physically or virtually, we can sate all our needs. Writing of speed, the no-timeness of our culture, the critic Susan George said in 1996:

In rich, industrialised countries, the seasons have virtually disappeared, anything is available at any time...Financial capital is pure speed and pure immaterial, profit. It makes instantaneous judgements on the values of national policies. If it doesn't like what it sees, it leaves, at the speed of bytes, leaving catastrophic consequences in its wake.

Susan George, 'Fast castes'[52]

There are many who urge us to consider inertia, slowness, the antithesis of the car, the Mach 3 or indeed the G3 computer upgrade culture;[53] there are others who can balance the speed-rush cocktail of drugs and house music or techno, or speed garage music (or the endless platforms of Playstation, Dreamcast and X-Box games) for hours if not days before final sleep.

This urge for speed will not dissipate. But now you are reading a book and that does not require speed. 'Sundial slowness' is one phrase we particularly liked. So, *Retailisation* is a book that tries to be of its time, which tries to be about the new speed, the new (and the next) economic models, the ineluctable processes of the free market, of fashion in everything from footwear to genetics. It is slower than the daily grind of paradoxical ft.com stories about the latest e-commerce initiative, or debacle, the next organ to be cloned, but faster than those five-year research projects that explore worlds long left behind.

While not wanting to be anachronistic, we have chosen to consider selective slowness without ever stooping to the New Futurism, that visionary, predictive, blue-skies writing and rhetoric we see and hear everywhere, which looks great in print for a while – have you read *Nineteen Eighty-four* recently, or *Being Digital*?[54] There is little about Shopping 2020 here, nor the 'inevitable' triumph of the machine over its architect. It would be a waste of time and print to speculate about a future when, because of the overt physical evidence of information overload all around us, we know we cannot know enough, or much, any longer.[55] On 23 November 2000 the *New York Times* reported

---

[52] Susan George, 'Fast castes', paper at the Netherlands Design Institute's Doors of Perception conference 'Speed', November 1996.
[53] Milan Kundera, 'Why has the pleasure of slowness disappeared?', *Slowness*, translated from the French by Linda Asher (London: Faber, 1996), p. 4.
[54] See George Orwell's *Nineteen Eighty-four* (Harmondsworth: Penguin, 1954) and Nicholas Negroponte, *Being Digital* (London: Vintage, 1996).
[55] Hunt, 'Dumbing down, the only way is up', p. 48.

that 'Retail battle returns to bricks'.[56]

Within six months the jazz of being a dot.com retailer was – with much old-school merriment – gone, and seemingly for good, the way many wrote it. And we thought it was all virtual now? That is the point. Things change so fast. Knowledge is circumscribed by economic climates; there will always be management consultants looking for the next thing to teach us. But now we don't even want to try and know everything.

So that was speed, choice, transformation, experience, and a few million confused asses. Now prepare to slow down – it is still going to be a bumpy ride.

---

[56] Bob Tedeschi, 'Retail battle returns to bricks', NYT.com technology, 20 November 2000, p. C12. 'Sleep is coming more easily these days to traditional retail executives, who by now barely become excited over the dot-com body count, or the latest e-tailing stock to drop below the buck. Gone are the days when they agonized about being "Amazoned", or blind-sided by a dot.com, and when the phrase "first mover advantage" conjured images of 20 year old Stanford drop-outs destroying their lives.'

Chapter 2 – Through the looking glass

Non nova, sed nove
Not new, but in new ways

Latin proverb

Mama had her morning duties, and daily drive, and the delightful round of visits and shopping which forms the amusement, or the profession as you may call it, of the rich London lady.

William Thackeray, Vanity Fair [57]

The linguistics of shopping

Chapter 1 is hectic, it is dense and it shows us how shifting and chaotic simple acts of buying and selling have become. So let us pause, slowly, and start from the beginning: what actually is shopping, what does it *do*? And what is retail? What connects them, what separates them and what defines them? It is important to answer these questions because if we are to understand retailisation properly, the myriad of spaces in which it takes place and the people who retail, we need to understand the meaning and connotations associated with the more basic and common terms 'shopping' and 'retail': their linguistics, if you like. In so doing we begin to trace the origins of the retailisation process – the process by which retail travels everywhere – and its development over the last 150 years to the confusing present. What are the shifts that have determined the state of retailisation today?

So, to begin. Shopping: a common term and an even more common pastime. But also, increasingly, a broad, open term that encapsulates many meanings, places and hours of the day. At the most basic level, and according to the *Oxford English Dictionary*, shopping is 'the action of visiting a shop or shops for the purpose of making purchases or of examining the goods exposed for sale'.[58] But this definition is from the 1989 edition of the *Oxford English Dictionary*, and 13 years is a long time in retail as it is in culture or politics. In 1989 the key words were 'Thatcher', 'Bush', 'Berlin Wall', 'negative equity' and 'yuppie'. The first British newspapers were a year into their 'direct' printing, via computers. It was long before the World Wide Web was around, long before we knew you could use a computer to buy a book, zap your television remote control across the Shopping Channel for your weekly food shopping, or buy goods from the reclining comfort of a London cab or the British Airways Club Class. Now, even if we don't take advantage of these possibilities, they are known to most of us – particu-

---

[57] William Thackeray, *Vanity Fair* (Chapman and Sons, 1848), p. 81.
[58] *Oxford English Dictionary* (Oxford: Clarendon Press, 1989).

larly retailers. In response, not only have retail outlets spread into spaces that were formerly purely civic and public; today spaces that were not traditionally associated with retail or shopping – museums, airports, schools, sports stadiums – all include a 'shop' in some form.

In the last 50 years major shifts have contributed to the redefinition of shopping as a term and as an activity. Socially, psychologically and spatially, shopping has become an all-pervasive and dominating presence in our lives. We no longer shop until we drop, we now – can – shop until we die.

The counterpart of shopping is retail. Defined as 'the sale of commodities in small quantities',[59] it is a term less commonly used by the consumer, and mainly denotes professional circles. It is used by the developers of outlets, outlet designers and retailers themselves. Retail is many processes. It is supplying to meet demand. It is creating demand. It is the business processes of distribution, marketing, and of not going bankrupt in a world of vicious supply and demand (which in the case of the generation 2000 dot.com world has proved more difficult than its vociferous young champions and their financial backers initially predicted). So we define retailisation as the nexus of these two processes. Retailisation is about the ways in which shopping (essentially the consumer experience) and retail (largely the organisational experience) have merged with design, technology and location to try and help buyer and seller efface time (to create a 'trance state' for the consumer, to speed up profits to the retailer), to sate the needs of 'demand' and shareholder alike.

Socially, shopping and consumer spaces have replaced the village square (which was arguably also a consumer space as it was the scene of markets and fairs) and the church. Designers of the world's largest shopping malls, such as the American architects Jon Jerde (the Mall of America) and Eric Kuhne (Bluewater shopping centre in Kent, UK), believe consumer spaces are the only place where people can still have communal experiences. That is one take: we will also show that aeroplanes, sports stadia and the Internet, to give but three examples, also lay claim to retail and communal experience.

Malls work to create 'place quality', spaces in which the use of historic and cultural references will allow communities to reconnect with each other and their roots. From the Southdale Mall in Edina, Minnesota, where formal balls were held as early as 1960, to the Galleria in Houston where 'mall-walkers', mostly old-age pensioners, meet to power-walk around the mall and the so-called teenage 'mall-bunnies' and 'mall-rats'[60] spend their free time, con-

---

[59] Ibid.
[60] John Hannigan, *Fantasy City* (London: Routledge, 1998), p. 89.

sumer space is increasingly the place where communities gather, if not always with the most communal of feelings. In Delaware Township, New Jersey, the local community even took such pride in its new Cherry Hill Mall – which had soon become the town's social hub – that it decided to adopt the mall's name, swapping Delaware Township for Cherry Hill.[61]

At the individual level shopping today satisfies not only physical needs, it also plays a significant psychological role, becoming a means of self-fulfilment closely related to self-image, our imagination and, if taken to extremes, addiction. David Peek, a British consumer behaviourist working on shopping centre developments in Britain and Europe and studying the psychology that lies at the basis of our desire to shop, sees clear links between shopping and our imagination. While he distinguishes two 'levels' of shopping – to fulfil basic needs and to fulfil imagination or 'perceived needs', he says that today the latter motivates the majority of our purchases.

"Once basic needs are fulfilled, shopping becomes an act of self-fulfilment; it is a means of expressing oneself, adorning oneself...By buying a painting to hang in his house, the consumer goes beyond real need, into the realm of perceived need. The purchase helps him imagining other lives and new possibilities. It is part of the idea that 'I imagine [myself as a better person if I have that painting] so I shop'...Taking that one step further there is also 'I shop so I can imagine': seeking new ideas and images in consumer goods and spaces. Here shopping becomes a lifestyle experience as well as a sensory experience where the consumer can touch, see, smell, taste and enjoy the goods but also imagine owning them. Increasingly, consumers today want more than just the product they come to buy; they want it to come with an experience or wrapped in illusion...People enjoy experiential shopping because it feeds their imagination. For example, a good Timberland shoe store is very atmospheric, so much so that you could almost imagine yourself in a log cabin with all these rugged men and women doing amazingly liberating things. By buying the pair of Timberland boots you somehow also buy into the illusion that this quality and atmosphere will rub off on you by osmosis, it stimulates your imagination in other words. Retailers need to do this because all too often the reality of the merchandise is that it is unfulfilling, so it needs to be wrapped up in a dream."[62]

---

[61] Margaret Crawford, 'The world in a shopping mall', in: Michael Sorkin, ed. *Variations on a Theme Park* (New York: Hill and Wang, 1992), p. 23.
[62] David Peek in personal interview, November 1999: all quotes are from interview unless otherwise stated.

> **In June 2000 the research group Retail Intelligence published a report that showed that department stores in the United Kingdom and Ireland were 'facing an uncertain future due to increased competition from discounters, hypermarkets and on-line stores'. They claimed the stores could 'save themselves' by increased differentiation, suggesting that design may play a key role enabling stores to reclaim market share.**
>
> **The research group also said that department stores are going to benefit from: 'the concept of retail theatre, the exclusivity of brands and high levels of décor and service'. According to the report, department store sales throughout Europe are in steady and continued decline.[63]**

Spatially, shopping has moved far beyond the shop; it is now an activity that has found a place in museums, airports, schools, universities, hospitals, sports stadia, homes and beyond this, off the ground, on cruise liners, in aeroplanes and in virtual space. Researching the global spread of shopping in a project with Harvard graduates, the Dutch architect Rem Koolhaas has calculated that the entire surface area covered by shopping worldwide is equivalent to 33 times the surface of Manhattan. Koolhaas says it has fundamentally transformed the urban condition today, as can be witnessed in New York's SoHo, for example, where buildings that were warehouses 20 years ago and galleries 10 years ago have now been taken over by retail, creating 'a blanket of pure commercial space'.[64]

Shopping, according to Koolhaas, is a phenomenon that has 'remained mysteriously invisible to the architectural eye'.[65] Its spread into urban and suburban fabric has gone widely uncharted in architectural circles, to such an extent that there is a clear divergence between the architectural profession and the phenomenon that Koolhaas qualifies as 'one of the most critical and...important contributions to urban texture at this moment'.[66] While this is certainly true, and there is a certain moral indignation surrounding the rampant spread of shopping space in architectural circles, the

---

[63] 'Department stores in Europe', *Design Week*, June 2000, p. 5, describing 'The Big Picture: Retail', a report published by Informa Publishing and Retail Intelligence.

[64] Rem Koolhaas, 'Start Again' lecture, Berlage Institute in Amsterdam, 7 March 2000.

[65] Ibid. Koolhaas explains that before starting the research project with Harvard graduates he looked for other academic research on the subject in the last 25 years. He found that in the Ivy League universities there had been just one project concerned with shopping, 22 years ago.

[66] Ibid.

refusal to acknowledge the importance of shopping in our society is a wider phenomenon.

Simply consider that in English there is only one term to describe the range of processes associated with this phenomenon. From the weekly trip to the supermarket for basic food supplies to an afternoon in town trying on clothes or surfing the Web for the cheapest deals in books and CDs, it all falls under the common denominator 'shopping'. The comment 'I'm going shopping', placed out of context, will almost invariably require some elucidation for us to know whether this is going to be a five-minute errand for bread and milk or an afternoon spree for new clothes or furniture. To distinguish between the different types of shopping and to create some sort of order in the chaos of endless moods, spaces, times, speeds and aims of shopping today, retail experts and academics have coined phrases such as 'chore shopping', 'research shopping', 'hobby shopping', 'top-up shopping' and 'leisure shopping'.[67] Applying these categories, the experts can then qualify the different types: chore shopping for food and basic necessities is different from leisure shopping, which involves browsing, trying on – and relaxation. Similarly, impulsive purchases serve a different purpose – perhaps to fulfil the imagination or a sudden desire, or as a treat or a reward – from planned purchases, which are more considered, often more functional and rational. But, while this type of classification is effective in subdividing the various types of shopping for academic and professional aims, it is unlikely that anyone else would go off to buy bread and milk from the corner shop and say: 'Just going to do some top-up shopping' or, when planning a trip to the local shopping centre: 'Can't wait to indulge in some experiential shopping on Saturday'. It would just be 'shopping'. There is too much information out there: we as consumers don't need to know this; retailers need to know everything – the problem for them is that we are on a fast-learning trajectory, following just behind their latest 'discovery'.

In French there isn't even one single word to describe 'shopping': the expression 'faire des courses' comes closest to the English word, though it is more reminiscent of 'running errands' and implies a certain necessity or obligation rather than a leisure activity.

From the agora to the Galeries Lafayette: the development of shopping as a lifestyle

Historically, the process of shopping has not changed so radically in the last 150 years. It is rather that the larger choice and better

---

[67] Larry O'Brien and Frank Harris *Retailing, Shopping, Society, Space* (London: David Fulton, 1991), p. 120.

informed consumer has created a new desire for 'point of view', for an edited version of the information available. As we have shown in the first chapter, media is one 'point of view', but increasingly retail attempts this illusion as well.

Shopping is as old as civilisation. We have shopped ever since the times of the first agora and the first caravanserai. The following piece from the 4th century BC was written by the Greek comic poet Eubolos, and illustrates that even the idea of shopping centres and supermarkets that sell a variety of goods and services is nothing new: 'You will find everything sold together in the same place at Athens: figs, witnesses to summonses, bunches of grapes, turnips, pears, apples, givers of evidence, roses, medlars, porridge, honeycombs, chick-peas, lawsuits, beestings-puddings, myrtle, allotment-machines [for random jury selection], irises, lambs, water-clocks [for timing law court speeches], laws, indictments.'[68]

While this description suggests that one really could find anything one wanted in the Athenian agora, the items on sale are all geared toward the fulfilment of needs rather than desires. Small segments of society may have shopped out of indulgence but it was certainly not a general trend. The broader shift that allowed a larger part of society to 'shop on a higher level' and satisfy (and also create) new desires only took place much later, in Britain during the Industrial Revolution and Victorian times. Indulgent shopping has been around since Biblical times,' says David Peek. 'It's a question of wealth: the shift from shopping out of necessity to shopping to fulfil desires and fantasies can take place as soon as the individual has money to spend after basic needs are met. For some this happened centuries ago: the emperor Nero, for example, had residual spending which allowed him to shop for giraffes. The Pharaohs were also very indulgent shoppers. At the same time, though, their subjects down the road couldn't even afford bread. Today this imbalance has evened out and it is no longer a select few, but the majority of Western society that can afford to shop indulgently.' Once a larger part of the population could afford to shop for pleasure – to create or sustain fantasies – retailers slowly began to discover the power they could wield over customers by presenting goods in more alluring and enticing displays and designing shop floors to lead customers past items they 'did not know they needed'.

Retailers in France, the developers of the *grands magasins* such as Au Bon Marché, Au Printemps and the Galeries Lafayette department stores in Paris, were the first to define the 'nouveau commerce' in the middle of the 19th century. Their success transformed Paris into 'a city not only of pleasure seekers but of keen and inde-

---

[68] Eubolos, fr. 74, quoted in *The World of Athens* (Cambridge: Cambridge University Press, 1992), p. 81.

fatigable shoppers' according to the *Manchester Guardian* in 1862[69] and retailers abroad soon followed suit, establishing Macy's in New York, Harrods and Whiteleys in London and Wertheim in Berlin. Design and layout in these stores were entirely focused on predicting and stimulating customers' desires and needs. Sophisticated layout and display techniques, and theatrical lighting and colouring effects all combined to coax the tentative customer gently into a dream state. Aristide Boucicaut, the owner of Au Bon Marché, knew about the power that fancy displays and subtle design detail could have on his shoppers. Just days before the opening of the new Bon Marché store in 1872 he justified a last-minute decision to rearrange his store's layout radically, saying: 'What is necessary...is that they walk around for hours, that they get lost. First of all, they will seem more numerous. Secondly...the store will seem larger to them. And lastly, it would really be too much if, as they wander around in this organised disorder, lost, driven crazy, they don't set foot in some departments where they had no intention of going, and if they don't succumb at the sight of things which grab them on the way.'[70]

The tricks of the trade: implementing *le nouveau commerce*

Ordered disorder and clever layout alone were not enough though: technological progress, improved transport links and new sales methods all played a significant role in the success of the department stores. As the price of electricity fell in the 1880s retailers could afford to install electric lighting and other 'modern devices' through-out the store so that the shop floor could spread further inwards but also upwards with lifts and escalators allowing expansion on to upper floors. Harrods in London installed its first 'moving staircase' in 1898 and, when a lift was installed on the premises of the Wylie and Lochhead department store in Glasgow in 1885, the *Glasgow Herald* described it as a 'very ingenious hoisting apparatus...not only intended to lift bales but also to elevate those ladies and gentlemen to the galleries to whom the climbing of the successive flights of stairs might be attended with fatigue and annoyance...[They] have only to place themselves on an enclosed platform or flooring when they are elevated by a gentle and pleasing process.'[71]

While all interior design was aimed at keeping the customer

---

[69] *Manchester Guardian*, 3 September 1862, p. 847/2.
[70] Rachel Bowlby, *Just Looking* (Cambridge: Cambridge University Press, 1985), pp. 5–6.
[71] Maurice Baren, *Victorian Shopping* (London: Michael O'Mara Books, 1998), pp. 7–8.

inside the store and encouraging further expenditure, the building's exterior was designed to attract passers-by and lure them inside. In 1935 the Dutch architect Marinus Dudok described his design for a new department store in Rotterdam as a 'trap' that customers should 'inadvertently walk into, like fish into a net',[72] implying that customers could, through clever design techniques and appealing displays, be baited and drawn into the store.

In his epic novel *Au Bonheur des Dames* about the rise of the *nouveau commerce*, the 19th-century French novelist, Emile Zola, also describes the efforts of his shopkeeper protagonist, Octave Mouret, to seduce the passers-by:

There outside in the street, on the pavement itself was a mountain of cheap goods, placed at the entrance as a bait, bargains which stopped the women as they passed by. It all cascaded down: pieces of woollen material and fabric, merino, cheviot, flannelette, were falling from the mezzanine floor, flapping like flags...Denise saw a piece of tartan at forty-five centimes, strips of American mink at one franc, and mittens at twenty-five centimes. It was a giant fairground display, as if the shop were bursting and throwing its surplus stock into the street.

Emile Zola, Au Bonheur des Dames [73]

> **In the early 1990s a change in UK law made for a new kind of seduction in the high street. Window frames in public houses were suddenly (mysteriously) allowed to grow in size. Why? Well, there are many theories. The result – so the owners of pub chains believed (and the new kind of pubs that began to grow: the Piano and Pitcher chain, All Bar One and the Firkin pubs) – was that women could see inside a bar and decide whether it was 'safe' to enter. Other changes to the pubs' ambience were a 'barification' of the interiors: sofas, light, pine floors, more kinds of drink, new kinds of hip music, the arrival of a selection of 'good' food – and then a huge range of 'good' food – a democratising of the locations where alcohol is consumed. A decade on, newspaper reports show that women are drinking more than ever before, closing rapidly on their male counterparts.**
>
> **Bars are the new pubs, they have a point of view (and architects rather than builders to design them). Most of all we can see into many of these bars, can be made to feel jealous rather than frightened – as well as thirsty. And when we are inside, we often feel the need to drink**

---

[72] Dion Kooijman, *Machine en Theater* (Rotterdam: 010 Publishers, 1999), p. 69.
[73] Emile Zola, *The Ladies' Paradise*, introduced and translated by Brian Nelson (Oxford: Oxford University Press, 1995, first published 1883), p. 4.

> **cocktails or expensive bottled beers from Belgium, rather than our more traditional pub diet of draught beer and lager. It is all about seeing – seeing in, and seeing what others are doing. In short it is (while we wait for the final barrier, an end to Britain's arcane licensing laws) the arrival of a European or café culture into our once-macho pub eco-sphere.**

But far more sophisticated than this lavish display of goods on the pavement was the development of shop windows and the creation of window displays. Denise, the heroine of Zola's novel who has just arrived from the province, stares at them in awe:

'I say!' said Jean. 'That beats Valognes…Your shop wasn't as grand as that.' Denise nodded. She had spent two years in Valognes, at Cornaille's, the main draper in the town; and this shop which had suddenly appeared before her, this building which seemed so enormous, brought a lump in her throat and held her rooted to the spot, excited, fascinated, oblivious to everything else. The high plate-glass door, facing the Place Gaillon, reached the mezzanine floor and was surrounded by elaborate decorations covered with gilding. Two allegorical figures, two laughing women with bare breasts thrust forward, were unrolling a scroll stretched along the Rue de la Michaudière and the Rue Neuve-Saint-Augustin, where, apart from the corner house, they occupied four other houses which had recently been bought and converted, two on the left and two on the right. With its series of perspectives, with the display on the ground floor and the plate-glass windows of the mezzanine floor, behind which could be seen all the intimate life of the various departments, the spectacle seemed to Denise to be endless.

Emile Zola, Au Bonheur des Dames [74]

Progress in the construction of iron and glass structures meant that larger sheets of plate glass could replace the small panes of 12 by 16 inches, effectively creating a new relationship between the street and the shop as the shop spilt on to the street, but the street also became a shopping space. 'This is one of the most important shifts in the last 150 years of retail,' says Paco Underhill, a New York-based retail consultant. 'For the first time, people could go shopping with a "look but don't buy" attitude; before, that had only been possible in outdoor venues like markets.'[75] Window shopping or, as the French so eloquently describe it, *lèche-vitrine*, 'window-licking', soon became a popular pastime and window-display artists competed to create tempting and fantastical scenes. Celebrities like the German artist and architect Frederick Kiesler, the film director Vincente Minelli, the artist Andy Warhol and the

---

[74] Ibid, p. 3.
[75] Paco Underhill in personal interview, March 2000; all quotes from interview.

author of *The Wizard of Oz*, Frank L. Baum, all began their careers
as window dressers. Baum, the editor of a journal called *The Shop
Window*, wrote extensively about the various techniques for catch-
ing the attention of passing window shoppers and turning them
into absorbed spectators:

How can a window sell goods? By placing them before the public in such a
manner that the observer has a desire for them and enters the store to make
the purchase. Once in, the customer may see other things she wants, and no
matter how much she purchases under these conditions the credit of the sale
belongs to the window.'
Frank L. Baum, *The Art Of Decorating Dry Goods Windows, 1900* [76]

Baum said the window dresser should have the talent 'for letting
objects tell some legible story', the knack for 'inducing trade', transforming the 'passive throng' in the streets into spectators: 'You must
arouse in your audience cupidity and a longing to possess the goods
you sell.' One of his recommended techniques was the use of the
so-called 'illusion window', which would never fail to 'arouse the
curiosity of the observer'. He gave the example of the display entitled 'The Vanishing Lady' in which 'a young beautiful woman, the
lower half of whose body is invisible to the spectator [would] disappear into the pedestal [then] appear with a new hat, waist, gloves,
etc. [while] everyone wonders where the rest of the person is'.[77] It
was these sorts of displays that boosted in-store sales as window
shoppers were inadvertently turned into shoppers and buyers.

Baum's experience as a window dresser is also reflected in *The
Wizard of Oz*, in which veiled references are made to the new consumerism in which people desire commodities they do not strictly
need. Upon arrival in Emerald City, the home of the Wizard,
Dorothy and her friends are struck by the fact that everyone is
wearing green spectacles and that all items on sale are green:

Many shops stood in the street, and Dorothy saw that everything in them was
green. Green candy and green popcorn were offered on sale, as well as green
shoes, green hats and green clothes of all sorts. At one place a man was selling green lemonade and when the children bought it Dorothy could see that
they paid for it with green pennies.
Frank L. Baum, *The Wizard of Oz* [78]

The residents of Emerald City are obsessed with the magical value
of greenness, as green in Oz symbolises the value of gems. The wizard who established the rule of the green spectacles essentially takes

---

[76] Quoted in Anne Friedberg, *Window Shopping, Cinema and the Postmodern*
(Berkeley: University of California Press, 1993), p. 66.
[77] All quotes in this paragraph from Stuart Culver, 'What manikins want: the
wonderful world of Oz and the art of decorating dry goods windows',
Representations, no. 21.
[78] p. 102.

on the role of the window dresser, a con artist and a fantasist who can give people what they desire and want but know they can't have. He thus promotes the desire and, satisfying it partially, capitalises on the Ozites' 'readiness to take the absolutely artificial as a substitute for the fundamentally unpurchasable...Thus consumption, under the influence of the green spectacles, becomes an endless cycle of visual fascinations and mistaken appropriations.'[79]

> **The World Wide Web has been very Wizard of Oz in the first five years of its life from 1995 onwards. Seen through the green spectacles of early adoption, the Web is revolutionary, changes everything, and moves us all ineluctably towards the virtual 'knowledge economy'. Often mistakenly, however, as the promises of the Web cannot yet be fulfilled while it lumbers with slow modems, appallingly uninteresting architectures and an utter lack of the third dimension. One of the biggest problems for e-commerce is that, with few current exceptions (such as online booksellers, of which Amazon is the best, as even the arch-critic of website design, Jakob Nielsen, attests), it is a complex business. We will frequently 'look' at a website but, lacking the seductions of light, sound, smell and other people, we often fail to act. We are but a click away from the latest football results, our stock prices and pictures of Britney Spears 'naked', after all. In many senses the Web is an 'endless cycle of visual fascinations', but in the manner of J.L. Borges rather than F.W. Woolworth, the founder of the Woolworth chain.**

On an urban level, the rise of the *grands magasins* in Paris also had far-reaching effects. Haussmann's reorganisation of public transport systems in 1855 and the subsequent expansion of the railway network meant more goods, and easier access to the new commercial spaces for potential customers. The architecture of these lavishly designed buildings was often inspired by the great monuments like the 1875 Paris Opéra building and spaces designed for the Paris World Exhibition in 1867. Ornate turrets on the corners and sculptural facades were designed to draw passers-by into the interior, where large atriums were decorated with elaborate ironwork and colourful, glass-domed roofs. The stores soon became destinations in their own right, landmarks in the urban fabric where one went just as much for shopping as to look – at the goods on display and at the other customers.

---

[79] Ibid.

Indeed 'looking' became a much more important part of the shopping experience as human interaction between sales personnel and customer was replaced by interaction with 'things', the goods on sale and the displays in the store. This was mainly due to the introduction of a fixed price policy, which transformed the consumer from an active participant in the retail scene, haggling and bargaining for better deals, into a passive onlooker. Money seemed no longer to be part of the sales transaction as payment took place in a separate area away from the merchandise. It also meant goods sold in the *grands magasins* were cheaper as the rapid turnover of stock meant they were able to undercut competitors with low profit margins. This, together with the concept of 'entrée libre' – which allowed customers to enter the space without being obliged to buy – and the introduction of a returns policy, fundamentally altered all transactions within the commercial and economical realm of shopping. These policies meant the buyer no longer had the same power in the realm of retail; the retailer still pandered to the shopper, but that was only flattery. It was 'take it or leave it' and there was no way of arguing the retailer's authority. The customer was still king but, as we will see, the retailer was a god. In addition, retailers now also ventured beyond their own stores, appealing to customers by advertising their brands and stores around town. As Rachel Bowlby explains: 'Stores, posters, brand-name goods and ads in the daily and magazine press laid the groundwork of an economy in which selling and consumption, by the continuous creation of new needs and new desires, became open to infinite expansion along with the profits and productivity which lay behind them.'[80]

While these techniques and retail philosophies were looked upon with disdain by other retailers who predicted the formula would fail and that these 'innovations' were merely 'du romantisme en boutique',[81] the *grands magasins* became increasingly popular. Not only did they sell a wonderful array and abundance of goods, they sold the dreams, lifestyles and beliefs of an increasingly well-established, upper middle class. In his book *Language and Symbolic Power*, the sociologist Pierre Bourdieu explores this theme in the wider context of social class distinction. He says: 'The Parisian department store played a leading role in the marketing of lifestyles that simultaneously demarcated and blurred class distinctions, encouraging everyone to aspire to a middle-class way of life.'[82] Thus, while the abundance and luxury of goods on display in the *grands magasins* only served to accentuate the working classes' feeling of poverty, the dazzling spectacle was often dan-

---

[80] Rachel Bowlby, *Just Looking*, p. 3.
[81] 'In-store romanticism'; quoted in Alison Adburgham, *Shops and Shopping 1800–1914* (London: George Allen and Unwin Ltd, 1964), p. 138.
[82] Pierre Bourdieu, *Language and Symbolic Power*, edited and introduced by John B. Thompson (Cambridge: Polity Press, 1991).

gerously entrancing, blinding them to the reality of their exclusion from this world and to the fact that this 'new worship of commodities and the spectacle of their display would function, like the old religion, as an opiate for the masses'.[83] The idea of shopping replacing religion as the new opium of the masses was also used by Zola to describe the processes that took place in the department store and in the customer's mind. Modelled on the Bon Marché and its owners, the Boucicaut family, Zola's fictional department store is owned by Mouret, an 'amiable god'. But: 'His creation was producing a new religion; churches, which were being gradually deserted by those of wavering faith, were being replaced by his bazaar...If he had closed his doors, there would have been a rising in the street, a desperate outcry from the worshippers whose confessional and altar he would have abolished.'[84]

Today, the religious metaphor in retail revolves not so much around the retailer representing God and the store being a place where one can be at one with Him; now we are the gods: the 21st century consumer is more independent and self-centred, seeking to find and define himself through the retail process. Our cathedrals are our homes – where we can define ourselves through objects, fashions, and location; where we can constantly 'do it ourselves'. In this sense, the highly successful Bluewater shopping mall in Kent, which was apparently considering charging visitors an entrance fee, though this has not yet happened, was looking for a 'donation' in the same way that our great cathedrals look for sponsorships to maintain their ancient flying buttresses or Giotto frescoes.[85]

The cathedral metaphor was commonly used in the description of new department stores with commentators drawing parallels between the 'new' and 'old' religion. An article in *Le Monde Illustré* of 1869 describes the newly opened La Paix department store as 'a cathedral' with 'a nave and side aisles' but also as an 'enormous vessel with flying bridges and suspended staircases'.[86] In the Netherlands, Marinus Dudok's design for a new department store in Rotterdam in 1929 was described by critics as a 'sacred space of modern architecture' that through its glass structure had 'taken the place of the cathedral'. At the same time it was compared to an

---

[83] Brian Nelson, introduction to Zola's, *The Ladies' Paradise.*
[84] Ibid., p. 427.
[85] '...an executive of LendLease, the Australian-based property developer, suggested that shopping at the company's Bluewater centre in Kent was just such an experience, and that perhaps the company should charge shoppers for admission instead of charging retailers rent.' Norma Cohen, 'Would shoppers pay to enter a mall?', *Irish Times*, 8 March 2000, Commercial Property p. 6.
[86] Jeanne Gaillard in the preface to Emile Zola, *Au Bonheur des Dames* (Paris: Gallimard, 1980): La Paix described as 'une cathédrale' avec 'une nef et des bas-côtés' also 'décrite comme un énorme vaisseau, traversé de ponts volants and d'escaliers suspendus'; *Le Monde Illustré*, 1869.

ocean liner with the view out to the busy traffic below giving the impression that one was 'on a cruise, far from the worries of daily life',[87] escaping responsibility and routine.

Customers could dream of other lives and other places, and even buy into them. Writing in 1894, the French writer Georges Avenel said: 'It seems that sales breed sales and that the most diverse objects, juxtaposed in this way, lend each other mutual support.'[88] Designing mesmerising, disorientating interiors and large spaces with a vast view of goods on sale, the 19th century *grand magasin* owner often managed to keep the clientèle in his grip for an entire day. Besides the endless display of goods, these stores also provided seating in the main atrium space, art galleries, reading rooms, refreshments and other amenities where the ladies go to rest or otherwise divert themselves and where gentlemen could wait for their wives to finish shopping. 'Elles sont chez elles', as Mouret puts it; although they were of course 'chez lui'[89] and entirely but deliciously at his mercy, away from their husbands:

'Women came to spend their hours of leisure in his shop, the thrilling, disturbing hours which in the past they'd spent in the depths of the chapel; for this expenditure of nervous passion was necessary, it was part of the recurring struggle between god and a husband, the ceaselessly renewed cult of the body, with the divine future life of beauty.'[90]

Providing such an escape for women, the concept of the department store introduced a new spatial typology into the city: a semi-public space aimed especially at a female audience. While the *flâneur* – a new breed of urban male who spent his time lazily ambling between cafés and brothels and strolling down the busy boulevards, crowd-watching and window shopping – had ready access to the whole city and the new pleasure zones, bourgeois women were still largely restricted to their homes. The safe yet public nature of the department store made it a new haven for women, replacing the church as a place between the home and the street where they could escape the restraints of domestic life and become *flâneuses* in their own right.

Overseas, in Britain and the United States, department stores like Macy's in New York and Harrods in London established themselves at the turn of the 20th century, modelling themselves on French examples of the 'nouveau commerce'. The French had started a worldwide trend: it wasn't merely a new building type, it was a

---

[87] Kooijman, *Machine en Theater*, p. 69.

[88] Georges Avenel, 'Le mécanisme de la vie moderne', quoted in: Bowlby, *Just Looking*, p. 4.

[89] 'They are at home', though they were of course 'at his place', says Mouret in chapter 9, Emile Zola, *Au Bonheur des Dames* (Paris: Gallimard, 1980).

[90] Zola, *The Ladies' Paradise*, p. 427.

lifestyle, which the United States in particular embraced with enthusiasm, soon appropriating the concept of 'shopping for pleasure', developing it until it became the American way of life. John Wanamaker, a Philadelphia entrepreneur, even went to the extent of building a life-size replica of the La Paix department store 'as a consolation for those Americans who can't go to Paris', turning a disused railroad depot into a popular department store. To increase shoppers' pleasure, other US retailers started introducing elements of entertainment into the realm of retail. The Siegel-Cooper department stores opened their doors at Sixth Avenue and 18th Street in New York in 1896 by offering an orchestra, art shows, tearooms and 'spectacular extravaganzas' in their auditorium. It also staged a summer festival, 'The Carnival of Nations', which featured shows like *Phantasma, The Enchanted Bower* using a grand *mise en scène* of lights and colours and a cast that included a Turkish harem with dancing girls, a 'genie of the lamp' and, slightly displaced but still exotic, a 'Cleopatra of the Nile'.[91] Following this example, Marshall Field's celebrated the opening of its State Street store in Chicago in 1902 with performances by six string orchestras on various floors.

Entertaining the shoppers: the role of theme parks in retailisation

As we move into the 20th century the role of spectacle and entertainment becomes more prominent in the world of retail. The invention of fantasy environments such as the Disney theme parks play an important role in this. When the film producer Walt Disney attended a convention of amusement park owners in 1953 he was, for all the books now critiquing him, merely continuing to build on our increasing awareness of and pride in our imagined selves. He was presenting a new idea, the concept for an entirely new type of amusement park: Disneyland. With relatively few rides, high maintenance requirements and a large amount of space that was left unused – and that would therefore not directly generate revenue – the idea was criticised as too self-conscious and unrealistic. It would fail, was the general verdict.

But Walt Disney believed in his idea; he had consciously left out the traditional rides and country-fair type attractions, striving to create a space that would appeal to visitors in a more fundamental way by evoking, or even inventing, an idea of America that existed only in the collective memory. His vision of what this park would be was so specific that the design produced by the two architects he hired did not satisfy him and he instead set one of his

---

[91] Hannigan, *Fantasy City*, p. 90.

studio animators to the task of re-creating his memory of small-town United States. Thus 'Main Street USA', the main axis that cut through the new park, was an idealised image of main streets in small towns around the United States, with old-fashioned, multi-coloured facades evoking a quaint, 'nice' version of the much less innocuous reality: 'This is what Main Street USA should have been like,' one of Disneyland's planners, or 'imagineers', says. 'What we create', according to another, 'is a Disney realism, sort of Utopian in nature, where we carefully program out all the negative, unwanted elements and program in the positive elements.'[92]

The themed 'lands' that existed around the park's central castle – a symbol to domesticity – offered visitors a collage of the American way of life that could be viewed all at once, since they could pass seamlessly from Frontierland into the magical realm of Tomorrowland. The fact that Disney had conceived a park entirely based on imaginary realms and places was entirely novel. Other entertainment and amusement parks like Coney Island were based purely on rides and geared towards fun or adopted single themes, portraying historical themes with educational purposes like Freedomland USA in New York, which told the story of American history. Disney did none of this. He just told stories; 'imagineered' adventures, replacing reality with fantasy and illusion. Thus Disneyland introduced an entirely new and ambiguous relationship between reality and fantasy. 'I don't want the public to see the real world they live in while they're in the park...I want them to feel they are in another world.'[93]

And they did. As other theme parks like Freedomland, Africa USA in Florida and Fort Dells in Wisconsin opened up around the country, *Life* magazine ran a cover story on the boom in amusement parks, announcing phenomenal growth figures for the 'fun spot' industry, with figures for 1959 rising by $250 million to $2 billion in receipts and visitor numbers growing to 50 million.[94] America was slowly starting to get a taste for the Disney environment, the secure, clean, predictable and fun spaces that were to spread throughout the country by the end of the century.

Disneyland's developers had looked to Europe for precedents of such enclosed and escapist environments. In his study of the origins of Disneyland, 'See you in Disneyland', the architect Michael Sorkin traces its origins back to London's Great Exhibition of the Works and Industry of All Nations in 1851, where Paxton's Crystal Palace was described by William Thackeray as:

---

[92] Sharon Zukin, *Landscapes of Power* (Berkeley: University of California Press, 1991), p. 222.
[93] Ibid., p. 64.
[94] John Hannigan, quoting *Life* magazine in *Fantasy City*, p. 39.

'A Palace as for a fairy prince
A rare pavilion, such as man
Saw never since mankind began,
And built and glazed.'[95]

Speaking in the inaugural address, Prince Albert said:

We are living at a period of most wonderful transition which tends rapidly to accomplish that great end, to which, indeed, all history points – the realisation of the unity of mankind...The distances which separated the different nations and parts of the globe are rapidly vanishing before the achievements of modern invention and we can traverse them with incredible ease; the languages of all nations are known, and their acquirement placed within the reach of everybody; thought is communicated with the rapidity, and even by the power, of lightning.[96]

An early version of the popular Disney tune 'It's a Small World', in other words. Sorkin describes the fair as 'the ur-theme of the theme park'[97] by gathering 'the wealth of nations under one roof' in a single architectural space and symbolising the technological progress that had allowed the construction of this, the largest greenhouse in the world. Previously winter gardens had been popular spaces for social assembly, offering an escapist environment and the idea of simulated travel, but the staging of world fairs offered the public much larger scope for imagination and mental evasion. Soon fairs evolved in size and content, adding different pavilions dedicated at first to themes like manufacture, science and transport, then national pavilions offering a higher proportion of entertainment and later corporation-sponsored entertainment and attractions. These utopian environments – particularly the City Beautiful Movement, which gained support at the 1893 Chicago World Fair – inspired the concept of the theme park as an introspective, controlled environment that offered escape from daily city life. In Britain the Garden City movement introduced the idea of a model community, advertising housing developments on the edge of town offering escape from the city and a reconnection to nature. Together, these two elements, the creation of a controlled, congruous environment and its location outside the urban realm, a place where people had to travel to, formed the basis for the creation of the Disney theme parks.

The organisation and scale of Disney World and the Disneylands is precisely that of the garden city. Located on the urban perimeter, they are, as phenomena, comparable to the office parks at other intersections in the highway

---

[95] Michael Sorkin, 'See you in Disneyland', in: Sorkin, ed., *Variations on a Theme Park*, p. 209.
[96] Ibid.
[97] Ibid., p. 212.

system, if sited now for convenience of access by leisure commuters. Internally they are also ordered according to a strict model. Radiating from a strong centre – occupied by the totemic castle of fantasy – the parks are arranged in thematic fiefs which flow into one another.[98]

Academics who study the Disney phenomenon today see it as the ultimate shopping experience, by selling a large quantity and variety of commodities, the prime one being the experience of the Disney landscape as 'the happiest place on Earth'. The British sociologist Steven Miles sees trips to Disney environments as shopping experiences that reinforce an escapism in which 'consumerism is all' and which provides the consumer with narratives, making consumption and experience indistinguishable, so the actual act of consumption does not need to be acknowledged.[99]

But it was more than just the familiarity of the Main Street vernacular and the escape into imagineered castles and pirate ships that made Disney's success. His cross-merchandising and the speed at which he branched out into different fields – film, television, toys, theme parks – meant that Disney was not only a destination in Anaheim, California, but also a mouse that entered into the realm of the home through the spread of TV and the creator of a series of adventures that could be viewed in cinemas around the country. By 1961 he had even branched into the domain of sports, building the 'Celebrity Sports Center' in Denver, Colorado with bowling alleys, a swimming pool, restaurants and shops. John Hannigan, a sociologist, sums up this inclusive character of Disney as the 'Davy Crockett phenomenon'. This hero of the American frontier became symbolic of Disney's ubiquity: 'Not only was Davy Crockett the first mini-series on television, but sales of his raccoon-skin cap were wildly popular and Americans flocked to Disneyland where Crockett lived on in "Adventureland".'[100] Today Disney is a clear leader among entertainment companies, with ventures in film, television, recordings, theme parks, live theatre and professional sports, and even retailing whole areas of cities (the New York 42nd Street development) with sales of more than $20,000m. in 1996.

However, Disney's all-round success also reflected shifts within US society and lifestyle: economic prosperity, the demographic changes following the baby boom, the expansion of the suburbs and sharp rise in domestic consumption, together with the spread of TV, meant that people had more time and money to spend on leisure, travel, entertainment and the adornment of themselves and

---

[98] Ibid., p. 215.
[99] Steven Miles, *Consumerism as a Way of Life* (London: Sage Publications, 1998), p. 65.
[100] John Hannigan quoting *Life* magazine, see his *Fantasy City*, p. 39.

their homes. Shopping environments today are often inspired by the Disney theme parks, which offer the visitor an escape into a fantasy environment that is secure and controlled, excluding any type of real risk or unpleasant surprises.

Settling into suburbia

Another factor that triggered the transition of shopping to become a leisure time activity was America's move to suburbia after the Second World War and the change in lifestyles that this entailed. The return of the troops in 1945 and the ensuing baby boom led to acute housing shortages in American cities. Helped by government subsidies, the implementation of low-cost mortgages and tax breaks, young families who had often been forced to live with their parents, moved to the suburbs. The construction industry embarked on a 'suburban building spree'[101] covering the American landscape with a carpet of low-cost, low-rise, detached houses surrounded by pleasant gardens – backyards – and paths – garage driveways. Offering deals that allowed the purchase of a home without down payment and low monthly payments, suburban growth rates skyrocketed. By 1954 nine million Americans lived in suburbia and the percentage of the metropolitan area occupied by suburbia continued to rise exponentially in the next 20 years: in Detroit, suburbs took up 64 per cent of space in 1970 as opposed to 38.7 per cent in 1950; in Philadelphia this figure rose to 51.8 per cent in 1970 from 30.8 per cent in 1950.[102] Houses were larger and people were keen to fill them with material belongings while turning away from urban culture and experience, concentrating instead on a new-found pride in the home and the family.

> **The building spree that created the suburbs finds a parallel in the World Wide Web. Construction work is everywhere, but transportation is still poor; so too in many cases the buildings we find. Everyone involved with the Internet talks of community building, of socialisation – and yet the Web's' greatest social achievement to date is the portal, whose equivalent in the real world is the Le Corbusier 'tower block', those socially exclusive constructions which are meant to create community and often evoke crime and destruction. The Web, for all its chat rooms, bulletin boards and 'personalisation', is a profoundly anti-social place in the context of any spatial experience. It will not always be, but the challenge for the next generation of Web designers and creators is to move towards the experiences that we have in our local store,**

---

[101] Ibid., p. 34.
[102] Ibid.

> **or at Disney World. The television can, at its best, do this – it is called Voyeur Television.**[103] **'Hello, Big Brother.'**

This demographic shift to the suburbs after 1945 led to a more generalised decentralisation. Discovering the cheaper real-estate prices in the suburbs, retailers deserted the city centre to move to virgin territories, unexploited spaces, on the edge of town, which were easily accessible by car. Dozens of shopping malls grew on the perimeter of American cities, leaving city centres deserted. The car played a central role in this context as it introduced the concept of travelling to 'destinations', theme parks, shopping malls and holiday resorts, to consume entertainment and commodities. 'The use of cars introduced the idea that people would travel to shop, causing a major upheaval in real estate and the cost of space. Retailers discovered out-of-town locations, creating pockets of artificial density outside towns and leaving city centres deserted.'[104] Indeed, until the 1950s developers of out-of-town malls focused on easy car access and the provision of free parking. Writing in his precisely named 1945 publication *Mistakes We Have Made in Developing Shopping Centres*, J.C. Nichols, the 'father of the shopping centre' and designer of the first shopping centre in the 1920s,[105] enumerated a list of 105 maxims that would lead to successful shopping centre development. The key, he believed, lay in the parking space around the malls: there should be lots, even too much, of it.

By the 1950s, though, designers saw that they could make more of the shopping trip than just a bland parking lot and strip mall. Inspired by the model of the 19th-century European department stores, which used a strong theatrical element, the American mall began to use other features that would draw customers and make them stay longer. Victor Gruen, an Austrian urban architect, was one of the first retail designers to introduce the concept of entertainment into retail in the United States. He was responsible for some of the first mall designs there in the 1950s and 1960s and aimed to add as many functions as possible to the shopping experience, believing that the ideal shopping centre should be 'a place to meet, walk and rest in a landscaped setting free of automobile traffic'; for him shopping centres should not be designed as 'machines for selling' but as 'shopping towns'.[106] Gruen's design for the Southdale mall in Edina, outside Minneapolis, was the first cov-

---

[103] Hunt, R. *Coffeehaus – clicketh here* (London, arehaus, 1999), p. 39.
[104] Paco Underhill in personal interview.
[105] The Country Club Plaza was built in Kansas City in 1924 and is regarded as one of the first malls.
[106] Victor Gruen quoted in Kooijman, *Machine en Theater*, p. 152.

ered shopping precinct in the United States and was, he said, based on the concept of the European shopping arcade. It was a fantasy world, a theatrical set staging 'retail drama',[107] with at its centre the 'Garden Court of Perpetual Spring', an atrium filled with tropical plants and flowers that 'bloomed even in the midst of the deep freeze of Minnesota winters'.[108] It was described by critics to be 'more downtown than downtown itself'[109] and Gruen believed that: 'Within such centres café tables are provided in the mall and here business deals are struck and social relationships made as they are in the street cafés of continental Europe. The difference is that the surrounding environment in the centre is carefully and consciously managed, unlike its counterpart in Amsterdam or Marseille.'[110]

While this was an innovative approach in the context of US retail design of the 1950s, in fact all Gruen was doing was tracing the meaning of the word 'mall' back to its 18th-century British origins. Indeed, 'mall' is etymologically derived from 'pall-mall', a game played with a stick, the mall and a ball, a cross between golf and croquet. Pall-mall soon also came to denote the place in which the game was played: sheltered grassy alleyways like The Mall in London or, more generally, tree-lined roads that were pleasant for walks. Later, in the 19th century, malls became promenades, in some towns even adopted as the proper names for thoroughfares. Inspired by the European passages with vaulted roofs and domed atriums, the importing of the concept to the United States led to the creation of the spaces we now know as the 'typically American' shopping malls.[111]

One fundamental difference, though, between Gruen's concept for the shopping mall and European arcades or 'passages' was that, instead of weaving itself into the adjacent street pattern and adding to the urban fabric, his mall was a fundamentally introverted, enclosed space, with no link to its surroundings. In that respect it was also different from the Parisian department store, which despite its inclusive character still engaged in the urban dynamic and became a landmark. Critics spoke of it as 'the inward turning shopping mall, which has abandoned the central city for the sub-urbs and whose fortress-like exterior surrounded by a moat-like parking lot turns its back entirely on its surroundings',[112] fearing the social consequences of exclusion and privatisation of space.

---

[107] Crawford, 'World in a shopping mall', p. 22.
[108] Hannigan, *Fantasy City*, p. 90.
[109] Kooijman, *Machine en Theater*, p. 135.
[110] Ibid., p. 153.
[111] Friedberg, *Window Shopping, Cinema and the Postmodern*, p. 111; *Oxford English Dictionary* (Oxford: Clarendon Press, 1989).
[112] Nan Ellin, 'Shelter from the storm, or Form follows fear and vice versa', in Nan Ellin, ed., *Architecture of Fear* (Princeton: Princeton Architectural Press, 1997), p. 14.

From creating townscapes and theatre sets in malls, retailers soon moved on to the design of cityscapes and urban atmosphere within the mall. Crawford describes how architects added glass-enclosed elevators and zigzagging escalators to create diagonal and vertical structures in the space.[113] They also used space and light to mimic the bustle of inner cities, thus creating a 'fantasy urbanism devoid of the city's negative aspects: weather, traffic, poor people'.[114] This also changed the nature of mall shopping as retail offered in the mall shifted from convenience stores – supermarkets and drugstores where people quickly dropped in to do an errand – to specialist and luxury outlets. US mall shopping became a leisure activity and shopping malls became destinations in their own right where people did not come out of need – for bread, milk and toothpaste – but for fun, to spend hours, if not days, wandering through fantastical landscapes, escaping the realities of the exterior world.

There seemed to be no limit to the success and expansion of shopping malls in the United States. In the first 25 years of their development less than 1 per cent of shopping malls failed as shoppers continued to flock mall-wards and the small group of entrepreneurs who owned most of the malls around the country became very wealthy developers. With numbers rising from 3,000 in 1957 to 17,000 in the 1970s and 26,000 in 1986,[115] malls became, in the words of the magnate developer, Edward de Bartolo, 'the best investment known to man'.[116] From the 1970s this 'malling of America'[117] started targeting city centres that had been deserted in the 1950s and were in need of regeneration. In San Diego, Horton Plaza was designed by Jon Jerde in 1985 using references to Hispanic cultures and 'semi-tropical, Southern Californian sun, deep shadow and colour',[118] in an attempt to rejuvenate the city's heart and attract people back to town.

The malling of Britain: shopping centre development in the United Kingdom

Meanwhile, back at the ranch in the United Kingdom, retail was looking to America for inspiration. While it did not re-appropriate the word 'mall', it did base the design of the first shopping centres on the American model of the 1940s and 1950s. With post-war reconstruction prioritising the construction of new housing, infrastructure and industry, the first shopping centres were not built

---

[113] Crawford, 'World in a shopping mall', p. 22.
[114] Ibid.
[115] Friedberg, *Window Shopping, Cinema and the Postmodern*, p. 111.
[116] Crawford, 'World in a shopping mall', p. 8.
[117] A phrase invented by William Kowinski in 1985.
[118] Jon Jerde, writing for the Jerde Partnership on http://www.jerde.com.

until the late 1950s. The first phase saw the development of open-air shopping precincts in towns like Bristol and Coventry. The first covered shopping centres like the Bull Ring in Birmingham (1956) and the Elephant and Castle centre in London (1965) were clumsy attempts at creating the pleasant 'shopping towns' that Gruen had conceived in the United States. Heavily influenced by the Modernist and Brutalist movements, these spaces soon became outdated as the stark lines of the design and the use of concrete made for harsh, uniform spaces that aged badly.[119]

The golden age for shopping centres in Britain came in the 1970s when designers became more sensitive and paid more attention to detail, while local governments began to support expansion into out-of-town locations. Encouraged by the free-market conservative ideologies, massive new regional shopping centres like Sheffield's Meadow Hall, Gateshead's Metro Centre and Dudley's Merry Hill sprang up around the country, heralding a new shopping culture. But the effect on city centres and their inhabitants was deadly, as a strong polarisation grew between the 'haves', who could drive to the out-of-town centres, and the 'have nots', who were obliged to shop in the deserted city environment. The case of Dudley, a medium-sized town near Birmingham, illustrates this well and serves as a good antithesis to the Cherry Hill example quoted earlier in this chapter. The decision to build Merry Hill shopping centre on the outskirts of the town proved an immediate success, attracting shoppers from Dudley and regions beyond. The consequences for 'downtown Dudley', though, were devastating, as all the major retailers – C&A, Marks & Spencer and BHS – moved away to Merry Hill only to be replaced by a 'rag-bag collection of discount stores, charity shops and struggling family businesses'.[120] With the number of vacant stores in the centre rising by 50 per cent between 1987 and 1994, locals who were left with the remains of what had been a thriving commercial centre renamed Merry Hill 'Merry Hell'.

Protagonists of these developments hastened to cite the case of Newcastle as a counter example. In Newcastle the town's Eldon Square shopping centre underwent extensive refurbishment to compete with the newly built Metro Centre on the edge of town, thus benefiting the town centre and the suburbs. In other cases transport links were improved, pedestrianised precincts introduced and traffic congestion in the town centre considerably reduced.

But Britain was not to be 'malled' the way America was, as government intervention in the 1990s led to restrictions on the development of more out-of-town projects. Political and especially environmental considerations – car pollution and urban blight – led the

---

[119] O'Brien and Harris *Retailing, Shopping, Society, Space*, p. 92.
[120] Miles, *Consumerism as a Way of Life*, p. 65.

government to draw up guidelines to restrict the use of cars and encourage the development of mixed-use projects in town centres.[121]

On the continent, the opening up of the former Eastern Bloc countries has led to a rush of retail development in the major cities there. As if to make up for the 45 retailisation-free years, East Europeans keenly embraced the Western brands and shops that flooded their high streets. Similarly, joint ventures between Western retail developers and their Czech, Hungarian or Polish counterparts led to the construction of out-of-town, American-style malls. They became hugely popular overnight, as customers – some of them sharing a ride with a car-owning neighbour, others willing to endure harrowing train, bus and tram journeys to reach the hallowed destination – crowded into the shops selling Adidas shoes, Armani jeans and Chanel perfumes, which most could only gaze at and covet without being able to afford them.

In the United Kingdom, though, at the beginning of the 1990s retail was set to return to the high street, with town centre regeneration projects encouraging retailers to invest in inner city locations.

Retailisation today

The invention of the Internet and the rise of e-commerce in the last five years has caused a great upheaval in the world of retail, where predictions that by 2005 the high street will no longer exist and we will all be wandering around in virtual malls have caused much concern to bricks and mortar retailers – much merriment, even Schadenfreude, too. The reality as we write this book at the beginning of the 21st century, however, is that while e-commerce is certainly a new player to reckon with in the retail landscape, it has not changed shopping habits in any fundamental way.

Still, shifts are taking place, putting the consumer in new positions of power and control and turning retail into an all-encompassing presence in the life of Western populations, be it spatially, socially or economically. So what are retailers doing? And what and where will retail go next? Back to town? To the peripheral spaces like the petrol station and the airport? Into virtual spaces, the television, the PC and mobile phones? Or is it the end? Are we finally going to get bored with shopping as a leisure activity, consumerism as a lifestyle and commercial space as the backdrop to our town centres and countryside? Where will it go from here? That's the million-dollar question. And the answers, predictions and forecasts are as diverse as they are short-lived.

There are endless reports from companies like Forrester

---

[121] Ibid.

Research (market research) and Hillier Parker (real estate development) painting pictures of retail and e-commerce revolutions to come in the next five years that will leave us shopping in places and ways we can hardly conceive of today. But then there is the expert consumer behaviourist, David Peek, who, in the face of the speed of change around him has stopped predicting and claims that 'every forecast about retail today is untrue...God knows where it will go now. It is totally unpredictable. We are now dealing with such experienced "floating voters" that shopping could go anywhere.'[122] And there is the architect Rem Koolhaas who has made an extensive study of shopping trends with Harvard graduates. He sees shopping as one of the most powerful but at the same time most threatened components of our urban fabric today and believes we are 'currently witness to the death knell of a big animal threatening to trample every activity in its agony'.[123]

For the retailers themselves, the current climate of change and shifting priorities is at the same time challenging and terrifying. Consumer tastes today move so fast that it is hard for retailers, especially those operating in bricks and mortar spaces, to keep up. Peek calls it the 'capital investment trap', where retailers have their capital tied in real estate or stocks and have difficulty moving them fast enough to respond to change. While the e-commerce bubble was temporarily deflated in the summer of 2000, the actual fight is only beginning as the process we are witnessing now is just the 'weeding out'. For every dot.com launched, there will be probably 10 more in the coming year. But in five years it is likely that the limitations of the Web – selling commodity information is hard, distributing products requires old-world skills, creating immersion seems impossible – means that the old physical players and the new ones will merge and create über-companies not unlike Wal-Mart or Volkswagen. The physical and the virtual will merge, with branding and spatial completeness; how this will happen is for the retailers to find out.

Peek, who in 2000 refused to acknowledge e-commerce as a real player within the retail landscape, now sees it as a real threat: 'the cheapness and ease of changing a website has left many bricks and mortar retailers at a loss'. Dr Jonathan Reynolds of the Oxford Institute of Retail Management (OXIRM) reports that it is one of the main areas of research these days: 'The question of e-commerce is worrying retailers. It is a great challenge for them to manage hybrid channels, to figure out costing, supply and effective methods of self-service that work both online and in bricks and mortar stores. The economics of it is very challenging. It's disconcerting for them;

---

[122] David Peek in personal interview, November 1999.
[123] Koolhaas, 'Start Again' lecture.

just when they have cracked the formula for successful bricks and mortar retailing, they are faced with a whole new scenario that has to include e-tailing.'[124]

One thing seems to be clear though, whether it is online, on the high street or in a petrol station: today the consumer rules more than ever. Retailers who fail to listen to their customers and keep abreast of changes minute by minute will fail to attract business, not only in the long term, but immediately, tomorrow. Witness Marks & Spencer, Britain's leading retailer 10 years ago, which in the last nine months of 1999/2000 lost many millions and several chief executives. And then it was anyone's guess if brands like Autograph and a new design for shopping bags would be able to save this household name, which has clothed and fed the British (and more recently Europe and the Far East) since 1888. Reynolds said at the time that Marks & Spencer had 'fallen off a cliff that brands fall off if they don't keep up consumer trust' and believed there was legitimate cause for concern about whether it would ever recover. Or is it not consumer power but the power of Gap or any other newer, trendier brand that nearly brought not just Marks & Spencer but also its consumers to their knees? This is the problem: for what seemed intractable amid the crazy daze of dot.com mania, now looks like a blip. By 2002 Marks & Spencer was doing well and everyone (in the UK) was happy again for a while.

The conspiracy theory that says that retailers, large brands and transnational corporations are manipulating us into buying, luring us into purchasing goods we don't need, is outdated. Vast choice, low customer loyalty and the ease of foreign travel have put customers in a strong position: they know that if they don't like it in this shop they will find satisfaction somewhere else – be it down the road or a plane flight away in New York or Stockholm. This is a daunting prospect for those who now realise that the previously clearly delimited playing field has been redrawn and that there are no longer any rules: today the competitor could be a furniture design boutique in a back street in Milan or a shoe shop in Barcelona. As Underhill puts it: 'Today's consumer is an 800-pound gorilla that goes wherever it pleases. Consumer behaviour has changed dramatically in the last decade or so: in the 20th century it was very much about consumers following, in the 21st century they lead.'

Jan Hol, Head of Public Relations at Ahold, the Dutch global food retailer that has stores in the United States, Latin America and Europe, says the secret of success today lies in the ability to gather and nurture knowledge about clients: 'I think the main message is to keep looking, every day, at your customer base. That's not as simple as it sounds: it is the most important and hardest

---

[124] Dr Jonathan Reynolds in personal interview, December 1999.

skill…which has to be ingrained into the bones of the organisation for it to remain successful.'[125]

We will look at the information about 'us' in chapter 8, when we consider branding, but remember now that one of the World Wide Web's greatest assets – its ability to monitor so much that we do – is also its greatest threat as privacy lobbies around the world line up to claim we are all now living under the spell not of Big Brother (apart from the television cult series now showing seemingly everywhere) but of Big Retailer.

Still, while it is important to know who consumers are and what they want, retailers also have to keep track of who their fellow retailers are, positioning themselves prominently among their competitors and communicating a clear identity to the consumer. Some call this brand image, others call it point of view; in any case it has to be strong and well defined for a business to build sustainable success. Tom Dixon, Head of Design at Habitat UK, is involved in what he believes will be a four-year process to rebrand Habitat and put it back into the leading position it held in the 1970s and 1980s. For him the main problem with the company now is that it has lost its edge and point of view, and that it is difficult to formulate a new one: 'There needs to be a single Habitat vision that runs consistently through all the aspects of the business. Unity is the most important thing in this competitive climate. When people want to put coffee shops into the stores, I think that's a nice idea, and the Internet is also a great thing, but it is not the answer. The answer is point of view. The point of view of a single person who knows what the essence of the business is.'[126]

Strong point of view but also being the first is the answer, especially for new brands that are trying to gain recognition in the already overcrowded marketplace. Thus the British digital shopping channel, Open TV (now Sky Active), launched in September 1999, positioned itself as an 'online mall', demarcating a virtual catchment area. Charles Ponsonby, group strategy and marketing director at Open TV, explained that knowing one's strengths and building on them is essential for the creation of a new brand. Open TV clearly positioned itself as a virtual shopping space that offered well-known brands. He realised, however, that Open TV would never be able to replace the 'experiential' shopping trip, the fun part of it – but then it didn't aim to. Open TV positioned itself in the realm of functional and planned shopping, an area of retail, says Ponsonby, where the largest share of wallet lies: 'People spend a large part of their money on grocery shopping throughout the year, especially families; we feel we can have a significant impact in this area.'

---

[125] Jan Hol, Ahold, in personal interview.
[126] Tom Dixon, Habitat, in personal interview, May 2000.

For Ponsonby, who describes himself as an e-commerce Luddite, a successful business can work anywhere, in cyberspace or in bricks and mortar stores as long as it has a 'strong proposition', that it knows who its audience is, what the brand stands for and which market it is trying to corner. 'Basically it is not about where you offer a product to the consumer, through what medium you offer it; it's about how you present it. You have to have a strong proposition.' He believes that the problem with many Internet start-ups is that they have been blinded by the e-commerce hype and think that because they are doing business via the Internet it will be successful. 'For me the high street is always the leveller. For any new business proposition I hear about, I imagine it as a shop in Oxford Street and I ask myself: "Will that work? Will it survive among all the other shops? Is it the kind of place you would go into to browse and buy?" And in most cases the answer is "no". And if it wouldn't survive on the high street, then why would it on the Web?', Ponsonby asks, describing the Internet as the Wild West.[127]

Once you have the strong proposition things get easier, as the food retailer Tesco shows. Leading the way in home shopping through their online branch, Tesco Direct, they seem fairly blasé about their fearless move into virtual spaces, embracing the idea of online retailing in 1995 and now leading the market with an annual turnover of £125 million.[128] Tim Mason, Marketing Director at Tesco, is down to earth about it, though: 'Online shopping, the development of the Web, was primarily about the development of another format for us. So far it hasn't impacted on existing business and it has been a fairly cheap shift to make.' He says that once the business model is right, moving into other formats, whether from out-of-town superstore to small, high street model in the 1990s or expanding with a 24-hour model in Swansea and online all around the United Kingdom, is just a question of logistics.

"Designing your business model so that it will work in different formats is the key. The difficulty then is to implement your ideas efficiently. Innovation isn't about good ideas in the first place, it is about strength and leadership and, of all the supermarkets, Tesco is most likely to have the capability and mindset in-house to implement these ideas. Once we decide to do something, we get on and do it. Many others suffer from debating. We have a strong leadership, which is what makes it work and gives us direction."[129]

---

[127] Charles Ponsonby in personal interview, January 2000; all quotes from interview.

[128] See tesco.com, corporate affairs.

[129] Tim Mason, Tesco, in personal interview, February 2000; all quotes from interview.

Having cracked the location problem by ensuring a presence in all locations, from the high street to the edge of town, the peripheral space of the petrol station and the virtual space online, Tesco is moving on to new areas, investing in the development of financial services by building on brand strength. 'Retail is becoming a broader concept and we see potential in a move into financial services. We will build on the brand and offer customers what they are used to from Tesco as food retailers: good service and good value,' says Mason. So, from covering all locations within the food retail sector, Tesco now aims to move beyond food into the retailing of intangibles, demonstrating that when you get the business model right you can take it anywhere and adapt it to a variety of situations.

Underhill predicts that this flexibility and ability to move between the physical and the virtual will be a crucial determinant of successful retailers in the future: 'The future of shopping will be about the integration of online and real-world retail – it won't be a choice between them. Well-known retailers were quaking in their boots a year ago. Now they're realising [that] bringing their brand online is much easier and less expensive than creating a brand from scratch as the pure play competitors must do.'

Conclusion

Retail is changing, that is an inescapable fact. But the changes we are witnessing today are not as radical or ground-breaking as they appear at first sight. Looking back over the last 150 years of retail it becomes clear that many features date back to the 19th century and that technological progress and social change have allowed for the refinement and popularisation of a process that was already in existence in 1850.

One crucial shift brought about by the gradual and seemingly unstoppable spread of retail in the last 50 years is consumer empowerment. Improved communication and transport links allow consumers to choose and move – physically or virtually – between retailers, putting them in a strong position and forcing the retailer to offer more for less not only in terms of product, but also in terms of service, environment and price. Choice is also limiting consumer control, however, as its overwhelming nature leaves consumers paralysed, unable to decide. This is the area where the retailers can regain control, telling confused consumers what is best for them and convincing them in their weak moments to just choose the retailer's brand. So at what point do consumers relinquish their power to the retailer? And why? Is it out of weakness, does the retailer seduce blind consumers? Is it tiredness, are consumers simply exhausted by the choice and do they want the retailer to decide? Or do consumers actually trust the retailer to make a better judgement because they have more information?

Chapter 3 – Science, enchantment and the voyeur

Shopping, for all we know about it, remains a mystery. Why does someone who walks into a store thinking IBM walk out lugging Compaq, or vice versa? What makes a shopper who decides to kill a few minutes in a boutique walk out $1,000 lighter but feeling more fashionable – more beautiful – than ever before? Yes, the simple answer is that he found something he wanted, but there's no easy explanation for why and how *that* happened.

Paco Underhill, *Why We Buy* [130]

With great dexterity, Monsieur Lheureux proceeded to exhibit three Algerian scarves, several packets of English needles, a pair of straw slippers, and to crown all, four egg-cups carved from coconut shells in filigree by convicts. Then, spreading his hands on the table, leaning forward, and stretching his neck, he watched, open-mouthed, while Emma looked through his merchandise, unable to make up her mind. Every now and again, as though to remove a speck of dust, he gave a flick with his fingernail to the silk of the scarves which were displayed at full length. When he did this they quivered with a faint rustling sound, and the gold spangles woven into their tissue gleamed in the green evening light like stars.

'How much are they?'

'The merest trifle!' he replied: 'Hardly worth mentioning! I don't mind a bit waiting for my money. Pay whenever you find it convenient.'

Gustave Flaubert, *Madame Bovary* [131]

Lheureux, Flaubert's 'dealer in fancy goods' and the ultimate example of the controlling retailer, combines 'the talkativeness of the southerner with the canniness of the native of Caux'[132] to coax Emma Bovary into buying his exotic wares. A shrewd and calculating character, he is courteous and polite but at the same time completely controls Emma, who is only too willing to give in to the seduction of his merchandise, which allows her to escape the boredom of the provincial Yonville and her married life to the town physician. As the story develops Emma comes more and more under Lheureux's influence, as he manages to keep her in constant financial debt and, after his discovery of her extramarital affair with Rodolphe, helpless fear that he might tell her husband.

Today, characters like Lheureux wouldn't have found it so easy to keep the bored housewives of provincial Yonville at their mercy. Everything is different now, as emancipation in the Western world and the establishment of a consumer society mean everyone can shop and has a wide range of choices as to where and how they

---

[130] Paco Underhill, *Why We Buy* (London: Orion Business Books, 1999), p. 157.
[131] Gustav Flaubert, *Madame Bovary*, translated by Gerard Hopkins (Oxford: Oxford University Press, 1991), p. 98.
[132] Ibid, p. 97.

do this. Emma Bovary's Algerian scarves and embroidered collars are available to all, in a range of qualities and prices. Emma could not only have chosen from a range of fashionable retailers offering her a variety of goods in her Yonville high street or her local shopping centre, she would have had access to the Internet, where she could have clicked on to global retail sites and found the best price. She could have driven her Renault Clio to Rouen or taken the first TGV to Paris to get away from the limited retail choice in Yonville and indulge in the dizzying spectacle of the boutiques on the Champs Elysées.

Still, even armed with all that knowledge, she could have fallen prey to Lheureux's gentle entreaties and the tempting display of goods. For whatever changes technological progress has brought – from electric lighting to the Internet – it will not change the human condition. We will always have conscious and unconscious desires that are waiting to be triggered. Even today, amid the plethora of shopping opportunities that present themselves to the consumer at every corner and everywhere in between, the sophisticated retailer can trigger those hidden desires through personal touch, playing on our conscious or unconscious weaknesses in ways that to date have not been replicated with our electronic, digital, substitutes.

Shopping today is about control, consumer control over the retailer, sometimes, but also the retailers' control over overwhelmed shoppers who wander through the physical retail space mesmerised by the environment or simply by the vast choice of goods that they could own. Consumers' control over themselves and their desire is what retailers are constantly trying to overcome, by creating tantalising images of better lives, by triggering desires. The Internet is interesting in this context as it gives consumers the illusion of control, but is in fact constantly drawing them into areas of a website or page where they initially had no intention of going.

Retail is about seduction as retail's imagery, environments and underlying messages strive to take consumers away from reality. Retail can convince consumers that they can have new personas – be it as an individual who will stand out or as an anonymous member of a group. The creation of retail space as a fantasy environment with spectacular and ever-changing features offers consumers an additional escape from reality, as they can momentarily – or indeed, for hours – forget the circumstances of their real life and imagine new lives.

In this chapter we will look at the relationship between the retailisers and the retailised from both points of view: that of the seller – today a professional seducer, seeking the fickle consumer's attention – and that of the buyer, an increasingly disloyal, adulterous (Flaubert was right!) creature. We will look at how consumers satisfy their conscious needs and desires and how they respond to retailers' techniques to trigger their unconscious desires. We will also look at the retailers' position and at the scientific and more 'spiritual' ways in which retailers try to win customers and keep their attention.

From the consumers' point of view there seems to be no end to the desire to consume. Retail is everywhere today and, instead of reaching saturation point, which some predict it will any day now, consumption is steadily growing. Expenditure by British households increased by 77 per cent between 1971 and 1995, with spending on durable goods like radios, televisions and video recorders increasing fourteenfold and spending on entertainment, leisure and education more than doubling.[133] Instead of getting bored with the consumer lifestyle, we are getting better at it, spending more time and money shopping. Today's consumers also expect more, though. They shop selectively, looking for quality, competitive pricing, good service, easy access and, often most importantly, pleasant and safe surroundings. As we have mentioned in the previous chapter there are different levels of shopping, the type that serves to satisfy conscious needs and desires, and the type that fulfils unconscious needs and desires. Each type elicits different behaviour from consumers and requires a different approach from retailers.

On the retailers' side, hard work is required to satisfy the differing needs, desires and expectations of consumers while constantly dealing with fierce competition from existing long-term rivals and from the nascent dot.com dangers. While powerful imagery in the form of branding and advertising go a long way in gaining the public attention, the retailer has to get much closer to consumers, try to 'know them' to be really successful. In an effort to gain a better understanding of the confusing mass of consumers, he is trying to create an order, some sort of hierarchy, that will reduce consumers to 'bite-size' chunks that are more containable and comprehensible. Endless techniques and systems have been introduced to create such an order; this is retailisation going scientific, number-crunching to keep up with the fluid mass of consumers that goes where it pleases. The difficulty is that today's predictions and assumptions remain valid only for short periods, consumer tastes change every week, and consumers get bored easily and are willing to embrace new brands and trends without hesitation. In addition, it is becoming increasingly hard really to 'know' and corner the consumer as some believe that each consumer is in fact two or three different people; thus British retailers are suddenly faced with not 60 million but 180 million consumers.

Even more problematic is that as retail companies 'go global' by

133 *Social Trends* (London: Office for National Statistics, 1997).

spreading a net of outlets around the world, high streets and shopping centres in London, Sydney and Hong Kong are beginning to look more and more alike. Inventiveness and creativity are the only answers to this 'emerging sameness and uniformity' of retail space. Designers are reaching for historic, fantastic or mythological themes in order to colour their designs with a touch of difference. As consumer behaviourist David Peek explains: 'This is the story-telling part of it, creating an atmosphere of magic to delight the consumer.'[134] This is where retailisation goes into the 'spiritual'.

Meeting conscious needs and desires

The shopping that fulfils conscious needs is of a rational nature, often planned, and places the consumer in a position of control: this is the shopping of the shopping 'to do' lists and the repetitive weekly trawling through the aisles of the supermarket, working through a pattern and mechanically throwing in 'the usual'. It is what the analysts and experts describe as 'purposive' or 'chore' shopping, clearly suggesting the no-fun aspect of it. But even conscious needs can involve pleasure or enjoyment. Daniel Miller, a professor of anthropology at University College London, has conducted extensive research observing the shopping habits of North London housewives. He concluded that, on a deeper level, this seemingly mundane form of shopping is an expression of love. Housewives shopping for their children and husbands will pay extra attention, buying foods members of their family especially like or that are healthy for them. Miller describes this sort of shopping as 'the outcome of a responsibility so basic that it does not need to be made explicit or reflected upon'. It is, in other words, a manifestation of love and care. He argues that the daily decisions that accompany such basic shopping trips may appear simple but they are in fact imbued with moral questions 'about good and bad action indicated in traits such as sensitivity as against style, or generosity against jealousy'.[135] Thus, the shopping for conscious needs can very easily cross the control barrier and become an out of control process, with the consumer giving in to personal desires or a desire to please, spoil or take care of loved ones.

The point at which the consumer 'loses it' and gives in to irrational desire has been identified in the world of retail as the 'Gruen Transfer', named after the Austrian urban architect, Victor Gruen, who in the 1950s and 1960s built some of the first enclosed shop-

---

[134] David Peek in personal interview, November 1999; all quotes from interview.
[135] Daniel Miller, *A Theory of Shopping* (Ithaca, New York: Cornell University Press), 1998, p. 19.

ping malls in the United States. It defines the moment when a 'destination buyer' with a specific purchase in mind is transformed into an impulse shopper. This is a crucial transition, immediately identifiable in customers' behaviour and body language as they slow from a determined stride to an aimless and sauntering gait.[136]

And that's when the shopping can start, when the retailer can cash in on cultivating irrational desire. Paco Underhill confirms that supermarkets are places of frequent impulse buying, with as much as 70 per cent of purchases being unplanned. Men are especially prone to reckless shopping patterns in supermarkets. In one of his studies Underhill found that while nearly all women carried lists, less than a quarter of the men did and that they shopped with 'a carefree abandon and restless lack of discipline for which the gender is known'.[137]

Shopping to satisfy conscious desires, though often planned, is not necessarily rational. There is no arguing that one needs bread, milk, washing-up liquid, and also a new winter coat when the old one is worn out, and a new bed when the old one collapses. But does one really *need* the latest model of trainers to replace last season's, which are now definitely not fashionable any more? Consumers' loss of control is a more deliberate process here as the desire is rationalised and transformed into a need. Also, this rationalisation process will make it appear that consumers are still in control, that they have made a considered decision, when in fact they have lost control and given in to the retailer's seduction.

We're getting into a blurred zone here, where the term 'need' is no longer clearly delineated, merging on the edges with 'want' or 'want to need'. While this is not the place to go into the depths of the linguistic or semantic value of the word 'need', it is clear that this term is very subjective. In today's consumer society, the abundance of goods on display and their 24-hour availability has redefined our idea of need. Take the example of bread: arguably it is a basic provision we all need. But the next decision as to whether one needs ciabatta, French bread or just a plain, white sliced loaf will differ for each individual, according to their idea of 'need'. And even if deep down we know that we don't really *need* something, it is very easy to rationalise the irrational desire in our minds.

Forgetting the meaning and interpretation of words for a moment, the process of shopping for conscious needs or desires is, whether it is rational or irrational, a considered process. Whether it is grocery shopping on Saturday morning or buying new Reeboks in the afternoon, these purchases will be part of a plan. And

---

[136] Margaret Crawford, 'The world in a shopping mall', in: Michael Sorkin, ed., *Variations on a Theme Park* (New York: Hill and Wang, 1992), p. 14.
[137] Underhill, *Why We Buy*, p. 101.

whether it is a plan to provide the household with basic necessities or a plan to improve one's idea of oneself or one's image to the world around makes no difference. The choice of the purchase will be determined by the same basic questions: what item?, which price range?, which quality range? and where?

The first question, 'what item?', will determine the generic nature of the object: 'what do I need, what do I want?' It could be toothpaste or cat food – or also trendy new trainers. Having determined the nature of the necessary or desired purchase, one moves on to answer the following three questions, which are interdependent. 'Which?' takes in two interdependent questions: 'which price range?' and 'which quality range?' Price and quality – or brand image – traditionally go hand in hand, but consumers' access to a wider range of information through the Internet could alter that.

From consumers' points of view, there is an increasing control over prices. Retailers are having to take into account that tools like the Internet allow consumers to check prices not just against the competitor next door on the high street, but anywhere. Jonathan Reynolds of the Oxford Institute of Retail Management predicts fundamental shifts in pricing as techniques introduced by the Internet become more accessible: 'I think there are going to be significant changes in pricing strategies throughout the retail landscape in the coming years. We will see a return to a type of bargaining economy with consumers bidding and buying for the lowest price available on the market. You can see this developing through companies like lastminute.com, expedia.com, letsbuyit.com and priceline.com. This auction mode of selling puts an onus on the retailers, forcing them to offer really competitive prices.'[138]

However, while auctions offer consumers new power to determine how much they will pay for what they want or need, they are also the ultimate place for giving in to desires and losing control over actual needs. The speed of the bidding process creates an immersive urgency and accentuates the desire for objects that would ordinarily, if they were simply displayed on a shelf in the back of a shop, not seem desirable or necessary. Indeed the full scope of this new bargaining economy became clear as we spoke to Michael Sastry, the revenue manager at the last minute online retailer, lastminute.com. Hardly pausing for breath he enumerated the features of these auctions for us: the new models, their advantages, their disadvantages. Thus we learnt the difference between Dutch auctions and English auctions, that online haggling (makeusanoffer.com) is good for consumer-to-consumer deals and could work for business-to-consumer transactions, that the community buy – where a group of buyers get

---

[138] Dr Jonathan Reynolds in personal interview, December 1999; all quotes from interview.

together to bid for a product (letsbuyit.com) – is good for shifting gadgets like Palm Pilots but no good for hotel rooms, and that there are also things called reverse auctions, descending auctions and floating price models. While this was explained flawlessly to us by an erudite 24-year-old who is making it big in the exciting new world of e-commerce, we did wonder whether we would ever hear our fathers, or even ourselves, say: 'Just going online to do a bit of reverse auctioning, I thought I'd get rid of that old radio.'

Choice of quality or brand is also being affected by retailisation. Reynolds explains that strong branding is increasingly seen as the key to gaining and keeping customer loyalty. 'Brands today have to be more customer-oriented without reinventing themselves too often. That confuses the customer base. Brands should provide a role of certainty that customers can trust. The most interesting thing today is to see how existing brands are evolving in the multiple retail channel environment, how they are translating their brand in electronic terms.'

After establishing the 'what' and 'which' of the purchases, the answer to the fourth question 'where?' will be determined by convenience and availability or range of choice. In a conscientious effort to establish the factors that will sway the consumers' choice of decision with mathematical precision, Reilly's 'Law of Retail Gravitation', which sounds rather like a law related to a physics experiment in school, but is in fact a law about shopping centres, says that 'if all factors are equal, shoppers will patronise the largest shopping centre they can get to easily'.[139] So people will choose Bluewater in Kent over a smaller local shopping centre because it is larger and, as we will see in chapter 4, easily accessible as long as you have a car.

Depending on the nature of the purchase, the importance of each of these factors will vary. For example, in the case of the new trainers, the price will be secondary and the brand image – the trust of quality the brand inspires or the image it projects to the outside world – will determine the choice. On the other hand, in the case of basic commodities such as sugar, milk or toilet paper, it is difficult to convince consumers that there is a tangible difference between brands. Thus the three factors price, brand image or quality and location will guide the shopping process for conscious needs and desires.

Triggering unconscious desires

Traditional economic theory defines the consumer as a 'rational human being who attempts to meet his or her needs by buying

---

[139] From Larry O'Brien and Frank Harris, *Retailing, Shopping, Society, Space* (London: David Fulton Publishers, 1991).

goods or services'.[140] Which is quite funny. Not in terms of the above, where consumers were indeed described as more or less rational beings, weighing their options and seeking the best deal. We are concerned here with consumers' irrational side, as illustrated in the passage below from Zola's 19th-century novel on the birth of the new consumerism, *Au Bonheur des Dames*:

[M]aterial was streaming down like a bubbling sheet of water...Women pale with desire were leaning over as if to look at themselves. Faced with this wild cataract, they all remained standing there, filled with the secret fear of being caught in the overflow of all this luxury and with an irresistible desire to throw themselves into it and be lost.

Emile Zola, Au Bonheur des Dames [141]

The *mise en scène* of such an 'irresistible' spectacle was the work of Octave Mouret, the owner of the department store whose 'sole passion was the conquest of Woman. He wanted her to be queen in his shop; he had built his temple for her in order to hold her at his mercy. His tactics were to intoxicate her with amorous attentions, to trade on her desires.'[142] Zola's Mouret and Flaubert's Lheureux reflect the growing number of 19th-century retailers who realised that they could do more than just fulfil the customers' basic needs. Using respectively visual and verbal seduction they understood that they could create a want where there had not been one before. Commodities, formerly on sale to fulfil human needs and desires, now created them, enveloping the merchandise in dreams and illusions of happiness. The Boucicauts, the owners of the Au Bon Marché department store, soon became aware that while they could make a decent living out of supplying customers' conscious needs, they could make a much better living by supplying a desire customers did not know they had until they entered the shop. Thus, the commercial principle of supply was replaced with the idea of consumer seduction, transforming the department store into a fantasy world, a dream machine, that Zola voraciously describes as devouring, disgorging, consuming and accelerating to the point of overheating and explosion during the sales.[143] These stores did not just sell goods, they sold dreams and illusions and the shopping experience as a sensuous and enjoyable pastime.

If you thought the 21st century consumer had evolved into a more sensible being, however, the following description of retailing practices in Japan, should set that straight.

---

[140] Ibid, p. 117.
[141] Emile Zola, *Au Bonheur des Dames* (Paris: Gallimard, 1980), pp. 103–104.
[142] Emile Zola, *The Ladies' Paradise* (Oxford: Oxford University Press, 1995), p. 234.
[143] Brian Nelson in introduction to Zola, *The Ladies' Paradise*.

Where there was order, there is chaos. Where there was clarity, there is confusion. The discount chain of stores Don Quijote, named after Cervantes' 17th century satiric novel, is thumbing its nose at traditional Japanese retailing practices. The retailer has abandoned the orderly layout and tender service on which most Japanese retailers pride themselves, offering instead narrow aisles with shelves piled high with goods and sections regularly moved about. Despite, or because of, the confusion, the stores are packed with shoppers shoulder to shoulder sifting through the vast selection of goods. The busiest time seems to be around midnight – the stores are open 22 hours a day – when a carnival atmosphere pervades. Everything seems to be for sale, from Louis Vuitton bags and big-screen televisions to groceries and slippers...Takao Yasuda, president and founder, says the company does not think of itself as a retailer but as an imaginative provider of space where young people can amuse themselves, especially at night. 'A lot of our customers are addicted to coming here. They're tired of going to karaoke clubs and bars and not many cinemas have late night showings on weekdays...'

Naoko Nakamae[144]

Narrowing down the aisles in a shop, Japanese retailers manage to create a shopping frenzy among customers who need to push and struggle to get to the merchandise. Yet these Japanese in 1999 and Zola's ladies in the 1850s are also, at other times, lucid, rational beings. But they have crossed the line, transferred into Gruen's zone where impulse buying is the only way of buying. On the wrong side of the Gruen Transfer then, consumers can, despite all their wisdom and knowledge of available choices, be lured into exactly the same naïve trap that Emma Bovary got caught in. Instigating such instant and irrepressible desires, understanding their motivation and setting them off at each opportunity, is retailers' main challenge. One of the basic tricks to create desire is based on 'indirect commodification', whereby the use of images, activities or objects that are not on sale encourages consumers to purchase. The principle of the 'adjacent attraction' uses the most dissimilar objects, which, placed next to each other, will incite purchases. Thus, placing a plain earthenware bowl in a window display of a Turkish harem 'transforms the pot into something exotic, mysterious and desirable'. The architectural theorist, Margaret Crawford, explains that 'this logic of association allows non-commodified values to enhance commodities, but also enhance the reverse process – previously non-commodified entities become part of the marketplace.'[145]

The dynamic of museum bookshops and gift stores is largely based on this mechanism, as visitors to an exhibition or gallery will want to take a tangible proof of their visit home with them. 'In the

144 Naoko Nakamae, 'Keeping shoppers amused is key to success: Japanese retailer Don Quijote uses an imaginative new approach to boost sales in the face of recession', *Financial Times*, 21 December 1999, Companies & Finance: Asia-Pacific, p. 28.
145 Crawford, 'World in a shopping mall', pp. 14, 15.

end that's what shopping at a museum is about: taking elements of the museum home with you,' claims James Gundell, the president of New York's Museum of Modern Art retail section. 'The only difference is that in the museum you are looking at a single piece, while in the shop we are trying to bring these elements to a broad public.'[146]

Manchester United über alles

It is a wet Thursday in early spring, but at the 'Theatre of Dreams', which is Old Trafford, home to footballing giants and world soccer brand Manchester United all is well. A good result the previous night in Europe is one thing, but in the offices of Steve Richards, Managing Director of Merchandising for the club, lie the plans for the latest Manchester United theme stores: they are to be built in the major cities of South-East Asia. The team, as with the Museum of Modern Art (MoMA)'s Picassos or Pollocks, is not just a work of art (if you support them) but also the most ruthlessly marketed sporting phenomenon in Europe and most parts of the world. (FIFA, world soccer's governing body, having placed the 1994 World Cup in America, has yet to see soccer play big there, really big, that is, like the US football, baseball or basketball teams.)

Oasis concert

The Gallagher brothers may hate each other from time to time, as their obsessive fans once again ask what's the story, boys?, or perhaps this is just a useful marketing spin happily sold us by the tabloid and music media to sell more albums; the last two CDs may have had fewer great tunes than the average muzak-filled shopping mall; the songwriter might not even be on stage tonight.

But that doesn't stop Sky Digital, Britain's leading satellite television provider, from bombarding us for two weeks in advance with promotional adverts on all of its channels: sports, news, features, movies, for the 'pay-for-view' Oasis concert 'Live'-ish from Wembley stadium in June 2000. The concert is so-so for the £12.95 we pay using our modem link bolted on to the satellite's decoder box. But what strikes, amid all the growling guitars (and guitarists), is the mass of merchandise on show as the cameras lovingly capture the tens of thousands of fans. Oasis t-shirts, hats, posters, are everywhere. This is not

---

[146] James Gundell in personal interview, March 2000.

> **so much a concert as another variant on MoMA's idea of 'taking the museum home with you'. The video and DVD were available within weeks.**

Such simple-minded tricks might seem insulting to our intelligence and we may hope not to get drawn into this trickery, but we do. Every time. And why? Not because we are stupid but because we want to buy into this deceit, believe the magic. We shop not only because we need to but, much more often, because we enjoy it.

There is a whole series of theories on 'why we shop', that is, what the motives are for this activity that makes up such an important part of our lives. The French sociologist, Jean Baudrillard, relates it to our quest for happiness: consumer society has imbued us with the belief that we can find it in the most banal commodities, like bath salts or an advert for the Canary Islands.[147] Others argue that in a society where family networks and strong community spirit have disappeared, consumption offers a sense of belonging and is an expression of social status. It is also said that we shop to express individuality or, on the contrary, confirm a sense of belonging to a particular group.[148] We shop to escape, to assume new identities and aspire to other lives. David Peek, who relates shopping to imagination, sees most consumers as in fact two, three or even five different people, depending on their moods. 'The bank manager who during the day wears suits and adopts the City look, may turn into a raver on Friday night and then again a biker at the weekend.' Paco Underhill takes a simpler view: 'We don't buy because we need to, it's just because we can; if you think about it, strictly speaking, most of us in the Western world have all we need to buy for the rest of our lives, all we really *need* is food. So when we buy a new car, it's not out of need it's just because we're tired of the previous one. It's a discretionary purchase, like most others. The social stratification of the 20th century is over. Everyone can shop.'[149]

We hope that by buying a new car, new clothes, a bigger house, we will actually become another person, even though subconsciously we know we won't. For the price of the house, the dress or the copy of *Wallpaper** lifestyle magazine, we buy the temporary illusion of a new identity that came with the car or that is portrayed in the magazine; we buy into the advertisements and brand image that suggest wealth, erudition and happiness. When the illu-

---

[147] Baudrillard, *Consumer Society* (London: Sage Publications, 1998), p. 139.
[148] John Hannigan, *Fantasy City* (London: Routledge, 1998), p. 34.
[149] Paco Underhill in personal interview, March 2000; all quotes from interview.

sion wears off, we get bored with the object and realise that we are still the same person, and we cast about for new dreams, new objects that still have the veneer of magic about them, until that wears thin, and so on, endlessly. Wrapping commodities in a veil of illusion – fantastic and unusual settings – not only hides their inherent plainness, it also serves a self-delusory purpose, allowing us to forget we are spending money on unnecessary items. Staging the simple act of buying in spectacular spaces, surrounding it with an experience, makes it possible for us to negate the actual act of consumption.

Tyler Brûlé, founder of *Wallpaper** magazine, now a style consultant, acknowledges that for many readers his magazine is 'a purely aspirational experience; it's their form of escape, their pornography in a sense'. He believes many readers are likely to follow all the fashion trends, up to the changing length of shirt lapels, without ever being able to afford to purchase any of the items shown in the magazine.[150] Shopping is not so much about actual ownership in the first place then; it is the whole shopping process, seeing the object, picking it up, coveting it and imagining ownership of it. In his book*, Why We Buy*, Underhill writes that possession is 'an emotional and spiritual process, not a technical one. Possession begins when the shopper's senses start to latch on to the object. It begins in the eyes and then in the touch. Once the thing is in your hand, or on your back, or in your mouth, you can be said to have begun the process of taking it. Paying for it is a mere technicality…'[151] This is even more true of large or rare items, a house, a designer dress or an antique book. Once we set our minds on owning such things there is the added twitching urgency that tells us that if we don't buy it now it might be gone tomorrow and there will be no duplicates or second versions – at least not quite as good as this one.

In her essay 'The World a Shopping Mall', Margaret Crawford explores the mental processes that take place in the preliminary 'just looking' phase of mall shopping:

By extending the period of 'just looking', the imaginative prelude to buying, the mall encourages 'cognitive acquisition' as shoppers mentally acquire commodities by familiarising themselves with a commodity's actual and imagined qualities. Mentally 'trying on' products teaches shoppers not only what they want and what they can buy, but also, more importantly, what they don't have, and what they therefore need. Armed with this knowledge, shoppers can not only realise what they are but also what they might become.

Margaret Crawford[152]

---

[150] Tyler Brûlé in personal interview, June 2000.
[151] Underhill, *Why We Buy*, p. 169.
[152] Crawford, 'The World in a Shopping Mall', p. 12.

> You are not, to paraphrase Jay McInerney, the sort of person who would watch *Survivor*. It's not just the larvae-eating contest...it's the gladiatorial concept...it's the machiavellian twist...it's the suffering, the mean-spiritedness, the humiliation.
> And that is why you are watching Survivor. And you, and you. More than 23 million of you, a phenomenal audience for summer-rerun season.
>
> *Time* magazine[153]
>
> Our 'just looking' phase may have been – academically – initiated by Roland Barthes' *Mythologies* and more popularly by John Berger's seminal seventies BBC2 classic, *Ways of Seeing*, but we are all now gazers, starers, invaders of all privacies, all taboos. For every vérité television series: *Big Brother*, *Survivor*, MTV's *The Real World*, there is, as Barthes writes, the knowledge of striptease that '[it] is based on a contradiction: Woman is desexualised at the very moment she is stripped naked. We may therefore say that we are dealing in a sense with a spectacle based on fear, or rather on the pretence of fear.'[154]
> So too us: we watch because we can, because it makes new celebrities out of people like us. Every tantrum, fight and sundry bad behaviour: it is us on a Saturday at Bluewater, or drunkenly picking an argument at dinner or in the pub. If media reflects us, and this new trend shows we like it, then retail must as well.

Oniomania, the compulsion to purchase

In extreme cases this need to seek a different identity and emotional satisfaction in the act of shopping veers toward the compulsive and becomes a mental disorder. An increasing proportion of consumers suffers from oniomania, the compulsion to purchase. Though it is not listed in official manuals of mental disorder nor widely recognised as a disease, several studies in the United States suggest that 5 to 10 per cent of the American population – 15 million consumers – could be suffering from 'shopaholism' with another 40 million suffering from overspending.[155]

While these figures look alarming, some see them as an overestimate. It all depends on your definition of shopping addiction and where you draw the line between a love of shopping and addiction.

---

[153] James Poniewozik, 'We like to watch', *Time*, 26 June 2000, p. 56.
[154] Roland Barthes, 'Striptease', in: *A Roland Barthes Reader* (London: Vintage Classics, 2000), p. 85.
[155] *Christian Science Monitor*, see the CSM archives at *http://www.tfccs.com.*

For Dr Adrienne Baker, a senior lecturer in psychotherapy at Regent's College in London and author of *Serious Shopping*, the line between shopping and addiction lies at the point when shopping becomes a total preoccupation and the person becomes convinced that it can change their lives. 'When it becomes an obsession, something you wake up with and that keeps you busy all day, then it is an addiction.'[156] Olivia Mellan, a recovering shopaholic and author of *Overcoming Overspending*, says it is not difficult to identify cases of shopaholism. She has drawn up a self-diagnostic quiz with questions like 'Do you buy things you want, whether or not you can afford them at the moment?' and 'Do you buy things to cheer yourself up or to reward yourself?' to help identify new cases.

The outward symptoms of compulsive shopping frequently mask deeper disorders, though studies confirm that compulsive shoppers try to counteract feelings of low self-esteem through the emotional high and momentary euphoria provided by impulse shopping. Purchases often symbolise the person's image of an ideal self and the act of buying temporarily fills an emotional void. Baker found that the media caricature of the 'shopaholic' as a middle-aged, middle-class, wealthy women is wrong. 'The problem concerns both men and women [though there are more women suffering from the disorder] and it does not always involve wealthy women.'

Baker explains that it works just like any other addiction, except for the fact that it is non-chemical and involves a more socially accepted activity. 'We are exhorted to shop, encouraged to buy, buy, buy,' she says. 'It is normal to spend most of your weekends in shops and therefore easier to conceal addictive shopping. Other than that it is exactly the same as any other addiction in every respect: it reflects the same emptiness and lack of emotional fulfilment that lies behind other addictions.' Baker's research also found that many clients had a history of addictiveness, both in their family and through previous addictions and also that they had a tendency to form relationships with other addicts – alcoholics, workaholics, drug addicts. 'Wives immerse themselves in shopping as a reaction to their husband's obsession with work, thinking "If you work, I'll shop."'

Dr Jerrold Pollak, an American clinical psychologist who has treated several shopaholics, argues that shopaholism seems to be a disease of an affluent society. 'Advertisers ... would like us to think that shopping is a reason to live,' agrees Dr Cheryl Carmin, another clinical psychologist. 'If you do not have the time or inclination to go to the mall or grocery store, there are catalogues, delivery services, home shopping networks on TV, and endless items to buy via the

---

[156] Adrienne Baker in personal interview, November 1999; all quotes from interview.

Internet.'[157] With US advertisers spending $233 billion – the equivalent of six federal education budgets – in 2000 to seduce Americans into buying ever more, it is being dubbed 'a health hazard that comes with America's unparalleled economic prosperity'.[158] Two years later, in the midst of recession, America remained the dominant global economy; when it stutters the global economy stutters.

However, Baker maintains that, although the interest and research into the subject may be new, the condition whereby one gathers things, the magpie instinct of hoarding and gathering to satisfy other needs, is not recent. Indeed, we need only to refer back to the beginning of this chapter and the case of Madame Bovary, who vented her frustrations by spending money she did not have on luxuries she did not need, to show it is not a new disease.

While Baker believes that this type of shopping could take place anywhere, from car boot sales to Harrods' jewellery section, she doubts that addictive shopping and the Internet could ever go together. 'A large part of the addiction lies in the instant gratification, the "hunt" for the item, the environment, the crowds, the lights and the buzz of the stores,' she argues (although shopping addicts usually shop alone and are totally oblivious to the people around them). 'They become totally immersed in the experience so that even shop assistants become peripheral. So, paradoxically, while they are trying on outward things, their shopping experience is a very inward experience. People and surroundings become blurred faced with the irresistible need to shop.' Baker describes how many clients described the buzz they get from finding the item they want as equivalent to an orgasm, saying that with 'this in your life you don't need sex'. It is also about control, and having a relationship with objects that shopaholics think they can control.

We will argue, however, that the Internet in 2000 has merely failed to gratify, instantly, because of its inherent distribution problems: mail-order shopping takes time to deliver, and the Internet's current e-commerce revolution is very often nothing more than digital mail order. Two companies that did attempt to change the Internet's 'time' problem, Kozmo and Urban Fetch, sold themselves to consumers and shareholders alike, by offering a motorbike delivery service off the back of an Internet site. Thus users in major American cities such as New York could order a pizza or a computer and it would be delivered within an hour. Problems began as the new technology share prices crashed, when it became clear that neither company could find enough good 'deliverers'. But that is merely an issue of time too: it won't be long before enough people are retrained to offer and excel in 'mobile' service, as provided

---

[157] Cheryl Carmin in interview with Sharon Krum.
[158] *Christian Monitor*: see the CSM archives at *http://www.tfccs.com*.

by say the RAC or AA, rather than the 'situated' service to be found in a store or a mall. Once this is achieved shopping addiction will, we think, arrive big time on the Internet and interactive television.

A study of 25 compulsive shoppers in the United States found that buying urges occur episodically in the compulsive shopper, from every few days to once a week, and the urges typically last one hour...although some subjects reported episodes arising as frequently as every hour or as infrequently as every month.[159] Researchers found that clients had the most buying urges at home, but they also felt the desire to buy at work, in stores, in malls and while driving. Although 22 of those studied fought the urge to buy, they were unsuccessful 74.3 per cent of the time. Typically, compulsive shoppers were unaware of what they would purchase when they entered the store to fulfil a compulsive buying urge and nearly all said they felt a huge relief, a climax point, when they found the item they wanted, immediately followed by acute feelings of guilt, depression and self-hatred at the moment of paying. More than half of the compulsive buyers reported that they never even removed the purchases from their packaging, returned purchases or disposed of the items in various ways. Baker found similar responses among her clients, with several of them admitting to entire spare rooms, garages and car boots filled with unused, unopened purchases.

Baker maintains it is a disease likely to occur in people with a very fragile sense of self, who seek confirmation of their identity in objects. 'One client said to me she bought clothes in the hope that putting on different, new clothes would make her a new person.' Treatment varies from weekly sessions with Debtors Anonymous, a self-help programme inspired by Alcoholics Anonymous, to psychological consultation that involves treatment of the underlying problems of self-image and anti-depressants.

In an ultimate ironic twist of the retailisation process, American pharmaceutical companies are working with researchers at Stanford University to develop a drug specifically aimed at shopaholics. While many doctors believe the disorder is part of a wider underlying problem and should be treated accordingly, multinational pharmaceutical companies are trying to 'create a market' for the new drug, a specific type of antidepressant (selective serotonin re-uptake-inhibitor or SSRI). And indeed, if one was a compulsive shopper shopping around for a cure, these pills could seem like a neat solution: the need for extensive soul-searching for other problems is avoided and the complete cure is provided encapsulated in one tablet.

---

[159] See Gary A. Christenson MD and colleagues, 'Compulsive buying: descriptive characteristics and psychiatric comorbidity', *Journal of Clinical Psychiatry*, 55 (1), pp. 5–11, January 1994.

Going scientific: welcome to the House of Fun

Drawing consumers today and keeping their attention is not as easy as it was back in the 19th century. Consumers of the 21st century are hard to impress: they've seen it all, 'been there and got the t-shirt' (and, increasingly, set up the rival dot.com or moved to Spain) and, moreover, have such a vast range of retail opportunities to choose from that they can afford to be fussy. A shop is no longer just a shop; for sophisticated New Millennium shoppers it has to be good value, clean, easy to get to, safe, pleasant with good service and most of all *fun*. Fun every single time they go there, which means the shop has frequently to adapt and offer new forms of amusement. To gain an understanding of what consumers want now and what they will want tomorrow, retailers are using all possible devices in the hope of getting ahead of the competition. Guesswork, intuition and the techniques of simply offering spectacles of lavish abundance to shoppers, employed by the 19th-century department-store owners, are no longer sufficient. To 'be a winner' in today's world of retail – as apparently today the situation is polarised between the winners and the losers – you have to build on solid facts about your customer base and their aspirations.[160] This is paradoxical in itself as aspirations and desires are inherently vaguely defined and hard to quantify and transform into flow diagrams or piecharts. Yet this is what retailers need to do to ensure the sustainability of their business model.

Employing market research companies and consultancies, organising focus groups, using psychographic research techniques, cluster analysis, tracking systems, loyalty cards and video recordings, retailers attempt to pin down their customers and put them in little boxes in the hope they will stay put. But how long do these data remain valid? Underhill believes that it is possible to predict trends in the medium term even though it remains hard to cater very specifically for individual tastes: 'Fashion is fickle and it is hard to predict individual trends like what the favoured Christmas toy will be...However, the study of demographic trends can predict the strength of the market for a product or type of store.' For Underhill the main concern today lies with the ageing population and the changes this will herald in the retail landscape. With 76 million baby boomers in the United States today and 25 million in the United Kingdom, the 'mature market' is a growing sector. 'We always talk about the cash-rich and time-poor, but as more people retire younger and the population ages, we have to think about the

---

[160] Dr Jonathan Reynolds, OXIRM, in personal interview, December 1999: 'There is a clear polarisation taking place between the winners and the losers. You can almost count the best companies on one hand.'

time-rich and cash-rich: where will they go?' he speculates. Underhill sees great opportunity in creating new concepts that appeal to a more modern, cool concept of 'senior' with products like hearing aids and incontinence products becoming sleeker, more sophisticated, and well branded so that they lose their stigma. The arrival of Mick Jagger on the cover of *Saga* magazine, the increasingly hip choice of reading material for the over 55s, and *The Times*' column celebrating all that is 'happening' in the lives of over 50s, suggest that something significant is going on. Viagra helps too, of course. And HRT and Botox.

At the Royal College of Art in London researchers at the Helen Hamlin Centre are concentrating on the development of such products for the elderly. Jeremy Myerson, co-director, has spent two years investigating this area helping product designers create new kinds of goods that reflect a cash-rich, time-rich sector of society. One key area he has concentrated on is the home worker, who could be a 22-year-old freelance journalist, but who could also be a 60-year-old retired bank employee launching a new website. 'In Britain today at least one employer in 10 employs some form of home-based worker and an estimated two million people now work wholly or partly at home ... Work at home has profound design implications, many aspects of which have yet to be properly understood.'[161] It is not just design – it is, as we shall see in chapter 5, also all about retail.

Similarly the youth market has blossomed in the last 10 years and consumers are getting younger all the time with more of a say in family decisions about consumption. In her book *No Logo* political activist and journalist Naomi Klein observes: 'Cool, it seems, is the make-or-break quality in 1990s branding. It is the ironic sneer-track of ABC sitcoms and late-night talk shows; it is what sells psychedelic Internet servers, extreme sports gear, ironic watches, mind-blowing fruit juices, post-modern sneakers and post-gender colognes. Our "aspirational age", as they say in marketing studies, is about seventeen. This applies equally to the forty-seven year old baby boomer scared of losing their cool and the seven-year-olds kick-boxing to the Backstreet Boys.'[162]

The American sociologist George Ritzer gives the example of toys that were originally conceived as miniature versions of adult tools (the toy hammer, the doll's house, the toy kitchen set).[163] The first introduction of toys designed specially for children came in the 1930s with the first Disney cartoon characters and this soon

[161] Jeremy Myerson, 'Create your own design for living', *Sunday Times*, 7 May 2000, New Work, p. 5.
[162] Naomi Klein, *No Logo* (London: Flamingo, 2000), p. 70.
[163] Ritzer, *Enchanting a Disenchanted World* (Thousand Oaks, California: Pine Forge Press, 1999).

evolved into an extensive children's market, which by the 1950s was marketing toys like Barbie and G.I. Joe directly to children through television ads. Today, adults know little or nothing about toys and have a hard time even keeping up with the latest cartoon character craze from Japan. Children have much greater control over what they buy and play with, as retailers have created a separate market segment to cater to them.

Retailers also need to take the race and gender of the customers into account in order to cater to their needs and habits successfully. Women and men shop in notoriously different ways, the most striking difference being that most men avoid it and usually dislike it, while most women love it. Underhill found that women don't only buy different items, they also behave differently, spend more time comparing prices and choices and are much more willing to engage in conversation or ask advice from sales personnel. Men are far more ruthless and focused in their shopping behaviour: they go straight for the item they want, try it and buy it. One of Underhill's studies found that while 65 per cent of men who tried something on bought it, only 25 per cent of women did.

Racial difference is also often an important factor. Underhill cites the case of a newsagent in New York who decided to expand the space in his shop devoted to magazines; however, the newsagent had ignored the fact that the majority of customers were Korean and Hispanic. Underhill therefore advised him to stock Korean-language magazines and popular South American drinks, after which sales rose significantly. Lack of attention to the ethnic background of customers even led Underhill to spot a drugstore in Washington DC that sold a wide assortment of hair dye products for blondes, while 95 per cent of the customer base was Afro-American.

Underhill, the founder of the New York-based retail consultancy, Envirosell, uses the simplest sociological field research techniques – freelance researchers armed with a clipboard and a pen tracking people's movement and gestures through the store, noting down every last detail, minute to minute – to solve major retailers' problems, sometimes just by moving a display five feet to the right:

...a bald, bearded man in a red sweater and blue jeans entered a department store on Saturday at 11:07 a.m., walked directly to a first-floor display of wallets, picked up or otherwise touched a total of twelve of them, checked the price tag on four, then chose one, moved at 11:16 to a nearby tie rack. Stroked seven ties, read the contents tags on all seven, read the price on two, then bought none and went directly to the cashier to pay. Oh, wait, he paused for a moment at a mannequin and examined the price tag on the jacket it wore. We'd mark that down too, just as we'd note that he entered the cashier line at 11:23 as the third person in line, waited two minutes and fifty-one seconds to get to the register, paid with a credit card and exited the store at 11:30.[164]

---

164 Underhill, *Why We Buy*, p. 15.

Simple, stupid, mundane, pointless even, it may seem. But it is by looking at the detail, noting down every hesitation, look and word that Envirosell has solved the problems of many retailers. And the solution, often, is so simple, so obvious that one wonders why no one thought of it before. Many of the principles underlying Underhill's idea of good shop design boil down to basic human anatomy: for example humans have only two hands, so don't make them carry too many loose items through the store, put baskets all through the store. Eyes tend to focus on what is straight ahead and what is at eye level, so place the items you really want to sell in the line of sight. Underhill also describes the 'decompression zone' phenomenon, which happens at store entrances. People usually walk into a store at a steady pace and take some time, even if it is only a minute, to adjust to the inside environment, unzip their coat, adjust their eyes, slow their pace. This all happens in the first few metres of store space, a sort of landing strip in which the consumer is not yet focused. Therefore: do not place items here, they will go unnoticed.

Founded in 1987, Envirosell has consulted for hundreds of retailers on how to improve their sales. Underhill calls it the 'science of shopping', invented in the aisles of America's large and small stores and successful because as competition heats up in the insatiable retail market 'there needs to be an edge'. It is not enough to just be a retailer any more, you have to be good and strive to be the best because, he argues, today retailers no longer open stores to meet demand, they are opening stores to steal customers from the competitor down the road.

So retail has gone scientific: it is the science of selling, the science of building spaces that will make people want to possess everything in it and the science of flattering the consumer. 'Shopping is science,' said Caroline Bos, the Business Manager and Co-director of the Dutch architectural practice, UN Studio, when working on the redevelopment of a shopping centre in the Dutch town of Emmen.[165] It seemed ludicrous at the time but it is not funny, she was right. It is not only a science; it is also an academic course you can study at various universities as an undergraduate or postgraduate, a discipline that is taught by economists, geographers, operations researchers, information systems specialists and planners. Senior military officers from the Royal Military Academy at Sandhurst have even been drawn into the world of retailisation, as plans are being made to teach young and upcoming managers the leadership skills, the strategies and the tactical moves that they would deploy in armed confrontation.[166]

---

[165] Caroline Bos, in conversation, 1999.
[166] Stephen Overell, 'The officer-training academy is to offer advice on leadership to business organisations', *Financial Times*, 11 April 2000, p. 17.

The Dutch architect Rem Koolhaas said: 'Shopping is war.'[167] To illustrate his point he describes a number of generals who, after having taken part in the Gulf War, immediately joined the directors' board of large retail corporations because retail presents the same logistic problems as warfare. In a similar vein, Jean Baudrillard writes that to celebrate victory in the Gulf War, General Schwarzkopf, the commander of the US forces, organised massive celebrations in Disney World, Florida. Baudrillard comments: 'The palace of the imagination was a fitting venue to celebrate the end of the first ever virtual war.'[168] It is a strategic game that is played today with such a confusing number of players on both teams and with so many rules and potential adversaries that you can't just bluff your way through the business, you have to know the retail landscape to conquer it. At the Oxford Institute of Retail Management at Templeton College (OXIRM), an executive MBA course applies abstract economic concepts to real-life situations to understand development patterns in the world of retail. Armed with an overview of the state of retail and an in-depth under-standing of the patterns that can occur retailers can then go back into the field after a year's course and face adversaries with more tactical knowledge.

Psychographic research is another weapon used by retailers and their consultants in the field to get into the psyche of customers and predict their movements. Defined as 'the study and classifica-tion of people's attitudes and aspirations',[169] it allows retailers to create categories of shoppers, identify their different tastes and shopping habits, and tailor the retail environment accordingly – from floor covering to staff profiles.

Calculating the Bluewater spirit

During the design of Bluewater shopping centre in Kent, the devel-opers and architect, Eric Kuhne, worked with consumer behav-iourist David Peek to consider everything from who their audience would be to what floor coverings to use. Using the results of the latter's psychographic research, Kuhne and Peek aimed to trans-form a simple shopping environment into a perfectly 'congruous', immersive and entrancing experience where one is prepared to spend money and time, over and over again. For Peek – a shrewd, stylish man with a background in marketing, psychotherapy and retail and whose sentences start with phrases such as: 'When I was

---

[167] Rem Koolhaas, 'Zorgelijkheid is moralisme', *NRC Handelsblad*, 26 November 1999, p. 25.
[168] Jean Baudrillard, 'Disneyworld company', *Archis* 1998/3, p. 52.
[169] *Oxford English Dictionary* (Oxford: Clarendon Press, 1989).

in the Arctic Circle last week with Porsche' – the success of retail environments entirely depends on the congruity of the space and its contents. 'The key to stimulating and delighting shoppers lies in ensuring that everything from the furnishings, the surroundings, even the psychological profile of staff members translates into a single experience. Once you achieve this you will be able to affect people and involve them on molecular levels. But one wrong look, one wrong smell or word can mean it is all wasted.' He sees shopping trips as 'four-hour holidays', a shorter version of a long weekend in Paris or Barcelona. The difference is that as it is a shorter period of time, the 'holidaymaker' will be more demanding and want every minute to be enjoyable. Thus staff's grooming and outfit should be perfectly in tune to the space they work in. To attune their behaviour to the space the new staff at Bluewater are sent on 'Hosting Excellence' training schemes to learn the 'Spirit of Bluewater' and 'personal development skills'.

Peek's work with focus groups allowed him to determine that neon lights in women's toilets discourage many women from shopping as the harsh lighting tends to make them look pale and drawn and gives them a bad self-image. Toilets at Bluewater have been fitted with bright theatre lighting instead, giving women a boost of self-confidence before they get out there to raid the shops.

On a larger scale, the spatial configuration of shops and the right mix of tenants was determined only after Peek had established six types of British consumers from the County Classics who are 'concerned about what others think of them' to the Young Fashionables who are 'in search of an identity' and attach more importance to visual health than to 'deep health', a class in which the British football player and 'brand', David Beckham, husband to a Spice Girl, and father, falls. Other types included the Club Executives, BMW and Boss Suits, the Sporting Thirties, 'interested in sport with a destructive element', and the Young Survivors for whom shopping can 'boost self-esteem'.[170] Based on these categories, six different 'streets' were designed, each aimed at a different kind of consumer Thus the West Mall has an 'aspirational and upmarket mix' and features 'King's Road-type retailers'; the East Mall, on the other hand, is more 'high street' with shops like WHSmith, Miss Selfridge and The Body Shop. Within these groups Bluewater management has also made a point of mixing individual and niche retailers with larger chains to mimic urban environments. Peek explains that the segregation of shoppers and shop types is necessary because people like to shop with PLUs, not, as we learnt, a new type of neon lighting, but an abbreviation of

---

[170] David Peek, 'Deadliest shopping species is the male', *Independent*, 13 March 1999, p. 12.

'People Like Us', people who dress, talk and act in the same way.

Peek acknowledges that the Sporting Thirties are the 'dangerous group' as they constitute a type of 'shopping saboteur', who 'don't really want to go shopping' and would rather go to the pub. This group is not only a danger to themselves, they also jeopardise the spending of their partners as research figures showed that such 'elements' will cause arguments (after 58 minutes on average) that cut short the shopping trip. This is why there are 43 things, ranging from sports bars, cinemas, bookshops and coffee bars, for men to do while their partner goes off with the credit card. So everybody's happy. Wife gets new shoes and dress, husband gets to watch the footie and they will spend an average of £121 each – with any luck more. It is just like dancing, Peek argues, these reluctant men need to be 'taught' how to shop, learn that it is Fun.

Identifying 12 stages in the shopping process, starting at home on the sofa and ending up in the same place, Peek was intent on bringing each part of the experience as near to perfection as possible. After all, any of these stages may be remembered 'for a next time' and therefore the congruity, the smoothness of the experience needs to start as early as possible. Based on the fact that the majority of shoppers are female, Peek conducted special focus groups to determine their fears and annoyances during shopping trips. He found dirt, confusing traffic situations and narrow parking spaces were the three main points that most women found disagreeable during shopping trips. This is why, on the way to Bluewater, no roundabout has more than two exits, parking spaces have been made extra wide to allow easy loading of bags and prams (and bad parking), and the malls are 'Disney clean', spotless in the style of Disney theme parks.

Systematised entertainment

Specifying everything, up to the maximum number of steps that anyone should need to take to reach a seating space (70), Bluewater is a place designed to extract maximum value from each visitor. And the best way to do this is to disguise this objective behind an elaborate *mise en scène* of slate floors, domed roofs, themed 'villages', potted plants and mythological references carved on the walls. In other words, pretending that this is not a shopping centre and coaxing the 'destination buyer' into a relaxed mood in which she or he will be willing to spend randomly.

The architectural theorist Margaret Crawford describes this duality of shopping malls, which on the one hand strive to establish a spatial order and on the other want to disorient and confuse shoppers to keep them inside for longer:

[A] double action – stimulating nebulous desire and encouraging specific purchases – establishes the mall's fundamentally contradictory nature. To survive profitably, it must operate within the enormous disjuncture created between the objective economic logic necessary for the profitable circulation of goods and the unstable subjectivity of the messages exchanged between consumers and commodities, between the limited goods permitted by this logic and the unlimited desires released by this exchange.

Margaret Crawford[171]

This disjuncture is reflected in mall architecture, which on the one hand uses 'familiar tricks of mall design – limited entrances, escalators placed only at the end of corridors, fountains and benches carefully positioned to entice shoppers into stores' but on the other hand uses architectural features that 'seem to contradict commercial considerations'. Thus atriums designed as 'huge floating spaces for contemplation', multiple levels with infinite vistas and mirrors bringing near and far together, create a 'weightless realm', which was described by the novelist Joan Didion as an addictive environmental drug, where 'one moves for a while in an aqueous suspension, not only of light, but of judgment, not only of judgment, but of personality'.[172] This is a paradoxical situation that all mall developers have to deal with and is a consequence of the commercial space becoming more uniform around us. The selling machines that Zola evoked in the 19th century today don't just grind away in a single space; they form networks of physical and virtual locations reaching into the home, the workplace and high streets around the world, reiterating the same formula. To control the working of this machine they have created, retailers have to systematise their business on a number of levels, from global expansion strategies to local, sometimes very local, customer surveys or focus groups that enquire into whether the canned fruit should really be on the top shelf. There has to be a hierarchy and an order to allow sustainable expansion.

The opposition between rationalisation and 'enchantment' is analysed by the sociologist George Ritzer in his book *Enchanting a Disenchanted World*. He calls the spaces that encourage unbridled consumption today 'the new cathedrals of consumption' and believes that it is these spaces that have dramatically altered consumer behaviour in the last 50 years:

As is the case with religious cathedrals, the cathedrals of consumption are not only enchanted, they are also highly rationalised. As they attract more and more consumers, their enchantment must be reproduced over and over on demand. Furthermore, branches of the successful enchanted settings are opened across the nation and even the world with the result that essentially

---

[171] Crawford, 'World in a shopping mall', p. 13.
[172] Ibid., p. 14.

the same magic must be reproduced in a wide range of locations. To accomplish this, the magic has to be systematised so that it can be easily recreated from one time or place to another. However, it is difficult to reduce magic to corporate formulas that can be routinely employed at any time, in any place, by anybody.

George Ritzer [173]

Ritzer goes on to argue that while retailers are doing everything to attract more consumers, the spaces they create are often 'disenchanting' despite efforts to instil them with magical qualities and that there is a real danger of people becoming bored by the 'machine-like efficiency' of their new cathedrals. The challenge, he says, is 'to maintain enchantment in the face of increasing rationalisation'.[174]

Rationalisation of the shopping experience is a development that retailers and designers recognise as a necessity, especially where large chains are involved. The increasing monotony and uniformity of retail spaces that goes with this rationalisation is forming a threat, though: Gap, Starbucks Coffee, HMV, Marks & Spencer — they are ubiquitous names and retail spaces that form a dull rhythm, droning along high streets in cities from Los Angeles to New York, from Helsinki to Rome. Reynolds argues that offering entertainment and combining retail with leisure is retailers' main weapon against 'the emerging sameness of the high street...The consumer is demanding more exciting environments for shopping and is willing to travel longer distances to find the added enjoyment of a leisure environment.'

But even these leisure environments are becoming boring and repetitive as familiar themes are reproduced according to the set formula. Rem Koolhaas believes that it is not just spaces of consumption that we are bored with, it is shopping as a whole. People are too busy or just not interested any more and the rise of e-commerce forms an additional threat. Most of all, we are bored with theming[175] as the whole world is slowly turning into a theme park. In March 2000 Koolhaas reported: '[There is an] internal erosion of enthusiasm that is beginning to affect what seemed to be one of the most vital and powerful incentives to the spread of shopping, namely the world of theming.' He argued that the receivership of the Planet Hollywood theme bar and the lack of interest in themed shops and attractions might mean that 'there is finally an uprising against the dumbness of theming'.[176]

Carlos Virgile – of Virgile and Stone Associates in London,

---

[173] Ritzer, *Enchanting a Disenchanted World*, p. 9.
[174] Ibid.
[175] The creation of spaces – parks, restaurants, pubs, shops and shopping centres – around fantasy themes.
[176] Rem Koolhaas, 'Start Again' lecture at the Berlage Institute, Amsterdam, 7 March 2000.

designers of the retail units at Volkswagen's new car theme park Autostadt in Wolfsburg and developers of the new retail concept at Schiphol in the Netherlands, among many other projects – believes that, while entertainment and theming have played an increasingly important role in retail over the last 10 years, theming is not the future. 'The concept of the 3D experience has definitely become much stronger and taken over interior design requirements... Clients want to create experiences to communicate their values, even if these values aren't clearly defined, in which case they will want us to define their values for them through our design. I think it's going to change, though. Very soon. People are already bored with the idea of the all-embracing experience. It is outdated. The 3D experiences that appeal to all the senses have desensitised people; it has limited their outlook on life.'[177]

Underhill also acknowledges that boredom is a threat. He says that we are 'over-retailed' and that 'too much is for sale, through too many outlets', but he believes that while boredom is a real danger customers will still visit themed environments:

The customer is more likely to tire of specific theme stores than the concept of retail as entertainment...This type of store's life cycle will grow shorter and shorter. Stores will have to work harder to be dynamic. If a girl visits American Girl Place in Chicago and returns six months later, there should be a new movie, activity, exhibit, a changing menu and whatever else the creative people can dream up to amuse, inform, and lure back customers. This is akin to the constant change that we're accustomed to seeing in amusement parks, which are always promoting a new scarier, larger, darker more modern roller coaster named after a super hero featured in a recently released blockbuster.

Another reason why theming will not disappear in the short run is that if retailers can no longer foster personal relationships with their customers around the world, they have at least to ensure that customers engage with the goods on sale and the environments they are sold in. While many claim that consumer space and shopping as an activity play a social role and reconnects communities,[178] the sociologist George Ritzer argues that people don't seek social contact – on the contrary, they want to 'get in and get out', do it fast and if not fast then at least with a minimum of human contact. This is contradictory, in the sense that most of the 'contemporary cathedrals of consumption' are purposely designed with the intention of attracting people's gaze. Ritzer says that 'interaction with people...is gradually being replaced by interaction with things, both great and small'.[179]

---

[177] Carlos Virgile in personal interview.
[178] The American anti-modernist architect Jon Jerde, retail architect Eric Kuhne and developers of retail schemes.
[179] Ritzer, *Enchanting a Disenchanted World*, p. 42.

Going spiritual

It is the growing blandness and uniformity of retail spaces that have incited retailers to package the 'act of consumption' and build fantasy worlds around their merchandise in order to turn what is fundamentally a mundane activity into an exciting and memorable experience. Through the creation of themed and artificial environments shopping is being transformed into a sensual experience, involving smell, sound, visual and tactile stimulation, 'delighting' consumers and stimulating their imagination. In addition, attempts to imbue the experience with spiritual values – be they mystical, mythical or historical – seek to create a sense of common heritage and tradition among shoppers who frequently have nothing in common save the space they choose to shop in. The following extract from an interview with the retail architect Jon Jerde shows how retailisation can go spiritual.

Jerde goes on to passionately explain his deeper thoughts behind his desire to bring people together. He believes in the truth of Gaia, he says, the idea that we are all part of the same 'thing' and that this is again part of a larger 'thing', etc. He was confirmed in this belief through a vision that he had 20 years ago, and that he calls white light. From that moment on he knew that everything was one, that humans should live in harmony with the earth and that it was his task to encourage unity and harmony by creating communal experience. 'We strive to give people the feeling that in the last ten minutes something significant has happened to them, something they might not understand, but which will give them a feeling of increased sensitivity and perception, the kind of feeling artists have. We do this by shaping the spaces between buildings in a sculptural manner and manipulate them in such a way that the perception of high and low for example is disrupted. In this way people are brought into a state in which they suddenly start to doubt the known, a state which is defined in art as "the suspension of disbelief". Then they are open to new, richer experiences, experiences of their own because I don't invent them for them. I just make them possible.'

Anna Tilroe[180]

Jerde's use of mystical and spiritual theories to underpin his work is part of a move to 're-enchant' the disenchanted world of consumerism, to use Ritzer's phrase. It is part of a wider phenomenon in which writers, thinkers and designers are trying to 'mollify the harshness of the modern world' using wisdom traditions of the native Americans, Semitic traditions and Buddhist cultures to revive the world around us. It is part of a new consciousness that exhorts the consumer to draw inspiration from spiritual movements that can 'help us to nourish wonder and hence to appreciate difference, the unique subjectivity of every being and community, thereby subverting the flattening process of mass culture'.[181]

---

[180] Anna Tilroe, 'Europe is a problem', *NRC Handelsblad*, June 2000.
[181] Charlene Spretnak, *States of Grace: the Recovery of Meaning in the Postmodern Age* (New York: Harper Collins, 1991), p. 223.

This is in reality – the real reality – little more than another attempt to escape the conditions of retailisation. Shopping malls, restaurants (the Rainforest Café, Planet Hollywood), casinos (Las Vegas) parks (the most obvious example being Disney) – are turning into themed and staged spaces, a feature that has been widely criticised in architectural and academic circles as observers see the world slowly 'Disneyfying'. The distinction between the fake and the real is fading as artificial and themed spaces become more common and we slowly lose the ability to distinguish between real reality and real fake. The Internet brings a hugely new take on this reality: what is more real, a Tesco store or its website? What is more human, an email, a phone conversation or a hand-written letter from a friend?

In the 1990s many sociologists wrote – in homage it often seemed to that chief mythologist, the American writer William Gibson – of the 'reality' of the merging of the human body and the digital world.[182] The architect and architectural philosopher John Beckmann wrote in 1998: 'To speak of, or even to attempt to visualise form now, one must contemplate its antithesis. Meta-attributes have replaced physical attributes: metaquery, metacontent, metasymbols, and metaspace. Though the dream is seemingly at hand, this electronic reality exists remotely – in the netherworld of earth-orbiting satellite links, communication servers, the Internet and intranets and so on. We have, in effect, fallen outside of ourselves, as the once hard distinction between remote and local stages become even further dispersed, and the exposure intervals between time and space, inside and outside, mind and body, imaginary and real are no longer quantifiable factors.'[183]

Beckmann is wrong: the distinctions are so quantifiable because they are still centred on us – consumers – and created by telecommunications businesses anxiously selling us the next technological revolution (or fad). The distinction between, say, a phone in the home and a mobile may have geographic interest (it does very much to the third-generation mobile communications manufacturers who want to know where we are, and can know via the 'global positioning service' or GPS to deliver relevant information, such as the location of the nearest Thai restaurant when we are visiting a new city) but it makes no difference to the telecommunications communications companies who just see increasing phone revenues accrue from data transfer, the Internet and mobile phone usage.

What is far more relevant, ironically, is an article in *The Guardian*'s Style section. Asking, quite rightly, 'Why shop on the

[182] William Gibson, *Neuromancer* (London: Voyager, 1995).
[183] John Beckmann, 'Merge invisible layers', in: John Beckmann, ed., *The Virtual Dimension* (Princeton: Princeton Architectural Press, 1998), p. 3.

Net when there's Bond Street?', the piece goes on to eulogise WCs
– or wearable computers. 'US company Charmed Technology
revealed its first collection of WCs...its mission is to showcase
smart clothes that think and perform...In the future a dress will be
more than a dress. It will monitor health, aid communication, provide instant access to information and more.'[184] Alex Lightman,
CEO of Charmed, concurs: 'The body and technology will become
one in the future. But people don't want to look like cyborgs when
it happens … Fashion is the answer. We aim to reduce technology
in size so much that it can be worn on the body. We want to personalise it [there we go again] so it knows and helps the individual. And of course we're going to make it look good.'[185] Fashion
will, it is certain, have more impact in this area on the everyday
consciousness than ever. Kevin Warwick, Professor of Cybernetics
at the University of Reading, is famous for embedding a computer
chip in his body as 'machines are already capable of doing many
things that humans themselves cannot do.'[186] Although Warwick
has attained a certain notoriety for his experiments in 'real'
human–computer interfaces, it is unlikely that his machine will yet
be able to tell a real Prada from a fake, or indeed a real orgasm
from its antithesis.

We stood wearing 3D goggles in a 'CAVE' at the SARA Institute
on the outskirts of Amsterdam. The CAVE is a 12-foot square real
cube, which simulates the exploring in real-time of the kind of
graphical landscapes one might see in the computer games Doom
or Quake; in our case it was a facsimile of the Grand Place in
Brussels, above which we were able to rise to the roof of the town
hall. It was all very nice: indeed useful too. The architect Rem
Koolhas, too busy to visit one of his many constructions in the
United States, took his client for a guided tour of the new building he has designed via two linked CAVEs, one in Holland, the
other in the campus of Iowa State University. Is this the future?
Well, it is real enough for the architect's client but, as Alex
Lightman says, who wants to look like a cyborg wearing clumsy
goggles when you could be wearing real, or fake, Dolce and
Gabanna sunglasses? William Mitchell, Dean of Architecture at
MIT, was more pragmatic: 'I think they [CAVEs] will remain in the
domain of specialised uses, mainly because of the cost. They are
very dramatic and effective but any technology that depends so
strongly on such a highly specialised environment will always
have limited use. You could compare it to the use of cell phones

---

[184] Hazel Curry, 'Smarty pants', *Guardian*, 26 May 2000, G2 p. 8.
[185] Ibid.
[186] Kevin Warwick, 'The man with x-ray arms – and other skin-ripping yarns',
in: A. Scammell, ed., *I in the Sky* (London: Aslib, 1999), p. 8.

and VR systems. VR systems are more expensive and require a more sophisticated technology and will therefore remain less common. I think that at the high end CAVEs work very well, though, for research purposes for example.'[187]

The height of fake in real space is reached in Las Vegas where replicas of an Egyptian sphinx, New York City, Venice and Ancient Rome sit unflinchingly side by side with slot machines, blackjack tables and country singers. In her book *The Unreal America* the architectural critic Ada Louise Huxtable describes the construction of a new hotel and casino complex, called 'New York, New York'. Featuring a pastiche of New York's famous skyscrapers from the Empire State Building through to the Seagram Building and the Chrysler Building, she describes it as a 'collage of pinstriped towers' laced with 'the airy looping curves of a giant roller coaster' – a reference to Coney Island. Further up, at the Forum Shops, moving sidewalks transport the visitors through six triumphal arches rising from cascading fountains into the streets and stores. 'Your typical Roman via', commented architectural critic Aaron Betsky at the opening, 'where the sun sets and rises on an electrically controlled cycle, continually bathing acres of faux finishes in rosy hues. Animatronic robots welcome you with a burst of lasers, and a Rococo version of the Fountain of the Four Rivers drowns out the sound of nearby slots.'[188]

The continuing success of Disney theme parks, Las Vegas casinos and themed malls and shops proves that artificial environments continue to satisfy people's urge to escape the everyday realities of their life. These environments have been described as 'hyperreal', that is 'overreal' or, as theorist Jean Baudrillard describes it, 'real without origin or reality'. In 'hyperreality' objects are not considered as 'unreal, or surreal, but realer-than-real, a real retouched and refurbished'[189] – in other words better than the real thing. These environments are simulations of the real place they refer to, which come to constitute a reality, leading to 'a death of the subject' – that is a death of the original reality. So for example simulations of China or Africa in Disney parks have become more popular than the real thing, making visitors believe the Disney versions of Africa and China to be reality.

In her essay *Shelter from the Storm*, architect Nan Ellin acknowledges that the development of hyperreality has led to successful urban projects like master-planned communities, shopping malls, theme parks and entertainment palaces, which all offer high-qual-

---

[187] William Mitchell, SARA, in personal interview March 2000.
[188] Ada Louise Huxtable, *The Unreal America* (New York: The New Press, 1997), p. 76.
[189] Quoted in Nan Ellin, 'Shelter from the storm or form follows fear and vice versa', in: N. Ellin, ed., *The Architecture of Fear*, p. 39.

ity design and opportunities for relaxation and entertainment. However, their existence alongside 'places of desperation and people who are unable to share in the hyperreal benefits certainly engenders shame, resentment, and fear in the haves and have-nots alike. To the extent that these fantasy worlds disguise real problems and thereby diminish the potential for resolving them, they contribute to exacerbating them.'[190]

The origins of the hyperreal can once again, as with so many features of today's consumer society, be retraced to the concept behind the Disney theme parks. In her book on the design of Disney theme parks Karal Ann Marling describes the 1950s as a period of duality between ascetic and austere modernism with an undercurrent of myth, magic and fantasy, as the thinking of Le Corbusier and Mies van der Rohe was counterbalanced by the thinking of Dalí and Frank Lloyd Wright. 'Fantasy – the bizarre, the eccentric, the grotesque, the unconventional, the unrestrained – filtered throughout 1950s America. But so too did impulses towards order, containment and control.'[191] The cultural historian Walter Susman describes the period after the Second World War in the United States as embodying a dual consciousness of 'abundance, opportunities, freedom, possibilities, and a new sense of liberation,' intermingled with anxiety, fear and edgy dissatisfaction. For Susman, Disney is the icon of this duality, 'a collective fantasy, an immense metaphor for the system of representations and values unique in postwar America'.[192] The obsession with fantasy signifies a search for new possibilities and alternatives, though many were at the same time apprehensive and attracted to these new options. In this sense Disneyland's imagineers subtly manipulated this duality, by creating a park built on the unreal in the context of extreme order and control.[193]

The sociologist Steven Miles sees Disney theme parks as symbolic of the tensions between reality and fantasy in contemporary consumer culture. He says that they are 'exciting and mystifying places which can be dismissed as serving to distort the real condition of social meaning and social relations. This is a key point. Consumer culture actively distorts reality for its own ends. Consumer culture works because consumers want reality to be distorted.'[194] He adds that by glorifying fake and stimulating a desire

---

[190] Ibid., p. 40.
[191] Erika Doss, 'Making imagination safe in the 1950s', in: Karal Ann Marling, *Designing Disney's Theme Parks: the Architecture of Reassurance* (Paris: Flammarion, 1997), p. 180.
[192] Ibid. p. 132.
[193] Ibid. p. 180.
[194] Steven Miles, *Consumerism as a Way of Life* (London, Sage Publications, 1998), p. 65.

for fake within consumers, the Disney concept is extremely effective because the reality of consumerism is always disappointing. This is a crucial point because, while it may appear at first that retailers take control of their relationship with consumers by creating these evasive environments, in fact they are responding to a type of consumer demand. The point is that we like fake, we like its safeness, its predictability and the evasion it offers us.

Tapping into deep cultural roots: Britain's Disneyfication

In Britain the Disneyfication of commercial and urban space is less pronounced than in the United States, though Bluewater shopping centre in Kent goes half the way using nostalgic themes and 'by tapping into the deep cultural roots of Kent's village heritage, using a fantastical range of metaphors to evoke the landscape, literature, formal gardens and historic buildings of rural England'.[195] Covering up the scientific detail that went into creating a congruent environment, decoration and other features distract the visitor from the ultimate goal of the place, which is to sell as much as possible to the largest number of people. We wouldn't want to be so blunt about it, though, which is why the American architect Eric Kuhne believes in myth-making. 'The domain of mythology is not the domain of the ancients,' he says. 'We have the capacity to create our own myths today.' Rejecting modernism as a style that 'robbed architecture of its storytelling quality', Kuhne sees himself not as a classicist but as an architect who 'pilfers readily across all the historical styles'. He believes that retail architecture is perfectly suited to this free style and allows people to identify with their surroundings while psychologically expanding their view of themselves.[196]

Thus Kuhne travelled around Kentish villages and countryside for inspiration and to make sure he would 'capture the spirit of the region' instead of 'imposing an international conceit'. The striking jagged roofline is inspired from the conical Kentish oast houses and the landscaping in the park was inspired by the painting *Carnation, Lily, Lily, Rose* by John Singer Sargent, depicting the English idyll. Inside, handkerchief domes at the mall's focal points, the leisure villages, are inspired by the interiors of Sir John Soane and Gilbert Scott, while quotes from Shakespeare, Dickens, Chaucer and Keats adorn the stonework on the interior and exterior facades. And as if that was not enough the National Gallery has now decided to organise one of its art exhibitions in Bluewater

---

[195] Bluewater promotional folder.
[196] Jeremy Myerson in interview with Eric Kuhne.

instead of central London.[197] Contemporary art is thus the new rock
and roll – and just as Chuck Berry, The Rolling Stones and
Aerosmith now routinely make it to the anodyne world of the easy-
listening music that fills our malls and shops, so too modern art is
deconstructed as a *signifier* of culture, *class*, the *upscale* world.

Yet the management at Bluewater believes that the presence of
civic art and educational references will help put an cultural element back into shopping, enhancing the visitor's experience and
conveying the message that Bluewater is more than the sum of its
300 shops. So for example the 24-hour World Clock in the John
Lewis forecourt aims to evoke a sense of place, with radiating lines
to 'great distant cities' providing a sense of connection to the rest
of the world. Whether Bluewater's visitors will pause long enough
to read such depth into what is, in the end, only a clock, is ques-
tionable, but these icons are only part of a wider effort to dissoci-
ate Bluewater from the traditional image of a shopping centre.
Kuhne explains: 'First and foremost, at Bluewater we had to build
something that was functional. Then we added the leisure components. And then, most importantly for us, we added the cultural
component.' Kuhne believes families will not come here for shopping in the first place, they will come for the experience and a 'cultural exchange'.

Tapping into the spiritual side of shopping Peek speaks of '[men-
tal] state management' and explains the power of design in inducing trance-like shopping moods. 'Everything must be specified or
the trance might break,' he says. 'We are state managers; we do
everything to get the customer in the right state of mind and then
keep them there. This is very difficult in the context of a consumer
space because with trance it is very much like sleep or hypnosis:
it's so easy to snap out of it.' He adds that it is not the amount of
design that makes a successful shopping environment, but knowing the effect of it, the outcome on the consumer masses. One of
the main dangers is that the more design you put into a space, the
more you risk losing control and getting counterproductive
responses. Peek cites the Mall of America, designed by Jon Jerde
in 1992 – the second largest mall in the world covering 4 million
square feet and attracting 35 to 40 million visitors a year – as a classic example of mall design gone wrong. With 32 per cent of the
mall taken up by entertainment and leisure activities, this is a marriage of the theme park and the mall giving birth to the concept of
the 'megamall'. Peek comments that while everything here is
designed, it doesn't work. 'The fact that it is so artificial will mean
people will have a tendency not to believe any part of it. If the

197 Maev Kennedy, 'Taking art to the people: National Gallery plans shopping
mall exhibition', *Guardian*, 21 July 2000.

materials are all GPS [plastic] or less, then what can you expect of the service or quality?'

Design on its own is not enough then, as is demonstrated by the car boot sale, a classically undesigned and uncontrolled retail space, which according to several focus groups and research reports that Peek uses are far more successful than many shopping centres – particularly with family groups who get more satisfaction and experience less tension than when they visit malls. 'The turnover there is huge, equivalent to that of shopping centres. So just get me a field and a hatchback on a Sunday afternoon and I'll put up your shopping centre for you,' says Peek. 'It proves that shopping without architecture can be emotionally more satisfying than with. It is the opposition between 0 per cent architecture and high satisfaction and 105 per cent architecture and very varying and unpredictable levels of satisfaction.'

Conclusion

The moral outrage at the importance of shopping and consumerism in today's society is misplaced. We are not being forced to shop, shopping centres and malls are not being imposed on our urban fabric – there is a demand. Retailers may be more sophisticated and clever, but they are, at the same time, still working to satisfy a demand – whether this be a demand to satisfy real or perceived needs.

If fake environments and themed experiences are what we want, then that's what we get. If we have been manipulated at all, it is because we want to be. Hell, we know there are only 10 actors in the summer blockbuster, *Gladiator*, the hordes of Roman thousands are all created by computer graphics. But we are oh so willing to suspend our disbelief. It is all too easy really.

Chapter 4 – Bricks, clicks and tricks

'This is real life. When you live in a place like Skem [Skelmersdale in Lancashire, England] it's all about survival. If you can buy something cheap, you do it.' Another resident, an elderly man called Tony, agreed. 'It's all about making your money go as far as possible,' he said. In his bag was a box of washing powder and four packs of Van Nelle rolling tobacco that he had bought from the club. 'The whole lot cost me a damned sight less than it would in the shops. And it means I've got a bit more for my beer.'

Mark Macaskill[198]

Once upon a time, retail in physical spaces, 'bricks and mortar' as they call it, was simple. You put together some bricks and mortar, placed a roof on it, mounted a couple of shelves and a counter, ordered supplies and waited for the customers to come. Shops like this still exist; you can find them if you look, tucked away in side streets, in villages, sometimes still on the corners of our streets. They are catering to the locals who have been coming there for years and know they will always be welcomed with a smile. The walls are covered with outdated ads, printed on enamel plates with rusty edges, selling brands that may not even exist any more, but that doesn't really matter. Faded letters on a plate behind the counter explain why: 'If we don't have it, you don't need it.' This is because they know that their consumers' needs when they visit are focused on particular wants: a newspaper or carton of milk, nails or paint remover – a packet of geranium seeds. The retailer here knows the needs of the local community and caters to them without fail.

It would be a seemingly perfect retail mechanism, were it not for one crucial point: retailers today need to cater to more than just our needs. To make ends meet they have to provide us also with the things we don't need, they have constantly to encourage us to buy more, convince us that our lives will be more complete with more 'things' in it. The local newsagent is now a Lottery card outlet, a mobile phone card store, a source of condoms, tights and razors. It stays open later than ever and opens earlier to entice us in the middle of the night and before the commuter rush. In the era before the car, the local store was paramount to providing us with the basic necessities, fulfilling our needs. Today the limits of our retail imagination have broadened through travel, through communication, and through media. It could appear that these kinds of retail outlet are doomed to the Betamax of retail history.

Building, furnishing and running a successful shop catering to our conscious and unconscious needs and wants goes way beyond

---

[198] Mark Macaskill, 'Black market takes over in slum towns', *Sunday Times*, 30 April 2000, p. 5.

the use of crude materials and supplying basic needs. It requires the fine-tuning of marketing, advertising, branding, distribution networks and sales techniques to be successful. Customers don't just want to get in and out; they want to have an experience and be able to take home a memory of that experience. As we have seen, this is nothing new: retailers in 19th-century Paris were already sparing no effort to create theatrical shop interiors. In the 20th century retailers only refined these techniques, turning the art of triggering desire into a science using the expertise of technologists, psychologists, architects, interior designers, photographers, 'personalities' and even *experts in smell.* Today, in the era of high-speed technology and infrastructure where interactive television, computers and mobile phones offer a chance to shop, old-fashioned, but oh-so-modern bricks and mortar shops are still the places where the consumer can have the most intense and effective sensorial experiences, and where the retailer can cash in best on impulse buys.

This chapter will look at the rich variety of shopping experiences in physical spaces available to consumers today, from the trip to the largest mall in Europe, Bluewater, to niche outlets where personal attentions lavished upon the customers make them feel they are among 'friends', or at least people who understand their lifestyles and wishes. Entertainment is playing an increasingly important role in bricks and mortar, particularly the larger and less overtly personal outlets, not just because it is the strongest weapon retailers have against the rise of the conspicuously 'unentertaining' but nevertheless pragmatic e-commerce, but also because if consumers are entertained they will stay longer, become immersed and also very probably spend more.

While malls aim to keep people in their grip as long as possible so that they spend money, individual stores, single-brand stores and particularly flagship stores, which represent a global brand spatially, are designed to sell not merely a branded product but, much more importantly, the brand name and its image. In flagship stores retailers don't mind if people just come in to browse or worship the brand and then go and buy it elsewhere. The key is to make them 'buy into' the brand and want to be part of the image, either by buying on the spot or by going home and clicking on to the website. Niketown, Donna Karan, Levi's, Disney, Calvin Klein, Sony, Waterstone's ... their flagships are all conceived to immerse consumers in their lifestyle vision to the point where they are willing to adopt it. And not merely adopt, but transform themselves through branding (to become not just Tiger Woods, but Tiger Woods, the Nike phenomenon). These brands are out to create customer loyalty and, frequently, to dictate not only what we wear, or how we furnish our homes but also what we eat and what we think. 'Just Do It' is, after all, the instruction of insensitive bosses all over the world, as well as Nike's global clarion cry to be an *individual.*

At the same time, we will look at the effect of shopping on the physical space around us, as public places are gradually being privatised and commercialised – a tendency some see as a positive movement towards the revival of alienated urban and suburban communities and that others abhor, believing the controlled and artificial environments created lead to exclusion of certain communities and fear of the other in general.

An odyssey to Bluewater, Europe's largest shopping mall (in 2000 anyway)

YOUR FREE TIME IS IMPORTANT
At Bluewater we acknowledge that, while most people come here to shop, having somewhere comfortable to eat, or something interesting to do is just as important, to really make the most of your limited leisure time.

'Discover Bluewater' pamphlet

Monday morning in December, stuck on a train between London Bridge and Lewisham. 'Ladies and gentlemen there have been some delays due to signal failures at New Cross, we have no idea how long this could last but we will keep you informed of any further developments,' comes the predictable announcement. Sighs and huffs throughout the train carriage. Silence. Waiting. The man in the suit sitting opposite us gets out his mobile: 'Hi. It's me. I'm on a train outside Lewisham and we're stuck. I'm going to be late; could you ask Michelle to cancel my 10 o'clock.' Ten minutes later we're still standing there. Ours seems to be the only train that is 'inconvenienced' by the signal failure, as we watch trains to our left and right chugging or even speeding past us.

Once we finally start moving the conductor announces that, due to exceptional circumstances, this train will terminate at Lewisham and we should all change to the train on platform three. It's 10.30 a.m. and still not light when we arrive at Lewisham but a fine rain, the type you can't see but that somehow makes you wetter than normal rain, gently soaks us as we stand on the platform. After a few minutes, an announcement comes over the loudspeakers telling us *not* to board the train on platform three – which is OK because it is not even there. Instead, we are told to cross the footbridge to platform one where a train to Gravesend will be arriving shortly. The small

group of passengers still left from the first train – those who haven't jumped into a taxi yet – damply traipse over the footbridge. Old ladies with plastic rain hats huff and puff across the bridge; mothers drag prams up the stairs, whining toddlers clambering up behind them. After 10 minutes a train pulls up to the platform and we all get in hopefully but after a couple of minutes the announcement comes: 'All change please, all change. This train terminates at Lewisham. The next train to Gravesend will leave from platform three.' Indignant sighs and the clatter of prams again accompany us as we cross the footbridge. Behind us, an old lady grumbles under her breath: 'Bloody scandal. Making us wait around like this in the rain. I'll have missed half the day by the time I get there.' 'There' we presume to be Bluewater, the new shopping centre that has been built in a chalk quarry in Kent. This is where we are trying to go as are, we suspect, most of the people with us on the footbridge in Lewisham. Opened in March 1999, Bluewater is being hailed as the cutting edge of retail: Europe's largest shopping centre, with 300 retail outlets. Its own publicity brochure, pretty much all there's left to read on this forlorn journey, tells us more. We learn that:

Bluewater combines retail and leisure in a new way. Whether you're looking for a quality restaurant meal, a stimulating environment for the children, where you can also enjoy a pleasant break, an exciting evening's entertainment, or something even more – or perhaps less – energetic, one of Bluewater's three leisure villages will cater to your needs.[199]

Back on platform three we are standing in the same rain, looking at the same tracks with no train on them. When we ask one of the conductors what the problem is, the unashamed answer comes: 'It's the rain.' Somewhat confused, we ask how this is possible, after all, rain is not infrequent in England. The answer, once again, is shameless: 'It's the type of rain. We can deal with proper rain, but this type of fine rain always gives problems on the tracks.' So if it's not leaves or snow, there is always 'rain' as an excuse. This shopping trip seems to be slowly turning into an epic journey of Odyssean proportions. One thing is clear: Connex South East is not fully conversant of the processes of retailisation.

---

[199] 'Discover Bluewater' pamphlet, November 1999.

When the train finally pulls up at platform three it takes another 20 minutes to get to a small station where a sign reads 'Greenhithe (for Bluewater)'. (It will – like Delaware township, which became 'Cherry Hill' named after its mall – surely soon be Bluewater station, as soon as it is revamped, and restyled.) Most passengers get off here; prams and babies and shopping trolley bags are all bundled off the train and through the exit, which is such a small, inconspicuous door that it almost goes unnoticed. It leads into the Greenhithe 'station hall', a 10- by 15-foot space more reminiscent of a storage room than a station hall, with a small ticket window and a makeshift newspaper stall where one can choose between a few dog-eared copies of today's *Mirror*, yesterday's *Sunday Mirror* or a Mars bar. Clearly, this is not the future of retail we came to see. It is, however, where until further notice the customers Bluewater claims to attract from France, Belgium and beyond will arrive. Large posters on the platforms and in the 'hall' announce that Connex South East trains are going to refurbish this station 'in the near future' to cater for passengers going to Bluewater. We'll see. It will probably rain and that could delay things for a couple of years.

Outside the station, a set of cracked concrete steps lead down to the bus stop where we wait, very wet now, for the bus that will whisk us off to this haven of delight that will, according to the ads, 'relax, refresh and replenish' us. Frankly, by this stage we're not too worried about Bluewater's facilities, as long as it has a roof on it, a restaurant or a bar (and my, do they) we'll be happy. Five minutes later we are smoothly cruising along in a blue Bluewater bus, grannies suddenly smiling and toddlers expectantly gazing out towards the chalk quarry where 1,400,000 square feet of retail space and 140,000 feet of leisure activities await us. We've taken three hours to get to a place that boasts a target audience ranging from any place south of the Thames in London to Bruges in Belgium. We should have come by car, after all that 's what malls are about: easy access, easy car parking and none of the hassles of shopping on Oxford Street. Enter the metaphysical brand experience.

'More than a shopping centre, a metaphysical brand'

Positioned just beyond the M25 on the edge between rural Kent, London (and, as soon as the Eurostar link at Ebbsfleet is established, Paris, Brussels and the rest of Europe), Bluewater shopping centre attracts a mixed audience of urbanites on a day out from London and suburbanites on a day out from suburbia.

Built by the Australian developers, Lend Lease, Bluewater was completed in just over three years, transforming Europe's largest industrial wasteland, the former Blue Circle quarry, into a retail and leisure destination that covers a surface area twice the size of Bath city centre and features a 240-acre park with a million trees, seven tonnes of bulbs and six lakes; 140,000 square feet of leisure with 36 restaurants and three 'leisure villages'; civic art in the form of poetry carved on the walls, 30-foot sculptural 'icons' and ornamental details inspired by English stately homes, as well as Britain's largest parking lot with 13,000 spaces. The project cost £700 million and managed to attract over 25 million visitors in its first year, generating £660 million in sales.

Yes. It is big; it is in the middle of nowhere and essentially it is a safe, clean, accessible, 'nicer' version of Oxford Street and King's Road placed in a pretty building. Yet developers, designers and management insist that this is not just another edge-of-town shopping centre nor an American suburban megamall imported to Kent. They believe it is a shopping centre with a difference, to such an extent that it will evolve to become 'a city rather than a retail destination'[200] in the long term.

The building's triangular plan, with three anchor stores – John Lewis Partnership, House of Fraser and Marks & Spencer – and three themed villages on each corner, further differentiates Bluewater from the conventional strip mall. Far from being a labyrinthine nightmare in which you walk around in triangles indefinitely and never know where you are or how to get out, the shape is intended to make life easier for retailers and shoppers. Backtracking, something shoppers don't like and that often makes them skip shops at the end of malls, is no longer necessary. Each retailer in Bluewater is in a theoretically prime position, as there is no beginning or end.

(It is perhaps interesting to consider at this moment a fragment from the notebooks of philosopher Walter Benjamin, chronicler over 15 years of the shop and arcade in 1920s and 1930s Paris: '[The] most hidden aspect of the big cities: the historical object, the

---

[200] David Redhead, 'Welcome to the pleasure domes', *Guardian*, 9 March 2000, Space p. 6.

new metropolis, with its uniform streets and endless rows of houses has given material existence to those architectures of which the ancients have dreamed – the labyrinths. Man of the crowd. Impulse that turns the big cities into a labyrinth. Fulfilled through the crowded passageways of the arcades.'[201] It is only a fragment of Benjamin's magnum opus on the Parisian arcades, but it points us to a key issue for physical and virtual retail: the vital role of the labyrinth in triggering our desire to buy *something*.)

On the whole though, despite being hailed as a shopping centre at the cutting edge of retail, Bluewater looks just like any other shopping centre, just newer and more groomed. And this is in a sense exactly what it wanted to be: a shopping centre with facilities attached. The perfection at Bluewater lies in the detail that one doesn't immediately notice but which imperceptibly contributes to the experience. The combination of Eric Kuhne's 'tapping into Britain's cultural heritage' and the efforts of the psychoanalyst and marketing expert David Peek to create a trance-inducing environment is designed to give the 'guests' a smooth and pleasurable experience. Kate Meyrick, Bluewater's spokeperson, explains that this is not a shopping centre but a brand, more than a brand even, a 'metaphysical experience'. Thus, shop fronts at Bluewater were specifically designed for the space and are all different from their counterparts on the high street. In fact the brands who appear in Bluewater *must* create a different environment from any other of their outlets.

Our main question, as we walked around in triangles in this metaphysical brand experience posing as a plain shopping centre, was: Is this really the future of retail? A pleasant environment offering shopping, entertainment, smiley people, lots of benches and plants and some token cultural references – even if it is a folksong called 'Old Father Thames' – carved on to stone-clad facades. Is that really what people want?

Meyrick is a woman with a mission. We don't so much ask questions as prompt a series of highly articulate responses from her, which often last for 10 minutes – enough time for a quick jog around the interior of Bluewater (though the security guard 'hosts' wouldn't let you). Following 1,500 focus groups and 22,000 home questionnaires Meyrick reports that the place is about 'more discerning shoppers ... about people bored by the simple shopping experience'. They don't want the formulaic nature of the modern town shopping centre where 'Dixons [the electrical retailer] is always next to Marks & Spencer [the clothes and grocery outlet]'. Here, she says, visitors are 'guests'; there's no security, just 'host

[201] Walter Benjamin, *The Arcades Project* (Cambridge, Mass., The Belknap Press for Harvard University Press, 1999), p. 839.

teams'; there are police outside called 'Park Rangers' and 'laddish behaviour…will be tracked down'.

There are astrological signs – icons – and poetry by Robert Graves and Rudyard Kipling among others and 119 music zones 'everything from Puccini to Robbie Williams', but perhaps the most fitting artistic analogy comes from Bluewater's architect, Eric Kuhne. 'At the outset, when faced with the question what could Bluewater's landscape be, a painting by John Singer Sargent seemed to capture the spirit of life that we wanted to achieve… *Carnation, Lily, Lily, Rose* depicts an almost fairytale garden; an English idyll.'[202]

That said, nicely, Bluewater isn't for the faint-hearted expecting a Pre-Raphaelite oneness with nature: with 80,000 people visiting or 'guesting' most days it is still a shopping centre, albeit one where you are never more than '70 steps' from a relaxation point.

The point in the end is this: men with money and a girlfriend are likely to get fed up after about an hour here: in fact 80 per cent of the time it is the man who wants to go home (he has usually driven the couple's car there). So if his girlfriend has a notional £100 to spend she will only have parted with £55 before the familiar male shopping strop. Bluewater, Meyrick explains, wants to keep her (them) inside for the three and a quarter hours it might take her to spend that £100. Solution: 43 different things for unenthusiastic male shoppers to do – cafés, bars, a natural history museum, a 'spiritual' room, even a cinema. There are jazz festivals and product launches: truly the 'man' in this Edenic idyll will have to be very, very difficult to keep happy not to hang around long enough for maximum purchase.

Bluewater seems a very modern retail experience, maybe not metaphysical, but virtual in the sense that the damp and epic three-hour journeys those without a car will endure to reach it makes it almost a pilgrimage destination. Its closest analogy? A Hindu temple in the middle of India, hugely busy with people taking whatever they can through prayer from their gods: money, fame, happiness, health – the spiritual.

Niche retailing: the point of view

Bluewater is only one in a million shopping experiences and a trip to a custom-made shopping centre is certainly not everyone's idea of a perfect shopping experience. There are still plenty of consumers who want to discover the hidden gems of the retail world, who want access to Benjamin's *labyrinths* – if only to find the per-

---

[202] Eric Kuhne, 'A very local landscape' in *Welcome to Bluewater* (Land Lease Global, 1999).

fect Arne Jacobsen chair from 1952. Tyler Brûlé, founder of *Wallpaper** magazine, is one of the people who doesn't want a ready-made shopping experience. 'When there is no sense of discovery, the experience becomes clinical and unsatisfying for me,' he says. 'It's about finding new shops, and having experiences that I wouldn't find on the regular high street. So it could be about finding a great charity shop with 1950s clothes or an off-beat menswear shop in a small town in Denmark. It's essentially about being able to go home with a sense of fulfilment, knowing that I've discovered something new that isn't mainstream.'[203]

Brûlé predicts a growth in small boutique and niche retailing in the coming years, as consumers are growing tired of the uniformity not only of the high street but of their surroundings in general. 'As the Gaps and Hennes & Mauritz but also the Guccis and the LVMHs [Louis Vuitton Moët Hennessy] of this world continue to grow and spread their global network, we have all started looking more and more alike and people are getting bored of this monotony. Whether it is the guy sitting next to you on a plane wearing exactly the same shirt and suit as you or the couple next door who have exactly the same kitchen as you, we are getting tired of sameness. You can see it in popular culture but also at the top end of retail where people are suddenly making concerted decisions not to buy the same luxury brands but to seek out something different. They'll choose to *not* go to Bond Street but to Barcelona, to break the pattern of sameness that surrounds them.' Brûlé foresees a comeback of niche retailing in the next 10 years with more 'butchers, bakers and candlestick-makers' – small businesses – grabbing the opportunity to 'be big fish in a small pond ... The high street is heading that way already: mega-chains are being passed by small businesses who can offer unique experiences and thus create loyalty among their customers.'

The Cross, a small boutique in London's Clarendon Cross, is an example of such a personalised fashion retail experience. Launched in the early 1990s by friends Sarah Kean and Sam Robinson, The Cross has expanded into mail order and the Internet but its physical location has proved pivotal to its success. Unlike most high street locations, Clarendon Cross is an oasis of designer calm in one of London's wealthiest urban communities. No Top Shop here, only other exclusive destination venues with a heavy focus on the feminine. 'Our clients like to shop away from the crowds, and it adds to the feeling that you're buying something unique,'[204] says Robinson. Which, of course, you are. Kean and

---

[203] Tyler Brûlé in personal interview, June 2000.
[204] Sarah Kean and Sam Robinson in interview with Alice Cicolini; all quotes from interview.

Robinson purchase a number of items on holidays overseas, and the designer labels they select for the store are bought in very small quantities and are snapped up by eager clients as soon as they arrive. The personal service – calls to clients' husbands prior to birthdays, anniversaries or just when something new from their favourite label arrives in-store – makes life a smoother, happier place both for their customers and the men in their lives.

The formula of The Cross has been widely emulated across the British high street, from Whistles to Marks & Spencer's new Autograph range, and has spawned a host of imitators attempting to differentiate themselves and thus bring us a niche 'point of view' through 'affordable' exclusivity. While The Cross may recognise competition from other boutiques, it certainly has no concerns about larger chains attempting to bask in its reflected glory. 'The high street stores are too large and too busy to be able to realistically offer the level of attention that our clients receive.' Nor could they ever afford to entertain the policy of small and frequent buying that keep The Cross's clients knowing that they are 'unlikely to see someone else wearing the same outfit'. We are back with Monsieur Lheureux, the canny retailer who seduces Emma Bovary with his personal attentions.

Buying policy at The Cross is based on the owners' tastes and desires. As a result it is unlikely to follow trends, more likely to initiate them. Both owners acknowledge the importance that their perceived status as design gurus affords them: 'because we buy so personally for the shop, rather than using any formula'. Thus the image of the owners themselves is central to the brand. 'It's important that we are seen. It adds to the down-to-earth feel of the shop and makes us as a company more accessible,' says Sam Robinson.

This division between niche and mass retailing is a reflection of diverging aspirations within the consumer mass (we're all individuals now) and perhaps also within each consumer. There are those who crave differentiation, want to stand on their own, and those who are seeking a sense of belonging, want to buy into an image created by a global brand. Jethro Marshall, the former marketing manager of Diesel UK, says the key lies in understanding the difference between fashion and style, and understanding which it is your customer wants. 'Those who want fashion will doubtless be lured by the "innovative, vocal, professional" approach of retail giants such as Hennes [& Mauritz, the Danish chain] and Top Shop, because they provide the balance between low-cost new product and an entertaining shopping experience.'[205] Squeezing out the middle-market, these stores offer transient fashion trends at prices that those who want the latest look can afford.

---

[205] Jethro Marshall in interview with Alice Cicolini; all quotes from interview.

One such middle-market retailer is, or was, C&A. Founded as a trading company in 1841, the C&A store first came to the United Kingdom from the Netherlands in 1922. Its retail philosophy of decent, mass-market clothing at cheap prices worked for many years, and in the 1960s 'everyone went there'.[206] But in June 2000 came the news that all 109 UK stores would close. Squeezed by supermarkets such as Tesco and Asda (with its George label), and more stylish, cheapish brands such as Gap and French Connection, C&A could not throw off its downmarket image in a world wanting style – and discounting. Indeed 'man at C&A' became an epithet for 'bad dresser'.

Those who go for style, on the other hand, are the consumers who have it already, who know where to go, what to get and when to wear it. Marshall cites the fashion label, Duffer of St George: '[They] have been producing highly marketable collections for the last 10 years, veering between the two most reliably stylish urban genres; skate and mod.' Neither fashion nor precisely style, Duffer has captured the retail hearts of a generation. Never oversold, the brand has quietly become the understated day-to-day label of London's creative heartlands. The secret? Well it helps to have a continual flow of celebrity through the glass doors who promote the label by just being seen in public wearing the clothes. These customers serve as kind of walking ads for the brand, and make the stylish consumer buy into the brand in the hope of indirectly buying into celebrity, or at the very least the realm of celebrity – 'I buy my clothes where Kate Moss does.'

Nan Ellin, Assistant Professor of Urban Planning at the University of Cincinnati, argues that The Cross and its imitators display that 'enhanced access to material goods through increasingly sophisticated means of production...[This] has put a premium on having something before anyone else has it. Being able to purchase an item that is fashionable no longer carries the cachet that having already had it before it was fashionable does. Retailers have accommodated this fascination for the old by resurrecting past styles[207] and by "wearing out" new goods in a mass-produced fashion through, for instance, multiple washings of clothes or special finishes on furniture or picture frames.'[208] The Gap's downscale brand Old Navy, with its $12 jackets, fine for a month or so, hit Gap's profit hard in the autumn of 2000, if not Old Navy's.

---

[206] Nigel Cope, 'C&A, a sad tale of the high street store that went from coats and 'ats to closure and acrimony', *Independent*, 3 June 2000, p. 3.

[207] Nan Ellin, 'Shelter from the storm or form follows fear and vice versa', in: N. Ellin, ed., *Architecture of Fear* (Princeton: Princeton Architectural Press, 1997), p. 28.

[208] For example, Jean Paul Gaultier's Fall 2000 fashion show was a re-run of Madonna's look circa 1983.

The niche point-of-view store doesn't exclude the other, mass-branded retailer: one consumer can buy from niche retailers as well as large global brands. The main difference is that, as the phraseology obviously indicates, 'niche' caters to small groups and large brands cater to the mass market. While the latter will no doubt make more money, the smaller retailers like Kean and Robinson at The Cross can create personal relationships with the customers and create stronger loyalty. Global retailers have a more challenging task as they have to communicate with the customer base through advertising, merchandise and shop design. It is also a task with higher risk levels as global retailers have to make sure their mass-produced product – be it Levi's,[209] Twister jeans or a new fragrance of cream at The Body Shop – has a market and will not fail to seduce the public.

Sociologist George Ritzer claims that the contemporary consumer wants minimal human interaction and a greater freedom to interact with 'things'.[210] He seems, however, to ignore the need for personal attention, which is the key to the success for niche retailing. While the huge spaces of consumption that attract crowds of people are considered by many to take up important social functions, Ritzer argues that they lend themselves equally to very individual experiences, as one is encouraged to sit, gaze at the setting, and watch other people without actually communicating with them or engaging in personal relationships. This is also, we would say, what the Internet chat room and voyeur television are all about.

It is obvious that niche retailing takes place outside this realm, 'off the beaten track', in spaces that need to be sought out by the more curious and adventurous consumer, catering to a more exclusive audience and offering, once you have found them, individual and unique experiences (as humans are involved). Shopping experiences in more mainstream settings on the other hand are, as Ritzer says, becoming increasingly commoditised as shop layouts are determined by set plans and staff are trained to reiterate the same phrases. John Hannigan, 'a regular patron of a downtown Burger King', as he describes himself, but also a sociologist, notes the 'concise, almost robotic four-question interrogation by the counter server: "What would you like? To drink? For here? Salt or ketchup?"'[211]

---

[209] Levi's is an interesting example at present: for many decades the jeans of choice for young men – and some women – it has seen its market share sliced away over the past decade by the combination of 'designer' jeans, street fashions worldwide, and merely the *ennui* that comes with seeing your mum and dad in Levi 501s at the weekend: revolutionary, it is not. The Twister jean played well at launch at the beginning of 2000 – but when trying to spot a pair at its end you'd be more likely to spot Elvis Presley first.

[210] George Ritzer, *Enchanting a Disenchanted World* (Thousand Oaks, California: Pine Forge Press, 1999), p. 186.

[211] John Hannigan, *Fantasy City* (London: Routledge, 1998), p. 81.

Customers come to appreciate this repetitive litany because of its predictability, but it also threatens to become too familiar and, eventually, boring. But while staff can be retrained, and phrases reformulated, it is harder to change interiors, refresh designs and sustain the magic of the experience over a long period. One answer is to play on the commodity in a post-modern way and make a virtue of the speed of service, the McDonaldisation effect, if you will. There is a noodle restaurant in Tokyo, for example, that charges for food not by the portion, but by the speed with which you eat it. The faster you noodle, the cheaper it is.

Building shopping experiences

Despite the speed-eating Tokyo-ites, more and more of shopping is about retailers creating 'environments' and building 'experiences' for us, leaving little space for imagination and discovery or unexpected encounters: they are replacing the labyrinth with what Peek calls the 'trance state'. We are being spoonfed ready-made experiences, herded along predetermined routes, lulled into quiet contentment as we wander through climate-controlled spaces on the backdrop of tuneless, soothing muzak.[212]

Spaces like the West Edmonton Mall (WEM) in Canada and the Mall of America in the United States, the two largest malls in the world, are the ultimate embodiment of such vacuum-packed, fun-filled and ready-to-consume environments. Built during the 1980s and 1990s, these mega-malls cover 4.8 million square metres and 4 million square metres of land respectively, attracting shoppers from around the world. The larger of the two, WEM – larger than 100 football fields – prides itself on two entries in *Guinness World Records*: the world's largest shopping centre and the world's largest parking lot. With 800 shops, 110 restaurants, an indoor skating rink, a 360-room hotel, 20 cinemas and 13 nightclubs – and a replica of Columbus's *Santa Maria* floating in an artificial lagoon, WEM claims that 'the entire world exists within its walls'.[213] Real submarines, imported coral, plastic seaweed, live penguins, electronically controlled rubber sharks, fibreglass columns crumbling in simulated decay, fake waves, real Siberian tigers, Ching Dynasty vases and mechanical jazz bands – WEM

---

[212] 'Music in arcades. It seems to have settled into these spaces only with the decline of the arcades – that is to say, only with the advent of mechanical music…Nevertheless, there was music that conformed to the spirit of the arcades – a panoramic music, such as can be heard today only in old fashioned genteel concerts like those of the casino orchestra in Monte Carlo: the panoramic compositions of David.' Benjamin, *The Arcades Project*, p. 838.
[213] Margaret Crawford, 'The world in a shopping mall', in: Michael Sorkin, ed. *Variations on a Theme Park*, edited by Michael Sorkin (New York: Hill and Wang, 1992), p. 102.

contains everything from real fake to fake fake. The architectural theorist, Margaret Crawford, describes it as a 'dizzying spectacle' where 'confusion proliferates at every level; past and future collapse meaninglessly into the present; barriers between real and fake, near and far, dissolve as history, nature, technology, are indifferently processed by the mall's fantasy machine'.[214] The concept behind all this apparent chaos was explained at the opening by Nader Ghermezian, one of the mall's developers: 'What we have done means you don't have to go to New York or Paris or Disneyland or Hawaii. We have it all here for you in one place, in Edmonton, Alberta, Canada,'[215] and ads for the mall exclaimed that it offered 'everything you've wanted in a lifetime and more'.[216] Tell that to a hypersensitive aesthete who goes to New York especially to visit four designer boutiques, and he would be horrified. On the other hand tell that to the millions of Americans who don't have a passport and it becomes frighteningly realistic.

London's Millennium Dome Experience
It opened 31 December 1999. It closed a year later. It was expensive. It smelt of bad food inside. It was patronising; the shop was rubbish – oh, and it lost a hell of a lot of money. It was supposed to be a great day out but its creators – a bureaucratic cabal whose governmental and corporate members never quite seemed ready to take the blame for the mess – managed somehow to fail in even the basics. There was no point of view, no sense of mystery, no history – and no transformation. In fact the Dome was like the painting of Dorian Grey, the ugly alter-ego of crisply capitalist Bluewater experience. Two years on the site has finally been sold. And nobody seems to care. The End.

Reducing the world to the realm of the shopping mall in this way is very reminiscent of Walt Disney's concept behind his theme parks. Built on the bases of success of the earlier amusement parks like Coney Island in New York and world fairs and exhibitions, Disney formally commercialised 'fun', eliminating all the 'seedy elements' that had given 19th-century amusement parks a bad name. Believing that in post-war America 'family fun' was as necessary to

---

[214] Ibid.
[215] *Time*, 27 October 1986, quoted in Michael Sorkin, ed., *Variations on a Theme Park* (New York: Hill and Wang, 1992), p. 4.
[216] Dion Kooijman, *Machine en Theater* (Rotterdam: 010 Publishers, 1999), p. 157.

modern living 'as a kitchen refrigerator',[217] Disney set out to design a park where parents and children could have 'fun together' by creating a tightly regulated and safe environment with a 'far more "moral" order'[218] than any of the predecessors. Ritzer says the Disney concept introduced a new morality into the realm of entertainment and amusement parks by offering safety and predictable, controlled fun with a moral twang instead of the 'moral holiday' that the likes of Coney Island, an amusement park associated with lewd behaviour, drunkenness and gambling, was known for. Similarly, contemporary shopping experiences are frequently set in controlled and artificial environments that, with the help of CCTV cameras, climate control systems, patrol guards and a whole host of cleaners, shield the consumer from the harsh realities of the outside world: dirt, rain, wind, beggars and pickpockets.

Shopping malls, Disneyland, television, are all examples of the new stage of hyperreality – the falseness that is better than reality. Reality always has its detrimental aspects like crime, homeless people, dirt. In a situation of hyperreality like a shopping mall, everything is reduced to a set of agreed upon themes, so people feel more comfortable here than in a real situation. The accurate urban reality is replaced by the falsehood of the shopping mall.

Margaret Crawford [219]

While safety and dryness are certainly advantages, many argue that the high levels of control enforced upon shopping malls infringe on consumers' privacy and dictate consumer behaviour and experiences.[220] The ideal mall as a civic space, a modern-day agora, which would serve social, civic and cultural needs as well as consumer needs, has been replaced by secluded, controlled environments.[221] Social, civic and cultural needs today fade into insignificance when faced with the creation of illusory needs one did not know one had.

The argument as to whether the shopping centre is a private or a public space has been the object of several first amendment lawsuits in the United States where various political and religious organisations were forbidden to hand out pamphlets or canvass new members in shopping malls – a case in New Brunswick in New Jersey is but one example of a religious group winning the right to use the public space that is a mall to disseminate its

---

217 Erika Doss, 'Making imagination safe in the 1950s', in: Karal Ann Marling *Designing Disney's Theme Parks* (Flammarion, Paris, 1997), p. 180.
218 Ritzer, *Enchanting a Disenchanted World*, p. 3.
219 Margaret Crawford 'Scenes from a mall', in: Susan Marling, ed. *The American Affair: the Americanisation of Britain* (Boxtree Ltd, London, 1993), p. 27.
220 For instance, sociologist Steven Miles, architectural critic Ada Louise Huxtable, architectural theorist Nan Ellin, and others.
221 Introduced to Southdale Mall in Edina, Minnesota, by Austrian architect Victor Gruen.

teachings. In her study of cinema, shopping and visual culture, Anne Friedberg describes the mall environment as a realm of consumption that banishes and ignores the realm of production, covering up the realms of management and maintenance from consumers' eyes. In a paradoxical way consumers are confined to the mall and become passive onlookers in the imagined space, but at the same time they are escaping, engaging in 'psychic travel' as she calls it, transported into the realm of illusion and fantasies. Further dissecting the mall dialectic, Friedberg quotes Mike Davis who, in his essay 'Panopticon Mall', compares mall design to Bentham's 18th-century model for a Panopticon Prison, a circular, tank-like space with cells around the exterior walls. The prisoners were always visible to the centrally positioned guards and the mall thus becomes a fortress, surrounded by fences, riddled with video cameras inside and out and motion detectors at every entrance, a giant 'seeing machine', gazing on the consumer, the prisoner.[222]

The concept of a tightly regulated, safe but heavily controlled space was taken the whole way in Disney's EPCOT (the Experimental Prototype Community of Tomorrow) Centre, of which Disney said:

It will be a city that caters to the people as a service function. It will be a planned, controlled community, a showcase for American industry and research, schools, cultural and educational opportunities. In EPCOT there will be no landowners and therefore no voting control. No slum areas because we will not let them develop. People will rent houses instead if buying them, and at modest rentals. There will be no retirees. Everyone must be employed.[223]

Disney died before realising this conservative utopian vision and EPCOT was never fully developed the way he wanted. Instead of being a town it became a temporary resort colony, with sponsored exhibits from corporate companies that opened only in 1982.

In a further Orwellian direction, Friedberg describes a new feature found in malls around the United States, a character called Anne Droid, a mannequin with a camera in her eye and a microphone in her nose, who watches as consumers gaze at her but also watches to see they are behaving as they should. Thus the 'shopper is dialectically the observer and the observed, the transported and the confined'.[224]

---

[222] Anne Friedberg, *Window Shopping, Cinema and the Postmodern* (Berkeley, California: University of California Press, 1993), p. 254.

[223] Pawley, 'Tourism: the last resort', *Blueprint* October 1988, p. 39.

[224] Friedberg, *Window Shopping, Cinema and the Postmodern*, p. 254.

Big Brother is not just a television programme

With the Internet such niceties as public and private space all but vanish. The 'cookie' is a code, an account number that a computer server sends to a users' browser to recognise us when we return to a website: if you have registered with any major site, Amazon, the *New York Times* or Tesco online, the home page will greet you with a friendly and personal hello. This cookie is then 'stored' on your computer hard drive. You will have either set up your preferences to be alerted to this, or – more commonly – not.

As the founder and liberal champion of the World Wide Web, Tim Berners-Lee, writes:

The cookie makes it possible to accumulate things in a [online] shopping trolley, or send items to the same address as last time ... the fact that cookies are often installed on a person's hard drive, and talk back to the server, without any form of permission is also valuable: it's the difference between going into a store and being recognised as creditworthy, and going in and having to fill out identification forms all over again ... some commentators see cookies as entirely evil ... the problem is that there is no knowing what information the server will collect, and how it will use that information.[225]

A few guesses then? Junk mail. Spam. Direct mail. Phone calls. And much, much, more junk mail. For Viagra, teen sex stars, money-making scams, you name it: from the real world it is landing in your email in-box as we speak. In response, many governments and the European Union have voiced fears for the undermining of consumer protection – a lynchpin of the retailisation world's 'Individual is King' mentality. As was noted in *The Economist* early in 2000: 'Consumer protection may be harder to enforce in a world where Internet gambling sites operate out of Gibraltar, porn rings are run out of the Caribbean and American patients are already using the Web to buy drugs in Mexico that have not been approved by the Food and Drug Administration.'[226] When we shop online, it seems, we forego the truly private – whatever Berners-Lee thinks ('people should be able to surf the Net anonymously, or as a well-defined entity, and should be able to control the difference between the two ...')[227]

One such Internet company most concerned about this private–public dynamic is the largest online advertising media group, DoubleClick. Its business model works by charging a premium to advertisers because it is able to direct adverts to consumers, users of the Internet, who have already shown a potential or real interest in buying certain products through their previous patterns of

---

[225] Tim Berners-Lee, *Weaving the Web* (London: HarperCollins, 1999), p. 157.
[226] *The Economist*, E-commerce survey, 26 February 2000, p. 41.
[227] Berners-Lee, *Weaving the Web*, p. 158.

Internet usage. What that means, in principle, is that you could be reading the *LA Times* or *The Economist* online and find yourself seeing ads for Audi cars because you have visited their site. In March 2000 DoubleClick hired two of New York's most prominent consumer 'advocates' in 'an effort to reassure the public, investors and federal and state lawyers that it will respect computer users' privacy rights'.[228] Right. The principle is that of an older marketing strategy, 'direct marketing', whereby people who have, say, bought a new car, are sent by mail many kinds of adverts for car products, even brochures for different types of car. Whatever the legal solution, this issue doesn't go away: it isn't just the Internet – interactive television, mobile phones, indeed the wired home all posit a computer database with learning agents underpinning our use of these technologies, helping us to make better, quicker, faster decisions. Nicholas Negroponte, Professor of the MIT Media Lab, named these 'agents' digital butlers, and it is not hard to see why. The problem is that these butlers have sneaky habits when they are back 'downstairs'.

The *Financial Times* was perhaps most balanced about this issue: 'nor is there any agreement about how much privacy people deserve in the online future, or how it can be assured. Personal economic and political freedoms are not a given priority in this new world.'[229] In the end privacy is a bit like the famous pronouncement of Potter Stewart, the Supreme Court Justice, when talking of pornography: 'I know it when I see it.'

Translating brand image spatially: flagship stores, immersive experiences

Conveying more coherent messages, brands are increasingly building flagship stores that offer entertainment but also translate a lifestyle vision and the 'brand image'. These spaces take the concept of the shopping experience one step further, as their main aim is not to maximise sales but to 'convert' a maximum number of consumers to the brand. These spaces are instilled with a certain religious value. Ritzer speaks of these spaces, which have mainly developed since the end of the Second World War, as 'cathedrals of consumption': enchanted spaces, often endowed with a sacred, almost religious character. To attract more customers, these cathedrals need to offer 'increasingly magical, fantastic, and enchanted settings in which to consume'. Thus, an employee at the opening

---

[228] Eric Lipton, 'Two hired to calm fears for web privacy', *New York Times*, Metro, 8 March 2000, p. B3.
[229] Richard Waters, 'Era of the intelligent dustbin poses as Utopia', *Financial Times*, 12 January 2000, p. 14.

of the Moscow McDonald's speaks of it 'as if it were the cathedral in Chartres ... a place to experience "celestial joy"', while trips to Disney World have been dubbed 'the middle-class hajj' and compared to pilgrimages to Lourdes.[230]

According to Matthew Brown, research manager of echochamber, an independent retail analysis company, brand success lies in the communication of simple and consistent messages to the consumer. He names Gap, who send out an 'undiluted' message in their advertising campaigns, which is also reflected throughout the store and the merchandising. Their messages have a single focus: 'Everyone in leather, khaki, that's what we're selling and nothing else.' Brown says giving consumers less to absorb dramatically increases the chance that they buy into it. 'If what you see on your television screen, on buses and on billboards is transposed to the store, each store becomes a miniature advertisement in itself and what it sells is instantly recognisable.'[231] Consumer behaviourist David Peek believes it is the simplicity of the Gap brand that makes it successful. 'It's like a uniform, a brand which says "I'm part of the Gap army"; like joining a religion or the Salvation Army without the same degree of spiritual commitment.'[232]

The experience offered at Niketown, the flagship store opened by the leading sport's retailer in 1996 in New York and 1999 in London, immerses the consumer deep into Nike's 'Just Do It' spirit. Everything in the space is geared towards the dynamism, energy and competitive spirit that Nike represents: giant screens in the atrium show MTV-style film collages, a multimedia show, which is scheduled every 15 minutes and consists of images of top athletes breaking records and winning competitions while wearing Nike shoes or outfits.

While Niketown still offers the possibility of buying merchandise, the Sony Wonder Tech Lab, also in New York, is purely aimed at entertainment while at the same time demonstrating all Sony's latest inventions. Rising impressively above the traffic on Madison Avenue, the Sony building houses the corporate offices, the Wonder Tech Lab and, on the other side of the spacious atrium, the Sony Style Store where the latest in plasma widescreen television, Walkmans and radios is combined with Starbucks Coffee and a Ralph Lauren-style suite. The Wonder Tech Lab is part of Sony's commitment to New York City to 'provide entertaining and educational experiences which lead to an understanding of communications, technology and entertainment'[233] but also goes a long way in

[230] Ritzer, *Enchanting a Disenchanted World*, p. 8.
[231] Matthew Brown in interview with Alice Cicolini.
[232] David Peek in personal interview, November 1999; all quotes from interview.
[233] Susan Sullivan in personal interview, March 2000; all quotes from interview.

buying customers, as the hands-on experience with the latest in Sony gadget and hi-tech apparel is designed to make even the most ascetic visitor weak with desire. Spacious display areas show the latest in hi-fi technology with everything from Minidisc players to AIBO, the electronic dog, in easy reach and ready to be switched on. Downstairs, re-created home environments with comfy sofas, coffee tables and plush cushions – all styled by Ralph Lauren – invitingly draw the customer to sample the latest product.

Athough the two experiences are separate, they have both become 'destinations' in New York, Sony Wonder Tech Lab receiving 285,000 visitors a year, while the Style Store has one million. Susan Sullivan, Head of Marketing for Sony Style and Sony Wonder, explains that both experiences are part of Sony's brand image and that both represent an aspect of the Sony brand, tapping into the latest hi-tech products in the field of the audiovisual but also exploiting the image of Sony as the provider of sophisticated home entertainment systems. 'The stores are branding statements providing the customer with the latest and greatest technology and entertainment that Sony has to offer,' she says, adding that this means both spaces need to be constantly updated and reinvented to keep on drawing visitors. 'If the [Wonder Tech] Lab is to feature the latest and greatest in Sony technology it needs regular facelifts...Sony Wonder will be undergoing a redesign soon; the new concept will also feature the current role technology plays in our lives, which is very different than it was six years ago when we opened our doors.'

Taking the concept of immersive entertainment further, Volkswagen has created Autostadt, a 250,000-square-metre theme park devoted to their car brand, in the small town of Wolfsburg near Berlin. The site, until 10 years ago a sleepy manufacturing town 'at the end of the track' 10 miles from the East German border, is today being reinvented by Volkswagen to represent the brand. 'Autostadt wouldn't have happened in Wolfsburg while the Wall was still up,' says Stefan Vogel, Volkswagen's spokesperson. 'It was the end of the train line, a town stuck on the edge. Since the unification Wolfsburg's position has totally changed: instead of being on the edge, it is in the middle between Hanover, Hamburg and Berlin.'[234] And thanks to the ICE, a 160-mile-an-hour state-of-the-art train that purrs along like an Audi in third gear, Wolfsburg is 56 minutes from Berlin, half an hour from Hanover and just two and half hours from Hamburg.

Stepping off the train, it is the first thing one sees: the huge Volkswagen logo on the facade of an imposing four-chimneyed power station. Outside the station large pieces of civic art – spon-

[234] Stefan Vogel in personal interview, May 2000; all quotes from interview.

sored by Volkswagen we hear later – are a further indication that Wolfsburg is back on the map of the new united Germany. The taxi driver confirms the first impression: 'Alles Volkswagen, alles ist hier Volkswagen,' he exclaims, as we drive at breakneck speed past the six square kilometres of the factory, then past research centres, test labs, another power station and an educational centre.

Established here in 1938, when Wolfsburg was little more than a village, this is where Volkswagen started production of the People's Car for the National Socialist regime. Today it is a town of 123,000, of whom 50,000 work for Volkswagen in some way. It remains the global headquarters for the group and is now also set to become a major tourist attraction. But instead of creating another out-of-town theme park experience in the style of Eurodisney or Alton Towers, according to Vogel designers have made every effort to make Autostadt a part of the town and the park's open nature symbolises the company's opening up to the public. 'It would probably have been cheaper to develop Autostadt further outside the town, but we really wanted to make it an organic part of the city, not an isolated theme park,' he says. Through the construction of a new pedestrian bridge over the Mittelland Kanal, the station and the town behind it will now be minutes away from the park. Organisers hope locals will flock to the Autostadt bars and restaurants as an alternative to venues in the town.

Wolfsburg is to a large extent already equivalent to Volkswagen, with most major projects in the town sponsored or owned by the car retail magnate. The shiny six-year-old contemporary art museum, the Kunstmuseum Wolfsburg, was created with support from the Volkswagen Art Foundation, which also curated the artwork near the station. Its permanent collection includes pieces by Jeff Koons, Nam June Paik and Tony Cragg. The Premier League football team, VFL Wolfsburg is 'a good team, sixth in the league, but it has no stars', according to a local fan, and is sponsored by Volkswagen. Every car in the town seems to be a Volkswagen or Audi, and the majority are. The Stadtmuseum, located in the old Schloss, a mile or so away from the centre, is adorned with banners for...well we needn't go on. Wolfsburg is Volkswagen.

Featuring art, architecture, an IMAX cinema, flight simulators, pavilions – 'brand embassies' – dedicated to the many Volkswagen-owned brands, restaurants, a five-star, five-diamond hotel, piazzas, bridges, lakes, kids' playgrounds, grassy knolls, a museum and two 120-feet-high glass towers, in which cars that have been built in the nearby factory are stored before being picked up by worshipping new owners, Autostadt is a car theme park with almost no cars. It is not about cars, its creators say: it is about ideas, images and values. It is about creating experiences, engaging emotions, evoking memories and serving the customer with a smile. So while there are pavilions dedicated to all of the brands in the Volkswagen group: Audi, Skoda, Bentley, Seat, Lamborghini and Volkswagen itself, they have experiences rather than cars on display – be they digital or cinematic.

And it doesn't stop in Wolfsburg. One hundred kilometres to the west, in Hanover, where Expo 2000 was held, Volkswagen has built a rain forest complete with South American bats and snakes – and a concert hall. In Dresden the finishing touches are being made to a 'transparent' Volkswagen manufacturing plant in the centre of town; in Berlin, on Unter Den Linden, a few metres from the Guggenheim, the three-level Volkswagen store is less like a car showroom and more like an exhibit in the Science Museum, complete with creches, bars, interactive panels, and cars to climb in and out of. Volkswagen is positioning itself not just as a major international car company but an important part of German *Kultur* and history, tapping into German collective memory and reminding the Germans that this brand stands for more than just quality and reliability; it is part of history, part of childhoods, adolescences and midlife crises. Vogel, who now drives a new Beetle, says: 'I grew up in the back of a Bug and then a Golf. This is something I have in common with 99 per cent of Germans of my generation.' Thus, Volkswagen maintains, Autostadt is not particularly part of a move to sell more cars; it is about offering better service and memorable experiences. This sounds laudable but in the end Autostadt is a rather Jesuitical exercise in the cultivation of customer loyalty and thus, indirectly, a way of increasing sales through the generations.

In Britain, the furniture design shop Habitat had such a grip over consumer psyche in the 1960s, 1970s and early 1980s when it had the power to dictate what a young generation of newly design-conscious Brits ate out of, slept in and relaxed on in front of the television every night. Set up in 1958 by Terence Conran, this was one of the first retailers to reach far into people's lives and define not only how they furnished their homes but also how they set their tables and which wine they drank. 'Habitat will sell not simply china, glass, fabrics, carpets and furniture – but a whole *look* in furnishing. The chances are if you like one thing, you're in the right mood and will like the lot...As our photographer Terence Donovan said: "It's the sort of shop where you go in to buy a skewer and come out with a butcher's block tucked under your arm,"' wrote Elizabeth Good in 1964 at the opening of the 6,000-square-foot Habitat store on the corner of Sloane Avenue and the Fulham Road.[235] Shopping at Habitat meant visiting the shops but also sit-

[235] Elizabeth Good, 'What the smart chicks are buying', *Sunday Times*, 10 May 1964, p. 43.

ting on the sofa at home and leafing through a catalogue to find new furniture and accessories. The famous Habitat catalogue, which came through letter boxes once a year, allowed customers to buy anything from dining room tables to bed linen and book cases. The Habitat catalogue archives at the V&A pay testimony to a whole new world vision for the generations born after the Age of Austerity. There are guides to how to use duvets,[236] make coffee and which wine to buy; there are posters of French Impressionists and (in 1973) prints by David Hockney and Peter Blake; there is the pantheon of great European and American design – everything from the Charles Eames chair – a 'snip' in 1965 at £65 – to the ubiquitous bean bag. As Terence Conran put it: Habitat had become the 'Mary Quant of shopping'.[237]

Habitat was also the first to introduce the real sense of globalisation and distant foreign travel to the British consumer as Conran wrote in the introduction to the 1977 catalogue: 'The irregularity of supply caused by such events as monsoon, cultural revolutions and what insurers like to call Acts of God make it impossible to catalogue them with the reasonable certainty that we can supply them to you.' He adds that he is just back from India and China while one of his buyers was in Czechoslovakia and another is just on his way back from Copenhagen via Frankfurt. But it was not only Conran who travelled; Habitat was steadily becoming a global presence, with stores open in 31 cities in 1978, from Paris to Edinburgh, New York to Brussels and Montpellier to London, spreading the 'Habitat style' around the world. The Habitat approach was holistic as the shops and catalogues complemented each other, making Habitat products available to all, in the way they wanted to obtain them. The 1987/88 France catalogue explained that there were three ways of shopping at Habitat: 'In town, it's just next door. Stroll around freely and pleasantly in the Habitat stores in the town centres'; at the 'grand Habitat', which was out of town and 'le plus grand', the biggest, but nevertheless 'nearby, practical and spacious' and 'there to make your life easier'; or, the third option: 'le catalogue: c'est Habitat chez vous'. Habitat from the home, with a simple phone call to place your order. The shops emulated the home environment, aiming to make customers feel relaxed and free to browse,[238] and shopping an

---

[236] In the first Habitat France catalogue of 1973 duvet use is explained to readers: '20 seconds to make a bed! The duvet has the shape of a large cushion, soft, light and comfortable.'
[237] Ibid.
[238] The first France catalogue of 1973 explained: 'Dans un magasin Habitat presque tout se vend en libre service. Mais si vous voulez un conseil, vous trouverez toujours quelqu'un pour vous aider. Il suffira de demander.' [In the Habitat shop almost everything is available through self-service. But if you want advice, you will always find someone to help you. You only need to ask.]

'impulsive, gay affair',[239] while the catalogue portrayed the shop but also the home environment through seductive imagery.

Habitat's popularity declined in the 1980s, though, as competitors started offering similar shopping experiences and merchandise. Today, the retailer is trying to relaunch the brand, a process that could take up to four years, according to Tom Dixon, the Head of Design at Habitat UK. He believes the main problem with Habitat today is that it has lost its strong point of view. 'We have to rebuild a brand that is unique, that can be set apart from the rest. This is harder today, because there are so many competitors on the high street with similar propositions. In the 1960s and 1970s, Habitat was the only one, it was unique, the first shop to offer high-class design on the high street. Now we have to work hard to refresh it.'[240]

Dixon says one of problems is that Habitat grew beyond its own capacity, both geographically and in the range of its merchandise. 'Habitat was successful because it was small, the problem is that it grew too fast, got carried away with itself. They wanted everything, and confused the point of view to the point where they were eventually unable to deal with the logistics of it,' he says, explaining that the frequent changes to the collection in the 1980s meant that Habitat was faced with huge problems in transport and packaging, eventually leading to the collapse of the catalogue system. 'We need to cut down on the number of outlets and the items in store: the system today is very hard to manage, with over 11,000 items. We are aiming to cut down to 6,000 this year and 3,000 by the end of 2001.' However, Dixon still believes that, with time, Habitat can regain a strong point of view and lead the market. 'Stores like Muji, Corso Como in Milan, Moss and Colette in Paris, they all have a strong point of view. At the moment everything is on offer to everybody, but there is still a lot of scope to do well. We have strengths to capitalise on. And when people want to put coffee shops into the stores, I think that's a nice idea, but it is not the answer. Similarly the answer is not the Internet. The answer is point of view. The point of view of a single person of what the shop is.' Dixon is at heart an elitist and Habitat's problems (its website does not have any e-commerce facilities, for example) are similar to those that beset any 'legacy' retailer.

Habitat's owner (whom it is, incidentally, trying to 'rise above') has none of these problems yet, as it is, for the moment, sticking to its philosophy. The Swedish furniture company, Ikea, which has been described as a 'missionary organisation', functions on the

---

239 Good, 'What the smart chicks are buying'.
240 Tom Dixon, Habitat, in personal interview, May 2000; all quotes from interview.

basis of a 'sacred concept', formulated in *A Furniture Dealer's Testament*, written by founder Ingvar Kamprad in the 1970s and described as 'a kind of catechism; its explanations are in the spirit of Martin Luther's teachings to the faithful'.[241] Indeed Ikea's mission goes far beyond just furnishing our homes; it aims to define our lifestyles and beliefs by inciting us to take control of our lives. Thus, the endless array of boxes, storage bins, shelving systems and bookcase units that fill the Ikea stores are an encouragement to organise the chaos that clutters our everyday life. The aim is to reach into people's lives and 'reach good results by little means'[242] by getting people to cut the clutter and 'throw out the chintz', as the Ikea ad campaign in Britain in the late 1990s encouraged.

Kamprad's vision is in fact so far-reaching that he does not just aim to improve lifestyles but the people themselves. He does this by giving the 'visitor' – not customer or consumer – great autonomy. Self-sufficiency is the key: in-store there is minimal service, you sit on the chair, lie on the beds, handle the kitchenware, you choose, carry the goods yourself, take them home yourself and also assemble them yourself. This is not just to keep cost and prices down: Kamprad believes it is *good* for you, and makes his visitors better people. The idea is based on a kind of 'sharing philosophy', where you take half the task of owning upon you. Shirley Jones, Ikea UK's PR manager, explains: 'The idea is that you do half. We will supply you with the design, the inspiration, the knowledge and the basic tools; your responsibility then is to go home, build it and use it.'[243]

The Ikea philosophy is about the 'real', not the fake; even children's toys are all made of solid, natural, materials, there is no plastic and the toy kitchen utensils are all oven-proof. Ikea's children are being prepared for the future. In stark contrast with any other shopping or entertainment environment, there are clocks everywhere in Ikea, signifying that time is precious and that, while shopping is fun, it should also be purposive. No Gruen Transfers here, then. This is the 'anti-image' image, almost the anti-consumerist image as the *Testament* exclaims: 'We do not need fancy cars, posh titles, tailor-made uniforms or other status symbols. We rely on our own strength and our own will!'

A visit to Ikea is unlike a visit to any other store in that the path you will take is mapped out. There is no question of just heading for the kitchenware section. You will go through the bedroom section, the dining room section, the living room section, the bathroom section and *then* you will arrive at the spoons. The *Testament*

---

[241] Stephen Moss, 'The Gospel According to Ikea', *Guardian* (G2), 26 June 2000, G2 p. 2..
[242] Ibid.
[243] Ibid.

declares: 'Happiness is not reaching your goal. Happiness is being on the way.'

Lost in the supermarkets

If you have waited more than ten minutes before your appointment time, please use the telephone in the waiting area to contact reception.

Notice on first floor of the Asda headquarters, Leeds, UK

We're all working together; that's the secret. And we'll lower the cost of living for everyone, not just in America, but we'll give the world an opportunity to see what it's like to save and have a better lifestyle, a better life for all. We're proud of what we've accomplished; we've just begun.

Sam Walton (1918–1992), founder of Wal-Mart

> **They are piping 'I was Born to Make you Happy' by Britney Spears across the in-house radio, when we arrive at the Leeds headquarters of Asda, one of Britain's leading supermarket chains, and now part of the giant Wal-Mart empire. Inside the vast – and, yes, supermarket-mall-like corporate atrium, a veritable cathedral in itself – there are helpful, casually dressed people everywhere – three alone ask if we want help with the coffee machine. The feeling is very, very young, and sexy in a Britney Spears, kind of way.**
>
> **'Breakthrough 2000' is the company-wide internal campaign under way – its aim, to make Asda–Wal-Mart the biggest and best retailer in the United Kingdom. It is, a child-like poster declaims, 'a massive programme of change affecting the whole company'. On another poster we read: 'It [Breakthrough 2000] will improve the way we do things, giving us more time to focus on our key values – selling and delivering great customer service.' There is even, on the studiedly unglamorous, we're-all-in-this-together first floor where the executives sit side by side with their staffs, a notice board headed: 'Heroes and Villains'. It tells of poor sales in parts of the company, bad news this month for the George fashion range of George Davis [the founder of the successful 1980s retail and mail order company, Next], it seems.**
>
> **Richard Baker is everything you don't expect from Asda, whose cost-cutting obsession is to be 20 per cent cheaper than any of its rivals. He is very young; he wears a rugby shirt and jeans that have seen better days. He is on the board, hints that he *could* be managing director next, and is head of marketing. When we joke about the Tesco executives and their international rugby jaunts,**

Baker says, 'Here the board still *plays* rugby.'[244] He hands over the folded A4 internal newsletter, entitled suitably enough, 'Who's Number One?' It informs all members of the management staff – from managing director to receptionist – that over the past month 'market share [of the United Kingdom's grocery market] has increased to 13.9 per cent, an increase of 1.1 percentage points', and that 'Primary Shoppers have increased by over 10 per cent since last year.' On the downside it adds: 'Safeway is performing strongly in Scotland and [the] North East with its deep discounting strategy.'

Across from Baker's open-plan work station a group of young executives are 'huddling', having one of their many face-to-face conversations – electronic orders or requests are forbidden at Asda HQ, you have to tell people looking them squarely in the eyes. 'Huddling' can include announcements of birthdays, holidays, or children's achievements – or news of success in the chilled savoury pie market. The key is for people to be together, and focused. 'Our mission', Baker says with none of the evangelical zeal one might expect, 'is to be Britain's best value fresh food and clothing superstore.' A lot of the new energy surrounding Asda comes, Baker admits, from the knowledge Wal-Mart is able to impart – much of it proprietary, secret, 'the crown jewels' is what Baker calls their ancient wisdom. Wal-Mart is, after all, for all the associations that come with it, one of America's best-established retail companies (its first store opened in 1962). It is also the biggest spending company in the world, buying goods to a value of around $165 billion per year worldwide: it has 3,500 outlets, employs more workers (1.14 million) than General Motors and has a long-term plan to triple in size. Employees are 'associates' who are charged by the spirit of founder, Sam Walton, to practise 'aggressive hospitality'. And ... it is the biggest seller of soap, children's clothes, toothpaste and many other everyday goods in the United States, and ranks high too with CDs, videos and books.

Asda needed help. For years 'Asda' meant downmarket, its groceries consistently bettered by more glamorous alternatives such as Marks & Spencer or Tesco. Asda also suffered from not having a major London presence. 'There was a lot of mismanagement in the late '80s at

---

[244] Richard Baker in personal interview; all quotes from interview.

Asda,' Baker says – this, at least, is no secret. 'It took Archie Norman[245] to turn it all around, he changed 150 of the top 200 people here.' With one exception the board is 30-something. And the casual manner? 'Well, it is dress-down Friday, but we'd love to do it every day.' The problem is that in this egalitarian company the people working in the stores *have* to be smart and so it wouldn't be fair if the non-people-facing workers got to be the only ones in the slinky combat pants or shabby Levi's. 'Customers like to see smart suits, and the customer service is the most vital thing,' Baker says.

Asda's success story is in many ways tethered to the increasing middle-class British society, its ever-forward upward mobility, for those who are in work, who have money. Its rivals (Sainsbury's, Tesco, Safeway, Somerfield and Kwik Save) have all had major problems in the past decade, and now they are all faced by a retailer that is aiming both to be cheapest and to provide the best quality. In March 2000, for example, a basket of groceries bought from Asda was 9.3 per cent cheaper than the industry average. In December 1999 the company overtook Kwik Save to become the consistently lowest-priced supermarket – for the first time. They have maintained this position ever since.

Asda is not really part of the new media revolution in the way that Tesco is, currently, but that's because they plan a more holistic approach. Asda's Chairman, Sir Archie Norman, believes the move into e-commerce needs to happen gradually: 'Home shopping is a recipe for losing money for the next 10 years.'[246] Baker reports that, instead, new media will be *in* many Asda stores: screens and proprietary barcode technology that will activate, say, short films about the wine or cheese being bought. More important, right now, are point-of-sale materials, signage, the trolley fleet – that's the great leap forward. 'You get the product range right, lower the costs, create customer loyalty and somebody else is going to die.' And we know the names of those somebodies, of course.

Key to this war of grocery attrition is the concept of 'Rollback', taking prices lower and lower in a kind of Maoist continual revolution. At an in-house get-together, a 'mass huddle' in one sense, employees donned Gallagher

---

[245] Sir Archie Norman, Asda Chairman.
[246] Sir Archie Norman, quoted in Richard Baker interview.

Brother (the singer and guitarist from rock band, Oasis) wigs and sang karaoke-style with new words: 'You've got to roll it back / We've got to sell it low ...'

And thus, presumably, to quote another Oasis song, 'Live Forever'. As Baker says, Asda isn't about 'yo-yo' prices, but about long-term commitment to being cheapest and best. According to the monthly bulletin, in the first 12 months of the Rollback 'main shopper perception of low prices has improved by 5 per cent year on year from an already high base of 87 per cent to 92 per cent. Furthermore, Asda is the only retailer to be seeing an improvement in secondary shopper low price perception compared to this time last year.'

It all sounds so easy. The devil – and the savoury pie – is in the detail. It is in cutting out 'promotions' offered by manufacturers, 'when they are over-producing something, ice cream in November, for example,' says Baker. Asda had 120 promotions in 1999, 45 in 2000 and will be paring down to zero very shortly. Baker is right: the customer wants the right things at the right time – discounted ice cream in August, for example. They look to the positions at the end of aisles (normally the location for the Asda-derided 'promotions') and treat them much as an old-fashioned newspaper editor, producing eight editions a day, might. Thus the aisle will have different offerings, depending on the time of day: the commuter first thing, school kids before school begins, mums with kids mid-morning, snackers at lunchtime, school kids after school ends, commuters coming home and thinking of dinner, late-nighters who need chocolate or just something to eat very fast.

Perhaps most interestingly, in the world of direct mail, online privacy debates and the value in 'knowing your customer', Asda has dispensed with loyalty cards. They aren't cost-effective, it seems, though Tesco, Sainsbury's and Boots clearly find much value in them. (Safeway also dispensed with loyalty cards in June 2000 after it found that customers had 'just got bored with the points', Simon Laffin, Safeway's Finance Director, said. 'Our job is to steal the competition's customers. We haven't got enough customers and loyalty cards are getting new customers.')[247] Baker argues: 'We believe people will come

---

[247] Alex O'Connell, 'Safeway to axe loyalty card that bores shoppers', *The Times*, 5 May 2000, p. 13.

because of our promise of value; they differentiate. Loyalty cards add to the price of goods in-store.' Which is not to say that in the United States Wal-Mart doesn't spend millions undertaking diary-based, focus-group work, asking a sample of customers old and young to fill in their diary for a year so that Wal-Mart can ensure the right goods are in the right place at the right time – and cheaper.

One would think this is a model custom-built for the World Wide Web, but Baker is not so much cautious as canny as he explains the Asda strategy: 'Clicks are going to work; we're going to be an in-house and clicks business, but our e-trade will merge with our stores, there will be no barrier between the two. For example, you could order everything you can't carry in the store and it could be delivered to your house. Men hate supermarkets, e-commerce could help change that, look at the demographics.' But men get more than this – pubs in-store are coming; cafés are already there, maybe it is not quite Bluewater, but Asda is trying. Baker added: 'Wal-Mart in the US has a barcode technology which allows the customer to listen to *any* CD, not just the ones chosen by the record companies for the music stores. So you can sample, *taste*, every product. Why not swipe this over a bottle of wine and see the vineyard, the vineyard owner, talking about his product on a flat screen in-store? These videos will be paid for by the manufacturers. Swipe a medicine bottle and find out what exactly the remedy does ... the Web technology will change the way we shop, but not necessarily how we think it might.' As it is time to go we ask about sponsorship, getting the message across in ways that don't involve advertising. 'We don't allow corporate hospitality,' Baker says with a smile. That's right, he plays rugby at the weekends, not 'cheer the wholesaler'. In the United States Wal-Mart underwrites local college scholarships, raises funds for children's hospitals and educates the public about recycling; nationally it provides industrial development grants to towns, encourages US companies to bring offshore manufacturing 'back home', and sponsors the American Hometown Leadership Award, which – as the Wal-Mart website informs us – 'salutes small-town government leaders who are mapping out long-term goals for their communities'.

On the way out we hope that the Asda radio is playing

> **'Down Down' by Status Quo; sadly it is only 'Dancing in the Streets' by Martha and the Vandellas – it is not a bad concept, though.**

Supermarkets rank low on Ritzer's 'enchantment' scale, as they are still mainly geared to providing the consumer with good quality and low prices in a pleasant environment. Tim Mason, the Marketing Director for the British food retailer, Tesco, says they are mainly trying to build up their image as reliable and quality food retailers: 'Tesco can't change your life, but we can at least try to improve the area of your life that we have an impact on, i.e. shopping, and make that easier for you.'[248]

But it is creeping in, even in the down-to-earth world of food retailing; retailers are realising that just offering the product will soon not be enough any more. Designers will have to think about how to make the conventionally mundane and tedious trip to the supermarket more exciting, entertaining or even educational, offering cookery classes and live preparations of recipes and turning supermarkets into destinations. More than anywhere else in the world of bricks and mortar, the physical space of the supermarket is threatened by the rise of e-commerce. Where e-commerce may not succeed in replacing a family trip to Bluewater or an afternoon at Niketown and Selfridges on Oxford Street, it is being welcomed by a growing number of consumers to replace the boring task of food shopping. This means food retailers have no choice about e-commerce: they have to develop it as a new format, resolving problems from website capacity to home delivery while sustaining their physical locations.

According to the retail specialist RPA, brand strength will become more important than ever, as food retailing will move across different channels and customers will have more and more choice as to where and when they shop. The increase in choice will also mean that customers' brand loyalty will lessen. RPA's retail strategy and planning director, Jeffrey McCall, believes the winners will be the ones who manage to convey their brand values in a consistent way across all channels. Yaron Meshoulam, the development director of design consultancy 20/20, predicts a rise in 'destination' stores that will provide added entertainment to shoppers: 'With more and more shopping via the Net, there will be a great need for supermarkets to get customers to and through the doors and to make the shopping environment more exciting.'[249]

This trend is already popular in the Netherlands where the food retailer Albert Heijn is trialling stores with restaurants in their cen-

---

[248] Tim Mason, Tesco, in personal interview, February 2000.
[249] Pamela Buxton, 'Big Spenders', *Design Week*, 24 March 2000, p. 19.

tre where customers can taste and watch the preparation of food by leading chefs. Meshoulam believes this trend will expand to the United Kingdom soon, with 'more excitement, more theatre' replacing 'the aisles and aisles of product'.[250] Thus, to animate a Tesco Pitsea store, RPA and the theatre contractors Scena introduced giant penguins above the frozen food section, washing lines over the detergents and corkscrews in the wine section, adding an element of play to the stores aisles.

But Steve Potts, the Director of Fitch Digital, still sides with the pragmatic view that supermarket shopping remains 'a necessary evil, a chore'. Being sensitive to customers' needs is the key to success amid today's price-driven competition. And our need to spend less time doing mundane things means that in the end virtual space and efficient localised distribution must be the way forward.

Retailisation of public space

Consumer environments today – whether they be branded shopping centres on the edge of town, flagship stores on the high street or shopping precincts in historic urban centres – are taking over urban space, leading not only to commercialisation of space, but also privatisation as public spaces are converted into areas that screen out the unwanted elements. In professional circles this tendency is being regarded with mixed feelings. While retail architect Jon Jerde and others see the shopping centre as a space for social interaction and community life – or 'vessels for a renaissance of the human communal scene'[251] as Jerde poetically phrases it – critics look upon the 'malling of America' with horror and fear. Horror at the vast areas covered by commercial space and fear that this seemingly unstoppable commercialisation will mean the end of public space. Indeed, increasing privatisation of space is leading to the exclusion of certain communities and catering to those with purchasing power.

Theorists Crawford and Ellin both evoke the language of this exclusion as spaces that could initially appear to be public are subtly labelled with signs that indicate who should be using it: 'We have the right to refuse service to anyone' or 'Areas in this mall used by the public are not public ways, but are for the use of the tenants and the public transacting business with them. Permission to use such areas may be revoked at any time.'[252]

Malls, theme parks and corporate office buildings, but also older redeveloped town centres, have been taken over by private agen-

---

[250] Ibid.
[251] From http://www.jerde.com.
[252] Crawford, 'World in a shopping mall', p. 14; Ellin, 'Shelter from the storm', p. 39.

cies who dictate and focus the usually consumer-orientated activity that takes place there, limiting access to those with ability to purchase. Referring to the controlled and secure environments where consumers are constantly being surveyed, either by cameras or security guards, the urban plannner Stephen Flutsy describes the transformation of public space into a space of paranoia:

> Traditional public spaces are increasingly supplanted by privately produced (although often publicly subsidised), privately owned and administered space for public aggregation, that is, spaces of consumption or, most commonly, malls. In these new 'post-public' spaces, access is predicated upon ability to pay. People without purchasing power, goods that cannot be mass marketed, more-than-passive activities, and ideas narrowly perceived as inimical to the owner's sensibilities (and profit margin) are unaccommodated or ejected by private security as quickly as they are manifested. Exclusivity rules here, ensuring the high levels of control necessary to prevent irregularity, unpredictability, and inefficiency from interfering with the orderly flow of commerce.
>
> Stephen Flutsy[253]

Jerde on the other hand argues that shopping spaces are the secret to new life and happiness in the bland suburbs and deserted inner cities of the United States. 'Bland, lifeless, proto-typical places cause perceptual organs to fall asleep...By using perceptual provocations we can open up the sensibilities so as to better see and sense the surrounding realm. We [the Jerde Partnership] don't rely on the visual, we think in terms of the visceral: heightened senses, textures, and stimulation.'[254]

The creation of downtown malls in the United States shows how retailers can create enclaves within the urban context, creating sheltered and controlled replicas of the exterior urban fabric and selling the space as an 'improved' version of reality. Thus, the Herald Center project in New York, which opened on 34th Street in the 1980s, offered consumers a sanitised and pleasantly predictable version of New York City within the realm of a mall. Each floor represented one area – Madison Avenue, Central Park, Greenwich Village – and contained a group of retail outlets to attract a particular type of shopper. Critics were not keen on this idea, predicting that 'to reduce New York to such calculated, stereotypical absurdity'[255] would not catch on, as New Yorkers – 'notoriously and irascibly fond of their city' – would not buy into any type of surrogate. In this instance, critics were right and the mall went bankrupt within months.

A few years later Disney bought up a whole section around

---

253 Stephen Flutsy, 'Building paranoia', in: Ellin, *Architecture of Fear*, p. 51.
254 Frances Anderton with Ray Bradbury, *You Are Here* (London: Phaidon, 1999), p. 139.
255 Ada Louise Huxtable, *The Unreal America* (New York: The New Press, 1997), p. 102.

Times Square in New York as part of the '42nd Street Redevelopment', proposing to turn the 'hot end' of it into an erotic theme park. The French cultural critic, Jean Baudrillard, at the time described it as an attempt to 'Disneyfy the girls in the windows and the hookers on the street corner to make them actors in their world of imagination and fantasy'.[256] This particular plan was not implemented but Disney did proceed to sanitise the area – covering 11 acres in mid-town Manhattan, which had been dubbed 'the sleaziest block in America' by *Rolling Stone* magazine – by investing in run-down real estate. While previous efforts to regenerate the area never got off the ground, Disney agreed to invest $8 million in the renovation of the New Amsterdam theatre in 1993, thus immediately attracting other big names to the area and leading to the establishment of theme restaurants, a 25-screen cinema, Virgin Mega Store, and the ubiquitous Starbucks Coffee.[257]

> **The NRA theme park**
> As the *New Yorker* elegantly described: 'If there's one thing Times Square stands in dire need of, it's wholesome entertainment for the entire family...so all of us here at four Times Square, the building that houses our office, were delighted to learn that [the] National Rifle Association is coming to the neighborhood.'[258]
> The plan, it seems, was to replicate the enormous success of the *ESPN* sports complex, which has bars, restaurants, mechanical horses to ride and hoops to slam dunk into, and a very nice shop filled with *ESPN* merchandise. Oh, and giant television screens everywhere to watch sport, sport, sport. According to the *New Yorker* the NRA complex will have 'a gift shop with t-shirts and ammunition belts bearing NRA logos; a restaurant, where the bill of fare will include dishes made from animals killed by guns ... and an arcade called NRA SportsBlast, in which a variety of electronic games will provide what a spokesman called "an exciting total shooting-sports and sporting-goods experience"'.[259]
> It makes sense, doesn't it? The customer with gun(s) probably does feel a little restricted in the new Sound of Music clean Times Square. And the customer is never wrong. It took Kate Muir of the *The Times* of London to

---

[256] Jean Baudrillard, 'Disneyworld company', *Archis* 1998/3, p. 52.
[257] Ritzer, *Enchanting a Disenchanted World*, p. 6.
[258] Hendrik Hertberg, 'Comment: bullets over Broadway', *New Yorker*, 12 June 2000, p. 29.
[259] Ibid.

articulate just how special this 'Hard Glock Café' could be: 'Venison Velouté – Succulent AK47 machine gunned Bambi in a spicy Redneck sauce; McGregor's Pie – We took the bounce out of this bunny with an M-16 rifle and packed him in shortcrust pastry for you ...'[260] Muir had also unearthed a retailisation joke: in a variation of McDonald's' slogan 'Over a billion served', she noted that Josh Sugarman of the Violence Policy Center has suggested the NRA strapline could be: 'Over a million killed'.

The only physical context in which the NRA's theme park seems at all sensible is that of the cavernous warehouse two thousand miles away in Kentucky where a new museum is planned by fundamental Christians, which will show – in a Jurassic Park kind of way – that the world and its creatures were created in six days. *The Sunday Times* reported that 'the dinosaurs on display will bear tags "Created on day six"'.[261]

In the United Kingdom the debate around the development of further shopping malls remains unresolved as protagonists see the potential to revitalise neglected urban areas whereas opponents would prefer a return to the values, whatever they might be these days, of the high street. Thus for Peek, who worked as a consultant on the Bluewater projects, the Bluewater scheme marks the end of an era in shopping development, representing the last out-of-town shopping complex in Britain – not only because of government restrictions but also because of a change in lifestyle.[262] 'People have more money to spend but work long hours to get it. Time allocated to shopping is a precious resource.'[263] This will mean that shopping centres will be evaluated according to the time it takes to get there and the choice of merchandise available, making town centres much more attractive than edge-of-town developments.

Peek, who is currently working in Asia, Europe and the United States, is focusing on inner-city regeneration projects in the United

---

[260] Kate Muir, 'That woman', *The Times* magazine, July 2000, Magazine p. 3
[261] Matthew Campbell, *Sunday Times*, 26 December 1999.
[262] Relevant planning policy guidelines (PPGs) – planning guidelines set by the government – are as follows. PPG3 on housing states that 60 per cent of housing in London should be built on brown-field sites. PPG13 furthermore outlines the policies to reduce the need to travel by car, an indirect encouragement to local shops. PPG6 on town centres emphasises the development of mixed-use projects and discourages the development of any further out-of-town developments. Together they encourage the sustainable and local development of retail spaces in Britain.
[263] David Peek, *Local Government News*, January 1999.

Kingdom and how to bring British shoppers back to town. As shoppers are confronted with an ever-broadening choice through online shopping opportunities and low-price airfares that broaden their choice, they become more sophisticated and critical of the choice on the British high street. 'We find that, influenced by cheap air travel and the media, people are discovering and learning to appreciate high-quality town and city centre environments ... Why, they ask, can't our city centres be like these?'[264] Peek believes that shoppers would transfer their loyalty to town centre shopping in Britain, if they were offered high-quality town centres. Issues of safety, cleanliness and accessibility are of key importance here, with shoppers expecting 'Disney Clean' streets, free of beggars, street vendors or louts and good transport links and parking facilities.

To achieve this the strategies for town centre shopping developments need to be thoroughly rethought, with branding being the main issue. The main problem is a conflict between the town's image, the 'host brand', and the brand of the proposed shopping centre. 'Developers see their projects as destinations in their own right. They are branded in the same way as, say, Walt Disney World,' says Peek. 'The town itself is in effect the host brand. Unless the two brands can achieve a clearly apparent congruity, the developer will not be persuaded to go ahead.' Thus town councils need to adapt to the image of the incoming brand rather than vice versa. This approach would essentially mean that the tight control enforced in shopping centres and out-of-town shopping malls would be exported into the street, creating artificial and themed urban environments. However, property developers have understood the value that commercial space can add to an urban environment, not only drawing further investment but also attracting people to such 'mixed use' areas, to shop, work and live.

The 'branding' of cities is becoming an important part of regeneration schemes and efforts to show cities in a new light. Thus Glasgow hosted several festivals in the 1990s, highlighting its architectural heritage and aiming to revive it as a centre of consumption and tourism.[265] Similarly, Leeds has been exploiting its heritage through consumer-led tourist attractions like the opening of the Tetley Brewery Wharf. Finding a strong brand for a city is not as easy as it seems, however, as the image must tap into the local heritage while at the same time showing the city as a place of the future. Working on the redevelopment of the medium-sized town Arnhem, in the eastern part of the

---

[264] Ibid.
[265] European City of Culture in 1990; host to the International Garden Festival in 1988; host to the Festival of Design in 1996 and City of Architecture in 1999.

Netherlands, the Dutch architectural practice UN Studio was asked not only to design the new station hall and bus station, but also to invent a brand for the town as a whole. 'Branding is now being extended into architecture and urbanism,' says Ben Van Berkel, UN Studio's director. 'We are now working as consultants to help Arnhem council set up a new profile for themselves, brand themselves in a sense. Instead of finding a brand for a product, we are trying to reinvent the concept of the city or the profile Arnhem wants.'[266]

Peek names the Brindley development in Birmingham and London's Covent Garden as the two major town centre redevelopments that work. 'In the Birmingham project they have gone back to using original materials. It is a very successful project; it is almost more congruent than Birmingham itself, an icon of the original Birmingham that definitely aligns and improves the existing townscape ... Similarly London's Covent Garden is a space that makes London more London.'[267] This may be true but at the same time it is little more than a post-modern melange of old and new creating a fantasy environment that has little to do with the past and even less with the present. Then again, this is perhaps to confuse historical veracity with historical inevitability.

Outrage at the dominance of shopping in urban and suburban space is increasingly complemented by protest from anti-consumer organisations who oppose the relentless retailisation of a society where everything revolves around shopping. This movement spans from highbrow academic indignation to out-on-the-streets campaigners picketing outside large global retailers and inciting shoppers to save their souls and stop shopping.

Conclusion

Bricks and mortar spaces still offer the ultimate shopping experience, just as Asda insists. From consumers' points of view it is here that they can shop in an indulgent way, touching, feeling, hearing, smelling and buying impulsively. From retailers' points of view this is where consumers can be observed and manipulated most effectively. Whereas the Internet rationalises the process of shopping and allows consumers to remain uninvolved and clear-headed about their choices and purchases, the bricks and mortar store can command a state of mind and drive the consumer to impulsive purchases. The tricks? Well, everyone can try them, from loyalty cards through replicas of Pre-Raphaelite paintings, through the cheapest goods to the most patronising exhibits

---

[266] Ben Van Berkel in personal interview, February 2000.
[267] David Peek in personal interview, November 1999.

(such as those displayed in the Millennium Dome). What counts in the end is that we as consumers have a great *experience* at Asda, Bluewater, or wherever, whatever time of day, whatever season we visit.

Chapter 5 – A house is not a home

The Internet Home will take the retail landscape right through the home environment, it will not just change some parts of our lives, it will affect all of them: how we live, work, live, play and learn. It is the way forward...

Mike Pilbeam, Cisco Systems[268]

Under Louis Philippe, the private individual makes his entrance on the stage of history ... For the private individual, the place of dwelling is for the first time opposed to the place of work. The former constitutes itself as the interior. Its complement is the office. The private individual, who in the office has to deal with reality, needs the domestic interior to sustain him in his illusions. This necessity is all the more pressing since he has no intention of allowing his commercial considerations to impinge on social ones. In the formation of his private environment, both are kept out. From this arise the phantasmagorias of the interior – which for the private man, represents the universe. In the interior, he brings together the far away and the long ago. His living room is a box in the theatre of the world.

Walter Benjamin[269]

Describing a shift in the role of the home environment under the reign of Louis Philippe in 19th-century France, Walter Benjamin talks of the home as a hermetic and essentially private space, which screens out commercial and social influences to allow 'phantasmagorias of the interior to flourish'. The living room becomes 'a box in the theatre of the world' in which private individuals can let their imagination and dreams about the 'far away and long ago' run freely. Today, the box is still there, but we no longer require the powerful forces of our imagination to gain access to the theatre of the world. And today it is not a box we find, so much as a gateway to a multiplex cinema, a travel centre, a shopping mall and a theme park. The shift from the home living room as a stimulus for our unconscious theatrical *mise en scènes* to the more consciously guided – auteur-like – world of modern communications technology[270] has a long history, well charted in the literatures of sociology and media studies. Indeed, even as Benjamin compiled *The Arcades Project*, between 1927 and 1940, the first technologies, radio and telephone, were already becoming the social lynchpin for families experiencing new kinds of home living. The role of the home has changed dramatically even since Benjamin's times, through the arrival of first passive and then increasingly active communications systems; through media. Through retail.

Where once the home was 'for life', now we move frequently,

---

[268] Mike Pilbeam, Technical Director of Cisco Systems, in interview at the Internet home.
[269] Walter Benjamin, *The Arcades Project* (Cambridge, Mass., The Belknap Press for Harvard University Press, 1999), p. 8..
[270] By this world we mean radio, gramophone, television, telephone, hi-fi, video, teletext, cable television, satellite television, the Internet and DVD.

for work, to accommodate children in a 'safe' environment, or merely to make money, trading on the lottery that is house price values. Today, the home has become as much of a commodity as the vast variety of goods and services we can consume in it.

At the same time – inside and outside our homes – we have been conditioned to think increasingly of ourselves as special, unique, individuals: we want more than a homogenous home, which is why do-it-yourself franchises prosper and every second television programme that isn't about food or gardening is about interior decoration. We also want more than a homogenous retail experience that could be the same in Stoke-on-Trent, Staffordshire, as it is in Dover, Kent, or Bangor, Wales.

Sometimes, in the midst of this all-changing, alienated, affluence-ruling world, we slump back to our homes beleaguered by the rush, the new, the Feng Shui-ed formal chaos of modern life and escape to our home 'theatre'. It is the same theatre almost everywhere now – '1,000 channels and nothing to watch' – all that is different is our *choice* of 'play' when we are behind closed doors.

In this chapter we will see how the once passive but imaginative 'theatre' we consumed even 50 years ago has become an active, personal experience, tracing the gradually changing role of the home in the last 150 years and the rise of home shopping. We will look back to the past to see how not everything that is being claimed as 'new' really is new. We will trace mail order through to its digital grandchild, interactive television, and we will consider the two-dimensional limitations of the Internet. We see how the couch potato has become the sofa-surfer. We are all home shoppers now.

The changing role of the home

In the middle of his epic novel *Infinite Jest*,[271] which tells the story of a tennis school for young, potential Gland Slam, sponsored-up, parent-divorcing tour-brats, the novelist and journalist David Foster Wallace digresses winningly on technology and the home. He posits the arrival and mass-acceptance of the videophone in our domestic spaces. He argues that with the sudden possibility to *see* the person we are talking to, a whole range of telephone subtleties are lost. We can't lie, we can't be doing three things at once, we can't phone the office with a hangover and plead food poisoning or 'sudden' flu. Hence the invention of computer-enhanced, software-driven faces that are real, and not so real. These 'faces' will be perfect for every telephone exchange. They can be manipulated to be happy, serious, sad, caring, loving; they can be, and in the novel are, spot and wrinkle free – they are, in short, a Platonic, ide-

---

[271] David Foster Wallace, *Infinite Jest* (London: Little Brown & Co, 1996).

alised notion of what we look like distributed outwards from the perfect reflecting mirror that is our home.

Quickly these telephone faces become popular among video-phone users – everybody wants to have a perfect telephone manner, after all. But they take off so successfully that a new domestic neurosis begins. Who can look as perfect as their computer-generated telephone face? Answer: none of us. People begin to stay at home more, become recluses living their lives through their telephones, home shopping and media consumption. Eventually, for this is a parable it seems, the videophone is abandoned as a technology and people can begin to go about their social, out-of-home, activities once again.

Let us compare the parable in Wallace's dystopian novel with the academic writings of George Ritzer. In his book *Enchanting a Disenchanted World* he writes of the post-industrial revolution shift away from the social normalcy of production and consumption of all our needs from our home, 'or within hunting and gathering distance of the home'. He argues that this hunting and gathering distance has grown significantly in the past hundred years through improvements in public and private transportation (Brussels to Bluewater is a journey of over 120 miles, after all). With the spread of the automobile, shopping was transformed, and people were more willing to travel long distances, to 'destination' shopping experiences to shop, but also to be entertained.[272]

At the same time there have long been efforts to eliminate the need to leave home, to turn the home into a place to obtain commodities (for example, the Yellow Pages campaign, 'Let Your Fingers Do the Walking'). And still, we think of shopping as largely an external activity, going to some other place (the market, the bazaar, the arcade, the exposition, the fair, the country store, Main Street, downtown, the supermarket, the mall). Home shopping, be it mail order or the door-to-door salesman in the past, or their younger siblings, e-commerce, television shopping channels and telesales, never managed to come close to the success of retail in physical spaces.[273] Still, over the last hundred years the retailisation process has successfully invaded Benjamin's hermetic and inward-looking home environment – partly because the home has become less closed to the exterior, and partly because its inhabitants are more keen to engage with the 'theatre of the [outside] world'.

The role of the home and the family has changed radically in the last 150 years: the large multigenerational family structure has been replaced by nuclear families who live in smaller houses, without

---

[272] George Ritzer, *Enchanting a Disenchanted World* (Thousand Oaks, California: Pine Forge Press, 1999).
[273] E-commerce figured in 5 per cent of all sales in UK in 2000.

servants. The role of women has changed beyond recognition as they are no longer expected to stay at home and run the household; they are now free to choose their lifestyle.

As this social and geographical shift took place, retail followed. As car ownership increased in the 1950s and 1960s, retailers in the United States and the United Kingdom and Europe discovered the potential of the cheaper, unexploited spaces on the edge of town, which were easily accessible by car. Retail became decentralised, moving to the suburbs and new towns on the edge of large cities. Shopping malls mushroomed on the perimeter of American cities, leaving city centres deserted. In Britain, the development of out-of-town shopping centres was less rampant, but town centres still suffered and large retailers moved away to the regional centres.

At the same time the home environment was changing, becoming less insular and more permeable as new technologies such as telephone, television and radio allowed the exterior environment to filter into the home space. But while mail-order retailers and telephone and door-to-door salesmen were able to introduce limited but effective ways of entering into the home environment in retail terms, using voice, by writing or in person, they had limited impact upon and penetration into the home life compared with the potential of newer technologies like the television and the computer.

The vacuum salesman, encyclopaedia seller, the milkman or the Jehovah's Witness at the front door is part of most of the post-war generation's collective memory. Nowadays we still just about have Avon[274] and Tupperware agents and sometimes we will let them in, though the sex products chain Ann Summers probably does better, and brands and politicians alike use the home for 'focus studies'.

But people ('faces' as Foster Wallace's tale would have it) no longer need to cross the symbolic threshold of our front doors. This process is, as Ritzer writes, 'rather primitive and expensive. It also requires face-to-face contact and interpersonal skills that people today may feel less inclined or able to practice.' Which is in itself interesting for several reasons: firstly that the most successful physical retailers – such as Wal-Mart, with its staff trained to display 'aggressive hospitality', or Sarah Kean and Sam Robinson, with their discreet, personal service to their select clientele at their niche fashion boutique, The Cross, in West London – are highly skilled at face-to-face communication. Secondly, some of the most highly marketed and talked about Internet-based retailers have failed not only because of poor distribution for their goods, but also because of the even poorer, less reliable, human distributors (be they on bikes, such as Kozmo, or in trucks such as Boxman) they employ.

However, this is to move ahead of ourselves. The front door is

---

[274] Avon is a door-to-door cosmetics retail company.

wide open now, metaphorically, thanks to mail order, the telephone, teletext, cable, satellite and the digital world. The home has become, as Ritzer writes, 'a, perhaps the, major site for obtaining goods and services'.[275]

The consumer world has now truly 'imploded' – spilt over – into the home environment, causing the disintegration of the boundaries between the home and the consumer world outside. Consumers are thus freer to shop when and how they want, while retailers have converted non-commercial space into a retailisation space.

The television, formerly already a type of retail outlet that featured ads encouraging consumption, will now offer a monstrous variety of shopping channels and networks, giving us access to cybermalls and high street brands from the sofa. Ritzer describes the ambiguity of this commercialisation of the home:

It is one thing to be trapped at the mall, but quite another thing to be trapped at home. No matter how trapped one is at the mall, one must eventually leave. However, most people do not have the option of leaving a home that has become commercialised. In any case, large numbers of people are quite happy with their commercialised homes and that contentment is likely to increase in the future as the possibility of purchasing more and more goods and services is brought into the home.

George Ritzer

He goes on to point out that even in home shopping there is spectacle, as snappy zapping and clicking technologies can make five bags of groceries appear on the doorstep while the consumer might have been relaxing in the garden or reading the Sunday paper.

How true this is. As we have shown in chapter 1, the home is now the Harrods of supply to us. But then, perhaps the implosion is not so radical. 'They say there's nothing new in retailing,' Dr Tony Parker of the Centre for Retail Studies at University College, Dublin, told the *Irish Times*, 'and in a way, what has been happening over the past three or four years, with more and more supermarkets delivering groceries to your home, is a bit like the grocer's boy on the bike from 50 years ago.'[276] We will argue that the *radical* is still to come; right now, remember, even in the United States, online retail only accounts for just above 1 per cent of all retail sales, while mail order accounts for over 10 per cent.

The role of the home is changing in more than one way as people are reverting to working from home, as in pre-industrial times. Clare Lees from the Henley Centre for Forecasting was quoted in

[275] George Ritzer, *Enchanting a Disenchanted World*.
[276] Arminta Wallace, 'Getting off your trolley', *Irish Times*, Weekend, 5 February 2000.

The Sunday Times positing a 'steady growth in home working – so that it will involve almost a third of the workers (31.5 per cent) in the UK by 2006'.[277] There are barriers to home working, though, and not everyone can manage it as the work environment spills and sometimes overflows into the home environment. Workers also often begin to feel isolated from the office environment and their colleagues, causing a lack of motivation. Lees says: 'Self-discipline is needed in large quantities, and home workers miss the social contact offered by office life.' (The same is true of home shopping, the reason for its limited success is that people will never get the same intensity of experience through the computer or television screen, let alone the mail order catalogue, as they do in physical spaces. It is primarily useful for bulk buying of groceries and commodities.)

Professor William Mitchell, the Dean of Architectural Studies at MIT, believes home working and telecommuting will become increasingly popular in the post-industrial era. Older cities – New York and Boston in the United States, Venice, Paris and Amsterdam in Europe – are eminently suited to this type of living–working combination. 'They are much more humane than cities such as Houston or Dallas that were designed for the car rather than the human being.' Mitchell describes the latter two as cities that are slowly 'turning into walled electronic communities with an undercity'.[278]

For Mitchell, digitisation will essentially mean more choice: we will be able to choose where we work – at the office, at home or even in a holiday resort in the Bahamas; we will be able to choose how we shop – using home shopping services for the bulk shopping and enjoying experience shopping in physical spaces; and we will be able to choose who we spend time with – perhaps more time with family or friends than in business meetings and trips. 'It will allow us to optimise our time, so that we choose who we have physical interaction, "face time" with; for some it will be family, for others friends.'

Mitchell also believes we will revert to antiquated service systems in which the 'human' delivery of goods and high-level household services will become valuable commodities. 'We are in a sense returning to a Victorian era of service,' he says. 'Today we don't just require high levels of service in the physical retail environment; as more of our home environment becomes automated and Web-based, traditional service professions like gardeners, cooks and builders will become more valuable. New York is a classic example: Lower Manhattan and the financial district could not function

---

[277] Carole Dawson, 'Create your own design for living', *Sunday Times*, 7 May 2000, New Work p. 5.
[278] William Mitchell, dean of Architectural Studies, MIT, in personal interview, March 2000; all quotes from this interview.

without the cheap labour that cleans the streets, the offices and provides basic services. I think this economic spillover is very important. The restructuring of the economy is very much about the shifting value of service.'

From the Yorkshire Dales to cyberspace

Home shopping is nothing new and has been with us for much longer than the Internet. Mail order, door-to-door salesmen and telephones all allowed the consumer to shop from home as early as 1900 – in some cases, long before. While primitive forms of mail order existed as early as the 15th century, when printers circulated lists of publications and sent delivery boys from village to village to deliver the goods, Aristide Boucicaut, the owner of the Bon Marché department store in Paris, was in 1865 the first to publish a catalogue of goods that could be ordered from the home.

Home shopping especially targeted rural populations who had little access to the stores in town. In the United States, where in the late 19th century few towns had more than 200,000 inhabitants and 65 per cent of the population lived outside town, mail order became particularly successful. Settlers and farmers who lived far from any town were able to order a diversity of goods including food, clothing, shoes, stoves, furniture, musical instruments, fishing tackle, bicycles, firearms and china.

Many of the first mail order and home shopping companies developed as a kind of accident rather than through strategic moves. Thus in the 1880s the station agent Richard Sears found that he had time to spare from his job at the station in North Redwood, Minnesota. He had already started selling lumber and coal to farmers further up the train line, but when he bought up a lot of gold-filled watches that a local jeweller didn't want, he realised the potential this business could have. Soon he was selling not only watches but all the items featured in a 532-page catalogue. By 1893 sales exceeded $750,000 per year and Sears had become a household name, selling to customers across the United States. Indeed, in the five years from 1888 to 1893 the annual rate of increase in sales was 25 per cent or more. It was only in the late 1960s that Sears' position as America's largest retailer was overtaken – by Wal-Mart, with its giant out-of-town superstores.[279]

Similarly, in the early 1900s the self-styled Yankee trader and inventor Earl Tupper distilled a product from the oil-refining process to form a material that was durable, flexible, odourless and light-weight. Using his invention initially to make gas masks during the First World War, he went on to develop consumer products, creating

---

[279] See *http://www.sears.com*.

the now-universal Tupperware. The tubs with the unique airtight seal were displayed in shops across the country from the 1930s onwards, but sales failed to take off as consumers were not used to such high-quality plastic household products and did not understand the functioning of the seal. It was not until the late 1940s when the product was introduced at a house party, that sales caught on, initiating the infamous Tupperware parties where sales people demonstrated the use of the product and persuaded women to buy it.[280]

In Britain, home shopping was already common in the Victorian era with many newspapers and local magazines carrying ads for goods and services that would be delivered to the home. In 1868 the publication of a weekly magazine dedicated to this type of shopping was published: the *Bazaar, Exchange and Mart* and the *Journal of the Household* were immediately successful. Publishers claimed the success was due to a hitherto almost unknown, or at any rate unrecognised, trait in the human race: an 'ineradicable love of bargains and trafficking'.[281] Until then, it had been assumed that if people traded at all, they did it from necessity, as a pure matter of business and not merely for the fun of it. It was Ellwood Brockbank, a Yorkshireman working in the market town of Settle, who pioneered home shopping in Britain, inventing and officially registering the term 'fireside shopping' in the 1880s while working for the Quaker firm John Tatham and Sons. Tatham's was like a department store, selling everything from bibles to Yorkshire hams and 15lb Wensleydale cheeses, and it was here that Brockbank opened up separate premises behind the shop for mail order service. The local trade paper described him as 'the inaugurator of a useful system for the distribution of goods at wholesale prices to retail customers throughout the country' [282] which was the ideal way of shopping without leaving the home.

Mail order and catalogue shopping services became increasingly popular after the Second World War, providing everything from home furnishings and accessories to clothing for every size and age available. In Britain, one of the most popular catalogue services in the 1960s and 1970s was Habitat, the furniture design company and shop set up in 1958 by Terence Conran. However, even Habitat, which soon became the first port of call for anyone wanting anything from a bathroom set to sitting room curtains, was faced with problems of distribution and delivery of goods. The 1973 Habitat catalogue apologised amid the images of movie posters, multicultural models, and bean bags, saying: 'we cannot tell you exactly on which day your furniture will arrive, but it will

---

[280] See *http://www.tupperware.com.*
[281] Maurice Baren, *Victorian Shopping* (London: Michael O'Mara Books, 1998), p. 105.
[282] Ibid.

be dispatched within six weeks of your ordering', while the 1976 catalogue urged: 'please don't leave your Christmas [mail-order] shopping to the last minute. It is so pleasant for us to know that you will receive your delivery on time.'[283]

To surf or zap, that is the billion dollar question

So we are here at last in the new era of home shopping, via tele-text systems, on our old analogue televisions,[284] on 'interactive television' through our satellite and 'digi' box and through the World Wide Web via the phone lines and our PC. This type of home shopping has been around for several years now and for almost every day of that time, e-commerce has been held up as the Web's commercial *raison d'être*. The early pioneers of the Web, such as Tim Berners-Lee, rightly highlight the medium's fantastic communication power and its liberating qualities. But the revolutions that have had most impact thus far are undoubtedly commercial.

Leading the way, as usual with the 'newer' entertainment industries such as video, CD-ROM, DVD, satellite television and the Internet, is pornography.[285] Just as video sales of 'adult entertainment' presaged the virtual end of the dirty-raincoat cinema, so too the Internet brought about the end of restrictions on the distinction between hard and soft-core pornography – and a much less embarrassing way of purchasing either. For an annual subscription of a few dollars to services such as AdultCheck or AdultSites, Web users worldwide can log into indexes and gateways to hard-core sex sites catering for every taste. In the physical world, in the United Kingdom almost all this material would be deemed illegal if it was in print, on video or in DVD format. 'Video is what really opened up and changed the porn market,' says author, journalist and once-only hard-core film maker (it was for 'research'), A.A. Gill. 'In the past fifteen years the home-movie market has grown enormously – the company I made *Hot House Tales* for has no idea how many movies it has in its backlist, but it's well in excess of 25,000, which is more than MGM has made in its history.'[286] The new way to 'watch' films, DVD, digital quality disks rather than tape, show no change in the

---

283 Habitat catalogues, courtesy V&A archives.
284 In 2000, Teletext accounted for 10 per cent of holidays and 15 per cent of flights sold in the UK; David Murphy, 'Open season for TV shopping', *Financial Times*, 29 February 2000, p. 18.
285 It is interesting to note at this point that many of the Web's most potent marketing weapons, banner advertising, selling clicks – shared revenue between two sites that are connected via hypertext links – originated in the adult entertainment industry on the Internet. Source: Richard A. Glidewell, 'Porn's parallel web universe', *Upside Today, the Tech Insider, http://www.upside.com*, 21 February 2000.
286 John Diamond, 'Freesex.com', *The Times*, magazine, Magazine p. 25; cited in Freesex.com..

trend: 'The new DVD format is being driven by porn, with ten porn titles produced for each mainstream one ... if your smart two-car, four-holiday friends have DVD they're almost certain to be watching porn on it.'[287] As one of Britain's foremost feminists – well, *Cosmopolitan*'s famous agony aunt, Irma Kurtz – told *The Times*:

As we divorce sex from reproduction, the motto will be 'make money, not love'. Sex will be an industry and I don't just mean pornography. We will all approach sex as consumers. Women worked very hard to argue that they should be seen as human beings, not as objects, but this new commercial approach means that people will become their own objects. If a woman has cellulite or her breasts are too big she will want to change them. We will be our own products, and sex will be colder and more humourless.[288]

Pornography made by far the greatest profits on the Internet in 1999 as 'commercial porn sites derived 20 per cent of their revenue from subscription fees, far more than for any other form of entertainment on the Internet, including sports, music or video'.[289] But it doesn't end there: these sites also sell videos, streaming video[290] from 'erotic clubs', 'exclusive' chat room playmates, and so forth. Almost nobody else has been able to charge for access to their site – not hugely powerful media brands such as the *Sun* newspaper or the BBC, the *New York Times* (it tried) or CNN. Not Harrods, not high-quality information sites such as *Time Out*'s global city guide, nor Manchester United's website. 'Information wants to be free' was the call from the first Net libertarians, and to date – with the exceptions of pornography and the *Wall Street Journal* (jokes are possible at this juncture) – nobody has made much from subscriptions. The former are not for access in the classroom, cybercafé, or office (though high-profile cases in the United Kingdom, Europe and the United States suggest that office emails contain all sorts of pornographic material). Internet porn is about home consumption.

It is not quite the same with groceries online. Sure, the Internet and e-commerce potentially offer home delivery, lower prices (no expensive stores to pay for), more information and wider choice. But home delivery is still a nascent British pleasure with less than five per cent of UK consumer spending going on home shopping in 2000.[291] The greater distances involved in American life make it more appropriate and figures are much higher here at around 10 per cent.

---

[287] Ibid.

[288] Irma Kurtz, *The Times*.

[289] From a report by DataMonitor quoted in 'Just because it's not clean doesn't mean it's not smart,' Paul Sweeting, *Revolution: Business and Marketing in the Digital Economy* (US), April 2000, p. 5.

[290] Streaming video is – before universal broadband access – the best way to watch video on the Internet. See *http://www.realplayer.com*.

[291] Quoted in Winston Fletcher, 'Decisions, decisions', The Business, *Financial Times* Weekend Magazine, 29 January 2000, Business p. 34.

Part of the problem is that with few exceptions e-commerce websites are badly designed, almost impossible to navigate, and in the United Kingdom don't offer enough range and depth for the home shopper to buy into. The architectural critic, Aaron Betsky, asked the founder of amazon.com, Jeff Bezos, why the front page of the Amazon website appears to be so chaotic. '[Bezos] pointed out that every square inch of that page, when viewed on a 13-inch monitor, was worth about $1 million in revenues through advertising and product placement. Each element the viewer sees on the screen has an active and continually changing relationship to the viewer's desires and actions.'[292] So apparently, as Betsky says, 'there is a logic to the architecture of the electrosphere' – even if the underpinning structure of that architecture is money rather than user-friendliness.

The Danish Web guru and communications expert, Jakob Nielsen, is one of the people seeking to improve people's experience of the Web and its usability. 'If you are going to buy something on a new website, you will fail. If you go to a new website you will not be able to use it. That's the average user experience.'[293] Some websites do work. Lastminute.com was set up in April 1998 by Martha Lane-Fox and Brent Hoberman with the ambition of cornering the 'last minute' market. 'We are aiming at an audience of cash rich and time poor people – which is ideally suited to the Web,' says revenue manager Michael Sastry. 'This marries well with the concept of selling "perishable products". Many airlines operate their high-cost services with empty seats; these are "losses" they can never win back, so our aim is to match customers' last minute needs with offers of goods and service providers.'[294] These perishables – they include: hotel rooms, package holidays, airline tickets, meals in restaurants, and tickets for 'big' events, such as a Robbie Williams concert or a trip on Russian MIG aeroplane to the 'edge of space' – play well with LastMinute's customer base 'mainly aged between 18 and 44, typically urban professional, with the bulk between 24 and 34 years old,' claims Sastry. This audience isn't at home much, though: orders are made late at night or at lunchtimes in offices; perhaps soon they will be made through WAP and third generation phones. These are busy people, not home-lovers (though they probably have lovely homes, too).

Other e-commerce sites are also successful. Tesco announced in January 2000 that its online shopping business was the 'biggest in

---

[292] Jeff Bezos quoted in: Aaron Betsky, 'All the world's a store', in: *brand*new*, catalogue of the exhibition at the V&A (London: V&A publications, 2000).
[293] Peter Catapano, 'Web guru: it's the user, stupid!', *http://www.wired.com*, 15 November 2000.
[294] Michael Sastry in personal interview.

the world', with annualised sales of £125 million.[295] Chief Executive Terry Leahy told the *Financial Times*: 'The growth over the last year has proved the enormous demand from our customers for this exciting venture.'[296] In January 2000 Tesco had 100 stores offering home shopping, and planned to increase this number to 300 – around half its stores – by the end of the year. At the same time the retail consultancy Verdict claimed that UK Internet grocery sales would boom from £165 million in 1999 to £2.3 billion by 2004.[297] Tesco Marketing Director Tim Mason told us that the success is 'about designing your business model so it will work in different formats. Once we decide to do something, we get on and do it. Many others suffer from debating. We have strong leadership, which is what gives us direction.'[298]

However, the year 2000 was one of high profile dot.com failures, such as boo.com,[299] clikmango.com, Boxman, and a raft of collapses and mergers in the United States, and it is easy to see why Internet home shopping isn't yet the mass-market preferred location for retail. It works for commodity shopping – if the delivery is good, and you are home – because of its ease. More often than not, though, delivery is *not* good, particularly around key dates like Christmas. Even Tesco is constantly encountering problems with its online branch. Tim Mason explains: 'The biggest problem is capacity [of transport systems], we keep knocking into our ceiling rate and having to adapt it. Essentially we have to learn to adapt our mindset: suddenly we're not just food retailers, we're in the trans-

---

[295] Julia Finch, 'Tesco leads the world in online growth and profit', *http://www.guardianunlimited.co.uk*, 20 January 2000.
[296] John Willman, 'Tesco to treble online stores to 300', *Financial Times*, 2019 January 2000, p. 1.
[297] Ibid.
[298] Tim Mason, Tesco, in personal interview, February 2000; all quotes from this interview.
[299] Boo.com's demise was greeted with smug, self-satified grins all over the press in the UK and US. An article in *The Independent* maintained: 'That spaceman lookalike Ernst Malmsten [the co-founder] with his poncey clothes, champagne lifestyle and glamorous partner had it coming to him, and there's the truth...It's the same sense of pleasure we get on seeing a Rolls-Royce wheel clamped, only better.' The online fashion company started by former model, Kajsa Leander and Ernst Malmsten – both Swedes – raised and spent around £91 million in their brief 15 minutes of Internet fame. In the good days the pair made the cover of *Fortune* magazine and met Tony Blair at Number 10. They persuaded backers such as the Benetton family, Goldman Sachs, JP Morgan and Bernard Arnault to stump up and they launched their site in seven languages and 18 countries, selling very smart fashion goods. The trouble was that the website didn't work. There was a 'great' well, wacky advertising campaign on television, but the site just didn't work on Apple computers and frequently crashed on PCs. An article in *The Sunday Times* stated: 'Boo's site was so high-tech that only the geekiest customers with the most state of the art computers could get into it.' (Dominic Rush, 'From boo to bust', *The Sunday Times*, 21 May 2000, Business Focus p. 5.) The author failed to add that such geeks normally favour the Gap or just about any utility clothes, not Prada or Armani.

port business, we have to think about buying vans and mapping routes. Another problem was site-robustness, as we started expanding rapidly, the site would crash because too many users accessed it at once.'

By April 2000 Reuters was reporting that 'UK supermarkets will lose more than £100 million (or $159.6 million) in 2000 on "costly and inefficient home delivery services".'[300] As we shall very shortly see, this is around five and half times less than the 'success', amazon.com, lost in 1999.

'Selling' the Internet as an experience

Why don't the venture capitalists just cut out the middleman, give the money straight to the advertising company to make some nice ads, and cut out all that website building rubbish?

The most asked question in London's advertising world between March and July 2000

Despite almost a quarter of the pre-Christmas 1999 television adverts being for computers, websites or Open Television, the profile of good UK retail sites remains fairly low. But the Internet has brought the scent of radicalism to the home consumer: it is faster to buy, if not to possess, things by using the Internet than by travelling to stores or posting off the mail order slip; the shop front can change from minute to minute so users at different times of day can benefit in the same way as do visitors to Richard Baker's Asda stores. Then there is the simple downward price factor: auctions for goods; last minute purchasing (lastminute.com); instant price comparisons, such as software that can tell you that Heinz baked beans are cheaper on the Tesco site than the Sainsbury's;[301] bidding for things, such as airline tickets; all these things *should* make online retail a huge thing.

The big stumbling block for online retailers is trust. This is particularly true for new companies who try to build their brand on the Internet without having any prior physical presence. Amazon.com – the books, videos, CDs and *whatever-next* online retailer – is one exception. Perhaps, because of its excellent, deep website and ease of use, it is *the* exception? And Amazon has never made any money despite having 25 million customers worldwide

---

[300] Kevin Drawbaugh, 'Supermarkets seen losing millions on e-commerce', *Reuters http://www.reuters.com*, 15 April 2000.
[301] The instore equivalent of this price comparison system on the Internet is barpoint.com. This is a PDA that allows consumers to swipe the barcodes of products in one store and discover via wireless access to an Internet-based price comparison engine if they can buy it cheaper somewhere else. 'You may want to run that maneuver past the security guard first,' wrote author Adam Fisher in 'Swipe this', *Wired*, December 1999 p. 109.

(well, in 150 countries according to *The Independent*).[302] For example, operating losses in 1999 were $896 million.

The ultimate (amazon.com) model as sketched out by top executives is a sort of one-stop shopping mall, delivered to your door in a single consignment and hopefully, to minimise shipping costs, from a single shipping point. Imagine ... being able to buy not just a video about barbecuing and recipe books, but also the barbecue itself, all in a single transaction. There won't be any reason to drive all the way to the mall, particularly when the mall, when you get there, lacks Amazon's two key advantages. The first is the focus on customer service, in Amazon-speak, the 'end-to-end, order-to-delivery customer experience'. Shipments tend to arrive when Amazon says they will, and a phone call or e-mail is responded to any time day or night.[303] Amazon Chief Executive Jeff Bezos is famous for using this 'service', which with many websites is so often non-existent, as a competitive differentiator.

The second is all about community. 'Customer experience is more important online than it is in the physical world, because online, the word-of-mouth impact is amplified. Every Internet customer has a big megaphone and, if we make a customer unhappy, they don't tell five friends, they tell 5,000. The reverse is true: you create evangelists ... Online your marketing dollars are best spent building great customer experiences.'[304] This is above even price or choice as a factor in Amazon's success, Bezos feels.

As in physical retail situations, convenience, safety, great experiences, ease of access (Bluewater's watchwords) and point of view are key to the success of online retail (ad)ventures. Perhaps this is why in July 2000 Tesco brought back 'pounds and ounces' dropping the metric values. 'It is time to turn the scales in favour of the British customer,' Tim Mason told *The Guardian*. 'Some 90% think in imperial. They tell us that when it comes to size, imperial matters. We're not anti-Europe, but we are pro-shopper.'[305] Spoken like a true Experience Economy Guru with a smart regional point of view.

Charles Ponsonby, the Head of Group Strategy and Marketing at Open, Britain's largest digital platform (known as Sky Active since 2002), says point of view is key to the success of any retail venture:

"It's not about how you offer a product to the consumer, through what medium, it's about how you present it. You have to have a

---

[302] Malcom Wheatley, 'Amazon.mom' *The Independent*, 7 June 2000, Business Review.
[303] Ibid.
[304] Ibid.
[305] James Meikle, 'Tesco puts old measures back on its shelves', *http://www.guardianunlimited.co.uk*, 18 July 2000.

strong proposition. I have to admit I'm an e-commerce Luddite, but we regularly get these small Web start-ups coming in to tell us about their business and saying things like 'We're going to sell cosmetics on the net, it's going to be great.' And we say 'Why? What brand is it, is it cheap, is it high quality, is it aimed at young people, older women ... what?' I believe the high street is always the leveller. Just think of Oxford Street and imagine that cosmetic shop among all the other shops. Would you go in there? No. You'd go to Boots or The Body Shop. The shop wouldn't survive. And if it wouldn't on the high street, then why would it on the Web? If you don't have a hard proposition then it won't work. The high street is always the test."[306]

Ponsonby argues that there is a discrepancy between shops with strong propositions and weaker ones on the Open shopping channel:

"Gameplay is an example of a very strong proposition...It's a company selling video games, targeted at a young audience and offering 20 per cent off high street prices. When you go to it on Open it shows you footage of the games in full motion; they offer a tight range of bestsellers and offer free delivery. It's very successful and that's because it's focused. When you imagine it on the high street you see it's a strong proposition that people would go to and buy from. On the other hand we have some large stores that are part of Open content that are weak. They have a huge range on the high street and on Open they only offer a small selection. Why? There is no strong proposition behind their range on Open. It's random, not thought-through. They should offer the '500 best products', the *Which?* best buys,[307] the best deals...they need to package their wares logically. The high street is always the sanity check."

The Economist quoted a Goldman Sachs forecast that online retail could account for 15 to 20 per cent of US retail sales by 2010.[308] This is bad news for the retailers of goods in the physical world. As Bluewater 'psychologist', David Peek, says: 'E-commerce leads to total commoditisation of goods. This is very dangerous because it short-circuits a whole sector: advertising, branding ... it breaks down the barriers of entry.' He tells the story of an acquaintance of his who bought a £60,000 car online, in five clicks, but then insisted on going in to see his travel agent to hear the reassuring voice of the lady who arranged family holidays to the

---

[306] Charles Ponsonby in personal interview, January 2000; all quotes from this interview.
[307] *Which?* is Britain's leading consumer magazine.
[308] 'E-commerce survey', *The Economist*, 26 February 2000.

Maldives: 'It shows that the Web can fulfil the procurement role but will never cover the experience role and the personal contact that comes with physical retail spaces.'

Online retail doesn't do taste, smell, touch, serendipity, face-to-face, or at present even really proper movement. These are the qualities that affect our choice of what retailers call 'high touch' goods, those things that we like to be tactile with, clothes, fresh vegetables, sofas. The Internet is also a private affair, which is presumably why pornography does do so well and why Saturday afternoon is still a time to crowd to Oxford Street and Bluewater to drown oneself in the mass of fellow consumers, instead of sitting at home and clicking through Top Shop online.

One group that is particularly keen on e-commerce is the environmentalists. 'More consumers shopping from home should result in less traffic congestion and less air pollution,' Simon McRae, transport campaigner for Friends of the Earth, told the *Financial Times*.[309] His point was reiterated by Russell Craig from Tesco who argued: 'Traffic congestion will decrease as consumers use the Internet for bulk shopping and browse at local stores for impulse purchases.'[310]

Local use of global Web
Despite the 'global nature' of the Internet, e-commerce sites still need to take local habits and sensitivities into account. Frequently this works in Darwinian ways as places that have no need for e-commerce facilities see it fail through lack of use. So, in Singapore, for example, e-commerce seems doomed to failure, despite the Singaporean love of shopping and consumerism: the high density of the urban fabric means it is still easier, quicker (and more fun) to pop down to the mall or corner shop. Until now, the limited success and profits of e-commerce have been blamed largely on the slowness of the current system. The new generation of the high-speed Internet access, ADSL (Asymmetric Digital Subscriber Line), which will broadcast over 'broadband pipes' allowing faster access and the display of film and text, has been heralded as the medium that will really make e-commerce take off.

The biggest boost to e-commerce over the next few years will come not from snazzier websites or snappier marketing, but from the proliferation of broadband Internet connections to the home

---

[309] Dan Bilefsky, 'Green Lobby welcomes shopping revolution', *Financial Times*, 20 January 2000, p. 3.
[310] Ibid.

as more and more people acquire cable modems or DSL lines, both of which are much faster than the dial-up modems in use today.[311]

Singapore, the ultimate wired city, has invested massively into providing every home, school and office with this new high-speed Internet access. And yet there has been a very low consumer response. Jason Tan, a director of the Singapore telecommunications multimedia group, explained why to the *Financial Times*: 'The narrowband [i.e. the spluttering, jerky Internet we know and almost love] meets the needs of most of the consumers at large, broadband is not yet a necessity.'[312]

On a more positive note, updating old customs to new technology in Argentina, the supermarket chain Disco in Buenos Aires now uses e-commerce in combination with its old home-delivery service system, giving customers a choice as to how they shop. Traditionally, Disco customers could go to the store and select their shopping or simply leave a list of items, which would be delivered later in the day by delivery boys who sped around town by bike in bright red t-shirts. Today the same service is still offered, but shoppers can also just place their order through the Internet and get shopping delivered to their doorstep. Jan Hol, the Head of Public Relations at Ahold, Disco's mother company, explains: 'The delivery model was originally aimed at customers in the Buenos Aires area who would drop off their shopping list before going to work and then pick up the groceries on their way home or leave instructions for them to be delivered at a specific time. This system is now so established that it has become part of the Disco brand image: students biking through town in red Disco t-shirts. It's like a pattern in the town that now also integrates the virtual facilities of e-commerce.'[313]

Similarly, in the Lebanese capital, Beirut, neighbourhood corner stores are adopting the role of Internet shopping delivery points. While these stores always played an important role in local community life, the advent of the Internet is expanding their importance, as people know and trust their local shopkeeper to look after deliveries until they get home.

---

[311] Ibid.
[312] Ibid.
[313] Jan Hol in personal interview, January 2000.

In the United States, where the tradition of mail order is more than 100 years old, people are embracing e-commerce with much more enthusiasm than anywhere else. Suburban living patterns and greater distances play a significant part in this. The shopping editor at *Time Out New York*, explains that fashion-conscious, suburbanite teenagers are particularly keen on the possibilities of e-commerce offers in keeping them looking trendy. 'As they don't have easy access to the latest trends, they are very keen on e-fashion. New Yorkers on the other hand are much less keen on it; they have most shops within a few blocks,' she says.[314] Her point is reiterated by Tom Watson, founder of the @New York website and email newsletter. Watson is old-school new media, there at the beginning and one of its Boswells for many years: 'Online clothes retail is all about the suburbs, kids who can get hip buying online, when they have nothing locally.' Watson has bought a car online, but won't again for a while: 'It's the service afterwards, you can't repair a gear-box online.'[315]

Not yet anyway.

Global e-commerce is not as straightforward as it might initially seem; being global sounds good but is hard to achieve as one is still dealing with local people. Tyler Brûlé, founder of *Wallpaper** magazine, thinks it's over-rated anyway. 'Personally I don't see where the great need comes from to be a global brand. What's wrong with being a super-regional brand?'[316]

Interactive television for online shopping?

So, if not the Web yet for mass-market online shopping, what of its digital sister, interactive television? Ask any American who has worked in new media over the past five years and the two words often evoke many emotions: horror, amusement and disbelief are the most frequent, though. Numerous attempts to make it work over the last five years have not yet resulted in acceptance of the concept.

Protagonists in Britain believe that television is a much more friendly medium through which to access the Internet. Open Television, one of the British interactive television services launched

---

[314] The shopping editor at *Time Out New York* in personal interview, March 2000.
[315] Tom Watson in personal interview, March 2000.
[316] Tyler Brûlé in personal interview, June 2000; all quotes from this interview.

in 1999, provides its users with a full range of media, telecommunication and financial services as well as a wide range of Internet shopping experiences to choose from. Its aim is to 'bring the Internet to middle England'. 'Open is a genuine populist service providing intelligent shopping with a strong proposition,' says Charles Ponsonby, the Group and Strategy Marketing Director at Open TV. 'Whatever anyone says, the Internet is still a niche market: only 15 per cent of homes have access to a PC so e-commerce excludes a whole section of the population. We are trying to get e-commerce out of this niche and offer it to middle England by packaging content and creating a purpose-built visual medium that gives people access to e-commerce through the most familiar piece of furniture in their home: the television. We believe there is a huge audience out there. If you look at figures, the average household in Britain watches four hours of television a day and there is [a] huge number of people out there waiting to be stimulated, interested and intrigued. Open is more spontaneous than the Internet. You can just switch on the television and sit back and use it rather than having to start up your PC, dial up and get on to the Web.' Ponsonby argues that the television is a much friendlier medium through which to offer e-commerce. 'We talk about "lean-back mode", where people can relax and are more responsive to shopping proposals. The other thing is that it doesn't require any skill: you just use the remote control and you don't have to deal with the PC.'

Peek agrees, saying that it is much easier to captivate an audience, or a consumer as the case may be, when they are sitting back in a comfortable chair, than when they are hunched over a keyboard – a position many people spend most of the day in and have no desire to resume when they get home. 'Physiology dictates the mental state,' he explains. 'It's very hard to hypnotise someone who is sitting bent over a keyboard; put them on a sofa in front of a colour television and you've got them, though: the urge to buy will be irresistible. This is why the television is an amazing tool for e-commerce.[317]

Open, described by Ponsonby as a 'virtual mall', offers access to shops from Woolworth, Next, Carphone Warehouse, Domino Pizza, Comet and First Choice, to name just a few. There are holidays to book, banking transactions to be carried out, books to buy from WHSmith, clothes to buy from Next, food to buy from a range of outlets … In fact, there are lots of things to buy, though the most useful one does seem to be home delivery pizzas, which could be ordered in a quarter of the time on the telephone, but that's not the point. The point is that the average person in Britain watches

---

[317] David Peek in personal interview, November 1999.

around four hours of television a day – and that's time that could be spend both watching and spending. And furthermore, as Ponsonby points out, Open is much more than a shopping channel: it is a shopping centre, a travel agent, a record store, a restaurant, an email centre, a bank and a games arcade all in one, packaged to be accessible to the home environment.

But what about the shopping experience, the entertainment, the fun of a Saturday spent on Oxford Street or in Bluewater? Simple: Open has no aspirations in this direction; it knows it won't be able to offer all the things physical retail space can offer, but it also knows precisely what it can offer and where its market lies. Ponsonby explains, drawing out a diagram to show the various 'modes of shopping':

"There's fun shopping and functional shopping and there's impulsive shopping and planned shopping. Fun shopping is very much about social interaction; it's often combined with other activities and we don't honestly believe that we can ever compete with that. We don't even try to. On the other side there is functional shopping, which is provisioning, so it's grocery shopping, household provisions. This part is very important, especially when you look at families. Here we feel we can have a significant impact. Impulse shopping is also an area that works very well, particularly when you think of interactive ads – you may for example watch a gardening programme, see a new model of a lawnmower, only to find you can buy it straight after the programme, just by using your remote. The important thing to look at here is share of wallet: if you look at what people spend their money on throughout the year, grocery shopping takes up a huge proportion."

A few channels along from Open, on Sky Digital, there are other ways to spend your money: 12 pay-for movie channels; a lot further along the Electronic Programme Guide there are another 20 or so ethnic channels to subscribe to; a little further still, under 'specialist', the 'Red Hot' brigade ply their adult ways. It's all made possible by a feedback mechanism built into the satellite's decoder box: a modem plugged into the phone, which allows for instant access to these channels, and instant purchase of Open's many goods and services. (QVC, the American television home shopping company, already turns over 70 million phone calls per year using such technology.)[318]

All shopping and banking on Open is handled through a central intranet, which is managed by HSBC. This means credit card and

[318] 'Open season for TV shopping', David Murphy, *Financial Times*, 29 February 2000, p. 18.

personal details never go out on the Web. All transfers go straight through HSBC, a trusted brand. 'It's much safer than the Internet,' says Ponsonby. 'Even the image of the television as compared to the PC is much more trust-inspiring. The Open environment is a controlled, purpose-built environment selling brand names and supported by brand names, while out on the Internet it's like the Wild West, anyone could see your details, and your information could be going anywhere.' Open's service is 'TV to doorstep' as Ponsonby puts it: it provides post-sales care, with a network of phone centres around the country, ready to deal with any customer queries. It underwrites customer fulfilment so that even if you buy from Next through the Open platform, Open is ultimately responsible for the timely delivery of the ordered goods.

According to a Fletcher Research survey, by 2004 all 13 million British interactive television users will cross over significantly with the 18.5 million Internet users then in place in the United Kingdom.[319] A Fletcher business analyst, Shobhit Kakkar, said:

Television is typically used for entertainment, passively viewed in a communal household location, and is rarely used in the workplace. The Internet, on the other hand, is used both at home and work, is an active medium, and is generally used alone for information content ... the usage patterns will evolve over that time [the 10 years to 2010 when all television will be digital in the United Kingdom, by government diktat] and TV viewers will become more active in their involvement with their televisions and, through the use of the Web, the PC will become more of a recreational tool. This will drive a need for providers of both PC and TV services to ensure compatibility and comparability across all platforms and interactive devices.[320]

Still, as Ponsonby and Peek have suggested, and polls confirmed, 42 per cent of consumers would or do feel more *comfortable* using television for home shopping, while 28 per cent prefer PCs. It sounds suspiciously like physical retailers needing to ensure their customer relationship management (CRM) by having Tesco-style stores suitable for every lifestyle need – and a great online service. It sounds suspiciously like everything is everything these days – or soon, anyway.

There are rivals to Open, such as OnDigital, FutureTV and TiVo; more still will come via the ADSL networks – and most will go as well. Some will deliver to the television, some to the PC. The most potentially exciting is TiVo. As the Director-General of the BBC, Greg Dyke, said at the Edinburgh Television Festival of September 2000: 'When you combine channel fragmentation with the introduction of new technology which makes recording programmes

---

[319] 'How Nearly 13 Million Households will use their Interactive TVs by 2004 – but it will augment, not kill PC Internet', *Fletcher Research*http://www.fletcher.com, January 2000.
[320] Fletcher Research *Press Release*, 6 January 2000.

and skipping the adverts easy, the medium-term economics of ITV, Channel 4 and Channel 5 [the main terrestrial commercial television channels in the United Kingdom] look fragile.'[321] TiVo is an example of the 'personalisation' culture that imbues everything from cars to home pages. It is a machine that allows for more than mere time-shifting of programmes; it puts control of everything viewed in users' hands so that they can watch just those programmes they want (at whatever time they want, without any adverts if they want). For example, Dyke reported that 88 per cent of adverts in programmes watched on TiVo boxes were skipped. The consumers' 'hands' are notoriously shaky, though: 'The question is whether people have really got enough mental agility to understand how to use a TiVo, having failed miserably to understand VCRs, which, you could argue, are much simpler machines,' Frank Harrison, Director of Strategic Resources at Zenith Media, told *Broadband*, the television technology supplement of *Broadcast* magazine.[322]

So could there be a future world with millions of shopping channels but no advertising? It is a model, but the reality, claims Harrison, will be incentives to watch television with cheaper subscriptions if you watch ads; profiling techniques such as those used with Internet cookies, which could offer one-to-one adverts to users. These *could* be useful to us as consumers; if, for example, during the FA cup final Ryan Giggs scores a goal, then in half time an advert will sell his boots and shirt – the 'Holy Grail of promotional and brand advertising,' as Ponsonby describes it. There's also more retail sponsorship of television now, taking us back to the days of US television in the 1950s when companies 'paid' for dramas – the real 'soap' operas. Finally, says Harrison, the adverts have to be so good they are 'must-see' events in themselves. Better start calling Ridley Scott now, then?

And all that is before the nirvana – or hell – that is the fully wired home. 'There's a serious risk of complete chaos,' Pagoda Consulting's IT Infrastructure Director, John Lane, told the *Financial Times*. 'To have a fully networked home, houses need a mass of wiring and there could be interference between wired and wireless systems.'[323] Spoken like a true IT consultant. More to the point, the chaos Lane speaks of comes not just from technology incompatibilities, but also from competing systems, a lack of true understanding about our imaginative and consumer desires as 'home shoppers'. There may be magazines in America, featuring the 'best Home Cinema installation under $150,000', but we don't *all* want to have the Odeon in our back yard.

---

[321] 'TiVo the end of commercial television', *Broadband*, October 2000, p. 10.
[322] Ibid.
[323] Joia Shillingford, 'House of the future could bring high-tech headaches', *Financial Times*, 5 April 2000, IT p. XIII.

But first, what is a wired home? Well, they exist already in the kind of pre-Web browser way that the Internet did: more James Bond than Bill Gates. London estate agents Dunster Properties, for example, had a brochure showing a £5 million Chelsea house in January 2000 complete with a front door security key, which can be opened remotely with a laptop or mobile phone (handy for the hackers), fibre-optic ambient lighting, television, audio and air conditioning activated by LCD touch units in each room, a swimming pool with an eight-foot wide DVD home cinema built on to one wall, and programmable under-floor heating. And it is not even a home – shades of Bluewater not being a mall, here – it is, according to Dunster's Managing Director, 'a concept we're selling here, not a house'. In other words, he wants the house to be yet another lifestyle accessory, like a Porsche or a Rolex or a pair of Gap Chinos.

In fact, however, the Dunster 'concept' is a mere mud-brick shack compared with Bill Gates' new home, one of the most expensive ever built, at $60 million. This house is fitted with the best technology available and allows him to choose the artwork on is walls out of a selection of works from the Louvre in Paris among others.

Blurring the boundaries of virtual and real: pushing technology forward

Pushing technology beyond that of the Dunster gadget house concept and even beyond Gates' private gallery, academics and architects working with new technologies are striving truly to merge physical and virtual spaces, creating an entirely new space typology for us to live in. And what will this space look like? According to some, it will be radically, unrecognisably different, according to others, nothing much will change. Prof. William Mitchell, Dean of Architecture at MIT, thinks the changes will not be so directly noticeable, it will be more like an invisible web of digital information and networks that will be superimposed upon the urban fabric: 'We will always need buildings; as long as we have bodies, we will need physical shelter. If you look at the development of the composition of buildings, you see it was first only a skeleton and a skin. With the mechanical revolution that all changed and now [with] the digital revolution we will be able to introduce the concept of digital nervous systems that will be integrated in the skin of buildings. They will then become truly responsive to our needs and actions.' Mitchell says spatial configurations – of cities and living patterns – will not change noticeably in terms of layout or appearance; it is rather the use of space that will change significantly.

On the other hand, Stephen Gage, a professor at the University

College London's Bartlett School of Architecture, believes fundamental changes will occur, as the architecture that surrounds us will be a hybridisation of the real and the virtual world. His postgraduate students and colleagues are developing such concepts through the use of embedded intelligence systems that use sensors and acceptors – the devices that are able to identify people personally. 'The technological changes of the recent years provide a huge conceptual challenge to architecture,' says Gage. 'Our whole perception and use of space is changing.'[324] He believes that these technologies will eventually allow a 'full blurring of the boundaries' between the virtual and the real, allowing us to step from one world into the next. Gage sees the beginnings of this blurring already happening to a certain extent: 'Today virtual representations of the world are strange, cinematographic images with their own reality and truth systems which are changing our world perception and our perception of the relationship between the virtual and the real. These representations of virtual worlds are increasingly feeding back into reality, so that the two are in a sense merging.'

The changes he foresees are so fundamental that it puts in question most of our contemporary lifestyle. How and where will we work? Where will we live? How will we run our households? Will we still travel – or will we just visit places virtually? Writing in a research report for the construction company Ballast Wiltshier, a group of architects and academics predicts that the home will become more important – as more people decide to live outside urban environments and work virtually in 'electronic cottages' – and at the same time more fluid, as the concept of the portable home becomes more common. The report tries to convince us of the latter:

On-line access to music, printed material and TV or video could allow you to listen to your choice of music and read your favourite book, magazine or newspaper, whilst watching your local news or much loved programme or film anywhere in the world. Wall to wall flat screen technology could allow you to be surrounded by your garden, living room or favourite view. Live video link ups would allow you to see your children or family after work, perhaps even eat an evening meal with friends in an on-line dinner party.

Landscapes of Change[325]

Electric cottaging may not be to everyone's taste. But the shift from the 'electronic cottage' to the home that can be packed away in a laptop and taken around the world will ensure that 'home, sweet home' will never be perceived in quite the same way again. 'The merging of the real and the virtual will thoroughly change our

---

[324] Stephen Gage in personal interview, November 1999; all quotes from interview.
[325] *Landscapes of Change*, a report commissioned by Ballast Wiltshier plc and undertaken by the Bartlett School of Architecture, 1999.

sense of place and our understanding of the world,' believes Gage. 'It is not easy to come to terms with this in architectural concepts, though we have to understand that the virtual can now feed into the world of reality and conversely that the exterior environment can feed into the worlds we have created.' Gage can even see a time when reality becomes one of the most precious commodities. 'When virtual reality surrounds us, reality could become very valuable. Thus, as virtual shopping becomes more common, the real experience becomes more valuable and rare as the consumer will have the rare treat of being able to see, feel and touch the merchandise.' Similarly, Gage believes physical tourism will soon be replaced by a virtual form of tourism. 'As virtual representations get better we will not need to make the effort to travel any more. This will be particularly valuable for visiting sites that are protected and may soon be inaccessible to the general public, like the Great Barrier Reef. We could just watch it from our living room.'

But, as with all media-based technologies of the past 40 years, technical issues of compatibility and market dominance will play an enormous role. Gage predicts a major increase in embedded intelligence in buildings in the very near future: 'The chips are so cheap now that it is a logical development; acceptors – the devices that are able to identify people personally – will probably also become cheaper soon.' Gage predicts that developing good sensors (devices that can monitor air movement and flow) and multiple actuation systems (which allow parts of the building to be shifted) will take longer, because it is difficult and still very expensive to make them accurate and reliable.

Images of Jacques Tati's 1958 film, *Mon Oncle,* and the mechanised Villa Arpel spring to mind here. Tati, who plays the protagonist, Monsieur Hulot, lives in an old village-like quarter of Paris and goes to visit his sister and brother-in-law in their fully mechanised, stark and machine-like villa in a new suburb. The villa is surrounded by a barren garden of pink pebbles with a temperamental fountain; its interior is cold and functional, filled with gadgets, which are meant to respond to each other or their users, often setting off catastrophic processes. The kitchen in particular is a dangerous zone, with self-opening and, more often, violently closing, cupboards, and an aggressive cooker.

At a more down-to-earth, less futuristic and more pragmatic level, John Lane of Pagoda Consulting foresees many practical everyday problems arising from such networked home technologies. 'They [builders] don't know what to install and there is no up-to-date domestic IT wiring standard,' he says.[326] Lane is also scep-

---

[326] Joia Shillingford, 'House of the future could bring high-tech headaches', *Financial Times,* 5 April 2000, IT p. XIII.

tical about consumer demand – do we all want to be a James Bond living on the edge of the physical and virtual? In this sense the drive to make the home a giant 'local area network', with all home appliances becoming more like the networked office PC, *may* be a mistake. 'Managing one's domestic environment is enough of a nightmare as it is ... there is so much kit from dishwashers to video recorders that can go wrong. But at least you can throw out your washing machine and buy another one without having to recon-figure the video recorder.'[327] Basically there is a dichotomy here between visionary theories that border on sci-fi and talk of 'digital skins' and 'webs of information' that will transform our lives, and home-comfort-loving techies and property developers, keen to embrace new technology as long as nothing changes *really*. As long as the sofa, the kettle and the television can stay in the same place, and the house can at least still maintain the pretence of being a home.

It's a weird, wired world
We are sitting on a flowery sofa in a suburban living room in Watford, a nondescript commuter suburb north of London, learning about the future. Not just of retail, but of living, working and life in general. The 'Internet Home', a cutting-edge concept that is set to revolutionise home design in the 21st century, was developed by Cisco Systems and the construction company Laing Homes and promises to 'show just how far Internet technology is part of our lives, while breathing new possibilities into everyday household appliances'.[328] Sitting here among the frilly curtains, fluffy wall-to-wall carpeting and gilded door handles it seems a little hard to believe. We were hoping for futuristic space capsule architecture, curves and smooth surfaces. But it is not. It is just your average Barratt Home, like any of the others in Watford: white-pebble drive to roll the BMW on to before it glides into the double garage, fake Tudor facade and neat little front garden with space for the garden gnome.
And yet, for all its apparent plainness, this is a house with a difference: wired-up, connected and tapping into all that is new and fast in the world of technology. This is a house that you can actually talk to and in which the various appliances – lighting system, water, heating, tele-vision, radio, washing machine and fridge – can talk to each other.

---

327 Ibid.
328 See *http://www.laing.co.uk.*

Through a personalised website inhabitants can control their Internet Home and what happens in it from a distance while the technology is also intelligent enough to figure out the cheapest way of co-ordinating the household. So, for example, in winter, when the inhabitant is at work, he or she can log on to the home site and turn on the heating – even program the bath to run – in time for when the family gets home. More conveniently though, it is possible to turn the heating off if one is unexpectedly not going home, thus saving on bills and heat. Four webcams installed throughout the house serve as security control but also allow users to zoom into the left-hand corner of the living room for example, where the video is, and program it to record a favourite programme from a distance.

Taking the technology to high levels of refinement, the next generation of washing machines will tune into the Internet Home system. They will not only be Web-enabled – controllable via the Internet; these new washing machines will also allow long-distance maintenance. Technicians will be able to assess problems online and either fix machines from afar through point-and-click technology or find out what spare part is required to fix it when they come to the house. These machines will even be so intelligent that they will select the cheapest time and electricity network on which to run cycles, bidding via server connections to find the best deal.

This means savings not only on a small, personal scale, but also on a national scale. For example, today, when the Football World Cup is being shown on television and there is an ad break, the whole country goes and turns the kettle on. To cater for these surges in electricity demand, power stations have to have back-up systems and employ dozens of people just to figure out when these surges are going to occur. On a national scale consumption during these periods costs millions. In a wired home, though, your television could communicate the imminent increase in demand on the electrical system to your freezer, which in turn could switch off for a few minutes to compensate. Mike Pilbeam, a technical director at Cisco Systems who worked on the development of the Internet Home concept, says: 'On the level of a single household the savings aren't great but if you look at the saving on a national level it means less power stations will have to be built to meet rising demand.'[329]

It all sounds a bit oppressive, a house that runs your life to a rigid clockwork, but we remain open-minded. We have, after all, not even started talking about retail. Indeed, as Pilbeam explains, the Internet Home is designed to manage the household, monitoring the contents of the fridge, the contents of the bin – to see what has run out – and draw up your weekly shopping list accordingly; it can even compile recipes, based on leftovers in the fridge. The delivery problems that many e-commerce ventures have been encountering will be solved by the storage box attached to the side of each house, which will allow delivery at any time of day and safeguard the goods until the owner returns. An Internet connection through the television will allow users to shop from the comfort of their armchair, replacing crowded supermarkets with home delivery. 'Retailers will now be able to penetrate to the most intimate parts of our lives, entering the home space through the Web interface,' says Pilbeam. 'At the same time consumers will be in full control as they will be able to control their shopping experience: it's all about being able to buy what you want and choose the cheapest outlet.'

Pilbeam believes that as e-commerce becomes more widely used, we will revert to old shopping models, in which we go out to buy fresh produce and choice foods ourselves and rely upon home delivery for standard items. 'The beauty of our concept is that the Internet is central to all operations and the general functioning of the home while at the same time remaining invisible; the house looks just like any other.'

So bins that scan your empty cans of peas, fridges that tell you what you can knock up with the cold pasta and tired contents of the vegetable drawer, and kettles that switch on as they hear the garage door opening? Will the future of the home environment really be dominated by household appliances that become 'lifestyle managers' and shoppers at the same time?

Conclusion

While Burt Baccarach and Hal David wrote the song 'A house is not a home' *(when there's no one there)* the domestic environment

---

[329] Mike Pilbeam in personal interview, February 2000; all quotes from this interview.

is fast evolving into a retail space (when there's someone there, even if it *is* only your refrigerator and your bin). The future prospects as interactive television and the Internet promise that those tedious and stressful trips to the supermarket and the shopping centre will be replaced by leisurely hours spent zapping on the sofa or clicking through the frozen food section on the family PC may come true. So too the futuristic houses that clean themselves or order frozen peas direct from the fridge, check our pulse and beam various visions from the Uffizi gallery on to our poolside walls each day. Seven years ago Nicholas Negroponte, founder of the MIT Media Lab, told us that one day the television screen in the kitchen would see that the dog was scratching itself and automatically order flea powder from the online grocery store.[330] A decade later the home is still waiting, more wag the dog, than watch the dog. It is, though, imploding, as Ritzer has it: all a matter of time. And money.

---

[330] Robin Hunt interview with Negroponte, *Guardian*, 1994.

Chapter 6 – Here, there and everywhere – peripheral space

Head for business
A Sikh businessman from Esher, Surrey, has raised £200,000 for charity by selling advertising space on his turban.

Guardian, Society, 29 March 2000

PHONEBOX R.I.P.
Kiosks for multi-media as the mobile revolution bites
The number's up for Britain's traditional phone box after nearly a century as a treasured national institution, BT said yesterday. Bosses admitted a 'noticeable' recent fall in the use of the country's 141,000 kiosks as more people buy mobiles. But they know scrapping the boxes would cause outrage – so they're reinventing them for the 21st century as 'multi-media centres' offering the Internet, email and even designer goods at discount.

Daily Mirror, 26 May 2000

It is April 2000 and we are sipping coffee, comfortable and relaxed as we sink into low sofas in the office of Tyler Brûlé, the founder of *Wallpaper** magazine, on the north end of Waterloo Bridge, London. The office interior is low-key, a stylish mix of soft beige, brown and cream tones and straight angles; slick, ceiling-high, cherry-wood bookcases line the walls, light-wood Persian blinds screen the space off from the rest of the editorial staff. Brûlé, a 30-something slick, tanned Canadian, is leaning back in his designer Eames desk chair, feet on the table, orange shirt and taupe trousers doing the sartorial talking – he's neither seasonally fashionable, nor out of fashion: he's *cool* in a Herb Ritts photograph kind of way. We're talking – again – about retail and, as Brûlé sips his Diet Coke, he explains how *Wallpaper** magazine is in a sense also a shop, selling a way of life. 'We have become a catalogue for living, but we are not trying to be global, we want to keep on functioning on the local scale, telling readers where they should go to find "that new spoon" in an off-beat store in Edinburgh or Stockholm.' This is not quite the case: *Wallpaper** is global in the sense that its extreme vision – its iconographic world is populated by stick-thin girls and seemingly over-heated, over-excited young men – appeals to a 'point of view' that finds favour in parts of London, Los Angeles, Miami, Milan or Stockholm. It is a world beyond the seasonal offerings from Habitat or Macy's. It is a world – a beige world, oft-times – of 'classics', be they new or old. 'Many retailers have actually pointed out to us how important *Wallpaper** has become for their image. I think it is hugely important to feature both niche and main stream retail in the magazine. And niche retailing is becoming increasingly important. As people get tired of global retailing, brands like Saks have become ubiquitous; they just keep on expanding, most recently into Saudi Arabia. Essentially you can find luxury brands in every resort town now – even in Manchester. People are bored of it.'[331]

As we quickly scribble down his words, we are both thinking 'peripheral space'; we're thinking 'brilliant example of peripheral space'. And indeed, it is. Peripheral space is our definition of the retailing that takes place 'in-between'; that is, not in the shop – that is the supermarket, or the mall, or the department store – and not in the newly digitally retailised home. Thus, peripheral space can include anything from the airport – which is no longer a functional ante-space leading to the plane, but a complete shopping labyrinth – to the virtual shopping spaces installed on Wireless Application Protocol (WAP) mobile phones (and their 3G, third generation, successors), which allow you to book train tickets, reserve theatre seats and get the latest football results. *Wallpaper** magazine fits right into this category, a peripheral space that sells a very particular lifestyle. It is the lifestyle for the person who skis in Prada, stays at hotels so discreet they never advertise, and probably looks a little like the actor Richard Gere did in *American Gigolo*.[332]

Just as we start asking Brûlé whether he could ever imagine doing all his shopping online, the phone rings. He it picks up and immediately puts on the loudspeaker.

'Your lot is next. Are you still up for it?' a woman's voice asks.

'It's number 1584, the Alf Swenson chair? Yes definitely.' He looks over and explains apologetically: 'I'm just buying furniture in an auction in Stockholm; all 1950s Swedish design pieces, just give me a minute.'

Bidding starts at 3,000 – we hope it is krone, not dollars or pounds (if it is pounds then the deal *Wallpaper** did with Time Warner, now part of the AOL empire, *must* have been good); you can hear the buzz of voices in the background, as the bids bounce around the room and the voice on the loudspeaker mechanically echoes 4,000, 4,500, 6,000, 6,500, 7,000, 8,000, while Brûlé hits the volleys back, determined to own this chair and offer the highest bid.

'Sold at 10,000,' we hear a distant voice, as the woman on the phone says: 'You got it.'

It is all over in two minutes and Brûlé is beaming, the proud owner of a new chair, showing us the photo in the catalogue. He thanks the woman in Stockholm, saying that he will be there in

---

[331] Tyler Brûlé in personal interview, June 2000; all quotes from interview.
[332] *American Gigolo*, 1980, directed by Paul Schraeder. Gere plays a male escort to older women in the Los Angeles area. He wears great suits, part of a lovely, colour-coordinated wardrobe.

person tomorrow to bid for the other chairs and tables he has ear-marked. He tells us he has just bought a house in Sweden and is furnishing it from afar through these auctions. 'They've really got nice pieces and it's good value,' he says, while we marvel at the speed and efficiency of this transaction. Even more to the point, though: what a beautiful example of peripheral space! Never mind lugging boxes home from Ikea or walking around antiques mar-kets; sit back wherever you are and furnish your house.

The point about peripheral space as we define it is that it emphasises the relentless intrusion of shopping into spaces that are initially entirely independent of the world of retail – Brûlé was in his office, but he could have been on the tennis court in Connecticut, in the dining rooms of the Sultan of Brunei or watch-ing performance art in Reykjavík's National Gallery of Iceland. That's the mobile 'revolution'.

But there is also a revolution in social and cultural spaces – the-atres, concert halls and, most of all, museums. They are no longer simply dedicated to art; they also offer shopping opportunities, sometimes entire retail malls, such as at the Louvre in Paris. Similarly, train stations, bus terminals, airports and petrol stations are now all cluttered with kiosks, boutiques; they are combined with malls and department stores or supermarkets – to such an extent that it is hard to distinguish what the function of the space is, travel or shopping? (One of the latest wheezes of charter airlines is 'scratch-cards', ostensibly for 'charity'; they nevertheless distract enough restless travellers to part with money in return for a five-second *frisson*.) In the museum, what is more important, seeing the original in the gallery or taking home the reproduction, be it in the form of a £500 lithograph, an ash tray, a poster or a postcard? An inversion of values takes place as retailisation enters the peripher-al space, taking up visitors' attention and distracting them from the essence of the program, whether it is travel, art or sport, and mak-ing them consumers of multiple messages and consciously desirous of more than one satisfaction.

Retailisation's colonisation of space, its movement into areas that were formerly entirely unrelated, such as education, arts, travel and sports and, most recently, the little-explored domain of virtual space, is seen by retailers as a necessity, a move to satisfy the increasingly demanding customer – or is that the demanding share-holder or trustee? It is retailing through hybrid channels in a vari-ety of formats, going beyond retail in the classic physical locations to spaces in between the high street, the edge of town and the home, which fills the interstices that were until now free from retail. From a consumer's point of view the move into the periph-ery makes retail both more accessible and inescapable – kiosks, touch-screens in communal spaces, shops where once there was merely a ticket office, mobile phones, PDAs[333] – the list is endless and will grow as technologies and retailers combine in ever more elaborate ways. Even now, as we illustrated in chapter 1, advertising has reached the bathroom; how long before we can relieve ourselves not just of our bodily fluids, but also of some more money as we 'take a leak'?

Opinions differ as to whether retail is a magnetic force in peripheral space, used to attract audiences towards one form of art, cinema or transport, or whether it is parasitically attaching itself to such programs, unable to sustain itself alone. The Dutch architect Rem Koolhaas believes the latter is true and that we are fundamentally bored with shopping. He sees the colonisation of peripheral space as 'the death knell of a big animal' that is 'threatening to trample every activity in its agony' with retailers associating themselves with other programmes to continue drawing customers. 'What was in the beginning a single band that was dissociated from living or from working is now becoming an infiltrating device, a fungus, that is part of any other activity known to man,' he says, describing it as a 'fundamental impurity' in architectural programs.[334] Similarly the writer Umberto Eco complains that even the domain of high art has been 'contaminated' by the presence of the museum gift shop, which sells copies of originals as though they were originals.[335]

Others would argue the opposite, that shopping is a catalyst that energises other elements of what are increasingly multimedia, multifunctional, mixed-use projects – projects that combine residential, office and commercial space. Thus Jon Jerde, designer of the largest mall in the United States[336] and projects like Universal City Walk in Los Angeles, believes the consumer space serves to reconnect humans with each other and that it is the secret to the success of any urban regeneration project. Property developers are also keen to involve a retail element in new developments or regeneration projects, partly because it is a guaranteed way of financing other parts of the development like housing, and partly because it will attract the public. Thus the regeneration of London's South Bank, the area around the Royal Festival Hall and the Hayward Gallery, combines the improvement and expansion of cultural facilities, the construction of new bridges and access routes, and a plan to 'Bring Streets to Life' by creating 'attractive street-level shops and

---

333 Personal Digital Assistants are hand-held units, which include diaries, notebooks and, in the most advanced types, modems allowing users to send emails.
334 Rem Koolhaas, 'Start Again' lecturevideo, Berlage Institute in Amsterdam, 7 March 2000.
335 Umberto Eco, *Travels in Hyperreality*, translated by William Weaver (New York: Harcourt Brace, 1990).
336 The Mall of America in Minneapolis.

cafés mixing arts and commercial use'.[337] In London's Canary Wharf development all that remains to cement its fixture as a 'must-visit' location, not just for the businesspeople, the newspaper reporters and the advertising executives who work there, but for all of us, is a new breed of peripheral space: touch screens offering restaurant booking, transportation and theatre ticket sales. It can't be long. Not now there is the utter splendour of the highly architectural Jubilee Line tube extension to Canary Wharf.

But how does retail in peripheral space differ from that in other spaces? Its association with other events and locations changes its nature to the extent that it has to adapt to the space it stands within or beside. This initial subordination to the adjacent 'program', as architects would call it, is often reversed at later stages when retail starts taking precedence – drawing more revenue or becoming the main attraction to the place. Thus airport shopping has now become so important to the revenue of airports that it generates up to half if not more of the total income.[338] Similarly, in New York the Museum of Modern Art's (MoMA)'s design store and museum store are so successful that a second store has been opened in SoHo, selling designer furniture and art books independently, while using the MoMA brand to sell their collection.

Shopping's association with other programs also makes consumers regard it differently. The act of consumption is disguised, put in the background. Thus while Disney theme parks are meant to be about fun and entertainment, they are in fact shopping experiences. The fantasy surroundings provide the consumer with narratives that blur the distinction between consumption and experience so that the actual act of consumption does not need to be acknowledged.[339] One of the (many) utter failures of the Millennium Dome project in London was that after the initial high outlay to get inside retail opportunities were left to so-so food outlets (McDonald's leading the way both physically and odour-wise) and a shop-full of cheesy mementos; the busy, trance-inducing (but the wrong kind of trance) exhibits had no adjacent retail or, we would have to say, cultural value.

The nature of shopping in peripheral space varies according to the event it is associated with. Thus, the shopping carried out in a station or an airport will be more tense and rushed – even if the

---

[337] 'Opening up the South Bank', information brochure published by the South Bank Centre and The British Film Institute, Spring 2000.
[338] In the case of Schiphol Airport in Amsterdam, the relationship between income from core business (such as aircraft landing rights) and retail in 2000 was being boosted from 50%–50% to 40%–60% in favour of retail. The spend per passenger at Schiphol Airport was £13.8 in 1999. At Heathrow, average sales totalled US$524.1 in 1995, or US$22.5 per passenger.
[339] Steven Miles, *Consumerism as a Way of Life* (London: Sage Publications, 1998).

consumer–traveller has time to spare – than in a museum book-shop where the experience takes on an almost virtuous value, as it is tinted with interest in culture or science. How so much better to walk away from Tate Modern in London with a print of a Bill Viola video installation or a Tate Modern t-shirt than without one. How so much better to walk away from the Rose Centre Planetarium in New York or NASA in Houston with a couple of packets of 'moon food' tucked into our Prada bag than without them. How so much better to leave Old Trafford with an embroidered framed facsimile of David Beckham than without one – even if his hair is wrong. How much better, now, to buy one at Beckham's new club stadium in Madrid!

The turnover of these peripheral retail spaces is often equal to or higher than that of prime retail space on the high street or in shopping centres. Thus income per square foot at Amsterdam's Schiphol Airport lies between £1,200 and £1,650 per square foot per year, while the new bookstore at Tate Modern at Bankside aims to boost retail revenue from £1,000 to £2,000 per square foot. The Metropolitan Museum of Modern Art in New York yields the highest income of any space in Manhattan, ahead of any *haute couture* boutique on Madison Avenue, let alone the run-of-the-mill suburban shopping centre. The difference in income per square foot in peripheral and 'pure' retail spaces also reflects the higher concentration of retail in peripheral spaces – there is usually less space to display the items and therefore a higher yield per square foot. At the same time, the higher concentration of goods in a small area makes it more tempting to shop, as the Japanese retailer Don Quijote has illustrated in its Tokyo outlet, which has become as much of a late-night hangout as any of the *karaoke* bars or restaurants by narrowing the aisles in the shop and encouraging spending urges among customers.[340]

The blurring of boundaries between retail and non-retail functions has been observed by cultural critics and theorists such as Jean Baudrillard and George Ritzer.[341] They describe it as 'implosion', a process in which boundaries of 'formerly differentiated entities collapse in on each other'. We have already explored how this affects the home; now we venture outdoors but don't quite make it to what was formerly known as the high street.

A series of such explosions has taken place in the area of retailisation, in a kind of chain reaction that has resulted in a 're-

---

[340] Naoko Nakamae, 'Keeping shoppers amused is key to success: Japanese retailer Don Quijote uses an imaginative new approach to boost sales in the face of recession', *Financial Times*, 21 December 1999, p. 28; see also chapter 3.
[341] Jean Baudrillard, *Consumer Society* (London: Sage Publications, 1998); George Ritzer, *Enchanting a Disenchanted World* (Thousand Oaks, California: Pine Forge Press, 1999).

enchanted world of consumption seemingly without borders or limits'. Thus malls offer a range of goods, services and experiences that were only recently available in separate spaces and Las Vegas, formerly a place one visited exclusively to gamble, now combines shopping malls, casinos and theme park attractions in single spaces like MGM Grand or Circus Circus. Jean Baudrillard defines implosion as 'the contraction of one phenomenon into another; the collapse of traditional poles into one another',[342] often blurring into a single huge undifferentiated mass. Everything is Everything, you see. Lauren Hill is right.

Come fly with me

'Think 10 years back to the time when an airport was a functional device where there was the shortest possible distance between entry and the gate and the trajectory between the two had maximum clarity.' Rem Koolhaas is lecturing a group of postgraduate students at Amsterdam's Berlage Institute, elaborating on the idea that shopping is spreading parasitically through all architectural spaces. He looks at the evolution of airports over the last 10 years, saying that what used to be a straight path is now a path extended past incredible intricacies, where the horizon is systematically blocked, where one cannot see the exits and the whole infrastructure is overgrown by shopping. This is, in Koolhaas' shopping lexicon, 'junk space', a space so cluttered with retail outlets, a 'crust of unclarity', that the observer can't make sense of the infrastructure of the space or the design. One of the features of Koolhaas' junk space is that it is incredibly ambitious and spatially rich, but at the same time, utterly unmemorable.

Airports like Stansted are a perfect example of junk space, crammed with visual noise in the form of kiosks, ads, coffee shops and signage posts, so that the underlying logic of the building becomes illegible. Because of the lack of coherence in these spaces passengers lose orientation, and eventually this can put them off shopping – even if it is tax-free. One answer, which Virgin Airlines has already adopted, is to book your duty-free on the Web and pick it up as you enter – or indeed leave – the aeroplane. Another comes from the Dutch architectural practice, UN Studio. This practice is working with the concept of 'inclusiveness', which aims to integrate a maximum number of functions in mixed-use spaces. Thus, their project for the redesign of the central railway and bus station in the provincial town of Arnhem in the Netherlands integrates functions like kiosks and small shops in the initial design. 'The main architectural goal behind our approach is to get rid of

---

[342] Ritzer, *Enchanting a Disenchanted World*, p. 153.

the clutter in places like Stansted and Schiphol,' says Caroline Bos, one of UN Studio's directors. 'Spaces that started off as beautiful, empty expanses have been cluttered up with kiosks, stands and other junk that conceals the building itself.'[343] If only they could have had a hand at the conception of London's Millennium Dome – perhaps second time around?

Clarity is paramount in retail spaces in airports, argues Johan van Streun, the Manager of Commercial Business at Schiphol airport in Amsterdam: 'When the passenger passes through the passport control gates he should be able to see immediately where everything is. With one look it should be clear that the perfume is *there*, the cigarettes are *there* and the jewellery is *there*.' He explains that shopping at airports is inherently different from shopping in the high street:

"The main aim of the visit to the airport is still flying, and therefore shoppers at an airport will still always have a certain tenseness, worrying about being on time, missing their flight. It's not like destination shopping; there is time pressure here, a certain stress, which means that the passenger will first make planned purchases and only afterwards, if there is time to spare, look around and browse and perhaps make impulse purchases. If the configuration of the space is not immediately clear to the passenger he will not put much effort into browsing or searching and go straight to the departure gate."[344]

Historically, retail at airports developed because of the price advantage that the tax-free zone behind the passport control could offer. Goods were 17.5 per cent cheaper than on the high street. However, since the European Union's Schengen Agreement has been implemented (in June 1999), the major European airports have been suffering losses rising to 90 per cent in countries like Germany and 66 per cent in the United Kingdom, as only non-EU passengers can benefit from tax-free rates. Still, at Schiphol Airport retail has become the core business,[345] while Heathrow has adapted to the new conditions by introducing special offer campaigns, such as 40 per cent off perfumes. And, with a bottle of whisky being sold every seven seconds on average, business isn't altogether bad. Globally, airport retailing revenue was estimated at US $3.4 billion in 1995 rising to US $7.2 billion by 2005.[346] With such astronomical figures, one would almost begin to wonder whether this still is peripheral space – they are certainly not peripheral earnings.

---

[343] Caroline Bos in personal interview, January 2000.
[344] Johan van Streun in personal interview, May 2000; all quotes from this interview.
[345] Schiphol still offers preferential rates to all passengers regardless whether they are from the European Union or not.
[346] Paul Freathy and Frank O'Connell, *European Airport Retailing* (Basingstoke: Macmillan Press, 1998), p. 32.

Imploding functions further, Schiphol – which has always aimed to offer more than just standard duty-free and the classic Dutch tulip bulbs – now also boasts a grown-up casino and a hotel. 'The casino caters to the passenger who has shopped, eaten and drunk and still has time to spare,' says Streun.

In Dublin's fair city, where the fans are so pretty

Manchester United, the hugely successful English football team, does not merely employ the services of English footballers. Indeed, its proud recent history is testament to its growing financial clout in buying some of the best players in the world (though not The Best, that privilege resides with the privately owned Italian and Spanish soccer sides, and, perhaps, Chelsea, basking in the largesse of their multi-billionaire owners). Ireland, both north and south, has long been a fruitful source of great United players – from the north, the legendary George Best, Sammy McIlroy and Norman Whiteside – from the south, heroes include current skipper, Roy Keane, and 1968 European Cup winner, Shay Brennan (even though the latter was born in Manchester). It is no surprise, then, that leaving Dublin's fair city by air involves not only a *flanêur*-style stroll through a shopping mall full of Irish merchandise, but also the opportunity to buy from a Manchester United retail outlet. The store is placed almost last in the mall and must be passed to reach the departure lounges for most European flights. Inside, the football strip, videos and books look out with Beckham-like sheen on to the music store opposite where Ireland's finest musical ambassadors (after U2, Riverdance and Daniel O'Donnell), the Corrs, gaze wistfully from point-of-sale posters. Ah, you think, if only David had married Andrea Corr the world would be a quieter place. Now, with Beckham gone to Madrid, United look to Keane, Ryan Giggs or the latest new star for its merchandising success.

Haven't you got any change? Or, Sorry mate, I'm going East

Meanwhile, in a black cab depot in East London, Peter de Coster is very pleased with himself. He has pinpointed the ultimate time

– London's near-continuous rush hour – and space – the back of a black cab – in which the consumer can be captured and lured into retailisation.

Passengers, however busy or rushed they are, are trapped with nothing to do but phone their secretary to say they are late and sigh in frustration at the congestion around them. So what better way to pass traffic-jam time than zapping between television channels and shopping? Believing that 'travel and boredom go together too often', Peter de Coster has designed a system, Cabvision, which he describes as 'traveltainment made by cabbies'. This comes in the form of a small television placed behind the driver's seat, which is passenger-controlled by remote-control panels in the arm rests. Four channels are on offer at present: Technology, 'because everyone is interested in it today'; Business, 'for the city types'; Lifestyle, 'for the ladies' (who make up 40 per cent of the passengers); and the London shopping channel, for everyone. Each of these channels caters to a particular audience. 'While we were putting it all together we constantly thought about what people would want. I kept thinking: "What would I want if I was a bum on that cab seat?" We had to think about bums on seats and also who these bums were. Because, for all of people's perception, tourists are not the main cab users.'[347]

With investment from silicon.com, Compaq, BT, Jaguar, Calvin Klein, sharepeople.com and Harrods, a trial version of Cabvision was launched in 100 cars around London. De Coster had the idea 15 years ago, but was unable to implement it in the old black cab models. It was only in 1997, with the introduction of the new design award-winning, TX1 model,[348] that de Coster saw his chance to fit a decent-sized television screen into the passenger space. Content includes travel, entertainment and listings information and is composed of four five-minute mini-programmes, which are updated once a month. 'With the average cab ride being about 20 minutes, we knew we had to have strong content that would captivate the audience. It had to be punchy, quick and well-rounded,' Coster explains. Anecdotal evidence – well, we heard about this from another cabbie who was trialling the technology – suggests that the system works: he told us of the American tourists who had landed at Heathrow 15 miles to the west of central London and insisted on going straight to the Marble Arch Marks & Spencer, which was being shown on the Cabvision screen, rather than to their hotel in Chiswick some eight miles from the airport.

[347] Peter de Coster in personal interview, June 2000.
[348] The TX1 model was also selected as a 'Millennium Product', one the 1,012 products designated by Tony Blair's Labour government as deserving of the title because of its design excellence.

While the technology is currently still on trial, Cabvision also has a further vision and is planning into the future, waiting for technology to catch up with de Coster's ideas. He wants to connect the cabs to the Internet using GSM-based mobile connections, creating a sort of moving network: 'Ideally we would like to download images from the Internet, really connect the cabs up, but at the moment that would just take too long. That's two years away. What we are looking at developing is an intranet, our own Internet which will give information on shops, restaurants, theatres.'

This system would then allow the passenger to arrive at Heathrow, get into a cab, browse through the theatre programme and book tickets on the spot – perhaps even printing out the tickets in the front with the ubiquitous 'chit' for the finance director. De Coster's idea may have been born small in an East London cab company, but he is planning to expand far beyond, first to Edinburgh and other British cities, and then the world. 'The theory behind it is that we install Cabvision around the country and then the world,' he says. 'Edinburgh has already expressed an interest: it is very comparable to London in that it is a fast-growing financial district with a large tourist trade; in the United States, where the Internet and buying online is more customary, there will also definitely be a market.' Imagine the possibilities, too, in Cairo or Bangkok; Tokyo or Rome. Cabvision is not just a great idea, it is a great reason not to have to talk to the cabbie.

And, forgetting the cab for a moment, what of the humble car? It is not just the Volkswagen group that has high hopes for new approaches to the selling and branding of automobiles. The latest Ford Windstar car available in the United States comes with the option of a console with colour television, VCR – make that DVD – and Nintendo nestled between the two front seats, facing the back-seat passengers. 'Entertainment centres, once strictly for the home, have hit the road, turning the minivan or sports utility vehicle into a family den on wheels. Since October 1999, when the television–VCR combination became a factory option, studies have shown it to be a high-demand accessory, said Frank Forkin, a partner in the automobile marketing and research firm J.D. Power & Associates in Detroit,' reported the *New York Times* in June 2000. It doesn't end there: the paper also reported that 'Chevrolet expected sales of a special-edition Warner Brothers Venture van, which features a television along with the company's logo and an image of Bugs Bunny, to account for about *10 per cent of Venture's sales for the 2000 model year*' [our italics].[349]

---

[349] Roy Furchgott, 'Where the TV room meets the road', *New York Times* Circuits, G1, 15 June 2000, Circuits p. G1.

The boredom-of-children factor is clearly at play here: Sony-In-Car TV replicates the consoles that almost entertain us on long-haul flights. The system allows children to watch movies via a portable DVD player or play Sony PlayStation games – and the sound is relayed via infra-red, cordless headphones. Entertainment – passive entertainment – has been leaping out from the home since the 1920s. Radio, eight-track cartridges (the boo.com of tape recorder formats), cassettes and CDs have all made the spatial jump to the car. Even televisions. (The first television installed in a car was in 1953. George Barris, known to some as King of the Kalifornia Kustomizers for his artistic car modifications, said he installed the first television in the 1953 Golden Sahara, a bubble-topped vehicle used in the Jerry Lewis movie *Cinderfella*.)[350] But it is with interactive services that the car really takes off. Talking to the editor of *Revolution* magazine,[351] Stovin Hayter (in the bar with the speaking urinal advertisements described in chapter 1), he mused: 'In 10 years time, you can imagine not buying a car, but getting one free with the services you buy.'[352]

Leading the way in this area is General Motors (GM) with its OnStar service. Originally conceived as a hands-free mobile service, which drivers could use if they had an accident, it has evolved to help them with directions, and now with bookings. So, for example, if you were driving from Tampa to Miami you could – while driving there – phone up to book a hotel, a restaurant and a ticket for the Jennifer Lopez concert. OnStar is but the beginning. Ford and GM have announced they will both partner with major Web companies in the near future, Ford with Yahoo!, the search engine and Internet provider. Ford Chief Executive, Jac Nasser, said: 'All future Ford models will be "communication tools". It means nothing short of a total reinvention of this company.'[353] Nasser was also reported in the *New York Times* with an even more grandiose vision: 'Henry Ford put the world on wheels in the 20th century. In the new century Ford Motor Company will put the Internet on wheels.'[354]

Meanwhile, GM is to work with America Online (AOL), and it doesn't stop there. Sirius Satellite Radio, which uses satellites to 'broadcast' to cars (navigation systems for now) plans to work with a company called ATX Technologies to 'let drivers buy the music

---

[350] Cinderella has always been a great – if inverted – tale of high-heeled retail. In this version, made in 1960, Jerry Lewis is the star and the film a farce. So all bets are off here.
[351] *Revolution* is a monthly media magazine.
[352] Stovin Hayter in personal interview, June 2000.
[353] Tim Burt and Nikki Tait, 'Ford and GM plan ahead for the online car'. *Financial Times*.
[354] Matthew L Wald, 'On the road. , on the web., in danger?' *New York Times*, Automobiles section, 10 March 2000, Automobiles p. F1.

they heard on the radio, ordering it as they drove'. As Professor William Mitchell at MIT told us: 'The automobile industry presents huge retailing potential, as connection to networks means you can deliver services and information to drivers. The items will mainly be guidance information and safety advice, i.e. intangibles.'[355] What he forgets is that Britney Spears record you could buy; that networked game of BloodBath Seven you could compete with on the car's PlayStation; that meal at the 'lovely French place' in Miami. What he forgets is retailisation in peripheral spaces.

Retailisation of the highway, motorway and its peripheries has been taking place ever since petrol stations started selling not just petrol and chocolate bars but everything from meals to be consumed in the adjacent restaurant to arcade games, books, magazines, car accessories and ready meals. Erik van der Meer, Shell's Marketing Manager, spends most of his time trying to invent new ways to attract people to Shell petrol stations. He says offering petrol and diesel isn't enough any more – petrol stations are increasingly 'logistic nodes' where people and goods meet. The next step was made when Shell started offering free Internet access: in most Shell stations you can now pick up free CD-ROMs, which give free Internet access. While Shell is not entirely sure how offering free Internet access fits in the portfolio of an oil company, van der Meer believes there are plenty of opportunities: as the Internet becomes a more integral part of people's lives, e-commerce and mobile communications will develop as well. 'We are constantly looking for new ways to attract customers. E-commerce could be part of that; we may become a link in the distribution of products bought on the Web,' he says.[356]

The concept of 'traveltainment' for taxis, cars, utility vehicles, or whatever, is often inspired by the developments in in-flight entertainment, particularly those evolved for boring, long-haul flights. The aeroplane is the perfect peripheral retail space – a trapped, bored group of people, some of whom will have arrived late at the airport and missed their airport mall splash. Here is an example of the rather 'classical' offerings from a British Airways long-haul shopping catalogue: 'Why do so many people choose to buy from *Shopping the World?*[357] The answer is simple: all the goods featured represent a superb choice, excellent quality and great value for money.'[358] And, if you pay using your British Airways charge card or credit card you can 'double your AIR MILES AWARD, by earning them on both your Executive Club Card and your BA charge or credit card'. There are

---

[355] William Mitchell, SARA, in personal interview, March 2000.
[356] Jochen van Barschot, 'Globaal denken, lokaal handelen', *NRC Handelsblad*, 28 December 1999, Economy p. 19.
[357] British Airways' in-flight shopping magazine.
[358] *Shopping the World*, March/April 2000.

gift ideas: everything from Lancôme skin de-stressing hydrations to teddy bears and Ray-Ban Elite sunglasses. There are perfumes and sun cares, there are watches and jewels; there are ties, pens and scarves; there are Walkmen and Psion Organisers, alarm clocks and toothbrushes; there are kids' things and model aircraft, bumper packs of Toblerone and cigarettes, and that old business-flight arrival dependable, the bottle of Gordon's Gin.

Meanwhile, at funkier rivals Virgin Atlantic, the in-flight shopping tone is somewhat different. Its catalogue is called *Retail Therapy*. Its strapline is not the somewhat colonial 'shopping the world' but 'Come on, you know you need it!' While the goods are not especially different in their range and scope – perfumes, watches, dark glasses, kids' stuff, booze and fags – they are younger and more trendy, everything from a tartan 'Daba Doo Small Animal Carrier' exclusive to Virgin Atlantic, and 'new generation' Furbys.[359] What sets *Retail Therapy* apart is its commitment to a kind of lifestyle journalism amid the products. All Saint pop star, Natalie Appleton, writes about her favourite smells; athlete Iwan Thomas on posing nude for women's magazines; Habitat's Head of Design, Tom Dixon, on why he loves American design; Paula Reed, style director of Condé Nast *Traveller*, on the international fashion circuit; James Dyson of vacuum cleaner fame on voice-activated technologies, and so on. In short, it is a mail-order catalogue for air passengers who are, as David Peek would say, 'people like us'. If we are young, style-interested, and a shopper, that is.

As communications technology improves and we no longer have to 'turn off all mobile phones and laptop computers' at take-off, we will be able to access the Web from the air. Here, the possibilities for retail are immense. Imagine being able, while in flight, to book the cab to pick you up on arrival, or to book that hotel room in Miami. Up, up and away in my beautiful, er, virtual shop. It is coming.

> **Cruise ships, the peripheral retail spaces of the ocean *par excellence*, are about to enter a new era as a new addition is made to the world's fleet. After the Disney cruise liner, a floating immersive Mickey Mouse experience, the new *Freedom Ship* will soon be navigating the oceans, catering not to pensioners and holidaymakers but to anyone. That is, anyone who wants to live on a**

[359] Film stars and retail wonders at the same time, the Furbys, reminiscent of the Star Trek brigade, have a new 'baby'. It has 'special baby-like personalities and baby vocabularies of more than 150 Furbish and English phrases ... They learn to speak faster than adults and have wider vocabularies ... (Please note, we cannot guarantee which colour Baby Furby you will receive in-flight.)' *Retail Therapy*, March 2000.

cruise ship 365 days a year, run their business from there, send their kids to school and later university on it and, best of all, not pay taxes. *Freedom Ship* will be a floating city of 40,000 people, with 20,000 homes, a school, a university, a hospital, a landing strip, a casino, 200 acres of open space and, of course, a shopping mall. Home prices range from $150,000 for a small apartment to $40 million for something a bit more spacious. Costing a total of $9 billion, the ship is being built in Honduras and will be nearly a mile long, 725 feet wide and 340 feet high. Roger Gooch, the Marketing Vice-President for the venture, hopes the vessel will become a 'global environment', with a mixture of nationalities and ages; it was not to be seen as a retirement cruise ship but more as a place where people could run businesses and raise their children. This then is not just taking retail into the peripheral space but into an entire town. [360]

Stand up if you hate Man U, Stand up if you hate Man U [361]

There are a huge number of girders being moved outside the stadium at Old Trafford; industrial trucks, too, are testament to the continuing growth of the ground. Inside at reception Manchester United TV 'MUTV' is showing a re-run of the triumphant 1999 European Champions League final victory over Bayern Munich. The first time an English soccer club had won something important for almost a decade. We have to wait for a while to meet our interviewee: 'He's with the Japanese people,' we are told. There is a long-standing joke about Manchester United that when the team won the UEFA Champions league in 1999 the bus-top reception shouldn't have taken place in Manchester, but in Bangkok or Sydney 'where the real fans are'.

In the unexpectedly modest office of Steve Richards, Managing Director of Merchandising at Manchester United, there are various icons scattered around. Not all are dedicated to his company or 'team', Manchester United, the most successful English football club of the 1990s.[362] There is a Darth Vader (the bad guy from *Star*

---

[360] Duncan Campbell, 'Nearly a mile long and 40,000 on board – the first floating city', *Guardian*, 6 May 2000, p. 22.

[361] Song usually chanted by the home fans at Manchester United's away matches when they come on to the pitch. (There are other chants as well, but these were deemed unsuitable for this readership.)

[362] In March 2000 it became the first football club to be valued at more than £1 billion. Matthew Garrahan, 'Man Utd breaks through £1bn barrier', *Financial Times*, 9 March 2000, Companies and Markets p. 26.

Wars), *South Park* memorabilia and a miniature All Blacks (the usually all-conquering New Zealand Rugby team) shirt. There are also framed cards of all of Manchester United's captains going back into prehistory, their images captured as if a Soviet propagandist artist circa 1922 was painting them.

Richards does not look like a football man; he looks like a retailer. He is. He began his working life at Marks & Spencer, worked at the tailors, Burtons, and was for two years managing director of the sportswear chain, All Sports. 'We're not like a normal football team – the core of the business will always be the football – but because of the hype, the history,[363] it colours the way we do things. We don't benchmark ourselves against other sides [football teams], we want to provide the best entertainment experience; be like *Star Wars*, Disneyland.'[364] Richards maintains that 'Manchester United has no barriers to entry, it's for all ages and for any creed' – though there are thought to be pockets of resistance in Liverpool and Leeds. No longer looking to rival teams for 'economic' competition', he allies his 'brand' with rivals such as Nike or Disney. Richards starts with the 'kids', the 'broadest appeal' for the club. Manchester United's retailing is positively Jesuitical here, never mind the 'give me a child at seven and we'll have him for life', this is virtually a cradle-snatching opportunity, one that would make Disney, or Gap for Kids, proud. Understanding utterly the importance of the domestic house, Manchester United has segmented the entire kids' 'home' experience. 'We follow them around,' Richards acknowledges. 'In the bedroom we have pyjamas, bedding, wallpaper, lights, alarm clocks.' That is to say, everything from the Fred the Red[365] romper suits in sizes 0–3 to 12–18 for children 18–24 months, through Fred the Red slippers, purses, fleece hats, scarves and mittens, to the 'Large Fred the Red Duvet' cover and pillowcase set, the 'Red Crest Fitted Valance set', the curtains and wallpaper, the 'Theatre of Dreams Duvet cover and pillowcase set', the lampshade or uplighter (for the classier touch, Tom Dixon would be proud), the

---

[363] A very brief history of Manchester United. 1877 formed as Lancashire and Yorkshire Railway Newton Heath, changed name to Manchester United in 1901. 1909 moved to Old Trafford. In 1958 11 Manchester United players and staff, and eight journalists, died in the Munich Air Disaster when the plane bringing them home from a European cup-tie quarter-final in Belgrade crashed after a refuelling stop in Munich. Ten years later, in 1968, Manchester United won the European Cup at Wembley, London. Manager Matt Busby, who nearly perished in the Munich air crash, was knighted by the Queen for services to football. In 1999, 31 years after its sole European triumph, United won again, this time in Barcelona, beating the German side Bayern Munich thanks to two goals in the last minute. Manager Alex Ferguson followed in Matt Busby's footsteps and was knighted in the Queen's Birthday honours list.

[364] Steve Richards in personal interview, May 2000; all quotes from this interview.

[365] Fred the Red is Manchester United's children's mascot, a little red creature with 'friendly' horns and an endearing little snout.

'Pop Tidy' – 'expands from flat for easy storage of clothes, toys and lots, lots more ...', the mini hi-fi, and the 'Red Crest & Star Bean Bag'. There are also dressing gowns, short or long pyjamas, 'child' and 'youth' slippers. And the 'Panelled Hat and Bootee Set'.

Richards continues. 'The bathroom ...': this means the towels – emblazoned with 'Beckham', 'Giggs', the crest or the pitch. 'Breakfast...': here we find many mugs, plates and bowls. 'School...': here we are looking at a variety of bags, from holdalls, through backpacks, drawstring bags and boot bags (in both the traditional Manchester United 'red' and its away strip 'black'). We are looking at watches, pen packs, pencil cases, notebook sets, an 'art' pack (presumably dedicated to David Beckham's passing ability), and a ring binder. 'Then there's lunch ...': lunchboxes, water bottles, 'sports' bottles, chocolate. 'Play – outdoors ...': footballs, t-shirts, hooded fleece tops, swimwear, 'pop-up tent', and 'Goalie Gloves'. 'Play – indoors ...': interactive Manchester United and 'I Support Manchester United' software; computer screensavers of the top players, mouse mats in the shape of the United crest; two hand-held computer games, 'Manchester United Subbuteo and Monopoly' and, for the very youngest, a range of Teddy Bears, though not one of Teddy Sheringham, once a United striker. Then are the books – every player seems to have 'written' an autobiography; both manager Sir Alex Ferguson and captain Roy Keane have seen theirs at the top of the hard-back bestseller lists in the United Kingdom – and the encyclopaedia, the *Official Annual*, and the *Complete Fact Book*. For the television there are videos galore, and for Sky Digital viewers a Manchester United television channel. (Right now it can't show live games.) We ask why not cereals or food? 'For every sector we provide for, we have to ask ourselves, "Do we have any right to be in that sector?" Right now with cereals we don't have the trust,' Richards says, 'but Kelloggs do.' Only a matter of time, then.

This plethora of retail goodies is available via mail-order, from the Old Trafford shop and the many other Manchester United shops around the world, and from a host of high street retailers: Woolworth, Argos, Debenhams. They are also available via the website. 'We're more proactive on the net,' Richards tells us. There is also access via the Open platform on interactive television and with new sponsors Vodaphone (one of the largest global mobile phone operators), no doubt via mobile phones, WAP phones and third generation units.

Is this classical retailing, is this branding, or is this peripheral space selling with multiple channels to buy? Who knows? We are reminded of the Chief Executive of Selfridges, Vittorio Radice, and his 'You go because you want to be in this fantastic place and the fact that you come out with a shopping bag is just automatic. You want to take a piece of this place home with you.' Not everyone can get to see Manchester United live – its games are invariably sold out and season tickets are like gold dust. So there are television, media and retail. 'We are a bricks and clicks company,' Richards says. His office floor is strewn with Manchester United retail building plans for 'China, Japan and Singapore'. He talks of retail partners in 'South-East Asia, South Africa, the Republic of Ireland and the Middle East'. There are 'big plans': 'four stores in London, the Café in Manchester, Dubai, Singapore, 15,000 square feet in Dublin, and Kuala Lumpur'.

Richards' retail experience means that United – often criticised for the speed at which they change their strip, or football kit, forcing parents to buy yet another 'official' shirt for their obsessed children – are all about attempting at least to follow 'best practice'; in this they are very Disney-like. It is no surprise that six months after this interview took place Manchester United signed a kit deal with Nike reputed to be worth £301 million over 15 years.

This 'best practice' mentality is lit all over Richards' responses. 'Even two years ago you could "brand slap" Manchester United on something and sell stuff,' he says. In the highly successful 1996/97 season, for example, United sold over a million replica shirts – and that's the official number – the copies and fakes probably triple this figure. 'Consumers are smart now, they are not content with second best.'

For we have not yet explored Manchester United's retailing to groups other than children. There is the 'Manchester United Collection' of fashion clothes. Modelled by the team members these wouldn't look out of place in Bluewater or at an 'Indie' music gig. There are t-shirts, shirts, Harrington jackets, cargo pants, twill chinos, shower jackets with very discreet branding, alongside the more overt football kit influenced clothes: sweatshirts, tops, fleeces, polo shirts and t-shirts. There are medallions celebrating famous victories, there are prints – oil paintings – of the top stars and, finally, there are, er, tickets to the games. Now those are one for a very good auction. 'Manchester United doesn't even have to win *everything*,' says Richards. 'It will always be a great brand.'

Another group that does *have* to win to be even a halfway awful brand is the England soccer team. The Football Association has to deal not only with its national team's perennial failure at major championships, but with the diabolical behaviour of its 'minority' of fans. Euro 2000 was a classic example of how England's finest players have consistently been let down by its least fine fans. The FA's commercial manager, David Smith, nevertheless focuses on trying to sell England as a brand and a concept – whoever the manager, and England has had many in the past few years. The latest, in a shock transfer move, is a Swede called Eriksson.

Smith describes the brand of retail products he wants to create:

"It's obvious that people will spend on the brand during championships and World Cups, but we want to create a brand of retail products that people will buy into outside of these peak periods. So we have joined up with several retailers who create in-store areas where they sell England products. During the previous World Cup in 1998, for example, Sainsbury's was the official World Cup store (it wasn't a sponsor but was more successful than many of the official sponsors). They sold licensed products like party packs, which included napkins, tablecloths, cups, a cake, so that children who wanted a football theme party could link their party to the FA. We also sold caps and t-shirts at Sainsbury's and we stretched the brand by going into other food items, like the official England meal', which included a pizza and a drink. We tried to really have fun with the brand so that we made meals that could be prepared during half time … we really tried to stretch it as far as possible…also for example selling 15 million medals through Sainsbury's."[366]

Try telling that to the fans down the pub watching on giant screens, but that is to digress.

Unlike Manchester United, whose fans appear to come from every corner of the earth, England has little appeal in, say, France. Smith describes the club's marketing focus:

"The brand is relatively successful in Canada, the US and in the Far East. It is harder to expand into other countries because we are a national team, not a club like Manchester United, for instance. We do sell, though, as there is a love of the English games in several countries, but we doubt whether we could ever go beyond product sales [which are largely through the Internet]. We are definitely focusing on the English market in terms of marketing. We were way behind in that domain for a long time. Looking at the routes to market we are selling our products through Marks & Spencer, Sainsbury's, JJB. In addition we have launched our own e-commerce site to market directly."

One major opportunity comes in the peripheral space that is – or rather, was – Wembley Stadium. 'This is an important element as well: especially once Wembley closes and England will be "on the road",' says Smith. 'We have our own retail units that can be set up at any game, and the website will also be very important during this period. We are now also looking into the design of a couple of flagship stores, at airports and in Carnaby Street'.

---

[366] David Smith in personal interview; all quotes from interview.

Next step is the 'flagship' store, so beloved of brands that actually mean something, such as Nike or Donna Karan. But the FA plug on, as resolute as 10-man England in their famous 'rearguard' action against Argentina in the 1998, *sans* one David Beckham, sent off for an act of petulance. Smith describes the flagship stores in the following way.

"The idea behind the flagship stores would be to offer the full range of FA products and to make these stores the only places where this can be found. In terms of branding, the flagship stores will be designed to sit above Premier League club merchandise, just as the England team is in another league from Premier League teams [yes, they're worse]. The FA product is more aspirational, and we don't offer the same breadth of merchandise as Man U or Arsenal, for example. We are thinking more along the lines of sunglasses, jewellery, luggage items, but not as overtly branded as Premier league merchandise. We want to sell Englishness on the gift market, so at airports, in Central London, people can buy the FA product as a souvenir or as gifts."

There are shades of Prime Minster Tony Blair's 'cool Britannia', which, though much derided in the United Kingdom, did make other countries notice Britain. England's football team as a global definition of Englishness has often meant hooligans, tattoos and (very) bad dress sense[367]. Smith doesn't agree: 'We are trying to look at the other areas that are not related to fan memorabilia but more to tourism. This is why we are locating ourselves at Heathrow, Gatwick and focusing on customers going on holiday or tourists who want to take home a piece of "Englishness".' The sound you might hear is Vittorio Radice turning in – no falling off – his designer chair at Selfridges HQ. Whether hip New Yorkers, fashionable Brazilians or cool Milanese will ever turn on to 3D England torso shower gel, England 'beach slippers', the 'England Celebration Cake' by Elizabeth the Chef Ltd (celebrating *what?*) or the 'Crowd and Grass Wallpaper with stick and peel England players' by Novasco remains to be seen. Or not.

Museums and art galleries: ready-mades 2000s

There is a perceived polarity (however artificial) between technology and the humanities, between science and art, between right brain and left. The bur-

---

[367] This was not the case in the World Cup of 2002: the combination of Japanese costs, policemen and some strange "transformation" in the psyche of the English fan led to the spectacle of "In-ger-land" supporters being liked, copied by the local fans. In short they had rebranded with some considerable success.   Then again, there's always Germany in 2006 to consider…

geoning field of multimedia is likely to be one of those disciplines, like architecture, that bridges the gap.

Nicholas Negroponte[368]

Art is today bridging another gap – that between the humanities and commerce. Six months before the opening of Tate Modern at Bankside in London, the mission of Tate Publishing was already clearly outlined: to become one of London's leading art bookshops, a destination that people would visit separately from the gallery, just for its fabulous book collection. Tate Retail Director Celia Clear claimed: 'We aim for it to be the best arts bookshop in London ... particularly as Dillon's Art Bookshop has closed down. It will be a feast of books, better than the typical museum bookshop with a sharp focus on books instead of souvenirs and cards.'[369]

Museum shops, retail spaces with one of the highest incomes per square foot, profit from the concept of the 'adjacent attraction', explained in chapter 3, where non-commodified objects add value to commodified objects. Thus, when visitors in the Louvre have just seen the original *Mona Lisa*, many come out of the gallery and want to take a bit of this experience, a tangible memory of the real painting, home with them. The real object will add value to any reproduction, even if it is not a direct copy. In his book *Travels in Hyperreality*[370] Umberto Eco explores how, in high art, the boundaries between original and reproduction have been blurred. Indeed, it is common to see originals, restored versions, reproductions and reconstructions all mixed together in exhibitions. This 'levelling of the past, the fusion of copy and original ... the flattening of real against fake and the old on the modern'[371] is extended into the museum shop where the availability of the reproduction, instead of making consumers want the original, makes them feel the original is less real and valuable. Just as in the hyperreal environments described in chapter 3, here the hyperreal object replaces the real object. 'Life-size scenes in narrative settings increasingly subordinate the thing itself to a dramatic re-creation. With nothing to recommend them except their often shabby authenticity, the real objects simply have less appeal than snappy simulations.'[372]

Taking home souvenirs of an experience is not only part of a desire to remember; the object also becomes a trophy that shows others that one 'has been there'. This also happens in theme pubs

[368] Nicholas Negroponte, *Being Digital* (London: Vintage, 1996), p. 81.
[369] Celia Clear in personal interview, February 2000.
[370] Eco, *Travels in Hyperreality*.
[371] Ibid.
[372] Ada Louise Huxtable, *The Unreal America* (New York: The New Press, 1997), p. 82.

and restaurants where branded badges and t-shirts testify not so much that one has been to the bar but to the town it is in. Hard Rock Cafe t-shirts and badges are today universal, showing off not only the number of towns in which the Cafe is based, but also that the wearer has been there.

So how did high art get the retail bug? The answers are tied up with the changing nature of the museum in the 20th century. As one example we will investigate New York's Museum of Modern Art (MoMA). Its first exhibition in 1929 featured installations co-ordinated by Alfred Barr, the museum's founding director (he didn't choose the work for the 'Cézanne, Gauguin, Seurat, van Gogh' show but he did instal them). As Mary Anne Staniszewski writes: 'Barr's installation method – neutral coloured walls, with paintings hung at a standardised height and with sculptures placed on white or neutral coloured pedestals...isolated the individual art object, creating a one-on-one relationship with the viewer.'[373] She continues: 'Barr envisioned exhibitions diverse in both theme and display methods that would deal with "primitive" and pre-modern art, popular culture, film, architecture, photography, design, and the modernisation of everyday life.'[374]

Barr's take on the curatorial approach was radical for its time. His proposal to the trustees included departments for painting and sculpture, prints and drawings, commercial art, industrial art such as posters, adverts and product packaging, cinema, theatre designs – sets and costumes – and photography. He always demanded a library filled not just with books but also with slides and colour reproductions. In 1941 Barr recollected: 'The plan was radical not so much because it was departmentalised (most large museums are) but because it proposed an active and serious concern with the practical, commercial and popular arts as well as with the so-called "fine arts".' [375] Today as the collisions of new and old media, physical and virtual retail, high and low art take place with giga-speed frequency this might seem quaint. But, with the history of the all-encompassing artistic vision came a new openness to commerce (the artist, van Gogh aside, always has this, of course).[376]

Almost a decade later, in 1938, Barr's MoMA mounted its first 'Useful Objects' exhibition. (In this case they were useful objects under the cost of $5.) 'Low-priced, machine-made, mass-produced

---

[373] Mary Anne Staniszewski, *The Power of Display: A History of Exhibition Installations at the Museum of Modern Art* (London: MIT Press, 1998), p. 70.
[374] Ibid., p. 72.
[375] Ibid., p. 72.
[376] For a thorough exploration of money and art in the Renaissance see Lisa Jardine, *Worldly Goods: A New History of the Renaissance* (New York: Bantam Doubleday Dell, 1996).

household articles were arranged in installations that evoked, in simple minimal style, both store and home.'[377] The show was successful, people came and the press were happy (they had all hated a previous Bauhaus show). The success was two-fold, however. 'Manufacturers and prices had been listed on the exhibition labels. As a result, significant numbers of visitors sought these objects from local distributors, with some consumers requesting them directly from manufacturers. Some wholesalers actually opened new retail exhibitions as a direct result of this exhibition. Manufacturers whose goods were not included in the show contacted the museum, requesting that their wares be selected if there was ever another such exhibition.'[378]

The show 'Organic Design', curated by industrial design director Eliot Noyes in 1940 featured designers' work for Bloomingdale's store in the lead and 12 other stores participating. The stores paid for the production of the work and then could sell them. 'Bloomingdale's Presents Organic Design Furniture and Furnishings ... Created for the World of the Present, Sponsored by the Museum of Modern Art ... Sold Exclusively by Us in New York,' was how the store marketed the show – and itself.

Several 'Useful Objects' later, manufacturers in 1945 were given the MoMA seal of approval, which they could use in their merchandising. As Staniszewski comments: 'The exhibition catalogue, which was distributed nationally, functioned as a consumer purchasing guide for useful things whose price was now capped at $25. The seal, the awards [there were three, described by the director of the Museum's Industrial Design department, as a kind of "Oscar"] and inclusion in the purchasing catalogue were coveted by manufacturers and received much publicity; the seal itself was an aesthetic version of a *Good Housekeeping* seal.'[379, 380]

It is now March 2000. James Gundell is the president of New York's MoMA Retail. He explains, with shades of Steve Richards at Manchester United, that the museum still comes first and that the items sold in MoMA stores have to fit the MoMA brand: 'There is a wealth of intellectual property which leverages the brand. This makes it sensitive. We are not so much in the retail branch as we are in the museum business. The product in the store has to reflect the museum's image.'[381]

Having successfully established two stores on location at MoMA

---

[377] Staniszewski, *The Power of Display*, p. 160.

[378] Ibid., p. 160.

[379] *Good Housekeeping* has a long history of being a shop disguised as a periodical. Think of it as *Wallpaper** without the pretty boys and girls.

[380] Staniszewski, *The Power of Display*, p. 164.

[381] James Gundell in personal interview, March 2000; all quotes from this interview.

on 53rd Street, MoMA Retail is now looking to expand to other locations in Manhattan, the first new location being SoHo, where 6,500 square feet of retail space combine the concepts of the current design and museum stores. 'The decision to move into the downtown area was strongly linked to the fact that the design store had become a destination store and we felt strongly that we could expand the retail base beyond 53rd St into Manhattan and beyond,' says Gundell. The new store includes more furniture and lighting items, art books with a focus on architecture, design, film, photography. 'The greatest part will be design objects, though, modern classics and contemporary design; we want to gain a better understanding of how to bring elements of the museum to the shop in these stores. In the end that's what museum retail is about: bringing elements of the museum home with you.' And thus culture moves into retailisation, selling a designer lifestyle to take home. Gundell still believes there is a difference, saying: 'In the museum you are looking at a single piece, in the stores we bring these elements to a broad public.' A quick glance through the MoMA 'Holiday Gift catalogue 1999' shows us what the public can buy: Le Corbusier chairs, Bauhaus table lamps, Aeron chairs (the Eames chair for the Internet generation) and Frank Lloyd Wright's Plate and Mug sets sit alongside Philippe Stark fly swatters, rubber radios and a CD of 'Jackson Pollock's favourite jazz recordings, including Louis Armstrong, Jelly Roll Morton and Coleman Hawkins'. Not to mention the less 'design'-style merchandise, such as umbrellas with photos of grass on the exterior, scarves (including a Pollock) and hundreds of Christmas cards.

Just as MoMA has – and still is – moving on, so Tate Modern in London has moved beyond its boundaries and colonised a retail space in Selfridges on Oxford Street, which will sell Tate-branded products including postcards, books and home accessories. Clear says the move is part of the rebranding of the Tate: 'It was time to have a presence in the heart of London. It will reach a wider, less committed audience than the galleries.'[382] Thus art and shopping are merging as museums become extensions of the department store and department stores become display galleries.

These two giants of peripheral retail, MoMA and Tate, are not just embracing new physical spaces, however, expanding beyond the doors of the museum to other locations. They are also moving into virtual spaces, setting up e-commerce ventures that will market their respective brands around the world. MoMA and Tate announced in Spring 2000 that they would be taking the leap into the virtual together, launching a joint website on which art lovers

---

[382] Damian Schogger, 'Tate opens standalone art store in Selfridges', *Design Week*, 17 March 2000, p. 4.

will be able to view parts of exhibitions, browse through the book-shops and buy gifts, and also research design archives and attend lectures and seminars through live webcasts.[383]

In her book *Landscapes of Power*, architectural theorist Sharon Zukin says the museum is becoming 'the extension of the department store and another display case for the big business of illusion-making'.[384] At Selfridges in London, though, it seems to be the other way round: the department store is becoming the extension of the museum. Indeed in Spring 2000, when Britain's oldest department store was having its facade restored, it commissioned a contemporary artist, the photographer Sam Taylor-Wood, to 'hide' the restoration and the builders by wrapping the building in a gigantic photograph. Entitled 'XV Seconds',[385] the work was made with a 360-degree camera and featured portraits of famous personalities, including the singer Elton John, supermodel Jodie Kidd, actors Ray Winstone and Timothy Spall. 'What we actually see is a frieze of familiar faces that travels around the building and that plays a witty game of snap with the famous art friezes of antiquity, notably with the Pantheon frieze itself,' wrote Waldemar Januszczak in the *Sunday Times*.[386] 'We are being reminded that Selfridges is a temple of shopping and these are some of our contemporary gods.'

Post-modernist architect Charles Jencks describes the modern museum in the 1990s as 'an old lady suddenly turned into an over-sexed teenager: she is pushed and pulled every way by hormones, exams and attractive, rich men on the horizon – promising everything, including ruin'.[387] He identifies what he sees as the six functions of the modern museum: 'To preserve and memorialise artefacts and events. To educate and reaffirm values. [To be] a substitute cathedral [Tate Modern must be St Peter's]. [To be] a place of entertainment for the whole family. [To house the] Blockbuster exhibition and shopping precinct. [And to be] the site of the culture industry.'[388]

This new hybridisation can be seen in many institutions. The Minneapolis Institute for Arts launched '*Star Wars*: The Magic of Myth' in April 2000. Evan Maurer, the museum director in charge of the collection, dressed as Hans Solo (the goodie played by Harrison Ford) for the opening. 'Art is still the point,' he told the

---

[383] Ashlin O'Connor, 'Tate Gallery and MoMA', CNET.com, 17 April 2000.
[384] Zukin, Sharon, *Landscapes of Power* (Berkeley: University of California Press, 1991), p. 54.
[385] A reference to Andy Warhol's comment on the brevity of modern fame.
[386] Waldemar Januszczak, 'Would you like that gift-wrapped?', *Sunday Times* magazine, 7 May 2000, Magazine p. 8.
[387] Charles Jencks, 'The contemporary museum', *Architectural Design*, Nov./Dec. 1997, p. 9.
[388] Ibid.

New York Times, 'but we want to make people feel they are coming in as wanted and welcomed guests, not as solemn visitors to a forbidding mausoleum.'[389] It should be noted that in the 12 years Maurer has run the Institute endowments from patrons have tripled to $120 million and admissions have doubled.

Across town, two other art institutions, the Frederick R Weisman Art Institute and the Walker Art Center, have had to follow suit. The Weisman collection, housed in a Frank Gehry building, is said to have 'some of the most gorgeous galleries on earth';[390] although it favours early 20th century painting it also has 18th-century Korean furniture and significant art by Roy Lichtenstein and Georgia O'Keefe on display. Director Lyndel King acknowledges the competition she faces with two important art rivals close at hand. 'We're also up against the nearby [Jon Jerde-designed] Mall of America … In our own ways, we've all had to start wearing our pink feather boas.'[391] Of the three institutions, the Walker is the most prestigious in contemporary terms with a track record that, according to the *New York Times*, 'has helped define contemporary American art for more than a generation'. Its permanent collection includes work by Jasper Johns, Chuck Close and the Flexus school. And yet in the 'Gallery 8' restaurant visitors can drink their 'Martini of the Month' as part of 'Walker After Hours'. An exhibition entitled 'Let's Entertain: Life's Guilty Pleasures' took its guided tour somewhat further with a multi-floor cocktail party and a football game played against visiting artists. Director Kathy Halbreich said: 'It's seductive and insidious, and I think this exhibition is a trampoline for people to bounce off their own questions.'[392] Cool.

But not as cool as Evan Maurer, whose once 'museumy' gift shop is now a bazaar, which sells $165 Roman glass earrings and turns a tidy profit. Refuting local press criticism – those pesky journalists, damn them – he said: 'You have to be a sorry case to walk in here and not see the difference between Rembrandt and Yoda.' Of course you would, Rembrandt only got into multi-channel marketing after he was dead.

The Louvre in Paris is one of the great shrines to the dead; like the National Gallery in London or the Uffizi in Florence, it is weighed down by what the dot.com league might call 'legacy systems'. In this case the legacy is the pantheon of great pre- and post-Renaissance painting and sculpture. But in Paris life moves on. While London's National Gallery got its vertiginous Sainsbury Wing – a very cod, post-modern James Sterling thing – in 1989 Paris went

[389] Neal Karlen, 'Displaying art with a smiley face', NYT.com, 19 April 2000.
[390] Ibid., quoting Herbert Muschamp in the *New York Times*.
[391] Ibid.
[392] Ibid.

in for I.M. Pei's glass pyramid, redolent of Egyptian colonies, history, and a glassy transparent future. Now it has an underground shopping mall, too, paid for by business. The 'Carousel shopping mall' was built in 1994 by multinational corporation Vivendi for £75 million in exchange for an 80-year management lease, which has already been sold on to mall management company Unibail. There are typical French rules about the kind of stores allowed – essentially they have to be *haut de gamme,* upmarket, which allows for a Virgin Megastore, a MoMA gift shop, and many designer clothes emporia. There's also a lot of world-cuisine fast food but, unlike the Millennium Dome, which attempted a similar concept, the tables here are difficult to come by at *l'heure du déjeuner.* 'Perhaps there are some people who go shopping and are then drawn into the museum,' Louvre administrator Wanda Diebolt said, with French understatement. 'But we're happy to have the mall there so long as it respects our guidelines.'[393] So that will be the Johnny Halliday retrospective soon, then (we know, he's Belgian, but he's big in France too).

The United Kingdom, also, has latched on to the exhibition as pop event; in October 2000 the staid, stately treasures of the Victoria and Albert Museum were disrupted to high media attention by its 'brand•new' show featuring a – pretty thin – investigation of what it is to be a brand. There was a nice shopping area at the end, though, with Lara Croft caps and Coke t-shirts in Russian – even a copy of Walter Benjamin's *The Arcades Project,* which we bought, naturally.

Virtual space: the (next) final frontier

I mean I was just trying to live my bloody life ... you know, get from A to B and do a little shopping! ... only to find that, in fact, life is controlled for me, by bits of bloody, bloody, buggery bits of paper! ... I mean, why can't life just be a little bit easier for everybody, you know?

Eddie, Absolutely Fabulous

Having begun the colonisation of the home environment through the fixed telephone, the television and the PC, retailers are now also colonising a virtual space even closer to consumers, a space in which they are always available, though maybe not always as receptive, a peripheral space ripe for people-mining. New mobile-phone technology now offers WAP (wireless application protocol), which in English means a connection to a selection of Internet sites through the mobile phone. With WAP, retailers can get to you all the time, at any time, as the mobile phone is an

---

[393] Alan Riding, 'A shopping mall at the Louvre? The French say bien sûr', NYT.com, 19 April 2000.

essential item that today travels with its owner from home to work, to the gym, to the cinema, the pub and on holiday. On the other hand, it also means consumers can have access to the world of retailisation, shop from the street corner, the train and on the beach.

Using WML (wireless mark-up language) instead of HTML (hypertext mark-up language), the basis of most websites, WAP technology offers a lighter version of the Internet, faster and more target-oriented. Users will be able to search for information from stock movements to football results and tonight's television programme. Mark Squires, spokesman for Nokia, explains: 'WAP is not suitable for browsing; people want much more instant information and data, which is why WAP pages will have to be very organised and streamlined, showing users exactly what they can find where, fast.'[394] How much this facility will actually be used remains to be seen but Squires seems convinced it will lead to a paradigm shift in shopping behaviour and relationships between consumer and retailer. 'It is the next step towards a mobile information society. We've never had such opportunity to address so many people: this is the most private direct medium to address people. PCs are different because you often share them, but you don't share your phone, that's personal.' No matter, WAP is an 'interim technology' awaiting even greater things.

Nevertheless, Squires excitedly explains the following scenario, illustrating the level of personalisation and the degree of penetration WAP technology will offer the retailer: 'Imagine you are at Heathrow airport; you walk past the duty free and your phone vibrates; you look at the message and it tells you: "Hi Mark! Welcome to Heathrow, you still have an hour before your plane leaves [because it will know this as soon as you check in], why not come and buy some duty-free? The duty-free whisky you bought last time you were here [because it will remember], is at half price now."' Similarly: 'If you're queuing outside a club where you've been before, you can receive a message: "Hi Mark, how are you? Great to see you again, don't worry about the queue, just press to buy your tickets and you can pick them up inside."' A scary vision: phones – actually retailers – talking to you and this time not just organising your home life as in the Internet Home, but suggesting retail choices and knowing your most intimate movements and preferences.

The point about WAP is that new technology adoption rates are getting faster and the migration from mobile communications (that's those pesky mobiles we just talk and listen to – or sometimes send a rude SMS (Systems Management Server) message to a loved one with) will in a very short time be mobile access units to

---

[394] Mark Squires in personal interview, May 2000; all quotes from interview.

the Internet. They will be far more user-friendly and nicer to consume than WAP phones. There are generations of people now, up to the age of 70, who are used to the ever-faster product replacement cycle. The Internet's Grey Panthers were an early 'blip' on expected consumption patterns, children buying mobiles for their parents so they could keep an aural eye on one another. Whatever the new units look like, they will be access points to useful things. And we, as consumers, will be driving the demand for features on them that are relevant to our lives. It won't be long before 'services retail', which we explore more fully in the next chapter, realises that the 'instant anything/everything' concept that supermarkets, call centres and, increasingly, websites are already beholden to, becomes the normal customer expectation.

Bidding in the United Kingdom for the next generation mobile licences, auctioned by the British government, raised close on £30 billion – enough to pay for the reprivatisation of the entire British rail system, should any government desire. That's how desperate telecommunications companies were to not miss the boat. Thirteen companies bid for the licences, which allow high-speed Internet access while on the move using the UMTS (Universal Mobile Telecommuncations Systems) standard. Most of the winners have seen their share prices much diminished by nervous shareholders in 2000, such were the high prices they paid.

It is important to remember that in late 2000, with the exception of North America, there were more mobile phone users than Internet users in the world. 'Two-way data messaging, a feature essential to e-commerce, is rare in the US,' says Katrina Bond, senior analyst with telecoms consultancy Analysys.

The beginnings of the mobile 'revolution' have some promising differences from the early days of the Internet: for a start it is being driven from the outset by business, the mobile phone industry and networks, rather than the academics who started up the Internet. As a result, it will be a profit-centred business, and that means getting products right for consumers in their many 'peripheral spaces'. But there are dangers. So much of the promise of the next mobile generation is that its units, whatever they are, will 'know' where we are through 'global positioning' technologies. That leads to the concept of 'locational spamming', sending 'junk mail' via email or, in the case of mobile phones, to people on the move who happen to be near a retail outlet.

Michael Sastry, revenue manager at the last minute online retailer, lastminute.com, has strong views on this: 'Spamming is dreadful on e-mail, but especially on phones and I think that soon SMS, System Management Server, spamming is going to cross a mark and really start annoying people. The point with this kind of advertising is that you constantly have to think of its *utility*. Online advertising models are changing fast as providers are more and more paying for eyeballs and targeted consumer viewing rather than just random displays.'[395] Utility, as with OnStar's in-car service, possibly yes; being told there are bargains inside every shop you pass on the high street, no.

Personalisation is also key. 'Personalisation and location is going to be another important field to expand into, because with WAP phones we will be able to know where the user is and, using a grid of reference points, we will be able to locate products in their vicinity,' says Sastry. 'Of course here you have to be very careful about the spam factor and provide the service purely on an opt-in basis otherwise consumers are going to go mental. SMS is a very sensitive device: messages sent through SMS are usually from friends and are sent to amuse; if advertisers start moving into that space, people will very soon get angry.' Yes indeed, but a lot of business plans are based on something not un-akin to this idea.

Global mobile access is expected to top a billion by 2003, which is one in six people in the world: it is an attractive market. It is also thought that by 2004 more people will access the Internet from mobiles than from office or home computers.[396] The Internet will not look as it does via Netscape or Explorer browsers; its new design paradigms wait to be created; no doubt design interface guru Jakob Nielsen[397] of Sun Systems will be working on tight guidelines as you read this. But these mobiles could also be payment cards – replacing credit cards, banking facilities, medical records, and probably marital guides as well.

It seems a long way from Waterloo Bridge, *Wallpaper**, and the aversion Tyler Brûlé has for 'a ready made shopping experience'. *Wallpaper**, now it is part of Steve Case's AOL empire, has a lovely looking website, and will be an e-commerce nirvana for those who like it, whether they are in Beirut, Buenos Aires, Stockholm or Tokyo. But for all the arguments about smallness and taste, *Wallpaper** is now a global brand. (Protesters against the capitalism and the global economy in general certainly thought so. Along with the usual targets for the protesters, such as McDonald's in Whitehall, they broke the glass to the *Wallpaper** entrance hall.)[398]

---

[395] Michael Sastry in personal interview, April 2000; all quotes from interview.
[396] Joia Shillingford, 'Ready to take off more rapidly than the Internet', *FT Telecomsinancial Times*, 15 March 2000, Telecoms p. XXV.
[397] Jakob Nielsen is probably the most famous academic and practitioner of 'web design'.
[398] This happened on May Day 2000, when protesters from organisations such as Reclaim the Streets, the Socialist Workers Party and the Anarchist Federation gathered on Trafalgar Square in London for an initially peaceful demonstration, which soon degenerated into full-blown riots during which shop fronts of large brands were smashed and the statue of Winston Churchill on Parliament Square was defaced.

'If we get it right we could create a proper e-commerce site,' he concedes. 'Building the alliances is not the problem and if we have the product and can bring in consumers from diverse parts we could really build something. And then we would be catering to customers in New Zealand, Brazil, Australia and Canada who are living out of town but have the credit limit to spend the money and the courier service who can deliver it to them.'

For, as even this aesthete of lifestyle will admit, 'there are those who will sit in their office in Chicago and order the stylish bed from Copenhagen, who will know the best lounge bar in Narita airport.' Yes, they will know their relatively obscure Swedish designers, their Swensons, Folk Ohlssons and Kurt Nordstroms, and they will buy them *wherever* they are.

The periphery is moving to the centre. How much longer this arena can be called a peripheral retail space is really for us to choose.

Chapter 7 – Beyond the product – virtual services

I am getting divorced over the Internet for a princely £75 and it is a piece of cake.

India Knight[399]

Ready, Steady, Click
Why wait in line when you can find virtually everything you need online – from gourmet groceries and cocktail recipes to mortgage rates and flu reports ... even sperm donors to sire your first e-baby!
Introduction to *Boston* magazine's top websites feature, March 2000

The discreet legal conference is held, symbolically, in London's County Hall. For many years the County Hall, a dominant 19th-century building, now somewhat dwarfed by the hugely popular, giant revolving London Eye next to it, was home to the city council that ran London long before it had a mayor. It was a centralised power base dealing with planning, education, transport, cultural and architectural issues City wide. It was also for a turbulent few years the centre of opposition to the House of Commons, to the Conservative government, the Parliament – whose buildings it faces across the water. When the Greater London Council was in full swing in the early to mid-1980s, everyone knew about its power. Its former leader, charismatic Ken Livingstone, is now the first London mayor.

Today, 15 years on, County Hall is, naturally, an upmarket-ish Marriott hotel, a Russian nightclub, an exhibition centre and a conference hall. Inside, a lobby of men and women just as powerful as the Greater London Council once was – a hundred times more, in reality – is in situ. Around 30 top City lawyers sit and sip fizzy water inside one of its new conference suites listening to a series of seminars about the Internet. We are a speaker – the man who has built websites. We have learnt early on from a piece of research that the average amount of money being spent per year on law websites in the United Kingdom in 1999 is between £2,000 and £3,000.[400] We are appalled.

The E-commerce Law and Policy survey revealed that one in three commercial law firms plans to offer online legal services in the future, but only as few as 6 per cent have listed income generation as a key objective ... 10 per cent of law firms are spending more than £10,000 a year on their websites, while a typical law firm's expenditure of websites remains low, averaging around £2,000–3,000, excluding partner time ... Almost three-quarters of those with

---

[399] India Knight, *Sunday Times*, 24 June 2000.
[400] Lindsey Greig 'E-commerce revolution is leaving law firms unmoved', *Legal Week*, 28 October 1999, p. 13.

websites do not know the volume of traffic on their site … one-third of respondents do not track the traffic at all.

We tear up our speech and start again.

We choose a well-dressed and slightly overweight partner in the front row. 'How much do you earn a year?' we ask. And when there is – obviously – no reply we speculate that it could be in the realms of $750,000. He does not look unhappy.

'Right, there are 30 of you in this room,' we continue, 'Let's take that sum as the average figure and let's throw in another $15 million to buy up law.com. That makes around $37 million, let's throw in another three to sort our some laptops and a network. Now, shall we walk over to the City and find some venture capitalists and ask for $40 million? Here's the pitch: law.com, the United Kingdom's first virtual law firm, all client meetings take place at their offices; 30 of the top legal brains in the United Kingdom, covering almost all sectors, plus no overheads like those fancy offices with busts of your founder. We reckon the VCs would pay up; we reckon you'd be a top five legal practice in the City within two years.'

There is little response. We have flirted around some of the key issues: how do you market such a service, how do you acquire users, how do you sell to them? But what we are trying to convince this august body of is a retailisation truism: virtual services are done better virtually, and this can still involve human contact. Even if it comes with a very establishment mien. Law, like sausages or George jeans, is really just a commodity like everything else. Law's brand is pretty high right now – like its rates per hour. We know: we use lawyers all the time, and $500 per hour is a bargain. Yet in some senses law is a piece of hypertextual publishing, a corpus of knowledge to be interpreted and used to ensure that the rules of a civic state are upheld, that there is a kind of justice. So in one sense lawyers are intermediaries, just as banks and financial service companies stand between lenders and borrowers, savers and spenders, so law firms stand between a corpus of knowledge that could empower us and keep us out of debt. Law is not easy, we are not saying that, but law is an organic body of knowledge, *information*, which most of us cannot easily access. In this sense law is about the *availability* of law and nice suits, about trust as much as accuracy. It is certainly about high profit margins.

Freeserve, the Internet service provider (ISP) set up with such stunning successes by the Dixons Group, had already had more than a hundred divorces by June 2000 through its Desktop lawyer service – amicable ones – undertaken with its downloadable forms. We all know that when we use our lawyers they are very often simply formatting precedent. Would you pay your lawyers the same rate as you would pay a Mac worker, a designer who is simply lay-ing out your words? Of course, a Mac worker and a lawyer carry out different kinds of jobs, but for the law of the mundane, wills, house-buying, simple divorces, we argue that they might as well be the same.

But we don't pay them the same amounts of money. We are looking in this chapter at the knowledge (and interpretation) pro-fessions who are, to date, the lucky escapees of the new economy: they benefit from email, from intranets, extranets and the mobile revolution, but they still keep those skyscraper buildings and those skyscraper salaries. By the knowledge professions we mean lawyers, accountants, insurance executives, bankers, even politi-cians: the 'professions' that have for many decades relied on the gravitas of personal contact, the old school tie, the social nexus. The digital world is no great respector of their lineage and who they know.

We turn to leave the seminar and a man in his 40s taps one of us on the shoulder. 'Can I come with you?' he asks. Two hours later we are mapping out his plan to set up a virtual law company – in South-East Asia. 'Business is very wired out there', he says, 'and unlike here everyone is looking for value money.' Given that he is a senior partner in one of the world's largest law firms, it seems sensible to hear him out. He has been trying to persuade his firm to make the radical step for some time and has given up – as so many talented managers have done in all retail sectors.

Law is but one of many services that will be radically trans-formed in the retailisation era. As with shopping, these services will rely on two key elements: trust and service. Law is so often seen as a terrifyingly mysterious and expensive product, yet its secrets are available in print and through massive Byzantine electronic databases – at one level, law is no different from the news from Reuters or the *New York Times*. So why not make it available to us all, easily? Why not set up websites that deal with conveyancing, divorce, wills and final testaments, tax, even acquisitions and merg-ers – the commodity factors of law, just as groceries, books and air-line tickets are the commodities of e-commerce? Answer: no rea-son at all. It hasn't happened yet, though, because law is not like supermarkets, law is not like entertainment or sport. Law is august.

What most lawyers won't tell you. Learn what the law is really about. What you can do for yourself is far superior to anything a lawyer can do. Learn how to reduce conflict, negotiate an agreement and stay out of court. Award-win-ning author, 25 years of proven success. All free!

The sales pitch to divorcehelp.com

Services do not require the high street or the mall; indeed, those spaces are not always appropriate for the kinds of retail we investigate here. And yet they do rely on many of the techniques of retailisation. Finance – long a virtual service in many senses – has increasingly less need of high street branches, and more than ever the need to create strong brands. But what of the other invisibles, the intangibles, that we are offered? What of education, health, politics, real estate, gambling opportunities?

In Manchester, England, Nigel Vaux runs a portal called ukline.com – which may be the great success of the Web, who knows? He is going for the service sector as his target market. 'I was fascinated by the social change brought on by the Internet,' he says. 'I wanted to have some kind of brand-ownership and I didn't subscribe to the dot.com mania, I didn't want to take a lot of venture capital and throw it straight at the advertisers. I am not blessed with the funds of the Abbey National Building Society who can create a brand like Cahoot, so I thought I'd take a range of generic names and add the word "line" to them. I have been in the computer industry for over 12 years.'[401]

He's been selling UNIX solutions and networks for years. 'Prior to the launch of ukline.com I was with Websites Ltd, who currently host all our domains, based on Hull University Campus. Equity is owned by a number of business people who have come to the business privately, but bring skills in the travel business, building production distribution and engineering. We consider equity participation from other VC companies or businesses. The framework for this is in place, as we've been approached by companies who have a specific interest in key line brands – filmline and haulageline for example.'

Ukline.com is merely a directory, then, but one that highlights how many services – everything from vets and doctors through divorce and school help – are becoming available online. 'I didn't want to have just one front door to the site – like lastminute.com – so I bought 220 generic names and added "line" to them. The more options I have the more I can gauge what works.'

Vaux is optimistic. His success will be measured by the extent to which we know about his services; if they appear on Open, Yahoo! and Freeserve, AOL and The Microsoft Network. If they are advertised on the big television channels, or in the major newspapers, nationally and regionally. If they are also physical – so were banks once. In fact, let's take every one of the professions and have a good think about how they might evolve in the new economy. Law, finance, education, health, politics, government, accountancy, architecture, science, you name it; the virtual is more effective, cheaper and often more consumer-friendly in terms of access to information relevant to us. This is retailisation of services in *no*

---

[401] Nigel Vaux in personal interview, June 2000.

space. So profound has been the movement of the physical to the virtual – whatever the major hiccups of the stock markets in 2000, the collapse of the dot.com bubble, and the corporate crisis of 2002 might suggest – that an analyst, Roger Bootle, felt confident enough to write in *The Times*: 'The strongest threat to the high street from the Internet surely comes not from the movement of goods [the shift of retailers to out-of-town depots or distribution outlets] but rather from the movement of the intangibles.' But he adds an interesting suggestion: 'One answer could be the establishment of high street "drops" where the net-ordered goods could be left for collection at a time convenient to the purchaser.' Most fundamentally he sees the partial demise of the high street as potentially a great boost for property development. 'Redundant retail space could be used for private housing. Indeed, in many towns and suburban centres, some of the property used by estate agents, banks, solicitors and the like was formerly in residential use. It could be moved back to residential use again.'

Intangibles or virtual services are by definition the great 'other' of the retail environment, the places where we don't necessarily come away with something physical; the services that don't need a physical product for us to take away. Their market value can only grow as retailisation kicks in.

Finance

It is no surprise to read the first words of a supplement of *The Economist* on the subject of online finance: 'The most remarkable thing about the effect of the Internet on the financial services sector is not how persuasive it has been; it is how limited a transformation it has wrought so far.'[402]

It is limited because for a very long time independent financial analysts (IFAs) have been carving up the financial market. Independent financial advisors are agents, middlemen, offering us a variety of choices for our house insurance or our life policies, which are scrupulous, fair, and very often based upon the kinds of commission available from the various companies wholesaling these services. In some case IFAs account for up to 60 to 70 per cent of a company's acquired clients in financial services. To put it another way, if one company's Internet strategy annoys them – where savings are promoted in company results to keep the shareholders happy – they could easily ruin that company in the period of time it takes to acquire a whole new online network of financial clients.

For agents and middlemen, read software agents and middlewear. The Internet revolution makes financial services – pieces of

---

[402] 'A survey of online finance', *The Economist*, 20 May 2000.

paper that guarantee that if 'x' happens, for instance your house is burgled, then 'y' is paid out in compensation – eminently suitable for web-based retailing. The basic premise of a policy can be easily explained – insurance companies have been creating leaflets and printed promotional documentation for years now. The long documentation required by the regulatory bodies can be embedded into the purchasing processes so that customers will have read all issues about their purchase. Systems of registration and approval, tied into credit card details about a customer's financial status are easily built into the system. Finally, all the data about such policies and policyholders is already stored on the computer databases of financial companies.

All that is missing is the human touch. But the human touch – the reassurance of the IFA's friendly gaze, the likelihood that he or she is making the right decision – has its flaws. Firstly, IFAs often choose the best deal for them, rather than for consumers. Secondly, the spread of information about financial services is not being promoted by the Internet, even though this medium has increased the transparency of information available. Old media has for the past two decades invested much time in personal finance journalism, illustrating the pitfalls of certain financial products, advising when things go wrong. We are, in short, far more informed about finance now than ever before. As with everything else these days, perhaps we are too well informed.

The advent of comparison search engines and online calculators also means that we can do our own sums. We can compare the offerings of one brand against another and make decisions based not only on our brand awareness but also on relative costs and services available. Many new Web companies, some without the reassuring parental grip of an established insurance or financial services company, can offer cheaper products simply because they have fewer overheads. Shareholders in all financial companies must, naturally, be kept happy – and further reduction in costs, which the digital retail of products and services promises, are clearly enticing. It is no wonder that TSB Chairman, Sir Brian Pitman, can say his company and all others are now going through 'transformations'.[403] Transformations brought about by the extreme retailisation process known as the stock market. 'One of the great advantages of shareholder value as a governing objective is that it demands continual improvement,' he said. 'There is no time when you can sit back and admire your achievements. The measurement is obvious to all, inside and outside the company. There is no hiding place.'[404]

---

[403] Sir Brian Pitman, 'In my opinion', *Management Today*, June 2000, p. 14.
[404] Ibid.

But for the five years of the World Wide Web there has been a hiding place for the financial services. For until the Internet is as ubiquitous as the telephone or the television financial companies cannot shed themselves of their symbolic relationship with their middlemen, the IFAs. Just as Volkswagen showed, with their special Dealer VIP lounges and suites in Autostadt in Wolfsburg, Germany, it is too high a risk to alienate dealers. Volkswagen made a huge play in our interview with them of their dealers' importance to selling cars. Well yes. Right now.

But it won't be long. We must prepare for a new kind of retail convergence – one that we explored in the classical retail world earlier. This convergence brings together physical spaces such as banks or building societies with virtual personae to mirror their real-world activities. It brings together online finance organisations looking for real-world outlets. Inevitably, this means fewer branches in the high street – as Barclays has already illustrated. It will mean the growth of call-centres selling 'open-finance'. That means they will become the Wal-Marts of finance, selling many kinds of service, including rivals' products.

Online insurance 'supermarkets' will emerge to dominate sales in the United Kingdom as consumers tire of filling endless forms to buy online, according to a report from Forrester Research. By 2005, about 20% of all general insurance sold to personal customers will be sold online, much of it through supermarkets, creating an online market worth £3.1 billion.

'Consumers' desire to comparison-shop is driving the creation of supermarkets in funds, mortgages and insurance,' comments Benjamin Ensor, analyst at Forrester's UK Research Centre. 'Built by a mix of start-ups, software houses and insurance brokers, supermarkets will undercut traditional insurance brokers by taking smaller commissions. They will distribute through websites related to cars, homes, holidays and health, displacing partnerships with individual insurance companies as they do so.'

It doesn't quite sound like that on the 23rd-floor boardrooms of the big financial service companies, whose reputations, often built over centuries, are based on a quiet, homely gravitas – and very comfortable profit margins. Now, as the baby-boom generation leads the way, unwilling to compromise in the face of old-fashioned monopolies, keen to be empowered and 'in control', we recognise that cost and service is everything, not the brand. We will go to the supermarket for anything – if what we want is there. We won't keep going to places where we know we are being cheated.

Britain's four biggest high street banks were on a collision course with MPs and consumer groups last night after it emerged that they are making excessive profits of up to £5 billion at the expense of current account holders. An unpublished report by a rival bank shows that Barclays, NatWest, Lloyds, TSB and HSBC, which have an estimated £85 billion in current accounts, are able to generate billions by paying customers a measly 0.1 per cent on those balances and effectively depriving each account holder of £136.24 a year. The study by Intelligent Finance, the Halifax's new Internet bank, suggests that the banks' profits are far greater than estimated in the Cruickshank report, which led to an industry row earlier this year by stating that banks give their customers a raw deal. It said that bank customers are paying up to £5 billion a year too much for banking services because of the dominance of the four biggest players.

Susan Emmett[405]

Forrester Research identifies two types of insurance supermarket emerging.[406] These are independent supermarkets, building new brands for the Web, and interactive television, using advertising and branded partnerships with other sites or other brands. We will see Nike finance, Manchester United, WestLife or Britney Spears credit cards, if they haven't already arrived before the printing of this book. Meanwhile, some other supermarket operators will partner with Web-aggregating portals, financial services companies and other kinds of brand-enhancing websites keen to help customers find low-cost insurance while keeping them loyal to existing players. In exchange for commission on transactions, these 'white label' operators will supply the insurance quotation engines and manage relationships with the insurance companies, but leave all branding issues to their partners. For example, unbranded technology solutions are already in place to enable Sainsbury's to have a bank – it is a 55:45 joint venture with the Bank of Scotland; Tesco's bank is held together by the back-end expertise of the RBS NatWest. Tesco's marketing director, Tim Mason, told us: 'The expansion into finance will build on the brand and offer customers what they are used to from Tesco as food retailers: good service and good value.' So potatoes or stakeholder pensions, all the same? Tesco has the virtue of its good service in store and Mason is determined that as his brand broadens its appeal and offerings this is not diluted. 'The brand is very important because of its strength. I think it is one of the strongest brands around because it speaks of reliability and dependability...It is stronger than the Virgin brand, for example [Virgin has moved solidly into the financial services market], because that's a *fun* brand and it's wild and reckless, and it doesn't have the *solidity* of the Tesco brand.'[407] *Solidity*, that is in the metaphorical rather than the physical sense.

---

[405] Susan Emmett, 'Banks cheat customers out of £136 a year', *The Times*, 27 May 2000, p. 5.
[406] Forrester Research.
[407] Tim Mason, Tesco, in personal interview, February 2000; all quotes from this interview.

Supermarkets will help consumers to find the best deal by pooling quotations from a large number of insurers and competing with each other on commission levels. Supermarkets will drive insurers to shorten the application process by simplifying their underwriting criteria, and help customers understand their insurance needs and the different kinds of policies available by providing editorial content, coverage-needs, calculators and simple decision trees for advice.[408]

The e-bank is obvious. Pay your bills, check your accounts, move money around in front of your computer screen – or the next generation of mobiles – rather than stand in a long queue, which is often followed by a lengthy physical exchange with banking staff who are little more than upmarket clothes' sale staff. Simple. So where does this leave the monoliths of the financial sector? Quite happy, probably. Their brands are to a large extent trusted by us. They have huge customer bases, which the digital newcomers do not. They have massive financial resources to invest in future technologies, which start-ups might do, but their backers will want to see returns far faster. But the boundaries of who is what, will transform. What a bank's function is will be determined by what its users need: insurance, brokerage, pension provisions, fund management – whatever.

Banks and other financial institutions can bring clout to a range of retailing options: Prudential's Egg, a company that hides effectively its parental lineage is one extreme; others in this field include Abbey National's Cahoot, the Co-op's Smile, and the Halifax Building Society's enigmatic If. Other banks simply leverage their name and reputation against a new, branded website. For example, *The Economist* reported that American Express used this transferred loyalty approach when it advertised its Web presence: 'online banking from a company that's been around longer than a week'.[409]

Both approaches could have one massive hidden bonus: 'equity transference'. This is where the realisation of the stock market can play massively. The established company – such as Prudential with Egg (which was valued at around $2 billion on flotation) – can spin off their new creations at high valuations, which can then help to fund the marketing, benefiting not just the virtual brand but the physical one as well.

As Jon Bond, co-chairman of Kirshenbaum Bond & partners, says:

For example if XYZ company spins off xyz.com, which gets a higher valuation, it can spend $50 million in advertising to build a shared brand name. At the same time regular old XYZ cuts its $10 million [advertising] budget to zero, at a stroke shifting all its marketing expenses to bottom-line profit, pleasing

---

[408] Ibid.
[409] *The Economist.*

Wall Street. To the consumer, xyz.com is almost the same as XYZ, so XYZ benefits from the equity built through the inflated valuation of its dot.com. Meanwhile XYZ is suddenly more profitable because it has no expenses. A double home run.[410]

Then there are the hidden benefits of knowing your consumer. In 2000, Barclays Bank, the largest in the United Kingdom, garnered a host of bad press when it simultaneously managed to alienate pretty much everybody by closing 190 small branches and also launched an advertising campaign with Sir Anthony Hopkins, Robbie Coltrane and Tim Roth among others, which proclaimed 'Big' was great. The Managing Director copped-off with bonuses of around $50 million. But then Barclays has around a million e-bankers right now.

As the world moves closer towards the day when a single plastic card will contain not only our credit ratings, and our means of payment for everything, but probably our DNA and our identity card – privacy campaigners not withstanding – the creators of these cards will also hold our consumer DNA. It is a powerful position to be in: few of us, whatever our retail decisions about clothes or cars, live without banks – or money. When, finally, the online world is no longer stymied by its inability to dispense cash directly from the personal computer, online jacket or merely a Super Mobile, the prospects for 24-hour personalised retail are awesome.

Credit may have been going in biblical times, and buy-now-pay-later a privilege of the rich for many centuries but, as Ken Kurson wrote in the millennial issue of *ID* magazine (the US design periodical): 'The tidal wave wrought on American culture by credit cards can't be exaggerated.'[411] They have come a long way in their 50-year history, having first appeared in the United States in 1950 when one Frank McNamara found himself embarrassed to be without his wallet at Major's Cabin Grill in Manhattan. (His wife paid, that time.) McNamara returned later with a cardboard card with his name on, calling it his 'diner's club' card. The Grill, who knew McNamara well, accepted the idea. Within a few more weeks, 200 of this ground-breaker's friends and business colleagues had cards and 14 restaurants in New York agreed to try it. Within a year 42,000 Americans and 330 businesses trusted the idea. (Diners Club is now owned by Citigroup.)
In *Enchanting a Disenchanted World* theorist George

---

[410] *Revolution* magazine, March 2000.
[411] Ken Kurson, 'The power of plastic', *ID* magazine, November 1999, p. 80.

Ritzer comments: 'Although most of the new means of consumption could exist without credit cards, it could be argued that their explosive growth has depended on the credit card.'[412] By this, Ritzer means that the mall, home shopping via the Web or interactive television, and the new forms of mobile 'retailing' using phones all rely on the credit card: not its physical existence, so much as its key numbers, and a good, healthy, credit rating.

In the 1950s, claimed an article in the *New York Times*, 'dapper men with moustaches and fedoras used them to settle their bills at Delmonico's, the "21" Club or the Copacabana. They were a novelty for the affluent and the urbane ... Today, almost as many people carry cards as have drivers' licences [in the United States] and three times as many have cards as have valid passports.'[413]

But this abundance of plastic – 157 million Americans have credit cards of some kind now – did, and continues to, spur the economy and breed a *carpe diem* optimism, which has carried through the 1950s to now. 'Even the average high-school senior knows that credit card companies offer bad deals (the average interest rate is 18.9% and the late fees average is $29),' *ID* reported.[414] But that doesn't stop us: the total US credit card debt at the end of 1999 was estimated at $572 billion – that's three and half times the annual revenue of Wal-Mart. New target groups include students: around 70 per cent of US students have at least one, with an average, revolving, debt of $2,000.[415]

In the United Kingdom credit card spending was £12.6 billion in March 2000, with the British Bankers' Association revealing that debt was rising to £29 billion, with an average personal debt per card of £675.[416] 'A spokesman for Barclaycard said: "What you are seeing is a surge in the number of people transferring their spending patterns away from cash and cheques and onto plastic."'[417]

---

412 George Ritzer, *Enchanting a Disenchanted World* (Thousand Oaks, California: Pine Forge Press, 1999), p. 33.
413 'Credit cards at 50: the problems of ubiquity', by the Associated Press in the *New York Times*, Business p. 11.
414 Ken Kurson, 'The power of plastic', *ID*, November 1999, p. 80.
415 Robert Manning, Georgetown University, cited in 'Credit cards at 50: the problems of ubiquity', p. 11.'Credit cards at 50', ibid.
416 Patrick Collinson, 'That'll do nicely to the tune of £12bn', *Guardian*, March 2000.
417 Ibid.

However, the credit card is a Trojan horse. 'Choose carefully next time you are flicking through the videos on offer in your hotel room,' Clare Gascoigne wrote in the *Financial Times*. 'If you settle the bill with your corporate credit card, your choice of viewing could become the focus of a management report.' Why? 'Not using the corporate card means that valuable information is lost and it is difficult for businesses to keep a grip on their travel policies [and, presumably, whether their senior managers prefer *Debbie Does Dallas* to *Autumn in New York*].'[418]

The *Financial Times* article highlighted a particular business need, but the credit card's utter traceability gives retailers, marketers and advertising specialists key information: every move and purchase we make. 'Information regarding what a credit card has bought and how its owner has paid is nearly as valuable to the bank that issues it as the profits it makes on transactions and interest,' Kurson concluded.[419] Now just imagine the potential of the mobile units we have discussed; these could become not merely information resources and communications tools, but also credit cards that know where we are – and, shortly, medical records and passports too.

It is perhaps no surprise that Web privacy lobbyists are now as prevalent as the common autumn cold. For the Web is but chicken-feed compared with the information gathering potential of the mobile, digital credit card. One such group, launched in April 2000, is the Personalization Consortium, which includes 26 Internet companies (DoubleClick among them). Co-Chairman of the group, Bonnie J. Lowell, founder and Chief Technology Officer of Younology, which makes a software program that allows consumers to see how they are tracked on the Web, said: 'I insist that we eat our own dog food.'[420] Well, that's real personalisation, we guess.

Right now, it could be argued that despite the Internet's 24/7 rhetoric, it is only the ATM that actually delivers this lofty dream. One day, very much as with video-on-demand and Professor Kevin

---

[418] Clare Gascoigne, 'Plastic that reveals all about you', *Financial Times*, p. 16.
[419] Kurson, 'Power of plastic', p. 80.
[420] 'Web privacy group to offer seal of approval', NYT.com, Technology Section, 3 April 2000.

Warwick's computer chip implant, there will be a standard 'smart card', which will fulfil the patent material obsolescence of cash. But not yet.

In the autumn of 2000 there were still 'legacy system' problems for the large extant financial organisations: the technologies put in place at massive expense over the decades, which served to organise transactions. These systems, however outdated they may now be, did have a few virtues, not least that, in general, they worked. When we were designing the website of a very large financial institution we used to sit in on their meetings. For several meetings running the argument came down to this: websites are easy to build, back-end systems that facilitate online insurance, banking, brokerage, whatever, are not. Therefore, said the Head of IT, a doyen of the company, first guest at the Test matches, a drinking companion of everyone on the board who mattered, we couldn't do it. Not for a few years, anyway.

So we let them. Two years on, their legacy-system-to-Web interface was taking four minutes to download; more time, in fact, than it takes to sign up for many of the new non-legacy financial sites. Security was the issue, as it is for all financial services companies, but there was a secondary one: security of the IT department, which for many years had run safe in the knowledge that its secrets – the techy savvy discourse that alienated so many from computers for a very long time – could bamboozle any can-do director who cared to ask.

How long does it take to build a database? Five years? IT departments in large corporations have long favoured the approach of cowboy builders, a purse of the lips, a sigh, and then an impossibly long time frame at vast expense. And by and large it has always worked. As the management guru, Tom Peters, puts it: 'In times of turbulence and rapid change, 95 per cent of the effort goes into preserving the status quo.'[421] There are real structural problems: banks' existing systems. They normally work with batch processing – the Web works in real-time. You check your account an hour after you've just bought that Dolce and Gabanna jacket and you might be temporarily richer than you thought. But 'real-time', as James Gleick shows us, is here to stay.

In the meantime, it is a stupid bank board that doesn't talk the new media world. For it is not just the consumers who will demand the transparencies of the digital, comparing, world: shareholders also will want to know that these companies are buying things – 'procuring' for themselves – in the most efficient ways. This is the world of e-procurement or business-to-business transactions. In other words, when Barclays wants to buy 100 new IBM Think

---

[421] See *http://www.tompeters.com*.

Book computers, how does it do it? When Tesco needs new office chairs for its middle management where does it shop?

The future in this business-to-business retail environment is about computers with e-catalogues; forget the middlemen who buy office chairs or stationery now these purchases can be made directly. In April 2000, 50 per cent of finance directors surveyed by Byline Research said that cost reduction was their most important factor in procurement issues and 92 per cent said that e-procurement was on the agenda for the next 12 months. For example, the $5 million global e-procurement system purchased by the Royal & SunAlliance group was expected to create savings in the region of $30 million. Moira Crabtree, the RSA's director of procurement, commented: 'Implementing e-procurement systems results in major bottom-line savings and substantial increases in efficiency.'[422]

A report by Goldman Sachs estimated that companies buying goods and services from the Internet rather than through more traditional sources could save between 2 per cent (in the case of the coal industry) and 40 per cent (in the case of the electronics marketplace). British Telecom stated that buying online would help them to cut the average cost of processing a transaction by a staggering 90 per cent.

So let's look at this slowly and rationally. The Internet reduces distances, brings people closer together. It should reduce costs. People, whether they are finance directors of Fortune 500 companies or individuals seeking out the best car insurance, will be able to compare electronically and choose the service that brings cheapness and reliability. The biggest beneficiary will be we consumers – which is why not all service professions are adopting the mantras of e-commerce as quickly as the consultants would like it. What the Internet brings is transparency, which leaves the service providers rather exposed. On the high street this has long been the case: shop for two hours in Bluewater and the relative merits of Gap, Diesel or Levi's are easy to see. Shop online for the best price for a Chevrolet or an Audi and it is the same. Try doing this with law firms or medicines and it is not so easy.

We are considering the middleman again. Just as we have seen car manufacturers to be keen to remove the costly dealerships (themselves a recent creation, being no more than 60 years old), so too the Internet lets us get to the information without interruption. That brings down costs. That reduces the barriers to entry. Competition should then increase, efficiency improve, resources move to their most effective place – and in general the economy gets stronger. That's the theory.

---

[422] Royal and SunAlliance global e-procurement system – a first for the service industry, at *http://www.royalsunalliance.co.uk/media/news*, 3 April 2000.

According to the financiers Lehman Brothers, moving money between bank accounts costs $1.27 per transaction if it is made manually by a teller in a bank, 27 cents per transaction if it is made at an ATM or cash machine, and one cent if the transaction is made over the Internet. And these days we all want the one cent deal. 'The growth of price-driven comparison-shopping will put further pressure on margins and drive more consolidation among insurers.'

Forester's Benjamin Ensor says:

"Pressure. Consumer pressure. That's what this kind of space beyond classical retail is about. But that pressure comes from knowledge, and there are some things we just don't know enough about."

The *Sunday Times* has obtained a copy of a secret hit list – compiled by consultants – that contains details of 109 areas where branches are being protected. Britain's big four banks – Barclays, HSBC, Lloyds TSB and NatWest – are thought to be using the list as blueprint for extensive branch closure programmes ... The hit list has been drawn up on the basis of the 'profitability' of the local residents. In order for a branch to remain open, it must sell a substantial number of mortgages and pensions. Therefore, areas with 'aged and settled populations' – such as coastal towns – and those with high levels of home ownership, are undesirable. Regions that are 'not attractive for shopping' will also suffer. A report drawn up for the banks concludes: 'In these locations, refurbishment will do nothing to increase business levels so branches with small catchments, where potential for new business is low, and where the shopping centre vibrancy is low, are the first candidates in the closure programme.' These branches may have served their purpose 50 years ago in acquiring customers and facilitating transactions, but today they are probably viewed as a drain on resources.[423]

The above is all about the human face of retailisation; on a macro-economic level, it is very different: 'The potential for cost savings and productivity gains from the Internet should be much bigger in the EU and Japan than in America. The impact of the Internet on growth could thus be more powerful in Japan and Europe than in America. This is because the Internet, by increasing price transparency and competition, will directly attack the inefficiencies in their economies.' [424]

The reasoning is that the United States already has a more cost-efficient economy than Japan or Europe. It is traditional industrially-based countries with high distribution margins that are likely to see the biggest price reductions and the biggest gains in efficiency. And

---

[423] Robert Winnett, 'Secret hit list threatens bank branches', *Sunday Times*, 7 May 2000, Money p. 3.
[424] *The Economist.*

that simply comes through the processes of globalisation. As soon as a firm, or a country, is exposed to more intense global competition (and all are), the Internet:

should force governments and businesses to rethink their old, inefficient habits and see new ways to get around or eliminate market inefficiencies ... The Internet allows producers and consumers to seek the cheapest price in the global market. This will make it harder to maintain higher prices and higher taxes. In Europe especially, by making cross-border purchase easier, the Internet will increase tax competition and so put pressure on governments to reduce taxes. Smaller firms in emerging economies can now sell into a global market. It is now easier, for instance, for a tailor in Shanghai to make a suit by hand, for a lawyer in Boston, or a software designer in India to write a program for a firm in California. One big advantage rich economies have, their closeness to wealthy consumers, will be eroded as transaction costs fall.[*]

Banks and financial services are one thing – trust and high street gravitas still have a part to play. In the world of betting, however, whether on horses, football, sport in general, even politics, we don't need and often would rather not be in the high street betting shops. The Internet, mobile phones and interactive television make gambling an ideal intangible or virtual service. Placing a bet is becoming more and more mainstream: it seems as harmless as doing the Lottery or entering the office sweepstake. Delivery of the information: how to bet, who to bet on, what the result of the event is, can be delivered without the 'white van man' – and at real-time speed.

This intangible is already predicted to be worth more than £2 billion by the end of 2002[425] and it is easy to see why. In the traditional, smoky, aggressive betting shops of our high streets around 1 per cent of bets are made on sports popular with the upscale new breed of punters. These sports include Formula One racing, golf and cricket. The new breed of gambler can try 'special bets'. These include soap-opera story lines, political events and the lives of celebrities. (One bet available in the spring of 2000 was whether French football star and L'Oréal brand guardian, David Ginola, following the footsteps of England's star and unofficial Mr Posh Spice, David Beckham, would have his hair cut in a skinhead style.) One of the new online gambling websites is firststake.com. Their site is for 'the kind of people who only make the occasional bet and very rarely make it to the bookies,' director Simon Grieve told the *Guardian*. Women are the obvious new target – and interactive television will bring that into millions of households in the coming years.

---

[*] Ibid.

[425] An article in Forrester Research's newsletter of 29 June 2000 reported that 5% of UK Internet users had bet, and 2% had done so in the previous three months. 'Women are more likely to be attracted, and the infrequent gambler,' it noted.

Health and healthy profits and prophets

The Ultimate Drive
In 2000 there will be about 182,800 new cases of breast cancer. An estimated 41,200 people will die from it. BMW of North America and Susan G. Komen Breast Cancer Foundation invite you to help find a cure for this life-threatening disease by participating in The Ultimate Drive. Two fleets of BMWs will tour the United States, making stops at more than 200 local BMW centers. In an effort to raise $1 million, BMW will donate $1 on your behalf to the Komen Foundation for each test-mile you drive.

Advert in New Yorker magazine, 12 June 2000

Junk mail in our in-box
SUBJECT: NEED ENERGY? LOSE WEIGHT? WANT TO BE YOUR OWN BOSS?
LIPOSUCTION ALTERNATIVE – LOSE WEIGHT, GAIN ENERGY
Researchers have found a way to incinerate fat from your body so fast, your friends will swear you had liposuction. Amazing new life altering pills work instantly blasting away unwanted pounds and inches all the while boosting your energy level and jump starting your metabolism. Do you need to shed some pounds and inches or just need more energy? To start losing weight by this weekend – guaranteed please visit *http://* ...
OWN A DIETARY SUPPLEMENT BUSINESS RISK FREE
Get your share of the billion-dollar dietary supplements market. This offer is for anyone or any organization – fundraisers, retired, college student, professional, entrepreneurs, housewife or househusband, full-time or part-time. If you know of people who need to lose weight or even if you don't YOU CAN EARN MONEY IN THIS BUSINESS. BEST OF ALL, WE SHOW YOU HOW.
For a very low start up cost you can own your very own turnkey business. We will show you how to succeed on and off the Net. We will show you how to sell, whom to sell to and how to get started. Quit making your boss rich. Work for yourself and reap the rewards of your time and hard work. When you succeed, we succeed. Interested in this opportunity visit *http://* ...
NOTE: This is not a get rich quick scheme. You will have to do work but we will help you every step of the way. When you work more, you will make more. Don't have a lot of free time? You can still prosper but it is all relative to the time you spend.

Email, 25 October 2000

An ageing population means a growing health crisis.[426] Queuing at a medical practice can now be a novel-reading experience. Waiting for a hospital bed can take months. But, as Peter Cochrane, British

---

[426] From: 'The marketing challenge – overcoming the stigma of age', Design Council, Design Horizons, website: *http://www.designcouncil.org.uk*. The over 50s control a huge 80% of wealth in Britain. However, while financial and leisure packages are rocketing, many companies are still ignoring this market. Likewise, discerning older consumers steer clear of many of the products that are designed for them. This may be because the dominant value in society is one of youth not age, which highlights the image problem associated with ageing and targeting older groups. This is reinforced by the fact that a lot of products targeted at this group lack the style that other groups command. Considering the potential of this market – in size and value terms – there are great opportunities for companies who can overcome the image problems associated with age and create products with real design integrity and style. See also Jeremy Myerson and the Helen Hamlin Centre at the Royal College of Art, chapter 3.

Telecom's Head of Research and Development, argued in 1998, technology changes things.[427] Or should do. In 1996 he wrote: 'Consider patient records; with the GP, nurse, specialist, radiologist, anaesthetist gathering the same basic information during just one illness. This is often repeated for successive illnesses and/or visits. The biggest single innovation in patient records during the last century has been to redesign the cart in which the paper is carried.' Now that is near at hand as websites for medicine grow at lightning speed. It has been estimated that a quarter of all US users of the Web look at the medical sites. According to Britain's *British Medical Journal*, 27 per cent of female Internet users and 15 of male use Web health information at least once a week. Health is Huge online – there are more than 100,000 sites and that number grows daily.

Here is a quick summary of the services provided by the major medical aggregating portal sites for consumers:

- health news and breaking stories
- online communities and discussion groups – webmd.com has more than one million people registered in online communities, from diabetes to asthma
  e-commerce – individuals can purchase healthcare foods, services or pharmaceuticals and over-the-counter medications online
- business transactions – users can interact with their health plan, and in many cases with their doctor, through an e-health website
- reference information – most sites provide searchable medical reference materials
- secure communications – posting medical histories and personal medical conditions must be kept private
- storing health-care records – major medical portals can sponsor individual websites for physicians and patients, allowing them to communicate with each other through the site, as well as make appointments and fulfil prescriptions; lab results and reports can be stored digitally at patient websites; aside from online research, storing medical records digitally may one day be the single most important advantage of the portal sites for consumers

'Nirvana for me would be if – from the time my kids were born – I could keep and control all the information about their health,' declares Rebecca Rarweel, Vice President and General Manager of onhealth.com, a consumer site targeted at women, which merged

[427] Peter Cochrane, *108 Tips for Time Travellers* (London, Orion Business Books, 1998).

220

with webmd.com in February 2000. 'A dream site for consumers would include functional tools to allow them to more efficiently and more cost-effectively manage their family's health. It would be a place where consumers could find multiple perspectives … Comprehensive sites allow users to consult with experts, and give them the ability to create a personalised online space that keeps medical records in a secure, private and safe place. You'll also be able to make appointments and even consult with your doctor through the site.'[428]

While many doctors feel that the Internet is just one more unwanted threat to their authority, the general reluctance of physicians to embrace the Internet may be changing, especially as younger doctors, accustomed to computers, enter the workforce. According to Saunders of healtheon.webmd, which is the owner of webmd.com and healtheon.com, there are well over 25,000 medical websites – and that number is increasing by 10 per cent every month.

Although the growth in the sheer number of health-related sites illustrates the undeniable thirst for medical knowledge by consumers, it does not mean that doctors are being cut out of the medical information loop. On the contrary, it will keep them in the loop. 'In the coming years, the top medical sites will allow patients and consumers to store highly personal information, share it with their doctor, and then have their doctor upload new information – a laboratory report, for example – into their medical records,' predicts onhealth.com's Rarweel. 'You'll also be able to have MRIs [MRI scans] and x-rays stored there in digital format, as well as detailed drug-interaction information. These personal sites will be controlled by the consumer, but they will also have a functional permeability – from the consumer back to physicians, insurance companies and hospitals.'[429] And this begs the question of privacy, and how the 'insurers', the financial services, in this cosy new relationship, don't become biased, premium-raising, now that they are armed with even more information.

This 'virtual service' brings other problems too. An article in the *Independent* put it concisely: 'Want an instant cure for your illness? Cancer; AIDs, even death itself? Look no further than the Internet.'[430] The problem here is self-evident, as no doubt angry lawyers, financial consultants and any other profession that is about to be 'commoditised' might argue. If we can access the same databases as our doctors and the new remedies available online, how do we know if the information is good or bad? Three

---

[428] onhealth.com press release.
[429] Ibid.
[430] Robert Baker, 'Ah yes, cancer: Just click here for a cure', *Independent* Section Two, 18 November 1999.

researchers in the *British Medical Journal* claimed the advice in the virtual sphere is variable, 'ranging from the useful to the dangerous'.[431] It leads to a classic physical human versus digital human conflict. 'Increasingly, patients are coming to their doctors with computer print outs advertising alternative treatments,' Linda Cuthbertson of the British Royal College of Physicians, told *The Independent*. 'Doctors just don't have time to sift the good from the bad.'[432]

On netdoctor.co.uk, for example, there is a 'depression test', which has been developed by the psychiatrist Ivan K. Goldberg. Using the 'simple' question forms on the website, 'you can see whether you have symptoms of depression or not'. Users are warned that: 'The test result is NOT a final diagnosis! The scale cannot replace professional help.' Filling in the forms one evening in June 2000 we discovered that: 'You have the symptoms of moderate to severe depression. The condition seems to cause serious problems in your everyday life, and you should consult a doctor immediately.' This rather frightening 'non-diagnosis', was signed by 'Medical Adviser, Jergen Holm, Specialist. Source and copyright: Dr Ivan K. Goldberg.'[433] Well, we didn't and don't feel depressed, yet honest answers solicited that response. Meanwhile, an article in *The Independent* reported:

Dubious cancer treatments that were briefly fashionable are popping up afresh on the Web. Essiac, Laetrile, Entelev, powdered Shark Cartilage, Hoxsey treatment, Greek cancer cure … the list is endless. All have either been tested and found wanting by conventional science, or have been thought too improbable to deserve investigation. All have numerous Internet sites making wild and unproven claims that they can cure cancer or other illnesses (for money).[434]

Perhaps online medicine has a little way to go yet. But almost every day news stories such as this are published: 'McKesson HBOC, the largest United States drug wholesaler, has formed an Internet unit that will sell software and services aimed at helping doctors use the Web to manage their office…[This unit will] compete with a growing number of other companies seeking to link doctors, patients and insurers online.'[435] And business wonders why the privacy lobby gets so uptight?

---

431 G. Eysenbach, E.R. Sa and T.L. Diepgen, 'Shopping around the Internet today and tomorrow: towards the millennium of sybermedicine', *British Medical Journal*, 18 November.

432 Baker, 'Ah yes, cancer: just click here for a cure', p. 9.

433 See *http://www.netdoctor.co.uk.*

434 Baker, 'Ah yes, cancer: just click here for a cure', p. 9.

435 *New York Times*, 20 June, Section C, Bloomberg News, 20 June, p. 11.,

Kidney, dear?

In a dramatic condemnation of globalisation's crushing tendencies, Benjamin Barber, Professor of Political Science at Rutgers University in New Jersey and author of the feted *Jihad versus McWorld*, posed academics at the London School of Economics a stark choice: 'It is a toss up whether a nine-year-old girl, born into poverty in Brazil or Thailand, can be more profitably exploited by selling her virginity or her kidneys.' He continued by responding to a question that had been posed in a headline in a *Newsweek* magazine, 'Who should own the code of life?' in the following way. 'If "God" strikes you as an insufficiently secular and hence insufficiently modern answer, surely private, for-profit, biotech corporations that have taken out patents on individual human genes they have "discovered" may strike you as an insufficiently humane and public answer. Under the rules of both democracy and morality, the code of life presumably must belong to some version of "us" rather than to some corporate "me".'[436]

Health is now at the centre of the retail world. With the arrival of the 'code of life' it is potentially the world's biggest business. As we move towards a world in which the ageing population becomes more and more dominant, the issues of health provision have moved beyond the statist, towards a world where personal responsibility for health – and for what we actually do to our bodies – is so much a matter of what we can buy for our bodies. So if you want to know what money can buy, try these terrifying predictions from the Millennial edition of the Panglossian *Wired* magazine.

If you are 100: The good news is that you have a fighting chance of hitting 110. You can guess the bad news.
If you are 70: Assuming you enjoy good health now, you have a respectable shot at 100. Your chances are better if you are a woman.
If you are 40: You're going to die, darn it, but some of what scientists are researching may be of use to you. Most of you push 85. More than a million of you will live to be a 100 or older. If most optimistic researchers are right, a significant number of you will live past the maximum human life span, possibly 135.
If you are 30: Close, but not quite. But, hey, you'll look great! Advanced plastic-implant and tissue engineering will give you access to augmentations and biologically matched replacement parts by age 80. Oral or injectable gene-based ageing treatments will ameliorate many of the diseases of ageing that plagued your parents. Some of you will then live to see 2100.
If you are 10: Immortalizing therapies will be available by pill and injection by the time you hit 40 – but you'll have aged, and the drugs are pricey and imperfect. The wealthiest of you will live to 150.
If you are minus 20: Bingo! By the time you are a gleam in your parents'

---

[436] Benjamin Barber, 'Can Democracy Survive Globalisation?', lecture given at London School of Economics on 25 April 2000.

eyes, they'll be able to choose germline engineering – tinkering with sperm and egg – to select for extended life-span. Though this won't address all possible variables, you will age much more slowly and take full advantage of available life-extending drugs later on. Many of you will be the first substantially augmented human beings. Can-do researchers figure that all these bonuses will combine to make life spans of 500 or 1000 possible. But just to be safe, write out that last will and testament no later than your 200th birthday.[437]

And this is not a one-off. As *The Sunday Times* reported: 'People will soon live twice as long as today, and have the potential to live 12,000 years.' The article quoted a speech made by a member of the British government's Human Genetics Commission, John Harris, which it summarised as: 'Advances in genetics will create a race of "immortals", bringing the threat of overcrowding and rivalry between generations.'[438]

Now this is retail beyond the supermarket, this is beyond the beauty race of cosmetic surgery vouchers, nose tucks and gym culture. This is beyond junk mail promising weight loss without liposuction. This is self-branding of the highest order. If we can buy into the right pills to pop. And believe such futuristic inventions … It is from the ever-forward looking *Wired* magazine yes; and yes *Wired* can sometimes be louche in its throw-away approach to the 'Better Future', but still …

Health provision has long been a target of the digerati. In 1996, Professor Peter Cochrane, Head of Research and Development at the British Telecom laboratories in Martelsham, hosted a press conference at the Telecom Tower in London. There, 500 swaying feet above the ground, he showed us 'remote medicine' as a doctor standing in London undertook a routine foetal scan analysis of an unborn child in a hospital in Bristol. It was great television. It was also symbolic of the Internet's new order. 'Why queue?', asks Tesco online. So why queue for hours at the doctor when remote sensory panels embedded in your home can monitor your health? Why queue for prescriptions at the chemist when you can buy them online? (Or 'Why stint yourself, when chocolate *is* good for you: Mars is patenting a new chocolate-making process, which it claims can help to reduce heart disease, and is using a new logo to promote it.')[439]

In the future health will be about websites as much as about

---

[437] Brian Alexander, 'From don't die, stay pretty', *Wired* magazine, January 2000, p. 178.
[438] *Sunday Times.*
[439] Compounds whose antioxidant properties can reduce the risk of heart disease. It is patenting a manufacturing process by which polyphenols can be retained in the chocolate. To promote the findings, Mars has created a 'Cocoapro' trademark, and is repackaging its confectionery with a new logo: a chocolate-coloured hand holding a cocoa bean.

doctor's practices. It is about white labels and brand names, queues and operations. As ever, it is about speed and choice. The four best-selling kinds of prescription drugs in the United States are smoking cures, fat reducers, anti-impotence treatment and baldness cures. They are all expensive. So, for the 45 million Americans not covered for these costs through private health care, there are retail options: mail order or the Internet. These are far less regulated markets. Even for the rest of the population, laden with medical cover, there are still many time savings to be made through virtual medicine: queuing, repeat prescription ordering, finding cures for common ailments, having access to the medical information that is most timely and up to date.

But, as far as we are concerned in the United Kingdom, the future of health retail online (of health as a virtual retail service) is mostly about DNA. The announcement about the breakthrough in DNA was hailed not only by scientists but also by President Bill Clinton and Prime Minister Tony Blair, whose governments had jointly supported the mapping effort. President Clinton, announcing the feat at the White House, called it 'one of the most important, most wondrous maps ever produced by mankind' – even more significant than the mapping of the American continent by the expedition of Meriwether Lewis and William Clark expedition in the early 19th century. 'Today we are learning the language with which God created life,' Clinton said. Prime Minister Blair, in a televised linkup from London, called the achievement 'a breakthrough that takes humankind across a frontier into a new era'. Blair said that it was 'almost too awesome fully to comprehend'.[440]

Indeed: but not too awesome for the pharmaceutical companies, which have been watching their market values rise with every part of the DNA code deciphered. For J. Craig Venter, a scientist who first began studying gene sequencing in the early 1980s at the National Institute of Health in Bethesda, Maryland, it was probably more than awesome. Venter stunned the scientific world when he announced that he and his colleagues at Celera Genomics could sequence the human genome ahead of the public consortium, backed by three billion dollars in public money. 'I guess people were puzzled that a business would set out to do something that publicly funded scientists have already embarked on,' Jim Kramer, a geneticist at Northwestern University Medical School in Chicago, told Agency France Presse in June 2000. 'But it makes sense in the business terms [as] it gives you a lot of visibility, and that attracts money.'

Celera (derived from the Latin word for swift) had a market capitalisation of 3.3 billion dollars at this time and has pledged to

---

[440] See *http://www.nytimes.com*, 26 June 2000.

publish and make freely available the raw data. But the proprietary software tools for viewing, browsing and analysing that information will be available only to paying clients on subscription. Celera's client list already includes some of the world's leading pharmaceutical companies: Pfizer, Pharmacia and Upjohn, Novartis and Takeda, as well as the biotech outfit Amgen.

'Our fundamental business model is like Bloomberg's,' Venter said. 'We're selling information about the vast universe of molecular medicine.' Venter believes, for example, that one day Celera will help analyse the genomes of millions of people as a regular part of its business – this will be done over the Internet – and the company will then help design or select drugs tailored to patients' particular needs. [441]

Thus, beyond the world of surveillance, the world of television shows such as *Big Brother* or *Survivor*, comes a new kind of surveillance, a new kind of information provision, which we will pay to be part of. Your special DNA, the 'bugs' in your own personal code, can be monitored by doctors to track how you are responding to treatment.

DNA is, after all, 'information'. Valuable information, for sure, but nonetheless for us, as consumers, that is what it is. In this sense Professor William Mitchell at MIT is completely right when he says: 'The basic product – digital information – is now like bottled water. It is not intrinsically worth much, but you can add value – often a great deal – by packaging and delivering it in the right ways. The structure of the entire information production and delivery chain will change as the new rules take increasingly decisive effect.'[442] So the future of our babies to come, commoditised like the amazon.com share price, is beamed to a million websites worldwide by Yahoo!'s personalised share monitor. Imagine, your DNA could be part of your Web personalisation on your home page. It could also be embedded, digitally, in your mobile phone.

Politics: the hand counting stops now

In 1996, just as the Web was getting going in the United Kingdom, Tony Blair, then a forthright leader of the opposition Labour Party, made a speech in Singapore. The speech comprised no more than 3,000 words, but was something of a landmark as it announced the arrival of the 'stakeholder economy'. The phrase and the concept have gone the way of many political dreams before them, though business has picked up on stakeholder pensions, and the rhetoric of most middle management meetings in the United Kingdom usu-

---

[441] Richard Preston 'The genome warrior', *New Yorker,* 12 June 2000, p. 66.
[442] William Mitchell, *e-topia* (Cambridge, Mass.: MIT Press, 1999).

ally passes over the 'key stakeholders' at some stage of the dreary afternoon.

After the speech, *The Guardian* newspaper decided to create a hypertext version of the Blair document, full of annotations, guides and cribs to show how this great new idea would empower us all in the great future ahead. The website took about a fortnight to create, by which time the newspapers and the policymakers seemed to have moved on to something else. However, it was *The Guardian*'s first fully fledged mini-website. Links reached out to EU websites, to American political databases, to Singapore City guides and the nascent Labour Party website. It was, at best, a limited success. One of the authors of the stakeholding ideals was *The Guardian* editor at the time, Will Hutton, whose book *The State We're In* was a national bestseller in the United Kingdom – despite (in 1996) having almost no reference to the impact of the digital revolution on our economy.[443] In 1997 Hutton agreed to respond to questions and debate on the *Guardian–Observer* election '97 website. The process was as follows: questions were monitored on a bulletin board, printed out, faxed across to *The Observer*'s editor's fax; Hutton read the questions, typed his answers, faxed them back and they were typed in, in 'real-time'. Nowadays Hutton is in charge of The Work Foundation (formerly the Industrial Society) in the United Kingdom, and uses the 'e' word with numbing frequency.

Indeed, nowadays, if you are interested in anything political there are thousands of sites. At c-span.org, a cable television and website, we have the ability to watch congressional debates and senate meetings. We can follow issues. We can, if we choose, debate issues. We can certainly get a little more information – if not the spin and analysis – than is available via traditional news media. And the global demand for democratic politics, as *The Economist* put it, 'has been as hot as for Pokemon cards'.

In his first ever Saturday webcast to the nation [on 24 June 2000], President Clinton today unveiled plans he says will move the United States government more firmly into the Internet age. The president touted firstgov.com, a website that he said will allow citizens to search all online government documents from one site. Firstgov.com will be operational in the fall, according to a message on the site. "When it's complete, firstgov will serve as a single point of entry to one of the largest, perhaps the most useful collection of web pages in the entire world," Clinton said during the Web speech, taped in Los Angeles.[444]

But politics goes far further than information provision and the opportunity to talk about state health-care policies. The Internet, that uniquely one-to-one branding medium, can sell you political

---

[443] William Hutton, *The State We're In* (London, Jonathan Cape, 1995).
[444] 'E-government Clinton wants to take public records to online forum', *New York Times*, 24 June 2000.

services too. The queues for television licences, the council taxes, the car licences, the number plates. It is all happening now, though not everywhere. Yet.

Why has it taken so long – well five years – for governments to catch up with the business world? Simple really: there is no choice about taxes, unless you decide to opt out of 'the system'. Access, too, is still an issue. But first and foremost are the issues of trust around giving amounts of information away. Despite these issues, governments are now beginning to realise – and their opponents probably realising more quickly – that they can reinvent themselves in the retailisation, digital world. Like most parts of the Internet, the virtual saves money. Unlike most businesses, branding issues are not so paramount. As with internal retail issues – 'procurement' – governments can make huge savings. Just as some of the largest American organisations are now saving around 20 per cent per year through electronic buying, so similar savings could be made in government, *The Economist* claimed (where, for example, the EU member states' procurement bill for 2000 was estimated to be almost $800 billion).

In 1999 we published a political pamphlet critical of many parts of the British Internet supply chain. The pamphlet was called 'Clicketh Here: the New Estate Agents'.[445] As part of the research we frequently emailed the British Treasury with some thoughts. As there was no reply to this activity, we then undertook the same task, asking for a regular response to a white paper about the new media. Eleven months later, this was the first reply we received:

We have recently discovered that a number of emails to the Treasury (of which yours was one) have, for technical reasons, not received an answer. We realise that your request may have been submitted some time ago now, for which we can only apologise. However, if we can still be of assistance, please resend your message to public.enquiries@hm-treasury.gov.uk or reply to this email. Thank you.

HM Treasury Public Enquiry Unit, 29 June 2000

So it is not easy. Governments don't have the same shareholder pressures that businesses do. Civil servants don't embrace change with the same flexibility as Tom Peters. However, government services will begin to come up to at least some of the standards being set by the leading retailers if government wants to keep any of its standing with the populace, us the consumers.

However constructed, government is a messy business, difficult to negotiate and chronically bureaucratic. At some stage, as Professor Benjamin Barber attests in chapter 9, government has to start showing itself in a better light to its citizens. In that chapter we will also see what some consumers think about government.

---

[445] Hunt, R. *Coffeehaus – clicketh here* (London, arehaus, 1999).

Singapore slings its bureaucracy online
Singapore is one of the most wired democracies in the world, and as such is a natural place for the beginnings for e-government. The government has instigated something called the IT2000 Masterplan, which wants to make all services, from delivery of information to the collection of taxes and everything that sits in between, fully available via digital means by 2010. It will, the government claims, 'transform Singapore into a vibrant and dynamic informations communications technology capital with a thriving and prosperous economy by 2010'.[446] Meanwhile, the rest of the world tries – at its differing speeds – to catch up.
The primary issue of this invisible, virtual service, is the most fundamental – universal access to the Internet in the first place. In 2000 it was still the case that if the world consisted of just 1,000 people then only one of them would have a computer; even in the United States, the number of people on the Web is still only around 50 per cent. That is why, as we have seen, mobile phones and interactive televisions are still such key technologies in the virtual world. But in Singapore, where so much has been spent to wire everything, it is clear that both sides can win: governments can save time and money allowing their people to sort out all their taxes online; and they can monitor those who haven't paid them.

There are tangible success stories that show government and its citizens working: a Democratic primary election for the 2000 presidential election allowed votes to be sent online. It caused a six-fold increase in the level of voting compared with normal returns.[447] More than 25,000 of Arizona's 843,000 registered

---

[446] From the Singapore Government Customs and Excise Department's handout.
[447] Richard Wolf, 'Democratic Party stages USA's first binding political election online', *USA Today*. 'Arizona voters click into history: With the click of a mouse, Monica Mims casts her ballot over catfish at Stacy's Restaurant. In the Sun City's retirement community, Betty Prince, 85, struggles with her friend Lola Boan's computer before recording a vote. 'Splendid,' she says. At the University of Arizona in Tucson, student Melinda Mills stages a chips-and-dip voting party. With a CNN camera crew filming from atop her roommate's bed, Mills clicks on Al Gore – and makes history. Move on, Amazon. Out of the way, eBay. Welcome to election.com, where the most important people aren't the candidates, but the voters. Their 15 minutes of fame comes courtesy of the Arizona Democratic Party, which is staging the USA's first binding political election conducted over the Internet. For the past four days voters have been

continued on next page

Democrats voted online during the first three days, which was double the 12,000 who cast ballots in the 1996 presidential primary, when President Clinton was unopposed. Democratic party officials quickly predicted an online turnout of 50,000 and a total turnout of 100,000. Behind the ground-breaking vote was a business: election.com, which now has offices all over the world. A six-fold increase in voting is good news for governments all over the world – particularly as only 51 per cent of people voted in the Gore–Bush election.

Upstairs downstairs, you rang m'lady?

Even at the cushiest hotels, the most [a] paying guest can hope for is a nice fruit basket, maybe a good-night mint on his pillow; how about a Bulgari watch on his pillow instead? The Ritz-Carlton has put together a special Millennium package for December 31, 1999, including his and hers eighteen karat chronis. The price: $100,000 for a minimum three-night stay (twenty-four-hour butler service, chauffeured Jaguar and bedtime mints included.

GQ magazine[448]

Then there are the things you didn't even know you wanted. Luxuries, once – physical for sure, but available as services digitally. Not just Pokemon or the AIBO artificial dog from Sony, but physical services, which, even a few years ago, we wouldn't have considered. We've already seen how the car is becoming a kind of Web browser in the chapter on peripheral space. But what about the boring stuff? In the centre of the United States, serving Boston, Chicago and Washington DC, streamline.com is now offering to do just about everything except brush your teeth. 'Our primary objective is to eliminate all of those errands the average family does on a Saturday morning between 8am and noon,' Gina Wilcox, VP of marketing at Streamline, told *Revolution*.[449] What that means is doing your grocery shopping, doing your laundry, preparing meals, processing films, repairing shoes and even recycling bottles. It will even install a fridge in the garage with a password – at no cost – so that its staff can leave foodstuffs. As in the United Kingdom, where Shell and Esso have looked at similar lock-ups at

---

continued from previous page

voting online – at work, home, public libraries, even the local Safeway – in a primary for the Democratic presidential candidate. Voting ends Saturday, when old-fashioned polling places will offer both paper ballots and computers. Proponents call it the future of democracy. They say it will raise turnout, reduce recounts, empower minorities, save time and cut costs. Besides, says party chairman Mark Fleisher, it's fun. "The sizzle is the vote at home in your pajamas at 10 o'clock at night," he says.'
[448] *GQ* magazine, December 1998, p. 28.
[449] *Revolution* (US), July 2000, p. 80.

petrol stations, Streamline is aiming at a kind of time-strapped consumer. Like the petrol station idea, this is primarily something for the suburbs, not for the centre of town urbanite.

And there is so much more: there are now 'virtual' green stamps[450] and there are estate-agenting websites, 'Real E-state', as Jay Romano describes them in the *New York Times*, with over a million homes for sale or rent. 'Buyers can electronically cull the listings of most of the houses for sale in a given area, and it is a rare real estate website that does not also make it possible for buyers to get up-to-the-minute mortgage rates, calculate mortgage repayments for various amounts at various rates and then visit an online mortgage broker or lender to get an application. "After years of consumers feeling frustrated and powerless, the Internet has cracked open the box and let consumers look inside," Bradley Inman, founder of Inman News Features, an estate agents news syndication service, told the *New York Times*.'[451]

There is Soar, the 'Searchable Online Archive of Recipes', which provides an enormous number of recipes, 'including Australian, Burmese, Chinese, Tibetan, Czech, Venezuelan and Eskimo'. The recipes are said to be described 'lovingly'. '"I'm in the process of making it even as I type," gushes the creator of Doro Wat, an Ethiopian stew, "and it's real good so far,"' John O'Mahony wrote in *The Guardian*.[452] The article notes many other sites, including speciality locations for Christmas, Thanksgiving and soups. Grocery retailers will have them all, very soon. Probably now, in fact. The website food.com can already deliver a meal and a video to the home in many parts of the United States. And that's not just pizzas or burgers: the deal done in March 2000 allows *any* restaurant to deliver via food.com. 'Anything I can ship out of the back door [of a restaurant] makes me money,' food.com CEO, Richard Frank told *USA Today*.[453] So, together with your Blockbuster video or DVD, comes something to eat. 'This is a big deal for us,' Blockbuster CEO John Antioco says. Based on consumer research in 2000, 'the appeal

---

[450] Michelle Slatalla, 'Clicks, not licks, as green stamps go digital', *New York Times*, 'Circuits', 9 March 2000, p. G1/G8. 'The S&H company recently went online with an Internet site, greenpoints.com, in an effort to resurrect one of the most famous icons of 20th-century shopping as a reward for online shopping.' The article goes on to show that the consumer needed eight books of stamps in 1962 to get a General Electric Waffle Iron, when each book held 1,200 stamps and 10 stamps were awarded for every $1 spent. Thus the waffle 'cost' $960. Today with greenpoints.com a cordless phone from BellSouth will 'cost' $2,520. Bargain?

[451] Jay Romano, 'These days, you can call it real e-state', *New York Times*, Real Estate, 12 March 2000, p. 1.

[452] John O'Mahony, 'Weblife: recipe sites', *Guardian*, 13 April 2000, Online p. 4; see *http://www.soar.berkley.edu/recipes*.

[453] David Lieberman, 'Food.com will deliver dinner, movie', *USA Today*, 15 March 2000, p. 3B.

(of home delivery) is very high and not just among active video renters. That makes us believe the potential is significant.'[454]

In one sense this shows how it is not just the professions which are behind. All big Hollywood films are now made digitally, yet when big films are launched in cinemas thousands of manual copies of the films are made, distributed to the locations throughout a country, then shown. Manual films wear out. Digital versions don't. Blockbuster, part of the Viacom group, won't one day be delivering their videos or DVDs by hand, but by pipes. When? Soon. Some day. And food.com will probably be delivering something else physical by then, anyway.

Or forget the food and vision and get to the virtual meat: 'When you're sitting in a cab, you could be sitting in a meeting. Because Orange lets you have a conference call with up to five people at once. Whilst faxes can be sent straight to your phone and printed later. So you can turn travelling time into time well spent at the office.'[455] Or forget your work and think about the other parts of your life: as William Mitchell says, the digital should bring about more face-to-face time with family and friends, thus avoiding situations such as this: 'My wife remembers with uncanny accuracy what we ate or wore 20 years ago. She remembers where I was when our first son was born (at the office working) and where when the second son followed (downstairs boiling the water). Things I choose to forget; just, alas, as I choose to let slip the time when she walked the hill to the hospital, carrying a suitcase, to have our twins induced (I was in the office working).'[456]

The Lady with the Fish and other tales from the download business

'Last week a friend e-mailed me, unsolicited, a short video clip,' John Diamond reported in *The Times*.[457] Not quite mega famous, the correspondent was nevertheless a television star: 'When the press talks about the chattering classes, this is the sort of bloke they mean,' he added. Then the punchline: 'The video clip showed a single shortish scene: a naked woman happily evacuating a medium-sized, live fish from her bottom.' (Diamond adds, touchingly, that 'As far as I can make out it's some sort of brown trout, but I'm no expert: it might well be a chub or small perch.')

Mucky films on the Internet, playground stuff – or adult entertainment for mature consenting individuals? Well, pornography

---

[454] Ibid.

[455] Orange advert, June 2000: 'Any space is your office space with Orange'.

[456] Peter Preston, former editor of the *Guardian*.

[457] John Diamond, 'Freesex.com', *The Times*, Magazine, p. 23.

now makes more money than Hollywood[458] and has moved ineluctably away from the dirty-mac brigade to the stuff of middle class acceptance and 'purchase'. Diamond writes: 'It seems to me that I haven't been to a dinner party for a while without at least a few of the participants – men usually, but not always – swapping details of pornographic websites. "Porn", a woman told me last night "is the new food."'[459] Not just food. Sex is everywhere, from $1,000-a-night hotels to Sky Digital Pay channels, the Internet, to the late-night fare of terrestrial Channels 4 and 5 in the United Kingdom. A virtual service for sure, but one that now brings in around half a trillion dollars worldwide.[460] Broadband access to the Internet is only going to make this more of a virtual service than a physical, buy-the-video one.

Sport will be the same, because of the unalloyed enthusiasm and loyalty it engenders from fans. Television currently screens sport when it wants to, often live, but we're not so easily trapped in front of the screen at the right time these days: we're time-strapped. Sports Internet sites are already very popular and soon they will be competing with traditional broadcasters. There are rumours that many of the broadcasting rights to the 2004 Olympics have already been bought by dot.com companies rather than traditional broad-casters. Stories of blank cheques and the IOC permeate many a boozy lunch with the agents brokering such deals. 'With the net it is entirely consumer-driven. You can get it when *you* want, and the content can be customised to your interests,' sportal.com spokesman, Andrew Croker, told the *Financial Times*.[461] Now sport is one thing for customisation, but the experience of being able to be the 'producer' of live football, which Sky Digital offers (on Channel 404), allowing us to watch the game from different angles from the 'real' broadcast, makes us recognise just how skilled the professionals are. With music, though, all bets are off.

It is midnight at the Tower Records store in Piccadilly, London, or Broadway, New York. The latest CD is being released at the stroke of 12 by Britney or Marilyn Manson or Radiohead or Madonna – it doesn't really matter who, they're hot and you've got to have the record. You've downloaded the sample from the Web, now you want the 'real thing'. Not much longer: the global music business may not have the gravity and augustness of the legal or banking fraternities, but they see an opportunity to make huge amounts of money. If, that is, they can stop, somehow, the down-

---

[458] Ibid.

[459] Ibid, p. 25.

[460] Ibid.

[461] Patrick Harverson and Matthew Garrahan, 'Entrepreneurs eager to put sport firmly in the net', *Financial Times*, 5 January 2000, Companies and Finance, p. 25.

loading of free music from the net. (When we were at MIT in Boston to see William Mitchell he told us that three-quarters of the Architecture School's computer server space was taken up with Napster files.)[462] Which is where the lawyers, for all their pitifully resourced websites, come back in. Copyright is the issue.

The Internet has always been a swapping medium: late in 2000 we were deluged by friends with emails of Bush-isms. Previously it had been jokes about Bill Gates, video clips of men smashing their computers, images of Brad Pitt naked, and so on. With music it is been different for a long time. In the 1970s, when recordable cassettes first arrived, the machines usually included a manual that reminded us to apply to the performing rights authorities before recording. We never did. Now, with the emergence and light-speed-fast acceptance of file-sharing software such as Napster, which (before all the law suits pulled the plug) allowed us to download music in a truly radical way, you can type in the name of song or artist you are interested in – and that's anyone, not just the unsigned Grunge band from Skelmersdale or the Reggae–drum'n'base combo from Syracuse – and up will pop a list of often thousands of examples. The music business calls this theft. Over the year 2000 Napster's fate was often in the balance. An article in *Time* magazine described its arrival as a 'millennial college trend ... provided another chilling glimpse into the dark void of a post-copyright economy.'[463]

But the music business is not stupid; maybe greedy and slow, but not stupid. It will, inevitably, use the Internet to distribute music, just as Blockbusters will use it to distribute films. As David Sinclair wrote in *The Times* in January 2000: 'Music will increasingly be delivered from the Internet, and in time the CD will become as marginal as the cassette tape is now ... Music business analyst Jon Webster predicts that the Internet will eventually bring about a "worldwide price" for recorded music. According to Webster "that price is not going to be an average of world prices, it's going to be the lowest price".'[464] (Incidentally, as of November 2000, when you could still fly Concorde to New York – for, say, £4,000 return, you would still be in profit if you bought 600 CDs in Manhattan and sold them at market prices in Piccadilly, London, such was the price differential.)

However, for most of the year 2000 Napster let us listen, for *free*, post download, to what we wanted, whenever we wanted. 'The position of students who use MP3 technology is morally and criti-

---

[462] The peer-to-peer music sharing software.
[463] Karl Taro Greenfield, 'The Free Juke Box', *Time*, magazine, 27 March 2000, p. 82.
[464] David Sinclair, 'Internet is the way forward', *The Times*, January 2000, p. 41.

cally respectable,' English professor and journalist John Sutherland argued in *The Guardian*. 'They want to mix and pick their own music. They want to form their own "interpretative communities", uncoerced by charts, playlists, DJ chatter, and MTV hype. They want a free range of aesthetic choice. Who is the better custodian of the soul of popular music: the American student body or big business?'[465]

We could also copy the downloaded files to a CD burner … the future did not so much look Orange for the music business as red as their profits burnt away. Edgar Bronfman Jr, CEO of Seagram, parent company of Universal, the world's largest record company, announced that unless something was done to stop people downloading his acts, like U2 and Bon Jovi: 'intellectual property will suffer the fate of the buffalo'.[466] Well, since then, the lawyers have played a big part in slowing Napster's business plans, if not its acceptance across the Web, until in November 2000 the company announced a joint venture with … Bertelsmann, one of the biggest music publishing companies in the world. Old and new joined; and the music probably won't be so free soon. Still, there will be another technology. And the good news for music businesses is that you can check up on people's personal Napster archives. Anyone could guess the kinds of music you might be buying next with that kind of information. Wonder what will happen next?

One answer is that the book publishers will jump on board as well. Using the well-tried midnight launching hour so favoured in the music business, Simon and Schuster and the Philtrum Press launched the latest Stephen King novel in March 2000 online. Users could download a 'free' net-only story, 'Riding the Bullet' simply by logging on and downloading – for a day. After this the book was available in a variety of computer formats including e-books (PDAs that sort of look like books) for $2.50. The result was carnage, pretty standard fare for King, actually. 'Connection errors and "time-out" messages plagued surfers seeking the 66-page tale,' *USA Today* reported.[467] Nearly 400,000 requests were made on that day. 'At one point we were experiencing 1.5 requests per second,' amazon.com spokesman, Paul Capelli, said.[468] King was quoted as saying: 'I don't think anything will replace the printed word and the bound book. Not in my lifetime, at least.' And he's right – but those downloads, the replacement of the physical by the virtual are going to keep coming.

---

[465] Quoted in John Sutherland, 'Free lunch with the net bandits', *Guardian*, 5 June 2000, G2 p. 5.
[466] Ibid.
[467] Dru Sefton and Jacqueline Blais, 'Frightfully slow download at "bullet" speed', *USA Today*, 16 March 2000, p. 1.
[468] Ibid.

It may seem another long journey from lawyers 'not getting it' in County Hall to Jon Bon Jovi not getting his royalties and loyal Stephen King fans not getting their 'Riding the Bullet'. But this journey represents the increasing powers we have to demand the best, cheapest, and most effective information from traditional professional services, and the quickest, most useful formats for the entertainment we watch and view. And if in the middle of all this digital communication somebody comes and cleans the kitchen for us as well, so much the better. No?

Chapter 8 – Burn baby, burn

Big names, you know, Chanel, Dior, Lagerfeld, Givenchy, Gaultier, darling, names, names, names!

Patsy, *Absolutely Fabulous*

And the hairdressers in Italy, my goodness! I began to wonder if I knew my own country! Now in my old favourite barbershop off the Via Veneto, they have new young men who ask me what kind of shampoo I want. I say, 'Just wash my hair, please – what's left of it!' 'But is it oily or dry, signor? We have three kinds of shampoo. Have you dandruff?' 'No!' I say. 'Can't somebody have *normal* hair these days, or doesn't ordinary shampoo exist any more?'

Count Bertolozzi, talking to the studious yet aesthetic killer of many men, Tom Ripley, in Patricia Highsmith's *Ripley Under Ground*

Because I'm worth it.

L'Oréal advert: Kate Moss, David Ginola, Jennifer Aniston et al

So far we have looked at how we are sold to, and where and at what speed. We have seen how spectacle and communal space can be used to sell us things. We have seen how these things don't need to be 'physical' but can be virtual services, can be 'information'. But what exactly is it that we are buying, wherever we are?

In most shopping experiences we are not necessarily 'buying into' physical things. Even when carrying out practical grocery shopping, which is increasingly about a weekly top-up, we are making a choice about where to go – supermarket or local shop, hypermarket or online – each has its own 'brand value' in a practical sense.

We are not, it is perhaps more accurate to say, 'buying into' physical things, we are buying into 'world views'. These created environments have been deemed 'brandscapes' by the anthropologist, John Sherry.[469] But whether it is a Volkswagen car, a holiday from lastminute.com or a soap powder from Unilever, what we are actually buying is a brand. We are buying a logo, a strapline, a vision, a way of looking at the world – in the end, something that defines us: who we are now, not who we were yesterday. We are buying the creation of part of ourselves. An advert for Nokia phones, for example, showed a slim, pretty young woman who says: 'I never copy other people's style but sometimes I notice that they copy mine.' Touché. That idea is what we all want to buy. We are the brand as much as the branded object – we are buying. We want to be first among equals, as it were.

What is odd about this relationship is that for the most part brands are invisible; made invisible by the everywhereness of their

---

[469] John Sherry, *Contemporary Marketing and Consumer Behaviour* (London: Sage Publications, 1995), pp. 3–10.

iconography, their advertising, their products. They are so all-consuming that, as authors and brand experts Barwise, Dunham and Ritson argue in their essay 'Ties that bind brands, consumers and businesses': 'We rarely question their nature and function.'[470]

Put more aggressively, as the American brand expert, Rob Frankel says in his 'prime directive' on his website: 'Branding is not about getting your targets to choose you over the competition. Branding is about getting your prospects to see you as the only solution to their problem.'[471] Now this is true and not true: there are many brands 'out there' that are not the solutions to our 'problems'. Yet they thrive.

Who are you (again)?

JEALOUSY
Why we need it as much as Love and Sex
THINK LIKE AN OLYMPIAN
& Improve Your Game
No-Fail Pet Therapy
Positive Psychology: The Next Wave
          Coverlines from the June 2000 edition of *Psychology Today*[472]

We are repeatedly told that we don't know who we are. Are we, as journalist and author, Michael Weiss, writes, 'part of a diversity in all its messy glory – from the yuppie enclaves of San Francisco to the ghettos of the South Bronx, to the prairie villages of western Minnesota'[473] – or the new media loft fortresses of Clerkenwell, East London, the dispossessed high-rise estates of Rotherham to the prairie lawns of Surrey suburbia? Do we fit into these clusters? Or do we sit in them uneasily, being many people who have identities that define us in other ways depending on where we are, who we are with, what we are doing, and what we want to get out of the situation? Are we not, really, a mass of contradictions where resolution does often come from consumption? That consumption might be of first editions of Proust or pirated copies of Playstation games, might be of *Prospekt* magazine or Playboy Online. We are what we do, not what we say – as political focus group research often seems to prove. This process is exacerbated by the requirements of a rapidly changing jobs market, which makes us need to be in a constant process of 'lifelong learning', a constant process of change. We are not only the things we do; we are also, literally,

---

[470] Patrick Barwise, Andrea Dunham and Mark Ritson, 'Ties that bind brands and consumers and businesses', in: *brand•new* (London: V&A Publications, 2000), p. 73.
[471] See *http://www.robfrankel.com*.
[472] *Psychology Today*, June 2000 (the issue included the first annual *Psychology Today* Mental Health Awards).
[473] Michael J Weiss, *The Clustered World* (New York: Little Brown, 2000).

what we do. 'I'm a computer programmer' wasn't so cool in 1989. 'I'm an Internet designer' *was* in 1999. (In the year 2000, the phrase was more of a 'whatever'.) We are how we self-brand ourselves.

The American novelist and writer, Sharon Krum, has explored the relationship between the brand and the individual: 'In America the movement to self brand is very hot.'[474] Her first novel explains how to become a celebrity in America – part one, perhaps, of the 'dream'. Its fiction is based on her knowledge of the worlds of American fashion and moviemaking, which she writes about for a range of upmarket magazines in the United States, the United Kingdom and Australia.

There are even seminars you can go to, teaching you how to turn yourself into a brand. The whole idea that you are your own best product is, I think, an extension of the celebrity culture that dominates today. Joe Citizen watches everyone get their Warholian fifteen minutes and he wants his too. But how do you do this? You outlay a thousand bucks for a computer, get on the Internet, build your own web page and suddenly you exist as a 'brand'. Once you are a dot.com you can then spin your presence in cyberspace into offline opportunities as well. (Joe Citizen, who collects matchsticks, writes a matchstick newsletter online once a month, gets quoted in the media and he is off and running and then gets an offer to market Joe Citizen matches – natch, the person becomes a product) because the perception is: a website confers legitimacy. I don't think it was possible to self-brand before the Internet. The amount of money and labour required meant it was only possible for movie stars to pull it off.[475]

This might explain why, one minute after Downing Street released the name of Prime Minister Tony Blair and Cherie Blair's youngest child, Leo, the website names leoblair.com and leoblair.co.uk were bought by a school teacher from Norwich, East Anglia. Diana George had already had an offer of 'a few thousand pounds' from a tabloid newspaper when *The Independent* – a far more upmarket brand – contacted her. She told the paper that she turned down the offer because she 'did not want to be associated with them'.[476]

This story has everything: competing brands, commerce, speed, legitimacy and illegitimacy (tonyblair.com is owned by a company in Portland, Oregon and registered two months before he won the 1997 general election).

It is argued that we may be moving towards a time when, as Tim Berners-Lee writes in *Weaving the Web*, we all become a node on a network, each representing who we are by the contents – not of our shopping basket – but of our hard drive. Well, maybe. We

---

[474] Sharon Krum in personal interview, June 2000.
[475] Sharon Krum, *The Walk of Fame* (London: Quartet Paperbacks, 2000).
[476] Charles Arthur, 'Blair tot.com Leo loses out in the rush to register his name', *The Independent*, p. 1.

believe the retail world will always be about the shopping basket and the hard drive, the physical and the virtual. What hard drive, for example, would we be looking at when we do the self-analysis? An IBM or a Compaq? This book has been written on two hard drives: a graphite, coloured Apple I-Book and a Topline, a Dutch PC. One is fashionable, Tyler Brûlé, the founder of *Wallpaper** magazine, likes them; the other a commodity PC. What does that say about the authors, us? Who knows? The branders do.

For, to be a brand ourselves, we have to consume other brands. At Autostadt, where the Volkswagen brand evolves into a kind of utopian arts festival cum entertainment zone, Stefan Vogel, the spokesperson for Volkswagen said: 'I don't understand why in the United Kingdom you advertise the Skoda car [part of Volkswagen empire] by saying "You needn't be embarrassed any more." In Germany the advertising says "You're smarter than Volkswagen buyers, because you're buying better value."' What Vogel is saying at one level is that Volkswagen is the stronger brand – and thus some of us will pay more to buy into its values for reasons of taste, exclusivity and brand-awareness. The same is also true for the travel website, lastminute.com. There are many websites offering last minute travel, but none has caught the imagination like LastMinute. Why? Perhaps the presence of its founders, Brent Hoberman and, particularly, Martha Lane-Fox, in the pages of every newspaper and magazine around for eight months helped. Weren't we all Brents and Marthas for a few heady days after LastMinute's successful flotation on the stockmarket? As Jared Sandberg wrote in *Newsweek* in May 2000, 'It's easy to drift into the latest American Daydream [it was everywhere, actually] ... The details may be sketchy, but the drift is clear: a new Internet business, lots of money and long stretches of vacation interrupted by short spurts of work.'[477]

Perhaps it was because the company's clientele were still largely London-based young professionals and LastMinute chose to spend their advertising money on the sides of London taxis, which, incidentally, young professionals often take? Perhaps because the name, unlike so many dot.coms, is accurate, descriptive and enticing?

A brand self-evidently has branding; this is not merely its advertising, nor the sponsorships it takes up, nor, as we have seen with Volkswagen, the sum of the football clubs, art galleries and theme parks it accumulates. Branding is the thing that cements these products and services in our mind and makes us look favourably towards them as we create our self-brand. Faced with the plethora of choice and speedy change we have highlighted in chapter 1,

---

[477] Jared Sandberg, 'The cult of the entrepreneur', *Newsweek*, 29 May 2000, p. 60.

brands fight hard to maintain and evolve their 'brand position'. Pepsi, for example, talks of share of stomach – its chief rivals being water, coffee and tea.

It is not easy; the wealth of information – and our gut reactions to products – suggest that many things we are sold are very similar to each other (just as we secretly know we are very like many other people, even if we are not being reinforced in this message by advertising and media, who are all telling us we are unique. In April 2000 *The Daily Telegraph* reported on a court case that made branding seem ever more necessary for manufacturers and retailers alike, and highlighted the new information with which we as consumers are able to counter brandings' seductions. 'Cosmetics and perfumes are "worthless" and the only difference between rival brands is the name, the former head of Yardley[478] told a tribunal yesterday.'[479] Richard Finn, who had been chief executive of Yardley, the perfumer famous for its lavender, sandalwood and other 'British' scents, said that such products were 'two a penny'. He added that: 'Where physically there is nothing to choose between your product and the next company's, all is determined by what the name brings to the product ... The value is in the name. You can get contract manufacturers to make them for you.'[480]

We don't any longer really believe there are great differences between a Big Mac and a Whopper, one brand of coffee chain and another: there is too much information out there for us to be that naïve – it is location and convenience that counts when it comes to fast-food and drink, and many other kinds of goods and services. That's why big brands often do so well: their 'branding' and their outlets are easily accessed, they simplify our lives, they are there in the high street in the best locations. That's why, when we're inside these kinds of retail outlets, our retailers look to create emotional relationships with us. 'The people who line up for Starbucks', Howard Shultz, CEO of the company wrote in 1997, are there for 'the romance of the coffee experience, the feeling of warmth and community people get in Starbucks stores'.[481] By this definition Starbucks Coffee is clearly a brand as defined by Jean-Noël Kapferer, an academic at the HEC School of Management in Paris: 'A brand is not a product. It is the product's essence, its meaning, and its direction, and it identifies its identity in space and time.'[482]

---

478 A cosmetics company bought by the German company Wella.
479 'Change the name the scent's the same', *The Daily Telegraph*, 3 April 2000, p. 3.
480 Ibid.
481 From Starbucks' promotional material, available in their cafés.
482 Jean-Noël Kapferer, *Strategic Brand Management* (London: Kogan Page, 1992), p. 11.

A brand is also a kind of watermarking, a trademark, name, even a shape (the McDonald's Fries pack is a trademark and copyrighted, for example). It is what helps to distinguish the differing meanings and associations we have for a brand as against a commodity (for example, the 'own label' colas or baked beans or coffee available in most supermarket chains). This is what is known as brand equity. If brands have good equity, it seems, they become our 'friends'. Brand Strategy, a London-based brand consultancy, surveyed 1,000 consumers in 1999 and asked them to categorise their relationships with brands – as either 'casual acquaintance' or 'friend'. 'Service brands – which rely heavily on human interaction – fared badly, whilst straightforward products did well. Least loved were telephone companies with an overwhelming 70% of respondents claiming them to be no more than a "casual acquaintance". Supermarkets and banks were also rejected – 60% put them into the casual category. Best loved turned out to be a favourite tea or instant coffee brand – 52% considered these products to be a friend.'[483] And with friendship come the three key ingredients of a successful brand: it is trusted, it is familiar, and it has a 'difference'.

So this isn't a chapter about branding, but about us as brands – the final virtual barrier. We are a brand too. Our real-life 'friends' are brands as well. To mirror Kapferer's words: we too have an essence, a meaning, a direction, an identity based on space and time. Symbolically, and firstly, this Me Brand requires outward signifiers. That is to say, 'We wear Dolce & Gabbana rather than Levi's to signify our sophistication, taste, and wealth.' That is to say, 'We drive a Volkswagen not a Fiat, because we are Germans and we have grown up inside Volkswagen cars, have been in Volkswagens for all our lives, and now we are a family, part of the Volkswagen family.' That is to say, more darkly, 'We will not employ that person because they wore Hush Puppies, not Church's shoes to the interview.'

There is a happy end for the Hush Puppy owner, though. 'It seems that, towards the end of 1994, there was a crisis at the Hush Puppy factory,' wrote Nigel Spivey, reviewing *The Tipping Point* by Malcolm Gladwell. Spivey continued: 'There was talk of discontinuing the brand. Then a couple of Hush Puppy executives encountered a stylist from New York who relayed the news that a gang of kids in downtown Manhattan had begun to sport the crepe-soled shoes anew. Designers included them in their spring collections; Hollywood icons called for pairs by the double. In 1995 sales rose to nearly half a million, and that was without any promotion whatsoever.'[484] Well, yes and no: being a 'brand' is precisely about PR

---

[483] Survey by Brand Strategy, 'Retail brands: foe, not friends', 23 October 1999.
[484] Nigel Spivey, 'How to move and shake the world', *Spectator*, 27 May 2000, p. 40.

companies persuading 'designers' to use, and 'Hollywood icons' to wear, your products; not just about promoting them using advertising on billboards or prime time television. As Barwise, Dunham and Ritson wrote: 'Nor is advertising essential to the development of brand equity. The customer franchise of brands like Microsoft, IBM, Mercedes Benz or Harrods has little to do with advertising in the traditional sense. A market such as petrol is dominated by the number, location and quality of outlets with price a secondary factor and branding probably only third. Similarly, with infrequently bought items such as cars or white goods, the product itself, its price and availability, *and the firm's general reputation* [our emphasis] (corporate brand equity) are considered to be more important than advertising.'[485]

Secondly, the Me Brand requires the internal signified. That is to say, 'We feel good that we wear Hush Puppies because Noel Gallagher from Oasis does – or did.' 'We use the graphite I-Book from Apple because other cool, creative people do.' 'We drive an Audi TT Roadster because we are design-conscious, style-conscious people.' These purchased signifieds have been bought because we have a self-image, a My Brand Awareness. This is why technology (the Internet in particular, mobiles following right behind) is now being used so stridently to create the idea of personalisation: we are in the era of MyBrand, My Yahoo!, the Daily Me, the personalised car, the unique home, the unique me. Our web home page can be made up of 'facets' of our lives: our weather – personalise it. Our stock ticker – personalise it. Our news – personalise it. Our entertainment – personalise it. Our online shopping mall – well, you get the picture.

But how powerful are we as we create this 'me', this 'self'? 'It is a marketing given by now that the consumer defines the brand,' said Unilever Director, Sir Michael Perry, in 1994. 'But the brand also defines the consumer. We are what we wear, what we eat, what we drive. Each of us in this room is a walking compendium of brands.'[486] An article by hip US cultural commentator, Douglas Rushkoff, helps put Perry's statement into its paradoxical context. Rushkoff, whose *Coercion: why we listen to what 'they' say* was published in 1999,[487] described in *The Times* being in a sports superstore and first observing and then interrogating a teenage boy who was in search of trainers.

---

[485] Barwise, Dunham and Ritson, 'Ties that bind brands and consumers and businesses', p. 7.
[486] Cited in Yianni Gabriel and Tim Lang eds. *The Unmanageable Consumer, Contemporary Consumption and its Fragmentations* (London: Sage, 1995), p. 36..
[487] Douglas Rushkoff, *Coercion: why we listen to what "they" say* (New York: Riverhead, 1999).

'He was slack-jawed and his eyes were glazed over,' Rushkoff wrote.

I slowly made my way to the boy's side and gently asked him, 'What is going through your mind right now?' He responded without hesitation: 'I don't know which of these trainers is *me*.' He explained his dilemma. He thought of Nike as the most utilitarian and scientifically advanced shoe, but had heard something about Third World workers and was afraid that wearing this brand might label him as anti-Green. Then he considered a skateboard shoe, Airwalk, by an 'indie' manufacturer, but had recently learnt that this company was, in fact, almost as big as Nike. The truly hip brands of skate shoe were too esoteric for his profile at school – he'd look like he was 'trying'. This left the 'retro' brands such as Puma, Converse and Adidas, for which he felt no real affinity since he wasn't even alive in the 1970s when they were truly and non-ironically popular. With no clear choice and, more importantly, no other way to conceive of his own identity, the boy stood there, paralysed in the modern youth equivalent of an existential crisis. Which brand am I, anyway?' [488]

And you thought it was tough out there as an adult? In this – somewhat absurd, but nevertheless accurate, reflection of what it is like to be a teenager obsessed by the right kind of cool – we can witness, depending on our position, both the consumer as rigorous self-inventor or as hapless victim. Let us imagine that we, teenager or grey panther; 40-something or four-year-old, are always both. That these polarities are merely examples of some of our many 'selves'.

We want to be an individual, and we want to belong to a gang called People Like Us – PLUs. While 'brand essence' is the term used to define how companies react with our world, our personal brand essence is about how their products are perceived by us both as individual consumers and as micro-cultures. And it reminds us that, while we are all unique individuals now, there are still many types of cluster analysis, locating us in Balkan-style tribes. The sexy ones usually make the newspapers. In *The Clustered World* Michael Weiss states that: 'According to the geodemographers at Claritas, American society today is composed of sixty-two distinct lifestyle types – a 55% increase over the forty segments that defined the US populace during the 1970s and '80s.' Some of the reasons given for the growth of these new descriptors include: 'Immigration, women in the workforce, delayed marriage, aging baby boomers, economic swings.'[489] These social shifts, together with the increasing power of technology to analyse them ('advances in database technology that link the clusters to marketing surveys and opinion polls'),[490] allow far more focused and accurate behavioural observation. Whether groups within Weiss's

---

[488] Douglas Rushkoff, 'I don't know which of these trainers is me', *The Times* Weekend, 6 May 2000, p. 4.
[489] Michael J. Weiss, *The Clustered World* (Little Brown, 2000), p. 10, 11.
[490] Ibid.

clusters, as he puts it, 'prefer tofu or tamales, Mercedes or Mazda, legalising pot or supporting animal rights'.[491]

The tribes change: time changes everything; some products and services have cycles, others vanish forever (until they are revived in ironic 'retro' chic) – the models and the products in the Habitat catalogues from 1965 to 2000 prove this. Gap clothes are advertised everywhere yet, beyond that clean, bright world of their posters and television adverts, the Gap brand represents 'cool, reasonable, consistency'. We know what we get from Gap, how we will look individually – and collectively. Its brand represents something other than aesthetics, though, something intangibly upbeat and clean. Gap sits alongside a number of 1990s brand and success stories such as Ikea – but, more fundamentally, it plays to our (current) sense (in the design-conscious cluster) of less being more. Of order in minimalism. Gap is not the Bauhaus, but Gap is like Nike or Starbucks Coffee in the strength of its brand. So strong, in fact, that many see its overweening brand strength as a reason to be fearful of it. And yet, Gap's figures in 2000 were poor; it concentrated too much on the youth skateboarding market; it launched Old Navy as a secondary brand and saw this take market share from Gap. Will Gap last, or will shareholders shortly be screaming to their brokers, 'mind the gap'? As the design writer, Stephen Bayley, wrote passionately in Blueprint magazine: 'Another chasm of ignorance [Bayley is very angry that the British retail design consultancy, Fitch, has sent out a press release claiming that "brands are the new religion"] is that the brand phenomenon has an indefinite life. I am not so sure. As soon as something becomes commonplace, intelligent people tend to look elsewhere. At one e-commerce forum, a debate centred on how to keep premium-priced products like Gucci *off* the net.' [492]

At the other extreme, in the past two years a host of dot.coms have used highly expensive advertising to promote their otherwise anonymous websites. As Leslie Kaufman wrote in the *New York Times*:

Last year, Web merchants came to the holiday retail party spending like the rowdiest of the nouveaux riches. They saturated television screens with obnoxious advertisements, sold goods at cost or below and panicked many established retailers into spending tens of millions of dollars and in at least one case nearly a billion to meet their threat. As Christmas 2000 approaches, the landscape has been transformed. Yesterday's high-profile, high-spending stars, including Pets.com, Furniture.com and Shoplink.com, are closing almost daily. Those that remain face fiercer competition in a market increasingly dominated by giants like Amazon.com and the online arms of traditional powerhouses Wal-Mart Stores, Target, the Gap and more.[493]

---

[491] Ibid.
[492] Stephen Bayley, 'Hallelujah, praise the brands', *Blueprint*, February 2000, p. 40.
[493] Leslie Kaufman, 'Testing the retailing net is critical for online merchants', nytimes.com, 21 November 2000.

As Ajaz Ahmed, the creator of the United Kingdom's first online and branding company, AKQA, told a First Tuesday panel on online branding: 'Many companies exist on the Web without any vision of building their brand and exciting the visitor.'[494] His point was emphasised by the CEO of the advertising agency, Leo Burnett. 'A brand is a promise. Name recognition is not enough. Start-ups should not underestimate the power of the old economy companies. They have established trust amongst consumers and that is a valuable springboard on to the Web.'[495]

So what would be a British brand that has lasted as long – and as fruitfully – as Volkswagen? We asked Autostadt's Stefan Vogel who, eventually, jokingly, said: 'Manchester United'. Now United are anything but commonplace, despite 100 years of fame as a football team, and their decade as The Brand in British soccer.

'Disney, *Star Wars*, Nike.' Manchester United's Managing Director of Merchandising, Steve Richards, is in no doubt as to his main rivals to his long-term Alpha Brand soccer side when we interview him. Rivals not for the Premiership soccer championship in England, nor the European Champions League. Richards is talking about the rivals to the brand 'Manchester United', the richest football club in the world. We have already seen in 'Here, there and everywhere' that there is a cradle-to-grave mentality about the marketing of Manchester United. As the schoolchild fan becomes the passionate teenager there are Man U designer clothes to wear and historic videos to consume. As the teenager gets enough pocket money, there is travel to matches to organise and there are season tickets to buy. But the branding's allure goes far wider than this. Footballers are cultural as well as sporting lingua-franca these days. Take England's, if not the world's, most famous current player, David Beckham. Carrying on Stephen Bayley's claim that intelligent people quickly bore of the commonplace, one of Britain's most famous broadcasters, the ITN news anchor, Trevor McDonald, introduced a profile of David Beckham and his Spice Girl wife Victoria 'Posh' Adams, as follows: 'From his underwear to her eating habits – we are spared almost no detail about the lives of David and Victoria Beckham, and although the opinion polls suggest we're sick of this never-ending media interest, newspaper and magazine editors know that celebrity pictures increase sales.'[496]

To prove this, the programme cited Nic McCarthy of celebrity

---

[494] Ajaz Ahmed, speaking at 'Old Economy Marketing services to play a key role in New Economy Brands' event; email from organisers, 18 February 2000, First Tuesday.
[495] Ibid.
[496] *Tonight with Trevor McDonald*, ITV, 4 May 2000, in a section entitled Becks Appeal.

magazine, *OK*. He said: '*OK* feature Victoria and David in the magazine because when we feature them, we sell more copies. Our readers absolutely love them, they're fascinated by every aspect of their lives. We sold well over a million and a half copies of the issues of *OK* which featured Victoria and David's wedding, and I think those sales figures speak for themselves.'[497] Meanwhile, Jane Moore of Britain's largest selling newspaper, the *Sun*, said: 'There's no greater hypocrisy sometimes than the public – on the one hand, they will say why don't you leave them alone, but then on the other hand they'll lap up every little thing that's written about them, and at the end of the day, newspapers are a business and they are its cause and effect, they are supplying what the public demands.'[498] And Dave Benett, a Fleet Street photographer, offered the most holistic response: 'You know, the thing about the two as a couple which is in fact unbeatable; David interests the whole of the back page buyers. Then you've got the other side of it, which is Victoria Beckham, which all the girls buy. Now, put together, you're actually taking the front pages, the middle pages for fashion and you've got the back pages for this guy because he, and you know, he's always scoring great goals.'[499]

We tested the theory the next day. The front page of the *Mirror*, the main rival to the *Sun* newspaper, a mass-market tabloid, featured a front page exclusive: 'Police probe "bullet in the head" death threat to Posh'. The story revolved around a death threat to Victoria Beckham in the form of a 'sickeningly defaced newspaper photograph ... [which] had a bullet drawn on it directed towards her'. On page 3 the newspaper celebrated the 'romantic break' the couple had taken – it was a 'second honeymoon' in the picture caption – in Florence, under the headline, 'Away from the hate ... Posh and Becks so much in love'. The story told of how the couple, 'took in the sights of the medieval Italian city before whizzing Brooklyn [the third party in the Posh 'n' Becks narrative, being their young son who was conceived in New York] round the shops in his buggy'. Although the sports pages didn't feature Beckham the footballer, the paper devoted three-quarters of its prized back page to an 'Exclusive Picture' describing Manchester United Football Club's new football kit for the 2000/1 season, with pride of place going to the logo for new sponsors, Vodaphone, the mobile phone company.[500] Indeed, the sponsors are name-checked in the copy and – without any criticism of yet another kit change – the article is almost a press release about the shirt: '[it] is expected to retail at

---

[497] Ibid.
[498] Ibid.
[499] Ibid.
[500] James Fletcher, 'You can put THIS shirt on United winning the title again next year', *Mirror*, 5 May 2000, p. 60.

around £39.99 to £42.99 for adults and £29.99 to £32.99 for children,' it concluded. Inside, the same journalist interviewed Steve Richards, who was able to inform *Mirror* readers about the new shirt, 'Richards insists the Club's hand was forced by the change in the £30 million sponsorship deal with Vodaphone,' the article states with little comment.[501] Richards, quoted verbatim for nine paragraphs, practically a novel by tabloid newspaper standards, was able to brand to parents, cost free – it must have seemed like the UEFA cup final all over again: 'if you take the kids' stuff, for instance, mums love it,' he said. 'It is wash and wear, kids live in it all day, it has to be pulled off at the end of the day to sling it in the machine. You don't have to iron it, it lasts forever, it is virtually bullet proof so from a value-for-money point of view it is fantastic … The mums say to me we don't like the price but we do get great value out of it. They can't wear it out – until they grow out of it, they have never got it off their backs. When you talk to people at the grass roots that is what they say.'[502]

In fact, within the 60 pages of that day's *Mirror*, not only did David and Victoria Beckham enhance their brand equity, but Manchester United received a free advert for its new shirt, Vodaphone received some pleasant coverage away from the City pages, and the man in charge of Manchester United's merchandising reiterated the trust and utility of his new product to his key market, parents. Now that's branding.

Just as we are brands, so are our icons. When we think of ourselves we also think of our role models, heroes or film stars. When television personality, actress and über role model, Oprah Winfrey, launched her own magazine, *O: the Oprah Magazine* in April 2000 it was not difficult to see why. Her image on the front cover of other magazines causes retail frenzy: 'When Ms. Winfrey appeared on the cover of *In Style* in November 1998, it was that magazine's best-selling issue ever, with almost 900,000 copies in newsstand sales. She was on the cover of *Vogue* the prior month, selling 810,000 copies on newsstands, and of *Good Housekeeping* in December, selling 1.4 million copies on the newsstand – best sellers for both magazines that year,' the *New York Times* reported.[503]

The magazine is aimed at women between 29 and 49 and is, as the celebrity says, 'a personal growth guide for women'. Explaining the fraught nature of the launch, as many editors tried to work out how to position the magazine to consumers, worrying about the 'diffusion' of the editorial vision, Winfrey took the editorial staff to

---

[501] James Fletcher, 'United's masterplan to stitch up the world', *Mirror*, 5 May 2000, p. 58.
[502] Ibid.
[503] Alex Kuczynski, 'Oprah Winfrey breaks new ground with magazine venture', nyt.com, 3 April 2000.

her Miami home and told them: 'Look, I know that to you guys the Oprah name is a brand. But for me, it is my life, it's the way I live my life, and the way I behave and everything I stand for.'[504]

Winfrey is right to be careful; we are all careful about how we brand ourselves. Branding is the 'trust' world value, which means we know what we will get when we eat McDonald's in Moscow or when we run in Nikes in the Newcastle marathon. It means a kind of economic and service-faced lingua franca. It is also ours, in meetings, travelling; even with friends. Naomi Klein writes that the success stories of the branding world 'integrated the idea of branding into the very fabric of their companies. Their corporate cultures were so tight and cloistered that to outsiders they appeared to be a cross between fraternity house, religious cult and sanitarium. Everything was an ad for the brand ...'[505]

Stephen Bayley was angry about the 'brands are the new religion' metaphor of Fitch: 'Have you seen what is happening to the established church?' he asks. 'Attendances are so low there are scarcely any relevant statistical tools to assess them. I mean: if you wanted to boost the brand concept, you would not choose a religious metaphor.'[506] Well, even religion can benefit from branding, it seems. The director of the International Advertising Association, Rupert Howell, told *The Independent* in February 2000: 'Party political broadcasts are probably as secular as you'll get to religious sermons and the ad industry has transformed them in recent years into interesting pieces of communication. I don't buy the notion that creative communication can only be employed in a commercial field. Toscani, the Benetton campaign photographer, was right when he said that the Sistine Chapel is the world's best poster and the Cross the greatest logo of the lot – the ultimate branding device.'[507]

The Cross via the soap powder is a mighty distance, ideologically, spiritually and commercially but Howell's reiteration of argument about the Cross does fulfil the branding criteria of trust, familiarity and difference. His analogy to politics is useful too. As advertising copywriter and member of the Christians in Media group, Chas Bayfield, pointed out: 'The local vicar is no longer the most educated person in town, so why would people want to listen to him preach for an hour?' No, but he is trusted. He is a brand with essence, meaning and direction – even if his demographic audience is dwindling.

[504] Ibid.
[505] Naomi Klein, *No Logo* (London: Flamingo, 2000).
[506] Bayley, 'Hallelujah, praise the brands', p. 40. Stephen Bayley, *Blueprint*, February 2000.
[507] Jade Garrett, 'Just how do you advertise God?' *The Independent*, 22 February 2000.

After God

Brands have imploded on to us, as George Ritzer would say. In a website interview he was asked: 'You have described the McDonaldised society as a system of "iron cages" in which all institutions come to be dominated by the same principle. So what sort of world would you like us to be living in?'

Well, obviously [laughter] ... a far less caged one. I mean the fundamental problem with McDonaldised systems is that it's other people in the system structuring our lives for us rather than us structuring our lives for ourselves. I mean, that's really what McDonald's is all about. You don't want a creative person clerk at the counter – that's why they are scripted. You don't want a creative hamburger cook – you want somebody who simply follows routines or follow scripts. So you take all creativity out of all activities and turn them into a series of routinised kinds of procedures that are imposed by some external force. So that's the reason why it is dehumanising. Humanity is essentially creative and if you develop these systems that are constraining and controlling people they can't be creative, they can't be human. The idea is to turn humans into human robots. The next logical step is to replace human robots with mechanical robots. And I think we will see McDonaldised systems where it is economically feasible and technologically possible to replace human robots with non-human robots.[508]

Here, we would argue Ritzer is wrong; we are not being turned into robots, quite the contrary. We are becoming home-focused, hero-worshipping, solipsistic consumers, not the slaves of brands; they are the slaves of our whims (or is it vice versa?). And yes, we do want routines and scripts at McDonald's because we want to trust and eat the thing we know.

It may have been cattle that first got into the concept of branding thanks to the hot iron, it may too have once been a sign of infamy, but now the associations are widespread. Which mybrand are you going to be today?

---

[508] George Ritzer interviewed by One-Off Productions, February 1997; see *http://www.spanner.org/mclibel/interviews/ritzer_george.html.*

Chapter 9 – Spaced out – the politics of anti-retail

May 8, 1998, The White House

Dear Benjamin,
Thank you very much for all your assistance with my State of Union address. Your thoughts and ideas helped make that special night a success …

Bill Clinton[509]

Democracy once lost is nearly impossible to regain.
Rousseau, The Social Contract

The rights of man?

We have travelled via the high street, the mall, the peripheral space, the theme park, the art park and the virtual words of e-commerce, interactive television, virtual services and branding to reach another kind of virtual state of retail space – *thought*. That's to say, political thinking, by us – well, by some of us – about the globalising world and the local economy, which is driven neither by branding, nor choice, but by individual ethics, however constructed. This isn't politics as defined by the Mark Penns or Philip Goulds, the interpreters of data, focus groups and people of this world, or indeed the Tony Blairs or George Bushes. This is about the thinking, abstract or engaged, that plays beyond party politics, behind the economics of real politics. This is anti-politics, if you like, which has an effect on retailisation, which has a significant effect on some retailers and manufacturers, and which might affect them all.

At one level the politics of the anti-globalisation movements can appear to be based on the thoughtless trashing of shop fronts in Seattle, Washington or London. 'Name and shame the rioters,' Tony Blair cried after May Day 2000 violence,[510] in a voice next used to describe the soccer hooligans who went on rampage at Euro 2000 in Belgium. But beyond this there are many, not just the shop window smashers, who talk of the new threat to 'civilisation' coming not from the bomb, or from despotic power, be it of the United States or Russia, Iran or China, but from the invisible corporations and their power over us. Their omniscience.

In the United States there has been a market cluster known as the 'off the grid' – they are the disappeared, the people who live beyond the credit card and the tax-office, living out their kind of

---

[509] Photocopy of a letter, posted on the notice board at the Walt Whitman Center for the Culture and Politics of Democracy, Rutgers University, New Brunswick
[510] Front page headline, *Evening Standard,* 2 May 2000, p. 1.

Gatsby myth. They are a new kind of underclass, which has chosen to pass by the splendours of the American Dream. This chapter looks at a few of those who actively argue against the global, brand-driven world.

Always Rutgers, always Coca-Cola

CHILDREN STOP SHOPPING FOR A MOMENT. Listen to me. Mickey Mouse wants to play. His bright red tongue looks like a nice ass, with the perfect butt crack. He reaches for us with three fingered hands. Mickey Mouse is the Anti-Christ. And we are in Hell now. Do you know the feeling? Do you feel the pain? It registers as a kind of minor happiness. Elton John is singing over there on the floor to ceiling monitor. All the Disney animals at the watering hole look up and smile at his sentimental junk. Winnie the Pooh and Tinkerbell are carried along on the backs of thousands of zebras – that's us. But the children, the tchotchkes in the Disney Store cause memory loss. And the question is, how many millions of us can forget our own lives and be forced here and there like water? The Disney magicians are amazed that we are still following their little smiling animals...There is only one sin, children!

> Bill Talen, aka the Reverend Billy of the Church of Stop Shopping,
> preaching his sermon in the Disney store in Manhattan in March 2000

We are sitting in the wooden chairs in a hallway on the stark fourth floor of the Walt Whitman Center at Rutgers University in May 2000, reading the departmental notice board and drinking iced tea from a can with a large logo. We are waiting for the man who reckons that globalised consumerism – he calls it McWorld – is making children of us all. We're not here because Professor Benjamin Barber is a retail theory specialist, a media studies junkie, or a Barthesian interpreter of the signs and signifiers of our visual, brand-obsessed, age. He is a hardcore 14-book, engaged fighter for political democracy. And he is very worried about retailisation.

Barber is part of a coalition – though not consciously or willingly; his own network is academic, governmental, think tanking – of individuals and organisations that respond to the 'free' world they see, not with an economist's glee or a reactionary's horror, not with an e-economist's bottom-line spreadsheet mind or a Pandoran hermitism, but with a thoughtful questioning of 'What is to be done?' Greenpeace, Seattle, No Logo, Adbusters, the Slow Food Movement, Unplugged – there are many trying to illustrate, deconstruct, the retailisation-speed processors of the global economy, and then ... who knows? Make it better?

One thing they are sure of, as Barber told delegates at the London School of Economics: 'The encompassing practices of globalisation have created an ironic and radical asymmetry: we have managed to globalise markets in goods, labour, currencies and information without globalising the civic and democratic institutions that have historically comprised the free markets' indispensable context.'[511]

Barber is one of America's leading political theorists; he's advised governments around the world about the democratic principle – right now he is vexed about the conference he has organised with Madeline Albright and eight other foreign ministers, which attempts to create the ground frame for an annual 'Davos for Democracy'. It is taking place in Poland later in the week and time – surprise, surprise – is short. For 30 years Barber has been investigating and articulating the broader issues of civic society: how we operate in the world, how we behave, the rights we should collectively be fighting for. He wrote once of democratic politics: 'It is precisely not a cognitive system concerned with what we know and how we know it but [a] system concerned with what we *will* together and *do* together and how we agree on what we will do.' Despite his fiercely academic defences of the philosophy of democracy he fights firstly for their practical applications. He is an organic democrat, not a foundationalist.

The Walt Whitman Center Barber founded at Rutgers in 1989 is dedicated to 'sustaining democratic theory and extending democratic practice, locally and globally'. What that means is striving for an ideal world in which our vigorous citizenry engages in the culture and politics of a free society. Listening to Barber's passion it suddenly seems a long way from the themed, arcaded, disengaged madness of Times Square – where the National Rifle Association plans to create a gun theme park – even though Manhattan is only 45 minutes away on the New Jersey shuttle.

Barber sees democracy as an organic, living thing, not a set of strictly political arrangements. It is not about governments' top-down pronouncements, Clinton or Bush, Blair or Thatcher, that he writes, speaks and fights; nor about us as individuals – creatures who only perceive self. He is interested in us, consumers – though he would never call us that – of collective, collaborative, democratic life.

He sees democracy – in the sense he defines it – not happening; he sees the world of global consumerism infecting every space, taking us away from civic responsibility, taking us away from common good, immuring us from fraternity and togetherness: the McWorld he sees is everywhere from the school bus to the home shopping channel QVC.

'Look at that,' he says, pointing to a red T-shirt, which hangs down from one of his many bookcases. It is emblazoned with the words, 'Always Rutgers, Always Coca-Cola'. 'That's worth $10 million over 10 years to the University. Since the University was creat-

---

[511] Benjamin Barber in personal interview, June 2000; all quotes from this interview.

ed freshman have always shouted "Always Rutgers, Always Rutgers", at the sports track. Now, they shout ...' He sighs grandly.

The Coke deal has been in place for a few years but has no part in the academic world, Barber argues, conceding that around three-quarters of the colleges in the United States have similar deals with corporate sponsors. 'When ordinary frat boys are pissed off, saying "Hey why can't we, *like,* buy Pepsi?" then you know we're onto something about it. Even under this onslaught there are pockets of resistance. The younger generation – the sons and daughters of the Reagan era, who are just beginning to turn up as undergraduates, are really rebelling. It is not even the really smart ones – they've always been off being *independent,* watching French films and all that – these are the unexciting kids, and they're saying we're sick of all this. It is not so surprising... Universities should be about freedom, independent investigation, choice, not bottles of Coke.' He laughs: 'Rather than selling the University's brand to get money in, why don't they get the girls to sell their bodies, it is less corrupting in the long run, and probably much less harmful – they're young, after all.' Just in case the PC lobby is twitching – this was a joke, though his position about Coke is not. 'Coca-Cola isn't about having a good education. It is another invasion of what should be a public space.'

I tell him about the Flatiron bar's urinal.

> **The chairman of Nike, Phil Knight, made news again in 2000 for the wrong reasons. Nike, one of the chief brands to be targeted for its 'sweatshop' practices around the world, drew further approbation for withdrawing a $30 million 'gift' to the University of Oregon.**[512] **The University's crime? It had not joined the Fair Labour Association (FLA), a coalition of colleges, the US government, human rights groups, businesses – and Nike. Oregon chose instead to join another lobbying group also operating on US college campuses, the Worker Rights Consortium (WRC). This group also wishes to change the nature of 'sweatshop' labour globally.**
>
> **These aren't the only groups: on the Web we find 'sweatshopwatch.org', a 'coalition of organisations committed to eliminating sweatshops in the global garment industry' in which hypertext links allow us to write a letter to the CEO of Gap to complain about 'Saipan Sweatshops' or write to Sears and Street Beat Sportwear to 'demand**

---

[512] 'Nike's sweatshops are to labor reporting what OJ Simpson's trial was to the legal beat: designer dirt.' Naomi Klein, *No Logo* (London: Flamingo, 2000), p. 351.

they stop selling products made under sweatshop conditions'. There is a form to 'Make Your School "Sweatshop Free"', there is information about the unionisation of workers, and links to a variety of other anti-sweatshop campaigns (though neither the FLA nor the WRC). There are many other links, also, and the relative success of Green (consumer) warrior Ralph Nader in the November 2000 Presidential elections shows that these issues are increasingly significant.

The Oregon case brought about an interesting response from the *New York Times*, reminiscent of so many liberal debates over the years in the United Kingdom. Thomas Friedman wrote: 'The natural assumption is that Mr Knight is wrong. The truth is, Nike has a shameful past when it comes to tolerating sweatshops. But on the question of how best to remedy those conditions in the future – which Nike has now agreed to do – Mr Knight is dead right and Oregon wrong: The best way to create global governance – over issues from sweatshops to the environment – when there is no global government, is to build coalitions, in which enlightened companies, consumers and social activists work together to forge their own rules and enforcement mechanisms. That's what the FLA represents and the WRC doesn't.'[513]

In the meantime, the University of Michigan and Brown University have also cancelled their deal with Nike. Michigan is negotiating with other sports' manufacturers, including Reebok, Adidas and Puma. As one Michigan athlete said: 'The swoosh [Nike's logo] is just a symbol. The person makes the player, not the shoes.'[514]

Undermining Barber's pursuit of a fair and just way to live comes his realisation – his moment of retailisation – of this new version of *The Invasion of the Body Snatchers* – where this time the enemy isn't from outer space but from the world of global brands, and their insistence is that to shop is to be *free*. 'How can we forge a *public* when everything says you are an individual: a heterosexual, Catholic, fly-fisher, for example? It's making people like cable TV channels, each one thinking themselves *different* because of what they buy. The management guru, Tom Peters? You know what he says? We are each to think of ourselves – as a brand! And then

---

[513] Thomas I. Friedman, 'Knight is right', *New York Times*, 20 June 2000, p. 25.
[514] Duncan Campbell, 'Nike gives universities the boot as student anti-sweatshop demands rise', *Guardian*, 6 May 2000.

somebody replied to his book and said, "No, no, we are many brands." *Now, come on.'*

Barber brings the politics of democracy to the spaces, physical and virtual, that define us. And as retail, as we have shown and Barber concurs, has invaded everything, every space, he knows there is a fight on and that governments show little sign of helping. 'Where nation states do try to act collectively and in effect pool their political sovereignties in order to contain and regulate multinational corporations and the social and cultural impact of markets, it turns out that their governments often seem more interested in protecting the autonomy and sovereignty of markets than insisting on their own citizens' public interests … Politicians', he says wistfully, 'say, "What is all this stuff about privatisation? It's ok." But they've all given up on the public.'

Barber is a retail solipsist. 'Shopping is a very private thing – we can do it alone, that's why e-commerce works,' he says. 'Mall shopping isn't really about togetherness; it's about get in – get out. But you can't just think in the box called *retail.* You need, for participation, to play up the municipal buildings and spaces. You need to have *public* spaces, you need a square. You need an art gallery, a church. What do people do in public spaces? They ogle each other, have fun, they talk – then they will shop together. Most of the malls around are so efficiency-minded, and numbers visiting are down. They'll all look for a gimmick.'

In Barber's book of collected essays, *A Passion for Democracy*, he writes:

Art galleries, theatres, and museums are all at their best, town halls made for the public, open to the public, constitutive of what public is. In small towns, the town hall is often itself a community hall, the amateur theatre, even the occasional gallery for a local exhibition. One of the tragedies of suburbanisation in America (over 55 per cent of Americans now live in suburbs) is the vanishing of public space. There are no town halls, no granges, no public squares, no downtown churches or galleries or schools, because there are no towns, no uptowns or downtowns, no centre cities. The few public dwellings that exist like schools and municipal works buildings are spread around everywhere, adjacent (literally) to nowhere.[515]

He points to a flip-chart: he's been doing some consultancy for an area known as Eton Town. It was a run-down area in a smart district and nobody knew what to do. The shops weren't working, it was a drive past. 'We had a look at the plan and there, just around the corner there was a library, there was some space that could easily become square, a public square. That's the answer to run-down places, get people in them, create spaces.'

---

[515] Benjamin Barber, 'The market as censor in a world of consumer totalism', in: Benjamin Barber, *A Passion for Democracy* (Princeton: Princeton University Press, 1998), p. 151.

Barber is pessimistic for the future – but in a reassuringly upbeat way. His next book argues that we have all been infantilised by consumerism; that aggressive, all-pervading marketing and branding has turned public citizens 'into self-interested individuals, individuals into consumers and, increasingly, both turning consumers into children and children into consumers'. He calls this new, defined-by-brand adult a 'kidult'. In psychoanalytic terms, he argues, we have adopted a position, like an infant child, where we cannot distinguish the self and the world. 'The infant is drawn to the twin illusions of totally mastering the world by supplanting it with the self, and totally merging the self with the world by yielding it up completely. Dominion or surrender,' Barber says, and we – consumers – do much the same. *We are what we buy.* 'The twin illusions of mastery over the material world through the power of consumer purchases and surrender to the material world through yielding to brand identity mimic the infantile illusions maturity is supposed to overcome.' Barber isn't a psychologist, merely using some of the ideas of psychoanalytic theory to investigate his larger theme: 'There is a natural tendency in humans for mental health, and that's through integration with the world – with people. It requires *balance.*'

We are back to Jean Buridan[516] – but now, instead of merely the inertia of consumer choice, Barber is making us consider the idea that our ennui with the civic world, the place where we take responsibility for the world, is in fact dangerous to our collective future: that we are right to be frustrated after 61 minutes into a trip to Bluewater; that David Peek's 'trance state' is probably not for the best of all worlds; that yes there are side issues to being on call 24/7; that when there is no escape from Gap, Coke or Yahoo! via our third-generation, GSM-positioning mobile phone and when we define ourselves through these things, that's when we are being uncivic.

So is the answer to market democracy like a brand? To become, as the Trotskyite philosopher Gramsci would say, an 'entryist'. To play McWorld at its oven game? 'That would mean a victory for marketing,' Barber says, gravely. 'You win by losing.' He posits an election where everyone is paid $100 to vote. 'Everyone goes, trust in government is up, the civic responsibility too. But it is not. You have to win a fight like this by making the right argument.' He is scornful of the selling of politics and politicians too. 'The

---

516 13th-century French philosopher who posited the following. An ass is hungry and there are two similar piles of hay in front of him, one to the right, and one to the left. The ass has an exactly equally balanced tendency to go right as left. Therefore, given such equality of choice, it will not be able to move and will thus starve to death. In chapter 1 we argued that the contemporary consumer is like the ass, paralysed by choice.

victim of this kind of politics is the public; they are disillusioned.'

(Later that night, back in our New York hotel room an advert is rotating on the late night chat show breaks for a website called I-Won. Its premise: each day money is given away to people who sign up. Once a year $10 million is on offer. 'Which would you choose, the one with the news, or the one with the news and the money?' the voice-over asks. 'The one with the money,' says a cheaply dressed Everyman dork in a monotone voice. *Just follow the money.*)[517]

What about the Internet's ability to disseminate information? It is out there, we argue, everything from philosophy through the codes to human life, to the bulletin boards and websites of counterculture, such as the anarchist computer network, Tao.

"Our generation, yours, grew up with the books. I grew to understand the tele-vision and video culture [Barber was born in 1939], you grew to understand the Internet. We both acquired all of the self-editing and research skills in rigorous ways. So, yes, for us, the Internet is a fantastic tool. It is a fantastic tool for the traditional generations now. But imagine a world where it is the primary source of all information – your first source. The world where there is no difference between Walter Kronkite and Matt Drudge. That generation is going to say – 'What's the difference?' There are no mediators, no masterwork, no pedagogies – it's just a chaos. The Internet looks like freedom, but it's chaos, it needs hierarchies. I – you – we can pick our poison, make the choices, but where are standard setters which leave us, the people, autonomous?

Democracy depends on deliberation, prudence, slow-footed interaction and lengthy (thus 'inefficient') forms of multilateral conversation and social interaction that by post-modern standards may seem cumbersome, time-consuming, demanding, sometimes interminable and always certifiably un-entertaining... Computer terminals, on the other hand, make process terminable, for electronic and digital technology's imperative speed. Computers are fast as light, literally. Democracy is slow as prudent judgement, which is very slow indeed."

There are those who would disagree, who would argue that there is methodology on the Internet, beyond that of e-commerce and unreliable narrators and speed-rush nausea, that we can find our own routes to the kinds of information we desire. Tim Berners-Lee – for example – the inventor of the World Wide Web, writes

---

[517] The catchphrase, if you will, from a movie about a previous generation's loss of faith in the American political process, *All the President's Men,* the Robert Redford and Dustin Hoffman take on the exposé by *Washington Post* reporters Carl Bernstein and Bob Woodward of the Watergate burglaries and, eventually, of Richard Nixon's complicity. 'Follow the Money' was the phrase used by a source, never yet revealed, to Woodward in attempting to help him unravel the cover-up.

inspiringly in his autobiography: 'The Web is more a social creation than a technical one. I designed it for a social effect – to help people work together – and not as a technical toy. The ultimate goal of the Web is to support and improve our weblike existence in the world. We clump into families, associations and companies. We develop trust across the miles and distrust around the corner. What we believe, endorse, agree with and depend on is representable and, increasingly, represented on the Web. We have to ensure that the society we build and the Web is the sort we intend.'[518]

So: weaving the Web?

Professor William Mitchell, Dean of Architectural Studies at MIT, and the author of *e-topia*, has an equally utopian view of these things, as he described to us.

"I think social polarisation due to technological developments is inevitable in the short term. That is always the way it works when new innovations come through. There is no point in wringing our hands about this, though; action should be taken to manage the inequities and I believe it is a major social policy issue which needs to be addressed to enable equal access. And when I say access, I'm not talking about having the plug in the wall, that's a detail in a sense; it's having the skill to use technology. If you look back to the telephone and its dispersion, most countries introduced an equal access system, giving one organisation the monopoly but obliging them to put the system in place throughout the community even in less privileged areas. Now of course this is not immediately transferable to the Net but I think a similar system needs to be devised to manage the spread of technology today."[519]

That is the position from which Tim Berners-Lee starts, and this is the position to which Barber has currently arrived: 'The Internet, a medium that holds out real promise for increasing the pluralism and liberty of our civic and cultural lives through its defining interactivity and (potential) universal access, is fast becoming one more zone for commerce,' he told LSE delegates. 'Click on whitehouse.com and you will get a porn site – a joke perhaps in the age of Monica, but a sad commentary on URL names nonetheless.'[520] There are clearly sides to this; the utopians and the liberal free-musketeers are at war.

A report by the Associated Press PARIS describes an example of this in April 2000.

---

[518] Tim Berners-Lee, *Weaving the Web* (London: HarperCollins, 1999).
[519] William Mitchell, Dean of Architectural Studies, MIT, in personal interview, March 2000.
[520] Benjamin Barber, 'Can Democracy Survive Globalisation?', lecture given at London School of Economics on 25 April 2000.

A French anti-racism group is suing Yahoo! Inc., claiming the Internet search and directory company hosts auctions of Nazi-related paraphernalia. The International League against Racism and Anti-Semitism, known by its French initials LICRA, filed its lawsuit on Tuesday against Yahoo! for having Nazi-related items on auctions websites that can be accessed in France. France has strict laws against selling or displaying anything that incites racism. Sales of such Nazi items are against the law. 'In the United States (these auctions) might not be illegal, but as soon as you cross the French border, it's absolutely illegal,' says Marc Knobel, researcher for LICRA. LICRA is asking Yahoo! to make all such auctions inaccessible to web surfers in France and its territories like Martinique and French Guyana, Knobel said. It has asked a French judge to fine the California-based company $96,000 (100,000 euros) for each day it does not comply. Knobel said there are currently over 1,000 Nazi-related items, such as pictures, coins and flags, available at the auction site at *http://www.yahoo.com*. That number was confirmed in a web search by The Associated Press.[521]

It may be significant that at the close of his book Tim Berners-Lee talks of the parallels between the Web and his discovery of the Church of Unitarian Universalism. This is a movement that uses ideas and philosophies from many types of religions and, as he describes it, wraps them 'not into one consistent religion, but into an environment in which people think and discuss, argue, always try to be accepting of differences of opinions and ideas'.[522] This, as we will see, is a description not dissimilar from the way some chose to see the anti-corporate movements categorised as 'Seattle' or 'Washington'. But then Barber's work is laced with a communal air of the humanist spirit, as well. It is merely that one person invented the World Wide Web and fights to keep it transparent; the other fights for a citizenship that, it could be argued, has never existed: more virtual even than Netscape or MyYahoo!

Benjamin Barber has the strangest allies – did he but know it. One such is Jerry Mander, the maverick organiser of the International Forum on Globalization (IFG), a think-tank of over 60 associates, including Ralph Nader, Martin Khor of the Malaysian 'Third World Network' and David Korten, author of *When Corporations Rule the World*. Mander wrote a famous anti-technology book called *Four Arguments for the Elimination of Television*; he feels we are cut off from the nature of our planet. 'The Internet and other global communication systems have empowered multinational corporations, made them faster, stronger and more able to co-ordinate their actions internationally. Now entire currencies can be destabilised at the push of a button. In ten years, we are going to look back and recognise that the Internet is not decentralising. It is the most centralising technology ever invented.'[523] Jerry Mander does not use email by the way. Another of Barber's allies

---

[521] Jason Strazioso, Associated Press PARIS (April 11, 2000 9:21 p.m. EDT).
[522] Tim Berners-Lee.
[523] Jerry Mander, *Four Arguments for the Elimination of Television* (New York: Morrow Quill, 1978).

is the leader of the Roman Catholic Church in England and Wales, Cardinal Cormac Murphy O'Connor. At the press conference announcing his appointment as Archbishop of Westminster he said: 'I think an attempt has been made to substitute the culture of consumerism for religion. This is a seduction that assumes that everything can be bought and sold and that even human beings are assessed by what they have rather than who they are...'[524]

Meanwhile, in 2000 that most egregious of market destabilisers, George Soros, wrote of the digital global: 'Global capitalism does not necessarily bring progress and prosperity to the periphery...foreign capital often feels more comfortable with an autocratic regime than with a democratic one. Foreign capital especially when it is engaged in the exploitation of natural resources [as the World Bank is!] is also a potent source of bribery and corruption.'[525]

After the interview is over Benjamin Barber drives us back to the New Brunswick station in his shiny BMW, the 'Beemer' he calls it. (The car has one of those anti-radar devices you only see in movies.) As we get out he jokes that he wrote a version of his last book, the best-selling *Jihad Vs. McWorld*, for the advertising agency J. Walter. Thompson, who called him in as the book began to become recognised as a key text about a kind of collective threat that nationalism and reaction on one side, and homogenised, global culture on the other, has for democracy. 'Know your enemy,' I say. 'That's why the advertising people want to know about it.' *Everything is Everything now.* 'They even published it in their house journal,' Barber laughs. We are reminded of the earnest advertising men in London who, flogging their latest bad British car to us over drinks, are enthusing wildly about Naomi Klein's thoughtful analysis of the politics of counter-consumerism, *No Logo.* It had been out a few days, and already it was their Bible.

On the platform at New Brunswick a middle-aged policewoman is smoking over her copy of the *New York Times.* 'Hey Annie, you can hear me,' shouts a drunk from the other platform. 'Give me a cigarette.' She looks up and smiles. Then waves. There's a civic duty done and there's a long walk to pass on a cigarette, and she chooses to stay sitting.

Some logos

'No junk mail'
> Sticker on the front door of the author and journalist, Naomi Klein

Ratio of number of people in the world who are underfed to those who are overfed: 1:1 (United Nations)

---

524 Clare Garner, 'New Catholic leader attacks the culture of consuming', *Independent* 16 February 2000, p. 11.
525 George Soros, *The Crisis of Global Capitalism Revisited* (Public Affairs Press, 2000).

Ratio of US corn exports to Europe over the last year [1999] to such exports in 1996: 1:220 (US Department of Agriculture)
Chance that a college student expects to be a millionaire by the age of 40: 1 in 2 (JOBTRAK Corporation, Los Angeles)
Number of acres of Brazil's Panambizinho region that the country's government promised to return to the Indians in 1995: 3,063
Number of acres returned so far: 0 (from Survival International London)

Harpers magazine[526]

On the highway verges from Toronto airport into town they are creating a new form of topiary: corporate logos made out of grass with concrete edging; there's a series of 10ft-long, coffin-shaped memorials to Amex and Arthur Anderson and about 10 others of the Fortune 500 as we speed along. It is almost cute, but this is the very last interview for the book, we're tired of retail and its viral everywhereness. At least – but that is the point – it is different from the 100ft-high, building-side billboards for Gap and Canadian airlines, for the television series *Sex in the City*, and Yahoo!, which loom up as Toronto city emerges. There is a 'no junk mail' sticker on the door to Naomi Klein's house; we are early and waiting on the porch like a digital decade, John Boy Walton. She arrives with her husband clutching groceries from the local market in brown paper bags: the pair look for all the world like a 2000 AD version of Redford and Fonda in *Barefoot in the Park*. You feel instantly uplifted by their ... *niceness*.

'There's a shop near here that's been here in Toronto forever,' Klein says midway through our interview. 'It's called Honest Ed's and it's full of cheap crap. Its store front is full of rubbish, neon, huge pictures, newspaper cuttings; there's a billion garish things. Ed's belief – he's called Ed Mirvish – is that you put "all of your money in the window". And I think, that's fundamentally what our culture is doing right now, we're just looking at the facade of it, not what it really means.'[527]

Klein is a young journalist whose book *No Logo: Taking Aim at the Brand Bullies*, published in 1999, catapulted her into the counterculture stratospheres. She is the Boswell to the Seattle generation now, but more than that: she is engaged with this world of anti-brand, of anti-global exploitation, not merely commenting on it. She is very critical of the way this new counterculture has been represented in the media as a group of reactionary rebel-rousers looking for some action. A Sunday newspaper article by an academic who should know about these things claimed that the 'long' 1960s revolutions were transforming and 'there were real gains: votes for 18 year olds (Britain 1968; America and West Germany

---

[526] All from *Harpers*, index, May 2000.
[527] Naomi Klein in personal interview; all quotes from interview.

1972; France and Italy 1974); the new feminism – abortion, divorce law and university reform; civil rights and equal pay; even an end to the war in Vietnam. The miscellaneous and contradictory movements of today, not being part of any general wave of emancipatory change, will achieve little more than broken glass, broken heads and temporary headlines.'[528]

Klein agrees with the contradictions, but not with their ultimate transforming potential. Klein wrote in the *New Statesman* that the problems of the new counterculture mirror those of both the Internet, and to an extent the retailisation world. There is, in short, too much choice of types of rebellion just as there are too many kinds of sunglasses. 'Despite…common ground,' she writes, 'these campaigns [of which Seattle is the most famous] have not coalesced into a single movement. Rather, they are intricately and tightly linked to one another, much as "hotlinks" connect websites on the Internet … Thanks to the Internet, mobilisations are able to unfold with sparse bureaucracy, decentralised power and minimal hierarchy; focused consensus and laboured manifestos are fading into the background, replaced instead by a culture of constant, loosely structured and sometimes compulsive information swapping.'[529]

What Klein argues is that the campaigns against global corporatism exhibit a lack of leadership precisely because they are 'not united by a political party or a national network with a head office, annual elections and subordinate cells and locales. [They are] shaped by the ideas of individual organisers and intellectuals, but [don't] defer to any of them as leaders.' As she points out, this makes it hard for normal working journalists, the media – as are all retailers, be they of sofas or counterculture ideas – to get a firm idea of what is happening.

What Klein critiques brilliantly in *No Logo* is the economics of brand: the shift from productions with fair wages to refined marketing that backs up sweatshop labour products. Just like Barber, Klein was soon approached by the very marketers she critiqued: she agreed to meet with one large brand consultancy only if she could take a film crew with her to record the event. Getting across the anti-corporate message is one thing, she argues, 'but being aware of how you collaborate, knowing what your actions could do' is another. The consultancy declined her offer.

Klein cites the repositioning of many of the 'enemies' in recent times: what some environmental campaigners have called 'greenwashing', the association of a big global corporation with an organisation that seeks to create social change. There are limits, though.

---

[528] Arthur Marwich, 'The spirit of 68? Not a chance', *Sunday Times* News Review, 7 May 2000, p. 7.
[529] Naomi Klein, 'War of the swarm', *New Statesman*, 24 January 2000.

'When some Disney workers used the image of Mickey Mouse with blood-coloured ears to criticise the company that was exploiting them, it then turned up on the cover of *Colours*, Benneton's house magazine. How can that be radical? I'm glad Toscani has now left Benneton to be a journalist because he was reporting from an imaginary world inside that company. The World Bank recently relaunched as an AIDS elimination organisation,' continued Klein, reminding us of other attempts at greenwashing: Volkswagen, with its Amazonian rain forest at the Hannover Expo, and Shell, advertising in the United Kingdom in 2000 using an earth scientist and a geologist from Shell. The comment: 'Three years ago they would have been fighting us, now they are on the staff.'

In the United Kingdom, supermarket chain Tesco has been working with Greenpeace for over a year now. 'We were approached by Tesco last year,' Lindsay Keenan, markets campaigner of Greenpeace United Kingdom told us. 'They invited us to work with them on sourcing the amounts of non-GM foods because we have rigorous traceability systems and we offer positive solutions to problems. For example, we introduced the Greenfreeze fridge technology[530] without CFCs and we got many supermarkets to adopt them.'[531] Keenan chooses his words carefully; Greenpeace is careful – except when it makes its 'statements'. The degree to which the organisation works with the supermarket is delineated with a pedant's care; this is not, he is keen to point out, another example of greenwashing:

"We are one of the main players in the field and we have been solidly campaigning for 10 years now on an international level. The international aspect is actually key in the GM issue because supermarkets are facing a problem that if they reject GM there is not much left. This is because the international commodity market is in the hands of [a] few large companies. There were serious supply difficulties for large quantities of non-GM sources. From our point of view we wanted to ensure non-GM foods in all supermarkets. Remember that Tesco only signed up last June [1999]."

[530] 'The UK Government and Ikea, the international retailer, are the latest to reject climate-damaging refrigerants, hydro-fluorocarbons (HFCs), and acknowledge the advantages of greenfreeze technology...Ikea's decision comes after a long-running campaign by Greenpeace's active supporter networks in Germany. For the last two years, supporters have been sticking "hands off" labels on to 134a fridges [they use the Greenhouse gas HFC 134a] in department stores and retail shops...Greenpeace Australia is also stepping up the pressure on McDonald's, Coca Coca-Cola and Unilever – three major sponsors of the Sydney Olympic Games – about their use of hydrofluorocarbon.' From 'Greenfreeze technology accepted as standard' *Greenpeace Business*, April/May 2000, p. 1, 7.

[531] Lindsay Keenan in personal interview, May 2000; all quotes from interview.

When GM doesn't mean motorcars

GM (genetically modified) foods are a contentious topic, particularly in Europe. The leading funding agency for research into this area, the Biotechnology and Biological Sciences Research Council (BBSRC), states in its 'inGENEious' pamphlet, which was part of a travelling exhibition, that the technology 'allows scientists to modify and regulate specific pieces of DNA that code for proteins (genes), and to move them from one organism to another...The debate about genetic modification revolves around a number of different issues...People are discussing the regulatory issues involved with applications of genetic modification. One of these is the maintenance of consumer choice by clearly labelling food products that contain GM ingredients. Another is about how GM crops and animals should be controlled and monitored at a commercial level, and how companies are developing applications of the technology.' It concludes by stating: 'Science cannot provide all the answers, but it does play a crucial role in underpinning developments in genetic modification technology.'[532]

There are other issues. ActionAid, the anti-poverty charity, wrote in February 2000: 'Large corporations are claiming patents on plant varieties and the most useful genes from crops which people have eaten and used to treat their family's illnesses for generations. Just by altering the plan's genes through genetic modification they can claim they "own" these plants and are the only ones who can profit from them.'[533] ActionAid 'confirms' a 'gene rush'. It sounds all too like the Code of Life all over again.

In 1999 Greenpeace described GM food as 'unpredictable, uncontrollable, unnecessary and unwanted'. It recommended: 'Ban genetic engineering in food and farming.' Because of the 'inevitability of cross pollination and genetic contamination, GM food and organic farming are incompatible. The health and environmental risks in genetic engineering in food and farming are unacceptable.'[534] More tellingly, in April 2000 Greenpeace published 'GM Statements' from food producers and retailers. Here are some of the responses they received from Asda and Safeway.

---

[532] InGENEious, the Science and Issues of Genetic Modification (BBSRC, 2000).
[533] Action Aid brochure:, 'Food patenting: crops and robbers', February 2000.
[534] 'The True Cost of Food', Greenpeace and the Soil Association, June 1999.

> We listen to our customers and they have told us that they have some concerns about Genetically Modified ingredients. We have responded to those and have taken action in line with their concerns. In fact we have now successfully removed GM protein and protein derivatives from all Asda own-brand products.
> Thank you for taking the time to share your concerns with us. I hope that I have been able to reassure you and that we will have the opportunity to serve you at Asda again soon.
>
> Allan Leighton, ASDA Chief Executive[535]
>
> **Meanwhile, the Safeway chain preferred the customer 'choice' route. Director of Technical Operations, Dr Alastair Robertson, wrote to Greenpeace saying:**
>
> Our policy on GM very much reflects the current concerns of our customers and our desire not to censor but to provide choice. I accept that this does not comply wholly with your organisation's aspirations regarding GM but as a major food retailer we have consider (sic) the views of all our customers before offering or removing products from sale.[536]
>
> **Tesco announced it was removing GM ingredients 'from products wherever it is practical to do so'. On 27 April 1999 Sainsbury's 'embarked on a project with the National Farmers' Union to establish the commercial and logistical implications for the supply chain'. Somerfield said it would 'follow a policy of avoiding GM foods and ingredients in all own label products'. Waitrose, the food shops of the John Lewis partnership, now 'avoid the use of genetically modified soya and maize as an ingredient' in their own label foods (and pet foods). British Airways 'exclude ingredients from GM crops from all meals offered within the United Kingdom or on services departing from the UK'. Burger King (Europe, Middle East and Africa) 'has removed all GM from its products which would require labelling under current EU legislation'. The list goes on, Coca-Cola Great Britain, Cadbury Schweppes and McDonald's all reply. Lobbying can work.**

Klein isn't taken with the Barber view of retail, brands and globalisation: it is too lofty, too academic. 'Branding is a childlike impulse for simplicity,' she says, echoing the words of Democratic media consultant Karl Struble, who, the *New York Times* reported, 'thinks of his candidates as brands, and as any marketer will tell you, a brand cannot afford complexity. "If you want to be popu-

---

[535] Documentation supplied by Greenpeace.
[536] Ibid.

lar," said Struble, "you're better off doing fewer things, and only one would be best."[537] This kid-simple culture is how branding starts now, as *No Logo* attests.

Fuelled by the dual promise of branding and the youth market, the corporate sector [at the beginning of the 1990s] experienced a burst of creative energy. Cool, alternative, young, hip – whatever you want to call it – was the perfect identity for product-driven companies looking to become transcendent image-based brands ... cool, it seems, is the make-or-break quality in 1990s branding. It is the ironic sneer of ABC sitcoms and late-night talk shows; it is what sells ... extreme sports gear, ironic watches ... post-modern sneakers and post-gender colognes. Our 'Aspirational Age', as they say in marketing studies, is about 17. This applies equally to the forty-seven-year-old baby boomers scared of loosing their cool and the seven-year-old kick boxing to the Backstreet boys.[538]

'By doing this, you are creating imaginary worlds, leading I'm sure to a bizarre life,' Klein says. She argues that opposing this branded world, reclaiming public, private space unencumbered by the cool surfaces of the retail world, 'is *The Issue* at colleges right now in North America. There are people who are willing to get arrested for it, they are ready to fight. It is almost a badge of honour now. Barber is so dismissive of this, but I don't think he sees enough of the struggle to understand it. It's the very opposite of the Jihad. I have made a choice here, obviously. I want to help those young activists that I believe in. I could, of course, very well be wrong.'

If Klein is wrong she at least has the breadth of knowledge and experience of the new campaigners to make a serious value judgement. 'Barber goes around spreading hopelessness,' she says, 'and I think that is counterproductive.' She reports that 'the cops are at every speech I make, these days, and that's not paranoid. The more I learn about these issues, the more you realise it is right to be suspicious of the cult of the personality and leadership.'

However, let us remember, this is not just a small-time academic bunfight about politicians and notions of citizenship, this is about the positioning towards us as consumers of every organisation that wishes to grow globally. How we think about globalisation, multinationals. How we find out exactly what we are buying – wherever we might be. We asked Jan Hol, the head of PR at the giant Dutch retail chain Ahold, how the company envisaged becoming a global retailer. He replied: 'Our policy aims for Ahold to be autonomous in our sector and grow independently of joint venture. We strive to set up collaborations around the world with the market leaders so that we can add their expertise to our network. That means that we work in Central America, South America and Europe, and in Asia, India and Africa to a lesser extent. Our

---

[537] Quoted by Greenpeace in interview.
[538] Klein, *No Logo.*

supermarket chains are connected from the back – in other words so that clients don't realise it – to form a network. We talk about being connected rather than unified.'[539]

And how does Ahold sell these supermarkets? 'Brands are very important, especially in food retailing,' he explained. 'There has to be trust in the brand because, in the end, food[s], like banking services are fragile commodities which you have to have complete trust in.'

David Peek puts it another way, 'chooses' a different tack: 'Local culture should also be taken into account, for example Asians are more likely to move vertically in malls, Europeans won't. Rapport-building with the locality is very important otherwise your shop won't work – unless you are a very strong brand like Gap. Unless you have absolute power you have to learn about the idiosyn-crasies and tastes of the locality.'[540]

Klein is 'very concerned' about the Internet. For while its glob-al communications facilities can enable activists to co-ordinate strategies, it is also a major threat to the regulation of trade. 'A lot of people see e-commerce as the solution, it's the way around trade regulations. As it advances so fast it becomes a free-trade zone, it de-regulates trade and standards – there are no reasons I can think of for three years tax exemptions e-commerce has in the US.'

Others take this position even further, even when they come from a technological background. Software engineer Ellen Ullman sees the marketing of the digital revolution as just another form of retail-isation's 'I'm ok if I'm consuming' mentality. She goes far beyond Klein in describing her 'problems' with e-commerce and mirrors Barber's more holistic view of consumerism, to address the micro-economics, rather than Klein's global concerns. 'In the Fall of 1998 … I saw it, a background of brilliant sky blue, with writing on it in airy white letters, which said: "now the world really does revolve around you". The letters were lower-case, soft-edged, spaced irreg-ularly, as if they'd been sky-written over a hot August beach and were already drifting off into the air.'[541] Governments (as Barber also notes) are good at trade deficits but bad at citizenship issues. Ullman comments: 'If it's time to protect profits, ways are found to do it. If it's time to protect citizenship, then nothing.'[542]

After we have finished our interview in Klein's garden, we go back inside to watch television with Klein and her husband. It is global sporting time, the European Football Championships, and

---

[539] Jan Hol in personal interview, January 2000; all quotes from interview.
[540] David Peek in personal interview, November 1999.
[541] Ellen Ullman, 'The Museum of Me', *Harpers* magazine, May 2000, p. 30.
[542] Ibid.

we're all rooting for our team, England. We plug into the live Canadian television coverage of the England versus Germany game, with its statistics-obsessed commentators and 'Jihad' is with me almost at once. We punch the sky when England score, and feel no kind of traitor to any cause, especially not myteamengland.com when after 34 years England finally beats the arch-rival, Germany, again (the last time was the World Cup final of 1966). We accept a Becks beer to celebrate from a range of brands proffered, and Klein's husband jokes: 'He's chosen a German beer, out of all the options.' We joke about the couple's new silver Volkswagen Golf, tell them about Wolfsburg and its 16-hour production cycles, its no-car thesis, which shocks Klein, who lists the company's actions at its factories in Mexico. 'They don't even own the factories in Mexico. They don't even own the factories,' she says, indignantly, coolly.

'The Golf was my decision,' says Ali Lewis, the dedicatee of *No Logo*, with an exonerating grin, 'and it took seven months to arrive – we *really* wanted the silver one.' Of course. And we wanted the silver Audi TT Roadster the moment we sat in it in the floor of the Unter Den Linden Volkswagen showroom. We wanted Naomi Klein's house, as soon as we saw it. Naomi Klein is merely the first of the anti-globalisation protesters to admit that retail can be irresistible; for heaven's sake, Benjamin Barber drives a slinky automatic BMW (his 'Beemer') and it is decked out with anti-cop radar, mobile phones and the usual technological paraphernalia, and that doesn't make him any less of a fighter for democracy, no less civic. There isn't any escape, not even for the committed, not unless they take to the trees.

With our Becks we are merely reverting to Logo-memory, and to Buridan's poor ass. We're wiped out by the range of views that retail subjugates, brain-dead to anything but the football Becks (who's married to Posh) and the Becks that eases my thirst. We choose what we *know*. On the flight back to New York it is easy to resist the Air Canada in-flight magazine, the 'complimentary' copy of the *Financial Times* and the swipe-card telephone.

> **The clean credit card, the online charity boom**
> **As with ethical shopping, ethical investment is booming in many parts of the world. There's around £2.8 billion, or 1% of all money in unit trusts, invested in the United Kingdom.[543] 'The increasing concern many people have about the social and environmental impacts of the activities of some companies is spilling over into the way**

---

[543] Liz Stuart, 'Clean money', *Guardian* G2, 29 June 2000, p. 14.

> **they think about their pensions and other investments,'
> Amnesty International's Peter Frankental told _The
> Guardian_.**[544]
>
> **In the United States $2 trillion was invested ethically in
> 1999. 'According to the Ethical Investment Research
> Service, EIRIS ... the most pressing concerns among
> savers are the environment, oppressive regimes and
> conduct in developing countries (whether the company
> buys from factories using child labour, for example).'**[545]
> **Elsewhere and online charity in some forms is working.
> The _Washington Post_ reported in October 1999 that a
> business man newly enriched through selling his com-
> pany to Microsoft decided to become a philanthropist.
> Peter Moutanos decided to enter the $174 billion dollar
> donations world that is the United States in an unusual
> way. He and a group of venture capitalists launched an
> $8 million website that features 'an online shopping
> mall and auctions'. Profits from purchases are shared
> with more than 2,000 charities.**[546]

Back in our hotel room it is impossible not to log on to _The
Guardian's_ website to see what the views are back home about the
football. It is all there in our virtual space, even though it is now
3 a.m. in the morning in England. Team England sponsors, Umbro,
will be pleased. We click through the hard drive and find that old
interview.

So basically we are trying to extend the England brand nationally and start to
build overseas. The brand is relatively successful in Canada, the US and the
Far East. It is harder to expand into other countries because we are a national team, not a club like Manchester United for instance. We do sell, though,
as there is a love of the English games in several countries, but we doubt
whether we could ever go beyond product sales. We are way behind in that
domain.[547]

---

[544] Liz Stuart, 'Clean money', p. 14.
[545] Ibid.
[546] Cindy Loose, 'On Internet, charity is the next big thing', Washington Post, 23
October 1999, p. A16. The website is at _http://www.charitableway.com_.
'Charitableway is the premier application service provider delivering
customisable technology solutions for more effective charitable giving programs.
Charitableway offers complete donation systems and management tools for:
Local United Ways: Learn how your United Way can open new channels of
giving ...
Corporations: Streamline your corporate and employee giving programs ...
Financial Institutions: Add philanthropic solutions for your high net-worth
customers ...
Nonprofit Organisations: Reach a new audience of online donors with zero
investment ...'
[547] David Smith, Head of Merchandising, English Football Association, March
2000.

Sales should be up tomorrow, then, in the in-store concessions. We go to sleep singing England's branded hymn, Three Lions,[548] and wake to the images of 450 English hooligans going mad in Charleroi on ABC's breakfast show. Jihad and McWorld again. And this time, even Klein would admit, it is depressing.

The riots merit around five seconds of airtime on the US network, though. Something much bigger is happening in the sporting world than the European Football Championships. There are adverts for today's Tiger Woods 'Nike' festival – he is winning by so far after three rounds of golf that it is no longer a contest – at the US Open to run, after all. (OK, we are watching ABC and that has the rights to broadcast the Open live.) Tiger usually doubles the TV ratings for golf and, like Michael Jordan, he's a Nike Man. In fact right now, 18 June 2000, he is The Man. It's quite hard, watching him win the US Open by a record number of shots with effortless ease, not to want to log on to the Nike site and buy some golf clubs. Except they don't make them.

Yet.

We're going to protest.

Naomi Klein, Benjamin Barber, Greenpeace and ActionAid all want a better world; they shop too. They shop with intelligence, knowledge – and with an ideological stance. They still have Volkswagens, BMWs and clothes from the big names in the high street. Meanwhile, the retailers are listening; but they won't be shouting their ethical engagedness from the street or the mall just yet though – not until it is *cool*, anyway.

---

[548] The unofficial 'theme song' of the European Football Championships of 1996, which were held in England. The song's combination of nostalgic lyrics and its sing-along jingoism (the chorus of 'It's coming home, it's coming home, football's coming home' – as if England owned football) made it not only a number one single, but also a terrace favourite.

Chapter 10 – Retailisation visions

We get the future wrong. History is so littered with dumb predictions – from there never being flying machines, through television never being a commercial success, to there being a world market for only about four computers – that anyone trying to peer forward has to start with some humility.

Hamish McRae[549]

History does not wait. It lays down an ultimatum.

Pitirim Sorokin, Soviet avant-garde thinker

This chapter is made up of two pieces by key contributors to retailisation. David Peek explores the retail of cars; William Mitchell investigates the retailing of information; each piece was submitted in the summer of 2000. We think they remain a fascinating take on retail. Undoubtedly Peek and Mitchell will have moved on ... everyone does.

Retailing passenger cars: future trends, by David Peek

At the time of writing (spring 2000) there are five key factors that will cause the method of retailing passenger cars to go through a revolution over the next few years, described below.

- *'Horrible to use / gorgeous to own'* The realities of car ownership involve the frustrations of congested roads, guilt about causing pollution, traffic management policies aimed to dissuade people from using personal transport, staggering increases in motoring costs, increasingly rigorous control of speed limits, lack of parking spaces, stress, tension and the constant concerns about damage and vandalism to unattended cars. In contrast to these realities, 'The Dream', which is promoted through advertising, implies freedom, excitement, self-expression, self-determination, status and convenience. Consumers crave for this Dream so much that, hitherto, they have been able to blank out the realities. Times are changing. Consumers are being forced to acknowledge realities. Therefore they need a more intense form of 'Dream Creation' if they are to be stimulated to buy in the future.
- *Deflationary expectations* Consumers expect every year to get a better product for a lower price. They are getting militant about this. Politicians are exploiting and encouraging this militancy to win votes.
- *Customisation* People will no longer accept the *manufacturer's*

---

[549] Hamish McRae, 'Globalisation, technology and the wristwatch television set', *The Independent*, 1 January 2000.

product; they want *their own* product customised to such a degree that makes it clearly distinguishable from other people's product even if it comes from the same manufacturer.

- *The business-to-business IT capabilities of the manufacturers* Car manufacturers now have sophisticated skills and technology to buy and sell electronically.
- *The shift in 'the tangibles–intangibles ratio'* Times were when people who bought cars wanted a machine that would transport them. It was a hardware transaction. Now people are searching for that brand and sub-brand (customised) that best projects them as the person they want to be seen to be. Consequently, relationship and emotional intangibles of car ownership are usually of greater importance to the customer than the 'hardware'.

As a result of these five key factors, retailing of passenger cars will shift from the traditional showroom method of retailing and split into three separate functions, namely:

- showcasing
- transactions
- post-purchase enjoyment.

'Trade-ins' will rarely be part of the process. These cars will be disposed of through auction and car supermarkets.

The split into separate functions will result in franchise dealerships ending as soon as motor manufacturers can extract themselves from dealership agreements. Motor manufacturers will then take fanatical control of the 'showcasing' process. They will allow un-franchised intermediaries to control the 'transaction', function on low margins, usually made possible by electronic retailing that may drive the existing dealerships out of business. Manufacturers will also probably sell direct.

Manufacturers will innovate to exploit locations that are best suited for 'showcasing' their brands and sub-brands. Wherever there is a concentration of potential customers in the right state of mind (mental state of potential customers will become more important than location), who also match the psychographic profile of a customer for a type of vehicle, there is potential for a showcase location. Expect to see showcases located in upmarket shopping districts, theme parks, tourist attractions, business airports, conference centres, major sporting venues, certain high-density office worker districts, stately homes and parks. Showcases will concentrate not on a manufacturer's whole range, but on model ranges.

As an example, an 'A class' Mercedes might be showcased in upmarket shopping malls, whereas the 'M class' might be found in leading locations for outdoor pursuits, while the 'C and E class' could be showcased in central business districts. Each showcase would have strict adherence to the manufacturer's core brand values but both the showcase (and the staff employed in it) would be carefully profiled to the image of the particular model range and its target customers. Also expect to see travelling showcases in the form of 'travelling circuses', which demonstrate the brand and, particularly, its heritage in the most dramatic way.

Showcases will have consultants employed by the manufacturer who will be rigorously trained in simplified psychology such as Neurolinguistic Programming (NLP) to identify enquirers' emotional needs. NLP technology will be used to align every 'sales pitch' to the needs of each enquirer. Thereafter that consultant will be responsible to drive the enquirer through any channel to complete the transaction phase.

The consultant will be responsible for arranging test-drives and other forms of demonstration such as cross-country for four-wheel-drive vehicles, or on a test track for sports vehicles. This will be in addition to using virtual reality to create the ideal car, which gives the most emotional satisfaction for the prospect. The consultant will also guide consumers to the transaction channel most suited to them, be it 'cheap and basic', whereby the transaction is done electronically and maybe direct with the manufacturer, or the 'pampered but expensive' route whereby a high degree of interaction takes place between the customer choosing the specification and taking delivery. Expect upmarket brands to start reintroducing factory collections of new cars and related holidays so that people can welcome their customised car off the production line, maybe try it at the manufacturers' test track, meet the people involved in its production and enjoy a short driving holiday getting to know their beloved purchase.

Car retailing of the future must be total retail therapy, otherwise 'The Dream' cannot be sustained. The total focus on therapy means that showcases must be like consultants' rooms. All forms of legal mood enhancers will be used: aromatherapy, subliminal messages, variable mood lighting and variable textures will be the norm. And what about the existing car showroom? Expect that to be as rare as a bank on the high streets of Britain by 2004.

Visitors will be astounded by the technology, levels of presentation, staff attention and pampering that the future car buyer will get at a showcase. Companies previously only employed to provide the showmanship for vehicle launches will be hired for every showcase venue. Showcases will have festivals and events that will get potential customers coming to have a good time and past customers to come and reaffirm their 'marriage vows' to the chosen brand that best suits their desired self-image.

The transaction element will be electronic. Most consumers will choose the 'cheapest is best' route and will electronically search the world for the best possible price and buy their vehicle through a safe, secure transaction process. They will probably do it late at night, during lunchtime at the office, or on a weekend. A barrage of phone calls, direct mail, gifts and emails (all in customised, rapport-building, psychologically evaluated language) from the consultant at the showcase, will ensure potential buyers don't get distracted and catch up on alimony payments, take out life assurance, have liposuction or spend their money on some other form of purchasing therapy.

Information retailing, by William J. Mitchell

The property metaphor

Information retailing as we have known it – the domain of bookstores, newsagents, record stores, video stores, encyclopaedia salesmen, media empires and public libraries – depends upon the credibility, widespread cultural acceptance, formalisation in legal language, political viability and enforceability of a metaphor. This metaphor has been remarkably durable and effective, but it is now being weakened by digital information technology. There are signs that its condition is terminal.

The metaphor is that of 'intellectual property' – the socially constructed notion that a chunk of information can be possessed and traded like a sack of wheat or a pair of boots. It is inseparable from industrial-era practices of mass-production and distribution of information containers such as books, newspapers, phonograph records, CDs, videotapes and videodisks. The subtleties and complexities of this concept have ramified, but the core notion is simple: information producers and intermediaries benefit from the sale of these information containers, consumers pay, and the interests of producers and intermediaries are protected by prohibition of 'unauthorised' copying and distribution.[550] Generally, the more information containers producers and intermediaries sell, the better they do.

Production and distribution systems based upon the intellectual property metaphor worked reasonably smoothly as long as production facilities (printing presses, television studios and transmitters, and so on) were few, expensive and readily controllable. But their inherent vulnerability was eventually exposed by the emergence of inexpensive, decentralised reproduction devices such as photocopiers and VCRs. And digital reproduction was to create a crisis for these systems.

---

[550] A weakness of the metaphor is that a passage of text is far easier to reproduce than, say, a pair of boots. The patch is to create legal barriers to such reproduction.

Traditional distribution strategies

The industrial production and distribution of standardised information containers had the additional effect, over time, of generating vast accumulations. Some containers (such as newspapers) were ephemeral, but others (like books and phonograph records) had long lives. Producers and distributors required strategically located wholesale warehouses, well-stocked retail locations, and sophisticated management and transportation systems to get items to the right places at the right times. Consumers needed their own storage facilities, ranging from modest home bookshelves and record racks to the enormous book stacks of major libraries.

To find what they needed within these accumulations, consumers had to apply search strategies – sometimes very sophisticated ones. These could be executed directly upon the accumulated containers; consumers could scan the spines of books in their shelves, browse through bookstores, or pursue their quarry among the library bookstacks. But where the relevant accumulations were particularly large, geographically distributed, or not physically accessible, searches were executed upon indirect representations such as library card catalogues, scholarly bibliographies, and the brochures of publishers.

Within this general framework, producers and intermediaries found that they needed to adapt their delivery strategies in response to the varying sizes of information containers and the time sensitivity of their contents. Some were like bottles of milk, containing small amounts of quickly consumed, highly perishable material. Others were like cases of good Bordeaux, containing larger amounts of material that did not quickly lose their value, and would be consumed over extended periods. The following figure summarises the various delivery strategies for these conditions, and gives some examples.

	Time sensitive	*Not time sensitive*
Small quantity	Stock quotes, weather forecasts	Signage, Haiku
Large quantity	Newspapers, magazines	Novels, opera CDs

Figure 10.1: Delivery strategies

Furthermore, the usefulness and value of information often turned out to be location-sensitive. Street signs and building directories only serve their purposes if they are in exactly the right places. Theatre programmes are meant to be used in the theatre – though they may have after-lives as souvenirs. Cookery books are most useful in the kitchen, law books in the lawyer's office, medical books at sites of medical practice, and tourist guidebooks at the places they describe. One standard strategy for dealing with location sensitivity – that of the lawyer's or MD's library – was to create accumulations at fixed points of use; these accumulations could be large, but they concentrated information resources in an inflexible way. The alternative strategy – that of the pocket guidebook – allowed a consumer to get access to information anywhere, but in strictly limited quantities. You could not have both quantity and locational flexibility simultaneously.

The lessons of Amazon

During the initial Internet boom of the late 1990s, amazon.com precipitated a major transformation of traditional information retailing systems. Amazon's business model did not challenge the intellectual property metaphor. Nor did it alter the character of the products – it offered the same books, CDs, videos, and DVDs as more traditional retailers. But it did revolutionise intermediation and logistics.

One key move was to disengage search and selection processes from physical collections of information containers. Instead of browsing through bookstore stock shelves and display tables, customers searched through an online catalogue. In some ways this was a straightforward extension of earlier uses of catalogues, but the online environment – combined with some clever software – yielded some overwhelming advantages. It could quickly, inexpensively and comprehensively reach an enormous, globally distributed customer base; old-fashioned print catalogues could never provide such coverage, and library card catalogues could not match this convenience. Through use of indexing and search engines it could provide efficient access to a much larger collection of titles than even the largest bookstore or the fattest print catalogue. And, through use of multiple classifications of titles rather than single-shelf locations, online reviews, and collaborative filtering, it could support extremely effective and engaging browsing processes.

A closely complementary move was to replace physical points of sale by online transactions – the famous 'one-click' purchase facility. This was quick and convenient, and was available to customers worldwide, anytime – not just during store opening hours. It was fully automated, so did not require a staff of retail sales assistants. It allowed efficient integration with credit card payment systems. And – less obviously to customers, but crucial to management – it provided numerous opportunities to automate back-office functions such as stock control, ordering and collection of marketing information effectively, and to integrate these functions with business-to-business e-commerce systems.

The third key move was to replace numerous, small-scale storage and distribution centres – that is, local bookstores – with many fewer, much larger warehouse and distribution centres located at national and international air transportation hubs. Publishers and wholesalers delivered books to these centres in larger batches than to local bookstores. Since the centres were in relatively inexpensive industrial locations, rather than expensive retail locations, they could be huge, and could keep far more titles in stock than any traditional bookstore. They could be highly automated and could achieve numerous economies of scale in their operations. And, since they dispatched orders by mail and package delivery services, they generated significant new demand for those services.

It seemed clear that amazon.com needed to operate at very large scale in order to succeed, and it aggressively pursued a strategy of achieving that scale. Investors were motivated to support this strategy by a winner-take-all argument – the proposition that there would eventually only be room in the market for one (or, at best, a very small number) of retailers operating at the necessary scale. And some interesting advantages of large-scale, Internet-based information retailing began to emerge; university presses discovered, for example, that Amazon's catalogue significantly increased demand for titles from their extensive backlists.

By the early months of the year 2000 it was obvious that – whoever the winners and losers in the online retailing battles turned out to be – the essential features of the Amazon revolution were irreversible. Jason Epstein published an eloquent elegy to the old ways in the *New York Review of Books*.[551]

The lessons of mp3

But that was just the beginning. At almost exactly the same moment, mp3.com and napster.com unexpectedly exploded upon the scene.

The brash start-up mp3.com was based upon the growing realisation that digital technology allowed information to be disengaged from its material substrates, and that this disengagement made tra-

---

[551] Jason Epstein, 'The rattle of pebbles', *New York Review of Books*, vol. xlvii, no. 7, 27 April 2000, pp. 55–59.

ditional information containers unnecessary. Books could be stored and distributed as digital text files. Photographs, films, and videos could be reduced to pixels and pumped around computer networks. And music could be distributed in the form of compressed, Internet-friendly MP3 files rather than on CDs.

Mp3.com quickly grabbed the music industry's attention by creating an online database of nearly 80,000 CDs in the MP3 format. As with amazon.com, consumers could search a catalogue and make online purchases. But, unlike amazon.com's book purchasers, mp3.com's CD purchasers could download CDs and play them immediately.

This was a direct – and, to producers and intermediaries, very threatening – challenge to the intellectual property metaphor, and to the cultural, economic, and legal structures that had grown up around it. Widely available, inexpensive, easy-to-use, microprocessor-powered devices made copying of digital information quick, inexpensive, and difficult to control by traditional means. Unlike analogue copies, digital copies showed no generational loss, so the traditional distinction between 'originals' and 'copies' ceased to have much practical meaning. Since digital copies could be proliferated endlessly, and distributed anywhere via the increasingly ubiquitous Internet, they lost any rarity value. Since copying was so easy, contention over availability began to disappear; images in a digital library were never 'borrowed' and therefore unavailable, like slides in a traditional library could be, and as long as there was server capacity books never needed to go out of print. If you could get ready access to information on a server, there was no motivation to create private collections in order to assure convenient and uninterrupted availability. Under these conditions, treating information as 'property', in the traditional way, seemed less and less convincing.

Debates and public policy battles quickly erupted along predictable lines. Those with interests in the old order desperately tried to shore it up by promoting draconian legal controls on digital copying and on cracking open encryption schemes designed to prevent copying, through aggressive litigation and by deploying a shrill, criminalising rhetoric of 'theft', 'piracy' and so on. Those with nothing much to lose, and an interest in the free flow of information, rallied behind the flag of 'consumer rights', coined slogans like 'information wants to be free', and began to invent radical new distribution schemes to by-pass resistant existing ones.

The lessons of Napster

Packet-switching, the TCP/IP protocol, and the Internet provided the underlying infrastructure for these new information distribution schemes. The HTTP protocol, World Wide Web, and Internet browsers made this infrastructure much more effective by supporting its organisation as a dynamic system of server sites (which publish information) and client sites (which allow users to find, download, and consume information). Napster – one of the cleverest of the new distribution schemes – took this logic a step further by allowing any site to function as *both* a client and a server.

These technological differences may sound like arcane details, but they fundamentally change the way things work. In the pre-Web Internet, files could be made available on File Transfer Protocol (FTP) sites, and downloaded by users at other sites, but you had to know exactly what you wanted and where to find it. The process was cumbersome and slow, and it was little used except by computer professionals. The Web, browsers and search engines broadened the appeal of digital information by providing unified, convenient access to files stored on countless servers scattered throughout the world; still, consumers had to spend time initiating searches, inspecting search results, and downloading – often a time-consuming and frustrating task. Then Napster went a step further by providing a multi-way sharing facility; users download and store collections of MP3 music recordings; these collections are accessible to other users, and if you want to play a MP3 that is not in your personal collection the software automatically finds it in someone else's collection and downloads it for you.

Within months of its introduction, Napster was so wildly popular that it was consuming huge proportions of the network capacities of most colleges and universities, with the result that many panicked and banished it. Recording interests saw it as a nuclear bomb, and did everything in their power to have it banned. But it was impossible to jam this genie back into the bottle; Napster had forever changed the rules of the information retailing game. And its importance was by no means restricted to recorded music; variants could work equally effectively for digital images, videos, scientific and technical papers, clip art for graphic designers, construction details for architects, software object libraries for programmers, and mapped fragments of the human genome.

Customised information services

One conservative feature of Napster, however, was that it traded in complete, finished, standardised information products – mp3s, exactly as if they were musical tracks laid down on CD, vinyl, or even Edison Phonograph wax. It relied fundamentally, in fact, upon treating copies of musical works as absolutely standard, freely interchangeable commodities.

This feature was a hangover from industrial modes of production and distribution, in which publication marked the formal completion of a work, established a definitive version, created a basis for scholarly precedence and subsequent citation (in the case of scholarly and scientific work), provided the application point for copyright protection, and allowed the work to enter libraries and archives. But under pre-industrial conditions, when information circulated aurally or in manuscript form, there was no such rigorous standardisation established at a point of formal publication. Similarly, in today's digital world, word-processor files, CAD drawings and similar productions typically exist in multiple versions and variants (which can easily cause confusion, and turn out to be a significant management problem). Furthermore, the contents of such files can readily be excerpted, transformed, and recombined to produce new works.

This inherent mutability of digital information, combined with its readiness for processing by whatever software and according to whatever parameters one chooses, opens up the possibility of digitally customised rather than industrially standardised versions. An online newspaper system, for example, may keep a profile of your interests and aesthetic preferences, select stories accordingly and lay them out for you in a style that you like. A digital videocast of a sporting event may allow each individual viewer, rather than the director, to select camera angles. As the new century dawned, it seemed increasingly evident that information retailing would become less concerned with mass-produced information products and much more concerned with highly sophisticated, customised information services.

Decentralised make-on-demand

Another inherent property of traditional publishing and distribution systems was the necessity of putting information into containers before distribution. Books had to go to the printers and binders before reaching the stores. Newspapers had to be printed in time for morning delivery. But digital technology can now reverse this; containers – when you still need them – can be filled *after* distribution.

The most obvious strategy is to connect large numbers of inexpensive, personal printers to the Internet. Thus your personalised newspaper might be automatically downloaded and laser-printed for you, every morning, at your home. If you were travelling, it might equally well be printed out by a machine in your hotel room.

More sophisticated devices can now download, print and bind books on demand. This means that, so long as the necessary files can be maintained on a server somewhere, books need never go out of print. Furthermore, wholesalers and retailers are freed of the need to keep and manage large inventories; their task becomes one of digital archive management. Contents can readily be extracted and recombined to produce customised compilations, anthologies, readers and class texts. And 'bookstores' lose most of their shelves, and are reduced to sites for electronic vending devices.

Yet another strategy is to fill special electronic containers with downloaded information. Thus, for example, the MP3 revolution quickly spawned a new type of consumer electronic device – the portable MP3 player. Less successful – initially, at least – have been hand-held, display-screen devices that serve as electronic 'books'. On the horizon is rewritable electronic paper that will enable the same physical pages to be refilled, as required, with new contents.

Location-sensitive delivery

Digital storage, networking, and processing capabilities have also yielded effective new ways of handling location-sensitive information. The traditional tradeoff between comprehensiveness and portability of information no longer constrains us.

Miniaturised digital storage devices now allow huge quantities of information to be carried around in portable devices such as PDAs, or in automobiles or other vehicles. Thus, for example, an automobile can now easily carry an enormous database of maps, street directories and guidebooks – sufficient to provide comprehensive information about whatever location it may reach.

A high-speed, wireless Internet connection has essentially the same effect. In this case, though, the information is maintained on a central server and downloaded as required. Such central databases can be larger still, and they can more readily be kept up to date. Hybrids are also possible; your automobile might download updated maps and directories, as an additional service, whenever it filled up with fuel.

To select the information that is pertinent to your current location, an electronic delivery system needs to know where you are. You might know your exact location and provide it explicitly – as when you call a taxi. Alternatively, a portable location-finding device – based upon GPS, cellular, or other technologies – may keep track of your location and automatically provide co-ordinates to an information-delivery system. Thus, for example, an automobile navigation system continually obtains GPS co-ordinates and uses these to show current location on a displayed map, and to compute efficient routes to desired destinations. In the future, as the necessary technologies evolve and the required locationally indexed databases develop, we are likely to see rapid expansion of services that provide for electronic summoning and delivery of location-sensitive information – maps, guidebooks, local health and safety information, advertising of locally available goods and services, and so on.

The future of information retailing

So the intellectual property metaphor is dying (though its demise may be delayed, for a while, by rearguard political and legal action), information containers are losing their traditional functions and roles, and information distribution channels are multiplying and taking surprising new forms. What does this mean, in the end, for information retailing?

The basic product – digital information – is now like bottled water. It is not intrinsically worth much, but you can add value – often a great deal – by packaging and delivering it in the right ways. The structure of the entire information production and delivery chain will change as the new rules take increasingly decisive effect. Publishers will retain an important role, since there will an ongoing need for informed collection and selection of material, and reliable certification of its quality. Large digital archives will be an increasingly valuable resource, and there will be businesses concerned with their compilation and management. Digital electronic delivery channels will continue to expand in reach, capacity and sophistication, and will carry vast quantities of traffic. And information retailing will mostly shift from offering standard products in stores to offering a variety of customised information services through digital electronic channels.

The success of customised information retailers will depend upon identifying those dimensions of value that customers are willing to pay for in the form of item-by-item charges, subscriptions, or acceptance of advertising. Some of the most obvious forms of valuable electronically delivered information are as follows (though this is by no means a complete list).

- *Time-sensitive information* Includes: instant stock quotes, current news, emergency medical advice, hot gossip, job listings, the very latest work of a fashionable artist. The value depends upon getting the information in time to make a crucial decision, or before competitors. Retailers need fast, secure delivery channels – typically to dispersed locations.
- *Location-sensitive information* Includes: maps and street directories, fastest routes, guidebooks and commentaries, local health and safety information, local advertising. Here, the value depends upon getting selected information to exactly the right place, just when it is needed. Retailers need geographically

indexed databases, and efficient delivery channels to mobile, locationally aware electronic devices.

- *Recipient-sensitive information* Includes: personalised news, custom-filtered classified advertising, collaboratively filtered book and music suggestions. In this case, the value depends upon selectively providing information that precisely matches the recipient's current needs, tastes and interests. Retailers need detailed information about their clients, subject-indexed databases, and sophisticated search, selection, and filtering technology.
- *Quality-critical information* Includes information that will be used as the basis for important decisions by scientists, scholars, medical practitioners, lawyers, engineers, and so on. The reliability and comprehensiveness of this sort of information is crucial, and the consequences of acting upon incomplete or erroneous information may be particularly severe. Retailers depend upon maintaining comprehensive databases, upon particularly strict quality-assurance practices and upon earning and retaining the trust of their clients.
- *Beautifully delivered information* This is distinguished by superior design, resolution, fidelity, or other such qualities. It is the domain of beautifully produced books, high-fidelity recordings and high-definition television. As long as there are aesthetically sensitive consumers, there will be retailers who are in the business of delivering beauty – but often in new, electronically mediated ways.

The information retailers of the near future will mostly represent themselves through an electronic presence on computer networks rather than a bricks-and-mortar presence on high streets and in shopping malls. They will deliver not just through PCs on desktops, but through a wide variety of electronic devices, ranging from wireless, locationally sensitive PDAs to point-of-sale printing and binding installations on university campuses, in traditional retail settings and in busy transportation terminals. They will compete on their ability to take imaginative and effective advantage of new digital technology, and to add value to information in many of these non-traditional (as well as traditional) ways.

Conclusion

Like the best and the worst of shopping malls – the smartest and the dumbest predictions for e-commerce and technology in general – Retailisation is a mixed bag. We hope that by ending our section with some other visions, some way of looking at retail outside the loop of the inevitable and ineluctable market, we might inspire you, shopper or seller, to create the next thing, the next success story, or bargain hunt; this year's Model Me.

It was a long shop to get all this information together; but then the shopping basket of life is never really ever full. Enjoy.

Index

Italic 'b' after a page number indicates 'boxed' content, and italic 'n' refers to a footnote. Names of people, companies and places have been indexed selectively.

A